AN INTERPRETATION OF WHITEHEAD'S METAPHYSICS

An Interpretation of

Whitehead's Metaphysics

by WILLIAM A. CHRISTIAN

Associate Professor of Religion, Yale University

New Haven: YALE UNIVERSITY PRESS, 1959

Acknowledgments

My study of Whitehead's writings has been helped by discussions with many friends, including some of his students, and by many silent debates with writers of books and articles on his philosophy. Robert L. Calhoun, Julian N. Hartt, Wilmon H. Sheldon, and Paul Weiss read the manuscript. For their encouragement and criticism I am deeply grateful to each of them. My wife and children have given me constant support.

An ancestor of Part One was submitted at Yale as a doctoral dissertation some years ago. An earlier version of Chapter 3 was published in the *Review of Metaphysics* in 1949.

I thank the publishers mentioned in the Sources and in various footnotes for permission to use quotations. Publication of this book has been aided by a grant from the Ford Foundation to the Yale University Press.

WILLIAM A. CHRISTIAN

Timothy Dwight College
Yale University
December 1958

Contents

PART THREE. God and the World

Sources of Citations from Whitehead's Writings, with Abbreviations

OT   *The Organisation of Thought.* London, Williams and Norgate, 1917.

PNK   *An Enquiry Concerning the Principles of Natural Knowledge.* 2d ed., Cambridge, Cambridge University Press, 1925 (a few notes are added to the first edition of 1919).

TSM   "Time, Space, and Material," in Aristotelian Society, Supplementary Vol. 2, *Problems of Science and Philosophy.* London, Williams and Norgate, 1919.

CN   *The Concept of Nature.* Cambridge, Cambridge University Press, 1920.

IDIN   "The Idealistic Interpretation of Einstein's Theory," in *Proceedings of the Aristotelian Society,* n.s., Vol. 22 (1921–22). London, Williams and Norgate, 1922.

PA   "The Philosophical Aspects of the Problem of Relativity," in ibid.

PRIN R   *The Principle of Relativity.* Cambridge, Cambridge University Press, 1922.

     "Uniformity and Contingency," from *Proceedings of the Aristotelian Society,* n.s., Vol. 23 (1922–23), London, Williams and Norgate, 1923, here cited from ESP.

SMW   *Science and the Modern World.* New York, Macmillan, 1925.

RM   *Religion in the Making.* New York, Macmillan, 1926.

SYMBOLISM   *Symbolism, Its Meaning and Effect.* New York, Macmillan, 1927.

TIME   "Time," in *Proceedings of the Sixth International Congress of Philosophy.* New York, Longmans, Green, 1927.

PR   *Process and Reality.* New York, Macmillan, 1929.

FR   *The Function of Reason.* Princeton, Princeton University Press, 1929.

AI   *Adventures of Ideas.* New York, Macmillan, 1933.

MT   *Modes of Thought.* New York, Macmillan, 1938.

SCHILPP   *The Philosophy of Alfred North Whitehead,* ed. by Paul
           A. Schilpp. 2d ed., New York, Tudor Publishing Co. for
           The Library of Living Philosophers, 1951.

MG   "Mathematics and the Good" (lecture delivered 1939), in
           ibid.

IMM   "Immortality" (lecture delivered 1941), in ibid.

ESP   *Essays in Science and Philosophy.* New York, The Philo-
           sophical Library, 1947. (The essays reprinted here are
           from various dates. Sometimes I have attached to a cita-
           tion the date of the essay from which it is taken.)

DIAL   *Dialogues of Alfred North Whitehead,* as recorded by
           Lucien Price. Boston, Little, Brown, 1954.

CHAPTER 1

Introduction

THIS is an analytical study of certain metaphysical theories advanced in the later writings of Alfred North Whitehead (1861–1947). These theories compose a remarkably subtle and original system of speculative philosophy.

1. Whitehead's later writings

Whitehead's writings fall into three main periods.[1] In the first period, while at Cambridge and at University College, London, he devoted himself to mathematics and logic. In the second period, at the Imperial College of Science and Technology, London, from 1914, he was concerned with the philosophy of natural science. In the last period, as professor of philosophy at Harvard from 1924, he turned his attention to "speculative philosophy," by which he meant "the endeavour to frame a coherent, logical, necessary system of general ideas in terms of which every element of our experience can be interpreted" (PR 4).

Since this study is an interpretation of Whitehead's speculative philosophy, it is based mainly on his later writings beginning with *Science and the Modern World* (1925). We should not suppose that Whitehead first began to think about metaphysical questions at that time. Just as mathematical physics led him into the philosophy of nature, so the problems he encountered in the philosophy of nature led him into speculative philosophy. He says in the preface to *Process and Reality* that he was undertaking to "compress the material derived from years of meditation" (PR x). This is easy to believe. However far back these "years of meditation" may have extended, in *Science and the Modern World* he

---

1. See, in Schilpp, Victor Lowe's study of Whitehead's development, and a complete list of his writings.

1

enlarges the scope of his thought and begins to philosophize in the grand manner. He then becomes occupied with the nature of individuality and the connections between individuals, with pure possibilities and their relation to things, and with the relation between God and the world.

Although Whitehead's later writings are the main locus for this study, practically all his writings since 1914 have been studied with some care. Chapter 4 contrasts his earlier theory of extension with his treatment in the later writings. Chapter 10 deals with the earlier theory of objects and events as background for the theory of eternal objects.

The most important of the later writings, and the most difficult to understand, is *Process and Reality*. Some philosophers would not agree that it is profound; all would agree that its meaning is obscure. It is difficult not only because of the novelty of his terms and the scope of his subject but also because of his aim at systematic unity. He warns his readers not to expect a conventional discussion of traditional philosophical problems. He intends "to state a condensed scheme of cosmological ideas, to develop their meaning by confrontation with the various topics of experience, and finally to elaborate an adequate cosmology in terms of which all particular topics find their interconnections" (PR vii). This aim at systematic unity, and at rigorous development of a categoreal scheme, is more characteristic of *Process and Reality* than of any other later writings. It is still effective in the more philosophical parts of *Adventures of Ideas*. In *Modes of Thought* and in the last lectures his philosophical stance is more relaxed.

Along with this aim at systematic unity Whitehead has another goal. The language of speculative philosophy is not a purely formal language, nor is it the language of science. "Philosophy is not a science" (MG 681). Speculative philosophy must offer direct illumination of concrete experience. Therefore it must connect its abstract categories with our concrete intuitions. So Whitehead undertakes to speak imaginatively as well as logically, to suggest as well as to state his meaning. Even his technical terms, he says, "remain metaphors mutely appealing for an imaginative leap" (PR 6). In this way his speculative philosophy has a kinship to poetry as well as to mathematics and science. This appeal to concrete imagination which shapes the language of *Process and Reality* and, to an even greater extent, some of the other later writings, makes an added demand on the reader. One must learn to understand both his poetry and his logic without confusing one with the other.

Finally, the organization and the style of *Process and Reality* are not without their faults.

For all these reasons it is not an easy book to understand. It makes demands on our patience and on our perspicuity. Often one finds clearer statements than one had hoped to find, sometimes in unexpected and unlikely places. But continual rereading, and collation and comparison of texts, are essential. It is easy enough to pluck verbal contradictions from Whitehead's pages. It requires some effort to distinguish verbal contradictions from real ones, those that lie upon the surface of his system from those that inhere in its structure.

Some of the obscurities can be seen through if one distinguishes three sorts of discourse. In some passages Whitehead is evoking and describing the concrete experiences he takes as his basic data. This we might call presystematic language. In others he is constructing and developing the concepts which compose his categoreal scheme. This we might call systematic language. Elsewhere he uses these systematic terms to interpret sense experience, the order of nature, art, morality, or religion. Here he is applying his scheme, and we might call this postsystematic language. These phases of his exposition correspond to the three phases of an airplane flight, with which he compares speculative philosophy. It begins on the ground; it rises into the air; and it returns to earth. Many blunders can be avoided if we do not mistake nonsystematic remarks for systematic ones.

Such a detailed study as this would be justified only if Whitehead's writings were not only difficult but important. One's judgment about their importance depends partly on one's view of metaphysics—though speculative philosophy in Whitehead's sense is not what metaphysics is sometimes taken to be. Just now philosophy is undergoing a drastic reassessment of its functions and limitations. One result may be a new way of understanding metaphysical statements. Revolutions in philosophy usually force us to reconceive old problems, and we may come to see the point of metaphysical problems in a new way. But I think these problems are not pointless and that they are important.

Metaphysics is important for two reasons. First, and more negatively, no adequate substitute has yet appeared. Neither science nor theology has yet learned to dispense with metaphysical categories. Certainly it is possible to avoid metaphysics by remaining strictly within the bounds of special languages, scientific or theological. The penalty for this avoidance is isolation of these disciplines from the world of ordinary experience and from one another, a penalty neither scientists nor theologians, on the whole, are willing to pay. Most scientists and theologians, it seems, hope to modify or at least to reinterpret common-sense beliefs. Second, and more positively, metaphysics is important because philosophy aims at clarification of thought, and because generality of thought is necessary for clarity. We understand a particular use of a term more clearly when we are aware of its other possible uses, including those possible uses which have as their context a coherent categoreal scheme.

For these reasons it seems likely that philosophers will go on asking questions analogous to the major questions asked by Plato, Aristotle, Augustine, Aquinas, Leibniz, and Spinoza. (They will also continue to ask questions like those asked by Kant, Kierkegaard, and Wittgenstein.) And I suggest, though this remains to be shown, that Whitehead's answers are acute, original, and coherent enough to deserve careful attention.

A third reason for offering this study of Whitehead's speculative philosophy, in addition to the difficulty and the importance of his later writings, is that among existing studies there seems to be room for one such as this. We have had some reasonably good introductions to Whitehead's metaphysics. We have also had some careful studies of special problems. There is a place for something more advanced than the introductions and more comprehensive than the special studies. This is the need I have tried to meet. I have in mind those serious students who, though attracted by Whitehead's generosity of spirit and incisiveness of mind, are perplexed about the structure and implications of his categoreal scheme. I have projected some paths through the thickets of his later writings and pointed toward some of their destinations. In this way I offer this study as a contribution toward discerning the shape of his thought.

2. The plan of this study

For the sake of analysis I have marked out and concentrated on three theories which together make up the groundwork of White-head's system. His theory of actual occasions, with which Part One is concerned, contains his interpretation of finite individual things and their connections. Here, we might say, he is dealing with the perennial problems of substance and causality. Part Two examines his theory of eternal objects or, as he also calls them, pure potentials. This is his alternative to the Platonic theory of forms and to the modern conception of universals. Part Three deals with his theory of God and the world, which again differs from some traditional conceptions.

In this way the scope of the study is limited. It does not deal fully or even systematically with Whitehead's applications of his scheme, for example his interpretations of space and time, matter, mind, knowledge, personality, science, morality, aesthetic experience, and religion. All these topics are touched on, but none is systematically explored. I have focused on the groundwork, not the superstructure, of Whitehead's system.

A preliminary sketch of the three theories we shall examine, and the questions they answer, is in order.

a. *The theory of actual occasions.* Whitehead construes the world as a plurality of real individual things ("as real as we are"), organically interrelated. He accepts both a plurality of real things, and genuine connections among these real things, as facts of experience. Speculative philosophy, he thinks, ought to devise a set of concepts in which these facts can be expressed systematically and coherently. His theory of actual occasions is the solution he offers. Let us explore a little further the problem he sets himself.

In a pluralistic theory of the world there must be a class of finite things with many members. These things must exist concretely, and each must have some irreducible self-identity and individuality. There must be many real finite individuals. Further, if a thing is a real individual then it is in some way *other than* all other finite individuals. Each of these things must transcend, in some way or other, every other such thing. Whitehead accepts this requirement. "It is to be noted that every actual entity . . . is something individual for its own sake; and thereby transcends the rest of actuality" (PR 135). So he must undertake to say *how* each finite individual transcends other finite individuals. He needs what I shall call a doctrine of *social transcendence* in order to make good his claim to a pluralistic philosophy. But this is only part of the problem.

In addition to the principle of pluralism, he accepts the principle of "organism." He usually speaks of his system as "the philosophy of organism." Though the sense of this phrase is not simple, it means in part that the things which make up the world are "organically" related. He takes a realistic view of efficient causation and perception. He holds that real things are "present in" other real things, not connected only in an external way. Causation, direct perception, memory, and personal identity, he says, "are all different aspects of the doctrine of the immanence of occasions of experience" (AI 237). So he must say just *how* a finite individual is present in other finite individuals. He needs to develop what I shall call a doctrine of *social immanence*.

In Part One, then, we concentrate on Whitehead's theory of actual occasions, taking it as a theory of the individuality and the real connectedness of finite things. We shall look for and examine his doctrine of social transcendence and his doctrine of social immanence. If his system is coherent, then the natures of the socially transcendent individuals will be such as to permit, if not require, their immanence in other individuals. Likewise social immanence will be so described that it permits, if it does not require, that the related things be socially transcendent individuals. We shall ask how well the theory of actual occasions meets these tests.

b. *The theory of eternal objects.* Part Two deals with Whitehead's theory of forms and things, that is to say with eternal objects and actual entities. One way to understand his problem is to see the alternatives he wishes to avoid. He means to maintain a firm distinction between possibility and actuality as irreducible modes of being. He means to avoid two alternative ways of dealing with forms and things.

i. One rejected alternative amounts to immersing forms in things. Things cannot be otherwise than they are. Real contingency is meaningless. Forms do not transcend the things of which they are forms. All that is possible is actual.

On this view there is no room for real novelty in the world of things. Creativity must be either denied or relegated to a putative beginning of the world. The world may or may not be said to originate. But there can be no genuine origination *within* the world.

Contrary to this view, Whitehead is committed to saying the world is in *process*. Actuality is in process of becoming. There is origination, creativity, novelty *within* the world of real things. Hence there must be possibilities which are not actual. Forms must transcend things. In order to interpret the world as *process* Whitehead undertakes to explain how eternal objects transcend actual entities.

ii. The world is not merely process. It is also *reality*. The second rejected alternative consists in attributing real being to forms alone. Things are construed as reflections or shadows of forms. Essence is beyond existence. The world becomes appearance, not reality, and philosophy becomes an intellectual flight from the world. Being is not "here" but "there." Things participate in forms and derive from them a secondary kind of being, but true being belongs to forms.

Contrary to this view, Whitehead is committed to saying the world is *real*. He will not subordinate things to forms. Forms are not being itself. Forms are possibilities for actualization, and reference to *some* actualization is part of the meaning of their being. Thus things do not participate in forms. On the contrary forms participate in things. All power is resident in things. This is the "ontological principle." It follows that Whitehead needs a theory of how forms are immanent in things.

His problem about eternal objects thus arises from some of his basic principles. The principle of process requires the transcendence of eternal objects. The ontological principle requires the immanence of eternal objects. Whitehead undertakes to meet these requirements. The realm of eternal objects "transcends, and finds exemplification in and comparison with, the actual course of realisation" (SMW 211).

> Eternal objects are thus, in their nature, abstract . . . To be abstract is to transcend particular concrete occasions of actual happening. But to transcend an actual occasion does not mean being disconnected from it. On the contrary, I hold that each eternal object has its own proper connection with each such occasion, which I term its mode of ingression into that occasion (SMW 220–2).

> Immanence and transcendence are the characteristics of an object: as a realized determinant it is immanent; as a capacity for determination it is transcendent (PR 366–7). [The context shows he has eternal objects in mind.]

So he needs to explain what sort of entities forms are, how they transcend actual entities, and how they are immanent in actual entities. Also his theory of eternal objects needs to be consistent and coherent with his theory of individuals and their connections.

c. *God and the world.* The problem with which Part Three is concerned is the relation of God to actual occasions. This problem arises for Whitehead in the following way:

i. He holds that, in addition to the multiplicity of actual occasions, there is an actual entity which differs in important ways from any actual occasion. (See PR 135.) Also he lays it down as a rule that the basic categoreal conditions of his system shall apply to God as well as to actual occasions. In other words, he proposes that God transcends actual occasions but does not transcend the categories.

ii. God also affects actual occasions. So a doctrine of divine immanence is needed, as well as a doctrine of divine transcendence. Further, actual occasions are genuinely immanent in God, so that they literally make a difference in God.

Thus we have here the basic problem of Part One over again— with a difference. The problem is again how actual entities transcend one another and how they are immanent in one another. The difference is that in this case we have an entity which is the "chief exemplification" of the categories but is, for all that, peculiar in some striking ways.

Whitehead must show how God is a real individual actual entity, exemplifying the categoreal conditions of actuality. He must also show how there are real connections, connections that make a difference, between God and actual occasions. And his theory of God and the world must be consistent and coherent with his theory of actual occasions generally, and with his theory of eternal objects. He must explain what the following passages, for example, mean.

> The notion of God . . . is that of an actual entity immanent in the actual world, but transcending any finite cosmic epoch—a being at once actual, eternal, immanent, and transcendent (PR 143).

> It is as true to say that the World is immanent in God, as that God is immanent in the World.
> It is as true to say that God transcends the World, as that the World transcends God (PR 528).

These problems are certainly descended from a long line of ancestors in European philosophy. But it would not be quite true to say they are old problems. Insofar as Whitehead introduces us to relatively new modes of thought, he forces us to think whether in the past we have put our questions in the right way. What might have been the problem of the One and the Many, of substance and causality, of the World and the Individual, or of internal and external relations, turns out to be subtly different from each of these traditional problems.

This study has a limited aim as well as a limited scope. It aims at exposing the structure of Whitehead's system, and is in this way analytical. It is critical in the sense that the analysis is undertaken with critical questions in mind, some of which become explicit as the study proceeds. Assessments of certain features of the system will also appear now and then. I have aimed at clearing the way for a full-scale critique of Whitehead's system. But I have not presented such a critique. For that, perhaps, the time is not yet ripe. Certainly it seemed a task beyond my powers.

I have not even tried to define Whitehead's place in the history of philosophy. But I have discussed his own attitude to the philosophical tradition, in order to bring out his views more clearly. His interest in this theme runs through his writings. In the preface to one of his earlier books he says, "Now the process of understanding new conceptions is essentially the process of laying the new ideas alongside of our pre-existing trains of thought" (PRIN R vii). And as readers of *Process and Reality* know, in Part II he lays his new ideas alongside the views of older philosophers, "in particular Descartes, Newton, Locke, Hume, Kant." With them, he says, "An endeavour has been made to point out the exact points of agreement and of disagreement" (PR vi).

In Part One of this study, Chapter 5 deals with his treatment of some traditional views of substance and Chapter 8 with his treatment of causality. In Part Two, Chapters 11–13 include his treatment of the Platonic theory of forms and some traditional views of universals, qualities, relations, and classification. In Part Three I have underlined some contrasts and similarities between his doctrine of God and some traditional views.

I do not suppose we should be content with Whitehead's estimate of his relation to earlier philosophers. But my primary aim is to bring out more sharply and clearly the logical structure of his metaphysical system, not to show its relation to the past or to estimate its historical importance. Certainly we need to judge its historical importance, and this means judging its philosophical value. Wise judgments depend on at least two conditions: first, understanding what Whitehead has said in his writings, and second, understanding what speculative philosophy can and cannot do. This study is a step toward meeting the first of these conditions. Indirectly it may also contribute toward meeting the second.

3. The point of view

I was tempted to call this "A Commentary on Whitehead's Metaphysics," since my immediate aim is to elucidate the texts. But that would suggest something less systematic than this has turned out to be. I find that from my study of the texts has come a sustained and more or less articulate argument about the shape of Whitehead's metaphysics. Since the existence of a system, even the existence of a systematic interpretation, is a likely sign of a point of view, I ought to say something about the kind of interest which led me to this project.

I began to study Whitehead's writings some years ago because they seemed to promise some new answers to theological questions. I had been reading a book by a German theologian, Karl Heim's *God Transcendent,* and was impressed by his plea for a new systematic interpretation of how God transcends the world. His own interpretation was not clear to me. So I proposed to see whether Whitehead's categories might be of help.

It soon appeared that one could not understand his theory of God and the world without understanding his theory of actual occasions and his theory of eternal objects. In particular, divine transcendence had to be seen in relation to the transcendence of one finite individual by another, and in relation to the way eternal objects transcend actuality. Since Whitehead leaves no room for any absolute transcendence, one had to consider modes of immanence as well as modes of transcendence. So the project took shape as a more comprehensive study of transcendence and immanence in Whitehead's metaphysics.

Many readers will not approach Whitehead with the same interests I have had or with the same presuppositions. But I hope my results will be interesting and useful to any serious student of his writings. I have tried to discover what they mean and to explain what I have discovered. Certainly I have had a number of surprises, finding at certain crucial points that they do not mean what I had thought they meant.

4. Some important systematic terms

Whitehead's formal statements of his basic categories are found in Part I of *Process and Reality,* chapter 2 ("The Categoreal Scheme"), though more illuminating statements are often found elsewhere, for example in pages 294–305 of *Adventures of Ideas.* His classical education and his respect for the philosophical tradition should be kept in mind in order to understand his choice and usage of terms. He says, "This nomenclature has been made up to conform to the condition, that, as a theory develops, its technical phraseology should grow out of the usages of the great masters who laid its foundations" (AI 301).

Actual entities are the real things (*res verae*) of which the universe is made up. An actual entity is an experiencing subject and is constituted by its experience. Its experience is its *real internal constitution.*

A *prehension* is an operation in which an actual entity "grasps" some other entity (actual or nonactual) and makes that entity an object of its experience. Whitehead relates this term to "apprehension" somewhat as Leibniz related "perception" to "apperception." A prehension is a "concrete fact of relatedness." It has a *subject* (the prehending actual entity), an *object* or datum that is prehended, and a *subjective form.* The subjective form of a prehension is the particular manner in which that subject prehends that object. Subjective forms are forms of emotion, consciousness, purpose, etc. A prehension need not be conscious—indeed, most prehensions are not.

There are *positive prehensions* and *negative prehensions.* Negative prehensions "eliminate" their data, so that these data do not make any positive contribution to the experience of the subject. A positive prehension is generally called a *feeling.*

The "becoming" of an actual entity consists in a *concrescence* (from *concrescere*), a "growing together" of various details of experience into a unity. This process of concrescence is organized teleologically by the subject's *subjective aim* at unity of experience. The *satisfaction* of an actual entity is the "concrete" unity of experience which the concrescence achieves. The living experience of an actual entity is its *subjective immediacy.*

Prehension of one actual entity by another means the *objectification* of the former for the latter. The former is then said to have "objective" existence. It exists and functions as an object, not as an experiencing subject. Whitehead employs Descartes's terminology and says the actual entity as objectified is that actual entity *objectivé;* the actual entity as an experiencing subject is that actual entity *formaliter* or in its "real internal constitution." The objective existence of an actual entity is its *objective immortality.*

Eternal objects are pure potentials. They are in fundamental contrast with actual entities. In themselves they do not determine in what actual entities they are *ingredient*. This is what is meant by saying that they are "pure" potentials. They are merely possible forms of definiteness. Prehensions of eternal objects are called *conceptual prehensions,* in contrast with prehensions of actual entities, which are called *physical prehensions.*

The term *actual entity* applies either to *God* or to an *actual occasion.* God and actual occasions are alike actual entities. God differs from actual occasions in two important ways: (a) The data of the conceptual prehensions of actual occasions are abstracted from the data of physical prehensions. Thus every actual occasion originates "physically." God's conceptual prehensions, on the other hand, are underived or primordial and constitute his *primordial nature.* This is his timeless "envisagement" of the multiplicity of eternal objects. God's physical prehensions are his experience of concrete actual occasions and constitute his *consequent nature.* Whitehead means to say God is one concrete actual entity, not two actual entities, for either "nature" considered apart from the other is an abstraction. (b) Every actual occasion is of limited duration. It is literally an occasion. When its concrescence has been completed it "perishes" or ceases to exist as an experiencing subject. God, however, does not "perish." He exists at all times as an experiencing subject. That is to say, God is everlasting.

Creativity is Whitehead's term for the most fundamental character of actuality. Creativity is not an individual thing and has no status apart from actual entities. By saying creativity is "ultimate," Whitehead seems to mean at least two things: (a) He means that any actual entity, whether God or an actual occasion, is not altogether derived from something else. There is an underived element in every actual entity. Every actual entity, not only God, is in some degree self-creative or *causa sui.* (b) He means that every actual entity is in some degree novel. The novelty of an actual entity is the uniqueness which results from its self-creativity. It is an essentially new unity of experience. Having in mind both of these meanings, it seems fair to say that an alternative expression for creativity might be "originality," in the fullest and most radical sense of the word.

PART ONE

Actual Occasions

PART ONE

Initial Conditions

CHAPTER 2

The Concreteness and Unity of an Actual Occasion

1. Introduction

As SPECULATIVE PHILOSOPHERS survey the various sorts of entities about which discourse is possible, they usually conclude that entities of certain sorts are more important than entities of other sorts. This judgment is reflected in the primacy of some categories over others in the systems they construct. For example, some philosophers have said there is one substance of which all other entities are attributes or modes. Others have said there are many substances (material, or mental, or of both sorts) of which other entities (for example, relations) are accidents. Other philosophers have said that what we regard as substances are really distortions of a formless flux of activity.

Whitehead poses a question of this sort by asking, What is concrete and what is abstract (PR 30)? What is there, from which entities of other sorts are abstractions? The answer he gives is different from those I have mentioned. There are many concrete things, not just one. These things are not substances, as sometimes conceived, for one is genuinely immanent in another. And while they are activities, the activity of each has a structure which makes it a real individual transcending all others of its kind. In Whitehead's system these many concrete things are called "actual entities." "The positive doctrine of these lectures is concerned with the becoming, the being, and the relatedness of 'actual entities'" (PR viii).

Part One of this study examines his theory of finite actual entities, which he calls "actual occasions" (PR 135). Part Three will examine his theory of the "primordial" actual entity, God, and the relation of God to the world of actual occasions. More immediately, Chapters 2–5 look for Whitehead's explanation of how an actual occasion "is something individual for its own sake; and thereby transcends the rest of actuality" (PR 135).

In the present chapter we consider the concreteness and internal unity of an actual occasion. Chapter 3 deals with the novelty and mutual exclusiveness of occasions as acts of experience. In Chapter 4 we see how these features of occasions are reflected in the theory of extension. Chapter 5 argues that Whitehead has in effect revised, not rejected, the notion of substance. These chapters are designed to bring out the main differences between Whitehead's system and those philosophies which picture the world either as the manifestation of a single universal being or as a formless flux of activity. They ask, Has Whitehead made good his claim to be a pluralist?

Then in Chapters 6–8 we turn to the other side of the theory of actual occasions, namely the doctrine of social immanence. These chapters ask, Do Whitehead's categories yield genuine connections among the many individuals? Finally in Chapter 9 the two sides of the theory of actual occasions are brought together. We must ask whether they are mutually compatible and what they amount to. For example, on Whitehead's showing, is the world of actual occasions an "organism"?

2. Concreteness and experience

The fundamental feature of an actual occasion is that it is an "act" or "occasion" of experience. Indeed, in *Adventures of Ideas* the expression "occasion of experience" supplants "actual occasion" and becomes standard usage. An actual occasion is an experiencing thing.

Some caution is needed in the use of this expression. It is notable that Whitehead deliberately avoids the term "experience" in his statement of the categories of existence, explanation, and obligation that compose the categoreal scheme (PR, Pt. I, ch. 2). The nearest approximations are "feeling" and "satisfaction." But both these terms are introduced by way of "prehension," which is freer from the connotation of experience. Where he might have spoken of experience or awareness, at various points in the categoreal scheme, he speaks instead of "implication in" or of "functioning" (PR 34, 38).

Whitehead avoids the term in his categoreal scheme for the following reason. He means to construct a set of categories to interpret *all* the items we find in our world. He wants to throw light on persons and animals, which we think of as having experiences, and also on plants and stones and electrons, which we do not think of as having experiences. Therefore he does not want to make "experience," with its restricted extension in ordinary usage, a systematic category. He uses it as a presystematic term.

Instead of using the term in the categoreal scheme, he takes certain features of its ordinary meaning and embodies these in his categories of explanation: (a) An experience is *of* something. It has an objective reference. And (b) the object experienced has significance for the subject. The experience has a reflexive function. These features of the ordinary meaning of "experience" are expressed in the categoreal notions of "prehension" and "immediacy." An actual entity is "a concrescence of prehensions" (PR 35), a process of activity in which many entities function as objects. The immediacy of an actual entity is introduced in the following categories of explanation:

> (xxi) An entity is actual, when it has significance for itself. By this it is meant that an actual entity functions in respect to its own determination. Thus an actual entity combines self-identity with self-diversity (PR 38).

> (xxiii) That this self-functioning is the real internal constitution of an actual entity. It is the 'immediacy' of the actual entity (PR 38).

"A is an act of experience," systematically interpreted, means therefore that A is a prehending entity and that its nature is determined in part by its own prehending activity. It does not imply that A is conscious of what it prehends or conscious of itself. Consciousness is a feature of some prehensions but not all (PR 35, 83).

It is therefore an open question whether Whitehead is a panpsychist or not, depending on what a "psyche" is taken to be. He does not attribute consciousness to stones and electrons, or to the actual occasions that compose them. He does attribute to these occasions a kind of activity which, presystematically, he calls "experience." He means to suggest an analogy with human and animal experience, but he explains he is giving the term an extension it does not have in ordinary usage, with the understanding that it can be given systematic interpretation in terms of the categoreal scheme. It is a useful term if the conditions of its use are understood.

So understood, we may say that in Whitehead's system the only entities that are concretely actual are those which have experiences. The mark of an abstract entity is that it has no experiences. In *systematic* language, an abstract entity is one which has no significance for itself (PR 38).

Here we take a first step toward explaining how an actual occasion is a genuinely real individual. Actual occasions are not abstract characters or collections of abstract characters. They "are not expressible by concepts in respect to their individual particularity" (PR 86). In a discussion of the "full concreteness" of an occasion Whitehead says, "It is impossible to complete the description of an actual occasion by means of concepts" (SMW 237). An actual occasion is a genuinely real individual because, in the first place, it is not abstract but concrete. It is an occasion of experience.

Another step toward explanation of the individuality of an actual occasion may be mentioned here. The experiencing which makes up the occasion goes on at a definite place and time. The occasion has a definite extensive region. This will be studied in some detail in Chapter 4. An occasion is an instance of experience going on at some particular "here-now."

If nothing more could be said about an occasion, then it would amount only to a flux of experience going on at some particular locus. But an actual occasion is a real individual in a much stronger sense than this. This "experiencing going on here-now" has a structure and a specific character.

Its structure is teleological. It has a "subjective aim" at "satisfaction." In the satisfaction the subjective aim is achieved and the concrescence becomes concrete. Its prehensions have grown together into a unity of feeling.

This internal unity of an actual occasion is essential to its being a real individual. So the next step in an examination of Whitehead's pluralism should be an analysis of this unity. One way and perhaps the best way to analyze the internal structure of actual occasions is to study the "satisfaction" of an occasion, in which its unity is achieved. That is the purpose of the rest of this chapter. We shall find that the satisfaction is of crucial importance for explanation of the individuality of an occasion, as the following passages suggest:

> This satisfaction is the attainment of something individual to the entity in question. . . . 'Satisfaction' provides the individual element in the composition of the actual entity (PR 129).

> In the conception of the actual entity in its phase of satisfaction, the entity has attained its individual separation from other things . . . (PR 233).

Here we begin our detailed analysis of Whitehead's system. The initial plunge may try the patience of the reader. For everything cannot be explained at once, yet each systematic term must be understood in relation to others. I hope the pattern of the scheme will become increasingly clear as we proceed, so that the reader's patience will gradually be rewarded.

3. The satisfaction of an actual occasion

In the categoreal scheme the term "satisfaction" is introduced in category of explanation xxv: "The final phase in the process of concrescence, constituting an actual entity, is one complex, fully determinate feeling. This final phase is termed the 'satisfaction.' It is fully determinate (a) as to its genesis, (b) as to its objective character for the transcendent creativity, and (c) as to its prehension—positive or negative—of every item in its universe" (PR 38).

When we study Whitehead's accounts of the satisfaction of an occasion we become aware of an important problem of interpretation. Now and then he uses expressions like the following:

. . . an actual entity has 'perished' when it is complete (PR 126).

Completion is the perishing of immediacy: 'It never really is' (PR 130).

[In the phase of satisfaction] Time has stood still—if only it could (PR 233).

. . . with the attainment of the 'satisfaction,' the immediacy of final causation is lost, and the occasion passes into its objective immortality . . . (PR 448; see 129, 355–6).

These and similar passages might suggest to an unwary reader that in the process of experiencing there is no pause for a final and consummatory feeling to take place before the occasion "perishes." From this point of view, the satisfaction would not add any absoluteness of achievement to the internal process. "Satisfaction" would be merely a name for the fact that experiencing terminates and objective immortality begins. This interpretation seems to agree with Whitehead's well-known emphasis on "relativity," "flux," "process," and "becoming" (SMW 102, AI 355, MT 131).

I shall argue that, though some passages may suggest it, this interpretation is a mistake. But first we should notice the reason why Whitehead's philosophy, so interpreted, would seem unintelligible. If the structure of an actual occasion is teleological, and if the realization of its aim is wholly extrinsic to the occasion, then we have a case of there being always jam tomorrow, never jam today. For suppose the satisfaction aimed at in the process A is realized *only* in the entities which succeed A, for example, B. Then the satisfaction of A will be a factor in the process of B. But this latter process aims at the satisfaction of B, which would in turn be realized only in C. Thus it would be true not only that the satisfaction of A is not realized in A but also that there would be no finite entity in which the satisfaction of A is completely realized. It would follow that there is always becoming, but nothing becomes; there is creativity, but nothing is created; there are relations, but no genuine terms; there is causation, but no cause and no effect. The point of this criticism is understandable. We must discover whether it is justifiable.

The interpretation of Whitehead's theory I would suggest may be stated in the following set of propositions:

a. The satisfaction of an actual occasion is both aimed at and attained in the experience of that occasion.

b. The satisfaction of an actual occasion is a feeling immediate to that occasion.

c. The satisfaction of an actual occasion is completely unified and determinate in relation to every other entity.

d. The satisfaction of an actual occasion is not a process of change.

e. The satisfaction of an actual occasion exists objectively for all occasions that supersede that occasion.

I shall explain these propositions and support them, and then examine their mutual compatibility. In this way we can get some light on the individuality of an actual occasion as an act of experience.

a. *Satisfaction as attainment.* The problem of the process by which an actual occasion comes into being is to bring a unity of feeling out of many feelings. The process is unsatisfied as long as its component feelings inhibit one another. The creative urge drives on the process until it is satisfied by the fulfillment of its potentialities of harmony and intensity. It has an aim at satisfaction. (See the "categoreal obligations" of subjective unity, subjective harmony, and subjective intensity, PR 39–41.)

In a sense therefore the satisfaction is present in the process from its beginning, but only in the sense that it is the ideal at which the process aims and by which the process is guided. "In its self-creation the actual entity is guided by its ideal of itself as individual satisfaction and as transcendent creator. The enjoyment of this ideal is the 'subjective aim,' by reason of which the actual entity is a determinate process" (PR 130; see 341–2). The subjective aim is a feeling of what the process may achieve, namely the satisfaction possible to it, together with "appetition" toward the realization of this relevant ideal. This envisagement of and tendency toward satisfaction gives unity to the many feelings in the concrescence.

The satisfaction is not, however, merely a flying goal, pursued but not achieved. The process actualizes its ideal. The notion of an actual entity involves "an attainment which is a specific satisfaction" (PR 129). The concrescence "reaches the goal" (PR 251) of satisfaction. An occasion "enjoys its decisive moment of absolute self-attainment as emotional unity" (AI 227). Whatever else the satisfaction of an occasion may be, it is clearly something not only aimed at but attained. It is indeed, in the earlier phases of a process of experience, an ideal. But it also becomes a fact. What sort of fact is the satisfaction?

b. *The immediacy of the satisfaction.* It is clear that the satisfaction is a *feeling.* The satisfaction is "the concrete unity of feeling" obtained by the process of integration (PR 322). It is "one complex unity of feeling" (PR 337). It is an experience which has "intensity" (PR 129), more specifically "quantitative emotional intensity" (PR 177). It is "subjective" (PR 82) and "immediately felt" (PR 235). In numerous other passages the satisfaction is clearly said to be a feeling (PR 38–9, 66, 71, 434; AI 298). Further, the satisfaction has all the components into which a feeling can be analyzed, namely a datum, a subjective form, and a subject.[1] It is distinguished from other (partial) feelings in that it unifies all the component feelings that have arisen in earlier stages of the process.

The actual occasion A is the *subject* of the feeling which is the satisfaction of A. The satisfaction of A is a feeling immediate to A and enjoyed by A. This conclusion is required by the categoreal conditions or "obligations" set forth in the categoreal scheme.

For example, the category of subjective unity is interpreted to mean that every feeling "is an episode in self-production, and is referent to its aim. This aim is a certain definite unity with its companion feelings" (PR 342). Now a unity of feelings requires a single integrative feeling. And if the subjective aim of A is attained in A, then the concrescence must result in such a feeling.

The same requirement can be deduced from the category of

1. For analysis of a feeling see PR 35, 355–6; AI 227, 297. On the datum of the satisfaction see PR 359, 434. On the subjective form of the satisfaction see PR 66, 233–4, 359, 434. On the subject of the satisfaction see PR 227, 234–5.

objective identity, stated as follows in the categoreal scheme: "There can be no duplication of any element in the objective datum of the 'satisfaction' of an actual entity, so far as concerns the function of that element in the 'satisfaction'" (PR 39). Whitehead explains this as follows: "The same entity, be it actual entity or eternal object, cannot be felt twice in the formal constitution of one concresence. . . . Thus objective identity requires integration of the many feelings of one object into the one feeling of that object" (PR 347; see category of explanation xxvi, PR 38–9). The process must produce finally a single feeling in which every object felt in earlier phases will have unambiguous status (PR 344–7). In the satisfaction each entity felt will be felt only "once."

Again, it is possible to deduce this requirement from the category of subjective intensity: "The subjective aim, whereby there is origination of conceptual feeling, is at intensity of feeling (α) in the immediate subject, and (β) in the *relevant* future" (PR 41). We need be concerned only with the aim at intensity of feeling in the immediate subject. Now a condition of intensity is that feelings should not inhibit but should mutually enhance one another. Achievement of the *maximum* intensity possible to an act of experience therefore would require a single integrative feeling in the immediate subject, in which all the component feelings would be adjusted to one another in a pattern of contrasts.

It seems clear therefore that whatever else the satisfaction of an actual occasion may be, it is a feeling immediate to its subject. It is an emotional experience of some positive intensity (PR 177) and is felt by its subject.

c. *Unity and determinateness.* The unity of the satisfaction has been explained, incidentally, in the discussion of proposition 2. The satisfaction is a *single* complex feeling, *unifying* all the component prehensions in the concresence. We shall return to this point in the discussion of proposition 4 below. Here it is enough to show that this feeling is completely *determinate* in relation to all entities other than its subject.

In the earlier phases of the process, the subject's relation to other entities in ambiguous. It includes more than one feeling of the same object, in somewhat the way that on a dark night one might be undecided whether a shape dimly seen is man or animal, friend or enemy. In this sense earlier stages of the process are "incomplete." In these phases the individuality of an occasion is only "nascent" (PR 230). By a process of progressive integration, however, "completion is arrived at—at least, such 'formal' completion as is proper to a single actual entity" (PR 248. See 44, 322–3, 327, 373; AI 247; MT 123). In the feeling of satisfaction this process of progressive integration culminates and all indeterminations have "evaporated" (PR 71). "All indeterminations respecting the potentialities of the universe are definitely solved so far as concerns the satisfaction of the subject in question" (PR 234). There is no longer any ambiguity about the relation of the occasion to other entities. The categoreal obligation of objective identity is satisfied.

The *datum* of the satisfaction is a complex unity of actual entities, eternal objects, and propositions, felt with corresponding complex unity of subjective form (PR 434). In this datum every item in the universe is implicated (PR 38). The actual occasion now has "a determinate attitude towards every element in the universe," and *in this sense* (and *only* in this sense, it should be added) "includes the universe" (PR 71–2). The feeling of satisfaction has a determinate reference to every other entity in the universe of its subject.

Some of the items "implicated" in the objective datum of the satisfaction are prehended negatively. That is, some entities are not positively felt, but are excluded "from positive contribution to the subject's own real internal constitution" (PR 66). "Feelings," or positive prehensions, "contribute their 'subjective forms' and their 'data' to the formation of novel integral prehensions; but 'negative prehensions' contribute only their 'subjective forms'" (PR 39, category of explanation xxvii; see 35). The items prehended negatively in the satisfaction are nevertheless implicated in its objective datum. Thus a negative prehension of X would have as its "datum" *not*-X, and this would add to the determinateness of those items that are positively prehended, as Y. While the "data" of negative prehensions may thus be said to be negatively implicated in the objective datum, the subjective forms of these prehensions make a positive contribution to the subjective form of the satisfaction. A negative prehension would contribute "aversion from X" as an element in the complex subjective form of the satisfaction. This element of subjective form would contribute to the way Y is positively felt by the subject.

All the objects prehended in the feeling of satisfaction are graded in "relevance." Most of them will be felt only vaguely (PR 66)—or perhaps it would be better to say only faintly—and each will be prehended only in a certain perspective. But each will be prehended in some determinate way.

This determinateness of satisfaction is required by the categoreal scheme. The categories of subjective unity and objective identity require that the occasion achieve a completely definite and consistent character. " 'Becoming' is the transformation of incoherence into coherence" (PR 38). Those same categoreal obligations taken together with the fourth category of explanation, namely the principle of relativity, require further that the satisfaction be completely determinate in relation to *all* other entities. The principle of relativity is "that every item in its universe is involved in each concrescence" (PR 33). The satisfaction must be determinate and self-consistent, and it must be related to every other entity. This is possible only if its relation to every other entity is determinate.

The satisfaction therefore establishes the actual occasion as a completely definite and self-consistent whole, with definite and unambiguous relations to every other entity in its universe. Nothing can henceforth be added to the experience of the occasion. ". . . the final 'satisfaction' of an actual entity is intolerant of any addition" (PR 71). No further adjustments within the experience of the occasion are necessary or possible. With the achievement of the satisfaction, the individual character of the occasion has been finally determined.

We now have to ask about the relation of this achievement to "flux" and "process."

d. *Is the satisfaction a process?* A number of striking remarks in Whitehead's writings might suggest that actuality and process are correlated in a direct and simple way. For example:

> Nature is a structure of evolving processes. The reality is the process (SMW 102).

> . . . we should start from the notion of actuality as in its essence a process (AI 355).

One main doctrine, developed in these lectures, is that 'existence' (in any of its senses) cannot be abstracted from 'process' "
(MT 131).

But a closer examination shows important qualifications on "the
primacy of process." The following passage is a good example:

That 'all things flow' is the first vague generalization which
the unsystematized, barely analyzed, intuition of men has
produced. . . . Without doubt . . . the flux of things is
one ultimate generalization around which we must weave
our philosophical system.

At this point we have transformed the phrase 'all things
flow,' into the alternative phrase, 'the flux of things.' In so
doing, the notion of the 'flux' has been held up before our
thoughts as one primary notion for further analysis. But in
the sentence 'all things flow,' there are three words—and
we have started by isolating the last word of the three. We
move backward to the next word 'things' and ask, What sort
of things flow? Finally we reach the first word 'all' and ask,
What is the meaning of the 'many' things engaged in this
common flux, and in what sense, if any, can the word 'all'
refer to a definitely indicated set of these many things
(PR 317)?

These qualifications need careful attention. "Flux" is not the
only "primary notion." Whitehead's insistence on the importance
of process does not mean that it is all-important.

First we ought to distinguish different meanings of "process."
Often it means (a) the temporal world, or the temporal passage
which characterizes the actual world, or the world of finite passing things. "The actual world is a process" (PR 33; see SMW 102,
MT 131). Here Whitehead is simply "taking time seriously." If
anything is in the actual world, then it is involved in a process
of change, but this does not imply that all actual things change
in all respects. I am not denying that the satisfaction of an actual
occasion is "in process" in this sense. The feeling of satisfaction
is certainly in process in the sense that it occurs in the temporal
world.

Elsewhere it means (b) activity or "life" (SMW 247, MT passim).

Any feeling, including the feeling of satisfaction, is a process in the sense that it is an "act." In this very general sense, every concrete actuality—that is to say, every act of experience—is a process. In this sense there is nothing in the universe which is not a process except abstractions. I am not denying that the satisfaction is a process in sense *b*.

Senses *a* and *b* of "process" are presystematic uses of the term. In these uses Whitehead is not giving the term a special meaning derived from his systematic categoreal scheme. He also uses the word "process" more systematically to mean (c) growth or internal change, or (d) change of status in relation to other things. In sense *c* process is the activity that takes place *within* an actual entity, namely the concrescence of its prehensions through various phases of integration into the unity of satisfaction. In sense *d* process is the transition between an actual occasion and its successor. In this transition the antecedent occasion "perishes" and the new occasion becomes (PR 228–9, 320, 326–8).

In both these more systematic senses the immediate feeling of satisfaction is not a process. The satisfaction does not undergo internal change. It is not in "becoming." It *is*. It is a complete feeling. Nor does the satisfaction as an immediate feeling undergo external adventures. As an immediate feeling, the satisfaction is not itself "in flux" in either of these specific senses.

This is not to deny that the satisfaction is *involved in* process. On the contrary, it is the outcome of the internal process of becoming, and it leads to the transition to the future. Thus the satisfaction as an immediate feeling stands between two kinds of process and is internally related to both. Yet it is not itself a process of either kind.

It seems that the satisfaction represents a pause in the midst of the flux. The pause is not empty; it is occupied by a single complete feeling. It is the "halt for attainment" (MT 139). ". . . the attainment of a peculiar definiteness is the final cause which animates a particular process; and its attainment halts its process . . ." (PR 340). It is true that Whitehead also says, "There is no halt in which the actuality is just its static self . . ." (AI 354). The clue to resolving this contradiction lies in the word "static." The latter passage asserts that the *occasion* is a process in sense *b*. It is an

activity of feeling. The former passage denies that the feeling of
satisfaction is a process in sense *c*. "In the conception of the actual
entity in its phase of satisfaction, the entity has attained its individual separation from other things; it has absorbed the datum,
and it has not yet lost itself in the swing back to the 'decision'
whereby its appetition becomes an element in the data of other
entities superseding it" (PR 233). This pause is not an instantaneous "moment," in the language of the earlier writings. It has temporal thickness, or duration.

Indeed the satisfaction contains, one might say, the whole of
the *temporal* duration of the occasion. For the genetic process
that produces the satisfaction is not itself in physical time. If we
think of "taking time" as a matter of filling up the gaps between
the earlier and later physical boundaries of occasions, then it is
the satisfaction that "takes time." It is by producing their satisfactions that actual occasions produce the temporally extended
world.[2]

The feeling of satisfaction becomes and perishes. But it is not
a becoming or a perishing. The satisfaction is *what* becomes and
perishes. Though it does not exist except in the context of processes of becoming and perishing, it is not itself such a process.
In an important sense it is not *process* but *reality*. It is by virtue
of this feeling of satisfaction, aimed at and attained, that any
actual occasion is a *real* individual, a genuine term in the universal
scheme of relatedness. "Thus Concrescence is useful to convey the
notion of many things acquiring complete complex unity. But it
fails to suggest the creative novelty involved. For example, it omits
the notion of the individual character arising in the concrescence
of the aboriginal data" (AI 303).

Let us look more closely at the relation of the satisfaction to
the process of concrescence. The satisfaction of an actual occasion
is related to the process of concrescence as the "outcome" (SMW
247) of this process. It is that state of complete coherence of feeling in which the "becoming" of the actual occasion terminates
(PR 71).

It is true that the satisfaction is often described as "the final

2. On the epochal theory of time, see CN, ch. 3; TIME; SMW 176–80; PR
105–8, 433–8; and Ch. 4 of this study.

phase in the process of concrescence" (PR 38; see 227–8, 323). But strictly speaking "the process itself lies in the two former phases," "the responsive phase" and "the supplemental stage," which are distinguished from the satisfaction (PR 323). With the attainment of the satisfaction, the creative urge which has driven the process of concrescence from phase to phase is "exhausted" or "contented," so that the internal process terminates (PR 335, AI 248). No phase of internal change succeeds the feeling of satisfaction. It is the final outcome of the concrescence.

This does not mean that it can be understood apart from the process of concrescence. In its complex subjective form the satisfaction embodies the history of its own becoming. The genesis and internal history of the concrescence have left their mark upon the final feeling (PR 354). The satisfaction, like any feeling, "bears on itself the scars of its birth" (PR 346). It is thus, but only thus, that the internal process of concrescence is involved in the immediate satisfaction. The way in which internal process or change exists in the immediate satisfaction is as *completed change*. The feeling of satisfaction involves no internal process within itself. It is the final act of "decision."

Now let us look more closely at the relation of the satisfaction to the process of transition. The satisfaction is not the transition, but it includes within itself "anticipation" of this process. The satisfaction exists before the transition takes place. The transition is *from* the occasion as internally complete by virtue of its feeling of satisfaction *to* succeeding acts of experience.

The crucial question here is about the meaning of "anticipation." According to the eighth categoreal obligation, "The subjective aim . . . is at intensity of feeling (α) in the immediate subject, and (β) in the *relevant* future" (PR 41). Therefore, "one element in the immediate feelings of the concrescent subject is comprised of the anticipatory feelings of the transcendent future in its relation to immediate fact" (PR 424–5). These anticipatory feelings express the urge to the future embodied in every actuality.

Sometimes Whitehead calls the satisfaction itself "the final phase of anticipation" (AI 248). But this is misleading if it suggests that the satisfaction is *merely* a feeling of anticipation. Anticipatory feeling is only one element in the complex feeling of satisfaction. It is the forward edge of the feeling of satisfaction. This would be the most relevant aspect of the satisfaction in a discussion of the relation of future to present, such as the context in which the above phrase occurs.

A similar ambiguity appears when he seems to distinguish between satisfaction and decision, as two "stages" in an actual occasion. "The final stage, the 'decision,' is how the actual entity, having attained its individual 'satisfaction,' thereby adds a determinate condition to the settlement for the future beyond itself" (PR 227; see 233). For if the decision is both immediate to the occasion and yet in some sense "after" the satisfaction, then the satisfaction cannot be the final phase of the occasion. It is better to look at decision as a feature of the satisfaction than as a phase succeeding the satisfaction. This would be more in accord with the treatment of decision elsewhere in *Process and Reality*.

"Decision" is used in its root sense to mean a "cutting off" of alternatives. This is "the very meaning of actuality" (PR 68), for the existence of an actuality means that some "pure" possibilities are excluded. "Immanent decision" is "the process of acquisition of subjective form and the integration of feelings" (PR 249). More specifically it is the occasion's creative determination of the subjective forms of its prehensions, including its "adversions" and "aversions" (PR 388, 399). This process both shapes and is shaped by its subjective aim functioning as final cause (PR 68–9, 343, 423). "Transcendent decision" refers to those decisions beyond the immediate occasion which have determined its data and thus govern the transition from the past to the present as its efficient cause (PR 75, 97, 248–9, 423).

Now the satisfaction is the culmination of the concrescence and thus the completion of the process of immanent decision. I suggest that the following sentences from categoreal obligation ix properly apply to the feeling of satisfaction: "This final decision is the reaction of the unity of the whole to its own internal determination. This reaction is the final modification of emotion, appreciation, and purpose" (PR 41–2). And I suggest that the "final stage" of decision referred to above (PR 227) is really the final valuation expressed in the subjective form of the feeling of satisfaction.

Now let us return to our question about the meaning of "anticipation" in relation to satisfaction. An actual occasion embodies
an urge to the future, a "principle of unrest" in the words of S.
Alexander (PR 42–3). In earlier phases of the occasion this principle of unrest is embodied as appetition toward completion of
the internal process. In the satisfaction this principle is embodied
as anticipatory feeling of the transcendent future.

We must note particularly that anticipatory feeling takes place
in the immediacy of the present subject, before its supersession
by other actual occasions. Anticipatory feelings are "one element
in the immediate feelings of the concrescent subject" (PR 424–5;
see 41, TIME 61). The feeling of satisfaction, *including* its component anticipatory feelings, therefore takes place before the present actual occasion is superseded. Anticipatory feeling is not a
feeling *in* the future. It is a present feeling *of* the future. More
exactly it is "a propositional realization of *the essence of the present subject,* in respect to the necessities which it lays upon the
future to embody it and to re-enact it so far as compatibility may
permit" (AI 248, my italics; see MT 228). It is a feeling that this
present actuality is as real as anything can be and must therefore
be taken account of by any future actuality.

The fact that the satisfaction includes anticipation of the future
is entirely consistent with the "internal completion" of an actual
occasion. Of course in one sense no occasion is ever complete. For
the process of nature is never complete. But this is not what is
meant by "formal" or "internal" completion (PR 248, 373; AI
247). The distinction is between "macroscopic" and "microscopic"
completion (TIME 61, PR 326–7, MT 60).

It is true that if anticipatory feelings were feelings of an actual
future, a difficulty would arise. If A anticipated B as an individual
occasion, then the internal completion of A would not be a fact
until B's process of actualization were complete. In the same way
B would not be complete until C had become complete, and so
on. The result would be that in the process of nature no actual
occasion would achieve internal completion. The process of actualization of A would require a series of feelings, all internal to A,
extending indefinitely into the future. The satisfaction of A would
then indeed be in transition. But anticipation is *not* feeling of an

actual future. Future occasions function in the feeling only prop-
ositionally or hypothetically. Since they do not now actually exist
they cannot be physically felt.

Indeed, the very nature of anticipatory feeling yields a reason
why the satisfaction is not a process of transition. A necessary
condition of there being a future beyond the present subject is
the perishing of the present subject. If what is anticipated is to
be actualized, the present occasion including its satisfaction must
cease to exist as an immediate experience (PR 44, 94; AI 227,
304–5). Anticipatory feelings require the perishing of their subjects. ". . . the fact that each individual occasion is transcended
by the creative urge, belongs to the essential constitution of each
such occasion. It is not an accident which is irrelevant to the completed constitution of any such occasion" (AI 249; see PR 327). It
is in this sense that "supersession" by other occasions is part of
the "real essence" (in Locke's sense) of a concrete entity (TIME
59).[3]

Anticipatory feelings therefore do not compromise the internal
completion of the satisfaction and are not evidence against the
proposition we are discussing. These feelings do not require further internal change in the subject. Precisely the opposite is true.
They prohibit further change in the present subject, because they
require the perishing of the present subject. This requirement
means that the satisfaction

> . . . cannot be construed as a component contributing to
> its own concrescence (PR 129).

> No actual entity can be conscious of its own satisfaction; for
> such knowledge would be a component in the process, and
> would thereby alter the satisfaction (PR 130).

> . . . the final 'satisfaction' of an actual entity is intolerant
> of any addition . . . (PR 71).

3. In TIME, but not elsewhere, "supersession" is used to refer to the succession of phases within a concrescence, as well as to the transition from one
occasion to another. In PR, though it is not a strictly systematic term, "supersede" usually refers to the process of transition (PR 68, 72, 91, 129, 233, 327).

It is in this context that the saying "Actual entities perish, but do not change" (PR 52) can best be understood (PR 92, 122; AI 262). The anticipation inherent in the present actuality involves a categoreal demand for change. The change thus demanded cannot be internal change in the present actuality. It can only be the cessation of the present act of experience, as a condition for its supersession by other acts of experience.

The outcome of the preceding argument is as follows. The satisfaction of an actual occasion is not a process of change, although it is related essentially both to internal process and to transition. It is related to the process of concrescence as the outcome of that process. It is related to the process of transition by including an anticipation of that process. Once attained, the satisfaction undergoes no further change in itself. "The occasion arises from relevant objects, and perishes into the status of an object for other occasions. But it enjoys its decisive moment of absolute self-attainment as emotional unity" (AI 227).

If this argument is valid, then we have gone far toward showing an important sense in which an actual occasion is a real or "substantial" individual thing. Whitehead clearly denies that an actual occasion is an "enduring substance," in the sense of an "unchanging subject of change" (PR 43). It *would* be true to say, however, that an actual occasion is an "unchanging subject." In the feeling of satisfaction, an actual occasion has become an experiencing subject which for a real duration, however brief, is unchanging.

In *Essays on Truth and Reality* (Oxford, Oxford University Press, 1914), F. H. Bradley remarks, "As to the duration of a self, that in principle need be no more than momentary. If we keep to ordinary usage a different reply would have perhaps to be given, but the usage, so far as I can judge, does not rest on any principle" (p. 416). If we leave out of consideration any other requirements for selfhood than that of real duration as a complete subject, then Whitehead, if we have understood him rightly, asserts of an actual occasion what Bradley requires for a "self."

To put the matter a different way, it is clear that in the actual world on Whitehead's terms "no subject experiences twice" (PR 43). This amounts to a denial of the "traditional" doctrine of substance. To determine whether there is left *any* sense in which an actual occasion is a real or "substantial" individual, we must ask the further question, Does the complete subject experience even once? If proposition *d* has been adequately explained and supported, the answer is affirmative.

e. *Satisfaction and objectification.* It is not the purpose of this section to give a full discussion of "objectification." Later we shall have to examine that notion more closely. At this point we need only indicate how the satisfaction of an occasion exists for the occasions which supersede it.

We have noticed that the subjective aim of an occasion is at intensity in the relevant future as well as in the immediate subject (PR 41). The occasion "wants" to be something for future actualities and thus to transcend itself. This is in accord with the principle of relativity, namely that "it belongs to the nature of a 'being' that it is a potential for every 'becoming'" (PR 33). To be is to be effective (AI 165). It belongs to the nature of an actual occasion that it should be effective beyond itself. The way this role is assumed is objectification.

"Objective immortality" is the term for the way an occasion exists after it has perished (PR 44, 94). Now it is the satisfaction which "embodies what the actual entity is beyond itself" (PR 335). Hence we may confine ourselves to asking in what way the satisfaction is "objective" and in what way it is "immortal."

Whitehead's use of "objective" seems to have been taken from Descartes: "Hence the idea of the sun will be the sun itself existing in the mind, not indeed formally, as it exists in the sky, but objectively, *i.e.*, in the way in which objects are wont to exist in the mind; and this mode of being is truly much less perfect than that in which things exist outside the mind, but it is not on that account mere nothing, as I have already said" (as quoted in SMW 104 n. and PR 118 from Descartes's *Reply to Objections I*, tr. Haldane and Ross, 2, 10). Whitehead says of this passage that it "practically . . . expresses the doctrine of objectification here put forward" (PR 118). The point to be noted is the contrast between "objective" and "formal" existence. "I will adopt the pre-Kantian phraseology, and say that the experience enjoyed by an actual entity is that entity *formaliter*" (PR 81). Objective existence is not the experience enjoyed by an actual occasion. It is not the way the occasion exists for itself. It is the way the occasion exists for other occasions.

Indeed, an actual occasion cannot exist as objectively immortal until it has ceased to exist for itself. That which is objectively existent is "divested of its own living immediacy" (PR ix). "The immediacy of existence is then past and over" (MT 131). The attainment of objective immortality means "the 'perishing' of absoluteness" (PR 94). When an actual occasion exists objectively, it is no longer an experiencing thing. "Its own process, which is its own internal existence, has evaporated, worn out and satisfied" (PR 336). It is now "dead" (PR ix); it exists as "dry bones" which future ways of feelings will reclothe with the flesh of "a real being" (PR 131).

It follows that when an occasion exists objectively it is no longer actual, in the strict sense of "actuality." For "actuality" is strictly correlated with "immediacy" of feeling.

> The actuality is the enjoyment, and this enjoyment is the experiencing of value (RM 100).

> 'Feeling' is used as a synonym for 'actuality' (RM 104).

> An entity is actual, when it has significance for itself. By this it is meant that an actual entity functions in respect to its own determination. . . . this self-functioning is the real internal constitution of an actual entity. It is the 'immediacy' of the actual entity (PR 38).

Thus when the satisfaction of an occasion exists objectively it no longer exists as an immediate feeling. That is to say it is no longer actual.

"Potentiality," not "actuality," is the term for the mode of existence denoted by "objective immortality." "The word 'object' thus means an entity which is a potentiality for being a component in feeling" (PR 136). This is why Whitehead speaks of the "pragmatic" value of the satisfaction existing objectively (PR 126, 134–5, 336). The satisfaction is now "an instrument for purposes" (AI 270), namely the purposes of those occasions which supersede it.

It exists as material for use by future acts of experience. In the objective existence of an actual entity, "the *esse* of its satisfaction is *sentiri*" (PR 336).

For this reason the objectified satisfaction is "divisible." It is a datum for analysis and abstraction. Formerly, as an immediate feeling, it was a complete unity of internal relations, an indivisible unity. Now some of its component feelings can be taken apart from the others. And this is what happens when other actual occasions prehend it. They prehend only some of its feelings, abstracting them from the full unity of its satisfaction. Objectification involves abstraction (PR 345-7, 359, 361).

The satisfaction of an actual occasion, when it has lost its immediacy, is not only objective but also immortal. The satisfied occasion persists and retains its identity as an object throughout its adventures in the future. The satisfaction is "fully determinate . . . as to its objective character for the transcendent creativity" (PR 38). "No entity—be it 'universal' or 'particular'—can play disjoined rôles. Self-identity requires that every entity have one conjoined, self-consistent function, whatever be the complexity of that function" (PR 89). An actual occasion A does not mean precisely the same thing for each occasion which prehends it. On the contrary, A will be prehended differently by each occasion according to its perspective standpoint. In each case, however, what will be prehended will be A, under those varying limitations.

The satisfaction in its objective existence is thus a "givenness" to which the future must conform in one way or another. It is a "real potential" not a "pure potential." Pure potentiality is the mode of existence of eternal objects. These are universals which have no particular local habitation. They tell no tales about their "ingression" into actuality. Real potentiality is the mode of existence of actual entities when they are objectively immortal. Such an entity has a local habitation, and in all its roles it is *that* actual entity objectified.

4. *Is the theory self-consistent?*

As a step toward finding out how an actual occasion is a real individual we are examining a crucial part of Whitehead's theory, namely the notion of the satisfaction of an occasion. The following propositions have been explained and supported as an interpretation of that notion.

a. The satisfaction of an actual occasion is both aimed at and attained in the experience of that occasion.

b. The satisfaction of an actual occasion is a feeling immediate to that occasion.

c. The satisfaction of an actual occasion is completely unified and determinate in relation to every other entity.

d. The satisfaction of an actual occasion is not a process of change.

e. The satisfaction of an actual occasion exists objectively for all occasions that supersede that occasion.

Now we must ask about the compatibility of these propositions. Two questions call for discussion. (i) The close connection between process and feeling prompts the question whether proposition *b* and proposition *d* are compatible. For it would seem that all feelings are processes of change. (ii) The fact that subjective immediacy and objective immortality are mutually exclusive predicates leads to the question whether propositions *b* and *e* are compatible. Otherwise the consistency of this theory of the satisfaction is fairly clear.

i. Let us test the compatibility of *b* and *d* by stating a difficulty. It seems that all immediate feelings are processes. For "immediacy" is defined as "self-functioning," and self-functioning seems to mean some kind of change within the subject. Thus it seems that if the satisfaction is a feeling immediate to its subject, then it must be a process of change within its subject. If the satisfaction is not a process of change, it seems to lack the immediacy of a living feeling. This difficulty is due not merely to faulty reading of what Whitehead says but also to the fact that many of his statements are mystifying or misleading. But I shall argue that it arises from a misinterpretation of his intention.

We should begin with categories of explanation xx-xxiii:

(xx) That to 'function' means to contribute determination to the actual entities in the nexus of some actual
world. . . .

(xxi) An entity is actual, when it has significance for itself.
By this it is meant that an actual entity functions in respect
to its own determination. Thus an actual entity combines
self-identity with self-diversity.

(xxii) That an actual entity by functioning in respect to
itself plays diverse rôles in self-formation without losing
its self-identity. It is self-creative; and in its process of creation transforms its diversity of rôles into one coherent rôle.
Thus 'becoming' is the transformation of incoherence into
coherence, and in each particular instance ceases with this
attainment.

(xxiii) That this self-functioning is the real internal constitution of an actual entity. It is the 'immediacy' of the
actual entity. An actual entity is called the 'subject' of its
own immediacy (PR 38).

First note the definition of "immediacy." The immediacy of an
actual entity is its "self-functioning." And self-functioning means
that the entity "contributes determination" to itself, "has significance for itself," or "functions in respect to its own determination." Self-functioning involves "self-diversity," so that the actual
entity "plays diverse roles in self-formation."

We can understand how this would apply to a "partial" feeling,
in those phases of the concrescence before the satisfaction. In any
such feeling the occasion plays diverse roles. The subject functions
as actual and also as potential. It exists actually as an incomplete
subject; it exists potentially as a complete subject. The complete
subject functions, in the earlier phases of the concrescence, as the
ideal toward which the subjective aim tends. In this sense, in a
"partial" feeling, the entity "has significance for itself" and "combines self-identity with self-diversity." It is this diversity of ideal
and actuality which in the earlier phases makes internal process
necessary. The actual must undergo change to become the ideal.

If the satisfaction is a feeling immediate to its subject, it seems
that the subject must play diverse roles in its satisfaction also.

But how is this possible if the satisfaction is a fully integrated feeling? For it would seem that in such a feeling the subject must be present in a single unambiguous sense. Self-diversity would seem to be a function only of earlier phases of the concrescence. Since the satisfaction actualizes the ideal and completes the concrescence it would seem to eliminate self-diversity. It would thus escape the categoreal demand for further internal process. But as a further consequence, it seems, it would fail to qualify as an immediate feeling. Insofar as it is not "in becoming," it seems, it is not immediate.

Some escape from this paradoxical conclusion, which requires us to say that the satisfaction is actual but not immediate, must be sought. One might say that the satisfaction of a given occasion exists as a "feeling" for those actual occasions which supersede it, in the sense that it is *given* for them as a feeling, even though it does not exist as a feeling in the immediacy of its subject. The satisfaction would then be a limiting case of immediacy. It would function only as an ideal in the experience of its subject. It would be a fact only in the experiences of other subjects. This is to regard the satisfaction as a feeling only in a Pickwickian sense.

There is another possibility. The satisfaction may be a limiting case of immediacy in the sense that it falls within the series of phases of its subject's experience as the last member in that series. This would be possible if in this last phase the self-diversity of the subject functions in another way than in the earlier phases. This can be shown.

The satisfaction is not a simple feeling. On the contrary, it synthesizes all the component feelings of the concrescence. It has a complex objective datum and a complex subjective form. Its objective datum is a synthesis of the data of the component feelings, while its subjective form is a synthesis of the subjective forms of the component feelings. Thus all the diverse roles which the subject has had throughout the concrescence, as the subject of each of the component feelings, are retained within the final synthesis. They are now in coherence with one another, but the identity of each of the roles has been retained. According to category of explanation xxvi, "Each element in the genetic process of an actual entity has one self-consistent function, however complex, in the final satisfaction" (PR 38–9). In this sense self-diversity of the subject is present in the satisfaction, which thus qualifies as an instance of immediacy. The entity in its satisfaction has significance for itself; it functions in respect to its own determination. The feeling of satisfaction is its final act of self-determination.

In the earlier phases there is disparity between the subject as actually incomplete and the subject as ideally complete. This disparity spurs on the process of integration. But the self-diversity of the subject in its final phase is a diversity within a *realized* unity. In this phase, and only in this phase, self-diversity does not involve a categoreal demand for further internal process of becoming. This is to say that propositions *b* and *d* assert, that the satisfaction of an occasion is a feeling immediate to that occasion *and* that it is not a process of change.

ii. Now consider proposition *b,* which asserts that the satisfaction is an immediate feeling, and proposition *e,* which asserts that it exists as an object. They seem to present a contradiction. For an actual entity which has objective immortality is "divested of its own living immediacy" (PR ix; see 94, AI 305, MT 131). How then is it possible to say that the satisfaction is both subjectively immediate and objectively immortal?

Before going further we should notice some passages where Whitehead seems to say that the satisfaction belongs *only* to the objective existence of an occasion. For example:

> The notion of 'satisfaction' is the notion of 'the entity as concrete' abstracted from the 'process of concrescence'; it is the outcome separated from the process, thereby losing the actuality of the atomic entity, which is both process and outcome . . . the 'satisfaction' is the 'superject' rather than the 'substance' or the 'subject.' . . . The 'formal' reality of the actuality in question belongs to its process of concrescence and not to its 'satisfaction' (PR 129).

> This terminal unity of operation, here called the 'satisfaction,' embodies what the actual entity is beyond itself. . . . It is the actual entity as a definite, determinate, settled fact, stubborn and with unavoidable consequences. The actual

entity as described by the morphology of its satisfaction is the actual entity 'spatialized,' to use Bergson's term. . . . Its own process, which is its own internal existence, has evaporated, worn out and satisfied; but its effects are all to be described in terms of its 'satisfaction' (PR 335–6).

Since these passages seem to identify the satisfaction with the objective existence of the entity, and since what is only an object cannot have subjective immediacy, these passages seem to contradict proposition *b* above.

My conclusion about these passages is that Whitehead has created a difficulty for his readers by failing to express his theory with sufficient care. For elsewhere it is generally very clear that the satisfaction is a subjectively immediate feeling. It is true that some qualifications mitigate the misleading impression. For instance according to the second passage the satisfaction is a "terminal *unity of operation*" (my italics). But the impression remains. Especially in the earlier passage there are sentences which flatly contradict what is said elsewhere about the satisfaction.

To see how both subjective immediacy and objective immortality might be predicated of the satisfaction without contradiction, let us look at some other ways of denoting these two modes of existence. One way is in terms of "privacy" and "publicity." As part of the immediate experience of its subject, the satisfaction is a fact private to its subject. "Thus the satisfaction is the attainment of the private ideal which is the final cause of the concrescence . . . [It is] a unity of aesthetic appreciation immediately felt as private" (PR 323). As an object for analysis and abstraction, the satisfaction is a public fact (PR 229, 443).

This distinction between privacy and publicity refers to diverse standpoints. From the standpoint of the subject, that is *for* the subject, the satisfaction is an immediate experience. As such it is a private fact. *In its own immediacy of feeling* the satisfaction is accessible to no other occasion than its subject. (This will be discussed in detail in Chapter 3.) From the standpoint of any occasion other than the subject, the satisfaction exists as a public fact, an object. It is still the satisfaction of *that* subject, but it has lost its own immediacy of feeling.

These standpoints cannot, so to speak, overlap. The satisfaction of A is an ideal for A, and it is enjoyed by A. But it cannot be a *given* fact for A. This underlies Whitehead's saying that "No actual entity can be conscious of its own satisfaction; for such knowledge would be a component in the process, and would thereby alter the satisfaction" (PR 130). The satisfaction of an occasion can be *pointed to* or *discussed* only from the standpoints of other occasions.

> The analysis of an actual entity is only intellectual, or to speak with a wider scope, only objective (PR 347).

> . . . the 'satisfaction' of an entity can only be discussed in terms of the usefulness of that entity (PR 130).

> When we consider the process under examination as completed, we are already analysing an active datum for other creations (MT 123).

These and similar passages do not deny that the satisfaction exists for its subject as an immediate feeling. They do assert that it cannot be an object for its own subject. It can be an object only for an occasion with some other standpoint.

Viewed in this light, the assertion that the satisfaction of an occasion is a private fact, and the assertion that it is a public fact, are not incompatible. The statement that "there is no element in the universe capable of pure privacy" (PR 324) means there is no actual entity whose experience does not *become* a public fact, *as well as* being a fact for itself. It asserts that every actual entity gets to be objectified for other actual entities. "The creative process is rhythmic: it swings from the publicity of many things to the individual privacy; and it swings back from the private individual to the publicity of the objectified individual. The former swing is dominated by the final cause, which is the ideal; and the latter swing is dominated by the efficient cause which is actual" (PR 229).

Another way Whitehead denotes these two modes of existence is in terms of "intrinsic reality" and "extrinsic reality," as found in the following single passage: "There is thus an intrinsic and an extrinsic reality of an event, namely, the event as in its own prehension, and the event as in the prehension of other events" (SMW 146). It is clear that in the context "event" is equivalent to "actual occasion." An occasion in its subjective immediacy as a private fact has intrinsic reality. It is something for itself. In its objective immortality as a public fact it has extrinsic reality. It is something for other actual occasions. I am arguing that the satisfaction belongs both to the intrinsic reality and to the extrinsic reality of the occasion.

Still another way of expressing the two modes of existence is in terms of "subject" and "superject." For example:

> An actual entity is to be conceived both as a subject presiding over its own immediacy of becoming, and a superject which is the atomic creature exercising its function of objective immortality (PR 71).

> An actual entity considered in reference to the publicity of things is a 'superject'; namely, it arises from the publicity which it finds, and it adds itself to the publicity which it transmits. . . . An actual entity considered in reference to the privacy of things is a 'subject'; namely, it is a moment of the genesis of self-enjoyment (PR 443).

Thus when the satisfaction is spoken of as "subjective" (PR 82, 135, 244), it is meant that the satisfaction is an immediate experience private to the occasion. When the satisfaction is spoken of as the "superject" (PR 129), it is meant that the satisfaction is a public fact expressing the objective immortality of the occasion in the future beyond itself. The statement that "the 'satisfaction' is the 'superject' rather than the 'substance' or the 'subject'" (PR 129) is misleading because it suggests that the satisfaction is to be identified *exclusively* with the objective existence of the occasion.

Propositions *b* and *e* are not incompatible if they refer to different modes of existence of the satisfaction, and we have noticed various ways in which Whitehead expresses this duality. It is intelligible to attribute these two modes of existence to one and the same entity because of two complementary considerations.

On the one hand the occasion aims at intensity of experience in other actual entities as well as in itself. But it cannot contribute to the experiences of other entities without ceasing to exist in its own subjective immediacy. Hence attainment of its satisfaction requires the perishing of immediacy and passage into objective existence. The subjective immediacy of an occasion calls for its objective immortality.

On the other hand, whatever the varied roles of the occasion as an object, there is a self-identity among them all. Wherever the occasion functions as an object, it functions as *that* particular actual occasion which came into being as an immediate subject and achieved its satisfaction *then* and *there*. Thus the objective existence of an actual occasion points to its previous existence as an immediate experience. The objective immortality of an actual occasion is "the superject *of its experiences*" (PR 43, my italics).

In these ways the two modes of existence require each other. The self-functioning of the occasion, in its satisfaction as well as in its earlier phases, has an essential reference beyond its own immediacy to its objective functioning. On the other hand its objective functioning has an essential reference to its self-functioning, including its achievement of a subjectively immediate satisfaction.

It thus appears that propositions *b* and *e* are not incompatible. The satisfaction of an actual occasion is an immediate feeling which, when it perishes, exists as an object for occasions which succeed it.

5. Conclusion: Process and reality

Our topic has been the individuality of an actual occasion as an act of experience. An occasion is more than a collection of abstract characters. It is a concrete thing in the only sense in which, in the philosophy of organism, anything is concrete, namely as an experiencing thing. It is actual, not abstract, because it is an act of experience. Again, an occasion is more than a mere flux of experiencing within spatiotemporal limitations, since it has a structure and an individual absoluteness of character we have attempted to understand in terms of its satisfaction.

In its feeling of satisfaction the occasion has become a complete and fully concrete thing. If an occasion were only a process of internal change, it would not be complete or fully concrete. In the following passage, taken from a section titled "Individuality" in *Adventures of Ideas,* Whitehead is in effect pointing out how the satisfaction is the basis for real individuality.

> The individual immediacy of an occasion is the final unity of subjective form, which is the occasion as an absolute reality. This immediacy is its moment of sheer individuality, bounded on either side by essential relativity. The occasion arises from relevant objects, and perishes into the status of an object for other occasions. But it enjoys its decisive moment of absolute self-attainment as emotional unity. As used here the words 'individual' and 'atom' have the same meaning, that they apply to composite things with an absolute reality which their components lack. These words properly apply to an actual entity in its immediacy of self-attainment when it stands out as for itself alone, with its own affective self-enjoyment. The term 'monad' also expresses this essential unity at the decisive moment, which stands between its birth and its perishing (AI 227).

An actual occasion is "something individual for its own sake." We now turn to the question of how an occasion, by virtue of its absoluteness of realization, transcends other actual occasions.

CHAPTER 3

Novelty and Exclusiveness

A GENUINE PLURALISM requires a theory of real individuality. Now a real individual is a complete and fully concrete thing that differs from all other such things. It is *this* concrete and complete thing, not *that*. A real individual is a particular thing, and is thus socially transcendent. In this chapter we ask how an actual occasion as an act of experience transcends the experiences of other occasions. In the next chapter we consider the spatiotemporal character of actual occasions and ask how Whitehead's theory of extension expresses his doctrine of social transcendence.

An actual occasion as an act of experience transcends other occasions by way of its novelty and by way of its exclusiveness. Our treatment of the novelty of an actual occasion will be brief. Most of this chapter deals with the exclusiveness of an actual occasion as an act of experience. Concerning this latter topic some important problems of interpretation arise.

1. The novelty of an actual occasion

Every actual occasion is a novel act of becoming. For the course of nature is a "creative advance" in which genuinely new things become. History never repeats itself in exact detail. Whitehead's realistic view of time leads to the consequence that every act of becoming is a novel act, and in every becoming what becomes is a novel thing.

> An actual occasion is a novel entity diverse from any entity in the 'many' which it unifies (PR 31).

> Every actual entity, in virtue of its novelty, transcends its universe, God included (PR 143).

This means that no two occasions are identical in their "real internal constitutions." They are not merely numerically diverse; each is different from all others in the structure and quality of its immediate experience. In each occasion there is a "novel determinateness of feeling" (PR 72), a "novel immediacy" (PR 207). In this respect an occasion transcends all others. Of course different occasions may have specific characters in common. But an occasion is not a mere aggregate of characters. As we have seen, it is a creative synthesis that fuses its data and subjective forms into a determinate unity of experience. The real internal constitutions of occasions differ in respect to (a) their data, (b) their subjective forms, (c) their subjective aims, and consequently (d) their satisfactions.

a. No two actual occasions have the same set of data for feeling. This is clear from the fifth category of explanation: "That no two actual entities originate from an identical universe; though the difference between the two universes only consists in some actual entities, included in one and not in the other, and in the subordinate entities which each actual entity introduces into the world" (PR 33–4). "No two occasions can have identical actual worlds" (PR 321). Two occasions may have some data in common. But every occasion is different from every other occasion in respect to the total set of data for its feeling. *What is felt* is different. In this respect every occasion is a novel act of experience.

b. Actual occasions differ also in their subjective forms of feeling. The novelty of an occasion is in this respect even more decisive than in respect to its data for feeling. For even where two occasions feel the same datum, they will not feel this datum in the same way. The "how" of feeling is different. "The essential novelty of a feeling attaches to its subjective form. The initial data, and even the nexus which is the objective datum, may have served other feelings with other subjects. But the subjective form is the immediate novelty; it is how *that* subject is feeling that objective datum" (PR 354).

c. The reason an occasion's subjective forms of feeling are novel is that it has a novel subjective aim. It aims at a specific satisfaction appropriate to its actual world. And its aim at this novel ideal affects the subjective forms of its feelings.

Incidentally this introduces us to one important function of eternal objects in Whitehead's theory of actual occasions. In the initial stage of a concrescence the datum for its subjective aim cannot be an actuality. The problem of the concrescence is to bring a *new* actuality into existence. Therefore we require a category of nonactual entities to serve as data of initial subjective aims. The datum of a subjective aim is initially an eternal object or "pure potential" which functions as the "form of definiteness" of the ideal satisfaction at which the concrescence aims. Thus eternal objects are needed for explanation of the teleological structure of an occasion. This function of eternal objects will be examined in some detail in Parts Two and Three.

d. Finally and consequently the satisfaction of an actual occasion is novel. The novel ideal at which the concrescence aims is finally achieved. All its component feelings are harmonized in one integral feeling with a complex datum and a complex unity of subjective form. The concrescence has produced a novel concrete actuality.

Thus we find one important sense in which an actual occasion is socially transcendent. Its total set of data for feeling, its subjective forms of feeling, its subjective aim, and its satisfaction differ from those of any other occasion. We have seen that an actual occasion is an individual in the sense of being a concrete and complete thing. It is something for itself, a unified act of immediate experience. We can now say that an occasion is an individual in the further sense that its real internal constitution is novel. In virtue of its novelty as an act of experience an actual occasion transcends all others.

2. Experiential exclusiveness

In the rest of this chapter we shall be concerned with another mode of social transcendence, namely the exclusiveness of an actual occasion as an act of experience. This we may call, for the sake of convenience, "experiential exclusiveness." It is important to make clear what will not be asserted.

It will not be asserted that an actual occasion excludes all other occasions in the sense that it is completely independent of them or isolated from them. This would plainly contradict Whitehead's doctrine of objectification, his theory of how one actual entity is "present in" another. Nothing could be clearer than the principle that actual occasions *are* present in other occasions. This is fundamental to the philosophy of organism. The positive meaning of objectification will be examined in detail in Chapters 6–8.

It is equally clear that when one actual occasion is said to be present in or immanent in another occasion, these statements are not to be taken in any simple sense. Whitehead's warning is worth repeating: "The philosophy of organism is mainly devoted to the task of making clear the notion of 'being present in another entity.' This phrase is here borrowed from Aristotle: it is not a fortunate phrase, and in subsequent discussion it will be replaced by the term 'objectification.' The Aristotelian phrase suggests the crude notion that one actual entity is added to another *simpliciter*. This is not what is meant" (PR 79–80). We are concerned with the sense in which one actual occasion as an act of experience is *not* present in another occasion. The issue is not whether or not one actual occasion is immanent in another. The only live issue is in what sense an occasion is immanent in another and in what sense it is not. A notion which Whitehead's philosophy is "mainly devoted" to clarifying can scarcely be a simple notion.

We shall be attempting to give some precise meaning to what is asserted in the following passages:

> . . . an actual event is an achievement for its own sake, a grasping of diverse entities into a value by reason of their real togetherness in that pattern, to the exclusion of other entities (SMW 147).

> The essence of depth of actuality—that is of vivid experience —is definiteness. Now to be definite always means that all the elements of a complex whole contribute to some *one* effect, to the exclusion of others. The creative process is a process of exclusion to the same extent as it is a process of inclusion (RM 113).

> The individuality of an actual entity involves an exclusive limitation. This element of 'exclusive limitation' is the defi-

niteness essential for the synthetic unity of an actual entity (PR 72).

All forms of realization express some aspect of finitude. Such a form expresses its nature as being *this,* and not *that.* In other words, it expresses exclusion; and exclusion means finitude (MT 107).

To understand Whitehead's view, it is as important to see how an actual occasion is exclusive of other occasions as it is to see how an actual occasion is inclusive of other occasions.

The interpretation I propose is that no two actual occasions have any immediacy of feeling in common. Among actual occasions there is no sharing of immediacy.[1] No two actual occasions mutually enjoy any feeling. No feeling "belongs" to the subjective immediacies of any two actual occasions at the same time. This is the most general sense in which the experiences of occasions are mutually exclusive. Further specifications of experiential exclusiveness can be explained in relation to contemporary, future, and past occasions respectively.

It will not be denied that there is "feeling of feeling." Whitehead clearly means to assert this. What is denied is that the feeling felt is in the same mode of existence as the feeling which "feels." It is suggested that the feeling felt is, when felt, in the mode of objective immortality, and that the feeling which feels is, when it feels, in the mode of subjective immediacy. Thus the experience of a subject as felt from within is private to that subject and is not, as immediate feeling, shared in by any other subject. It is the intrinsic reality of that subject. What is public is the objective existence or extrinsic reality or superject of an occasion. The private experience of a subject will become a public or objective fact, the superject. So that no fact, if we consider its whole career, is a purely private fact. But the subjective immediacy of any feeling is private and unsharable.

1. In a conversation in 1942 Whitehead seemed to endorse the phrase, "no sharing of immediacy," as an epitomization of his view on this point. But this interpretation is proposed as an interpretation of his *writings.*

3. The exclusiveness of contemporary occasions

Generally it is clear that an actual occasion does not influence its contemporaries. Actual occasions contemporary with A do not, as concrete units of experience, affect the experience of A. Whitehead expresses this mutual exclusiveness of contemporaries in terms of causation and in terms of perception.

Any two contemporary occasions "are not in any direct relation of efficient causation" (AI 251). Contemporary occasions are "causally independent" of each other. In fact, "It is the definition of contemporary events that they happen in causal independence of each other" (AI 251. See TIME 62; PR 95, 188, 482, 489).

Likewise there is no direct perception of contemporary occasions. In "presentational immediacy," the mode of perception in which the contemporary world is apprehended, the subject perceives a contemporary region but not contemporary actual occasions. The "particular occasions of the contemporary world, each with its own individual spontaneity, are veiled from the observer" (AI 280. See TIME 62; SYMBOLISM 16; PR 96–7, 188, 484, 498; AI 281).

Thus if P is an actual occasion contemporary with A, then P and A are causally independent of each other, and neither perceives the other as an individual unit of experience.[2] This separation between the experiences of contemporary actual occasions means quite clearly that there is no sharing of immediacy, no mutual enjoyment of feeling. It seems that no two contemporary occasions have the subjective immediacy of any feeling in common.

2. Whitehead does not identify (a) the set of actual occasions causally independent of A, with (b) the set of actual occasions prehended by A with presentational immediacy. Set (b) constitutes the "presented duration" (TIME 63; PR 256–7, 486–90). The former set, namely those occasions which are causally independent of A, includes the latter set. But the former set also includes occasions which are not members of the latter set. Note that if P and M are both members of the former set, they need not be contemporary with each other, though both will be contemporary with A. This is Whitehead's way of providing for alternative time systems, which he understands the physical theory of relativity requires.

. . . the immediate activity of self-creation is separate and private, so far as contemporaries are concerned (AI 252).

. . . the contemporary entities do not enter into the constitution of the percipient subject by objectification through any of their own feelings (PR 484; see 188, 489).

For the sake of completeness we must ask whether this mutual exclusiveness of contemporary occasions has to be qualified in any way. For instance, Whitehead says there is "relevance" between contemporaries in spite of their causal independence. Does this entail any sharing of immediacy? Relevance is said to occur in two ways.

a. There is a mutual relevance between two contemporary occasions in that they participate in a common locus, a "now" which is spatially and temporally extended. For each of the occasions this "now" extends indefinitely beyond its own basic region, which is here-now. It is there-now as well as here-now. Thus "there is a 'unison of becoming,' constituting a positive relation of all the occasions in this community to any one of them. The members of this community share in a common immediacy; they are in 'unison' as to their becoming: that is to say, any pair of occasions in the locus are contemporaries" (PR 189).

But this does not say nearly as much as it seems to say. The "positive relation" between the occasions consists only in the fact that they are contemporaries. Neither of two such occasions prehends the other *as* an individual actual occasion contemporary with itself. For either occasion, what is given is simply a locus ("now") whose members are in unison with it. The expression "share in a common immediacy" is therefore liable to be very misleading. It belongs, in its context, to a series of statements intended as equivalents. It means merely that the pair of occasions are contemporaries, in "unison of becoming." It does not mean that they have any mutual enjoyment of feeling.

For occasions of a relatively high grade of complexity, a contemporary region may be given in presentational immediacy. That is, the region may be perceived as the locus of sensa, and as subject to mathematical relations (PR 96-7, 188-90, 193-4, 472-86, 498;

AI 253). But the sensa and the geometrical relations in terms of which the "now" is "spatialized" are not contributed by the contemporary occasions. They are derived from the subject's own past and "projected" (PR 472–90) by it on the region. The "illustration" of the contemporary region is thus "subjective" (PR 189). The "spatialized world" of the "presented duration" is "objectified for M by M's own conditioned range of feeling-tones which have been inherited from the causal past of . . . M" (PR 488–9).

In any case, whether there is perception in the mode of presentational immediacy or not, the duration shared by contemporary occasions is not defined *for* an occasion *by* its contemporaries. It is defined by the occasion's own experience of itself. Contemporary occasions enter into the definition of the duration only as hypothetical actual entities. No specific facts about any individual occasions in the locus are directly given. This kind of "relevance" does not entail any direct prehension of any contemporary by another, and *a fortiori* it does not entail any sharing of immediacy.

Some of Whitehead's discussions of presentational immediacy have caused some confusion. For instance: "Presentational immediacy is our immediate perception of the contemporary external world, appearing as an element constitutive of our own experience. In this appearance the world discloses itself to be a community of actual things, which are actual in the same sense as we are" (SYMBOLISM 21). Language like this seems to imply direct disclosure of some features of contemporary occasions. Usually Whitehead's account of presentational immediacy is more careful. Victor Lowe's explanation of the confusion is that such language is a vestige of Whitehead's earlier philosophy of nature,

> . . . in which causality was little analyzed. A contemporary world of things was assumed as a datum, and the characteristics of the sense-data were related together by a primarily atemporal theory of their multiple inherence in events. . . . On passing from examination of perception to examination of experience, he adopted the view that it is the *antecedent* environment that is the datum for an occasion of experience. Then there is no awareness of absolutely contemporary occasions: *they* constitute no datum for the present. But after

that we find, as we must expect, that some of Whitehead's discussions of the contemporary world retain language which, as ordinarily used, is appropriate only if that world is considered as a datum (Schilpp 100–1).

b. Whitehead also speaks of another kind of relevance between contemporary occasions, an "indirect relevance" (PR 98–9, 484–5; AI 252, 280). No two occasions have identical past actual worlds. But two neighboring contemporary occasions may have past actual worlds which are *practically* though not completely identical. In the case of contemporaries remote from each other, the difference between their pasts will be important. In ordinary human experience the difference is practically negligible. Such occasions inherit from what is for practical purposes a common past. It is thus possible for a subject to make fortunate guesses about the nature of its contemporary world.

Whitehead goes so far as to call this "indirect prehension" (AI 280) of contemporaries. But it should be quite clear that what is *directly* prehended is not contemporary actuality but past actuality. Judgments about the contemporary world are not derived from any direct intuition of contemporary actuality; they are pragmatic judgments for practical purposes. "The animal body is so constructed that, with rough accuracy and in normal conditions, important emphasis is thus laid upon those regions in the contemporary world which are particularly relevant for the future existence of the enduring object of which the immediate percipient is one occasion" (PR 99). This indirect relevance of contemporary actual occasions does not imply any sharing of immediate experience.

Another question arises from the following passage: ". . . so far as physical relations are concerned, contemporary events happen in *causal* independence of each other" (PR 95). The limiting clause, "so far as physical relations are concerned," suggests there are some relations between contemporaries, other than physical relations, to which the assertion of causal independence does not apply. It is difficult to determine just what this passage is meant to imply. Two possibilities may be suggested:

i. The implied relations *may* be those relations indicated above under the first type of relevance between contemporaries, namely the relations of being in unison of becoming, and of participating in a common system of geometrical relations in the extensive continuum. These are not "physical" relations in Whitehead's sense, since they do not involve prehension of individual actual occasions. On this interpretation, no qualification of the experiential exclusiveness of contemporaries would be required.

ii. On the other hand, the implied relations to which causal independence does not apply *may* be relations between the mental activities of contemporary occasions. This interpretation might find support in what Whitehead says about the possibility of telepathy. These remarks are usually *obiter dicta,* and they are not numerous, but they must be taken into account. For example, ". . . we must also allow for the possibility that we can detect in ourselves direct aspects of the mentalities of higher organisms" (SMW 209). He regards it as a "more natural" hypothesis than its contrary that direct "transmission of mental feeling" may occur between noncontiguous occasions, although direct transmission of physical feeling always occurs between contiguous occasions. He adds, "This conclusion has some empirical support, both from the evidence for peculiar instances of telepathy, and from the instinctive apprehension of a tone of feeling in ordinary social intercourse" (PR 469; see 468).

In most of the passages referring to telepathy Whitehead has in mind the possibility of direct objectification of mental feelings of noncontiguous *past* actual occasions. Mental feeling is said to be transmitted by "hybrid prehension," and "a hybrid prehension has as its datum an antecedent occasion objectified in respect to a *conceptual* prehension" (PR 469). In this passage, which amplifies the earlier and more tentative statement in *Science and the Modern World,* the transmission is from the past to the future. So these passages do not support the suggestion that mental feelings of *contemporary* actual occasions are directly prehended.

The following passage, however, refers to the contemporary world:

> Perhaps in the mutual immanence of occasions . . . the relations of the mental poles to each other are not subject to

the same laws of perspective as are those of the physical poles. Measureable time and measureable space are then irrelevant to their mutual connections. Thus in respect to some types of Appearance there may be an element of immediacy in its relations to the mental side of the contemporary world. . . . If such be the case, some types of Appearance will have a more direct relation than others to contemporary Reality (AI 318).

At first sight this seems to say that an actual occasion may prehend directly mental feelings of some contemporary occasions. If so, then it conflicts with Whitehead's general treatment of the subject. So interpreted it would assert what he generally denies, namely that there is direct influence between contemporaries. As far as I can discover, no other passage makes this suggestion. And further study of its context leads to a different interpretation.

The clue to a better interpretation lies in the meaning of "appearance." In this part of *Adventures of Ideas,* appearance means the contribution of the mental pole of the occasion, its valuations, syntheses, and transformations, to the objective datum of the satisfaction (AI 268–70). The "difference between the objective content of the initial phase of the physical pole and the objective content of the final phase, after the integration of physical and mental poles, constitutes 'appearance' for that occasion" (AI 270). Appearance is therefore important only in organisms where mentality is important, and means simply the contemporary world *as it appears,* "the world presented to us for our enjoyments and our purposes. It is the world in the guise of a subject-matter for an imposed activity" (AI 271).

In chapter 16 of *Adventures of Ideas,* where the problematical passage occurs, Whitehead defines truth as a qualification of appearance, namely "the conformation of Appearance to Reality" (AI 309). And he is distinguishing between direct and indirect truth-relations. Now, "Within any type of truth-relation a distinction arises. . . . The Appearance of the contemporary regions has its truth-relations to the past, and its truth-relations to contemporary Reality" (AI 317). It is clear enough that truth-relations to the past may be direct. But truth-relations to contemporary reality "can only be estimated by an imaginative leap, which has as its basis for justification the truth-relations to the past and our experience of the stability of the types of order involved" (AI 317–18).

Thus our passage may suggest an exception to the indirectness of truth-relations to contemporary reality. There may be in some cases a direct truth-relation of appearance to contemporary reality. There would be a direct meaning for truth. But direct truth-relations do not necessarily involve direct perception:

> . . . the infant feels its mother's cheerfulness as a datum, and feels it conformally, with that affective tone. The *datum is derived from the past, the immediate past*. It is precipitated upon the present region occupied by the nexus of occasions which constitute the complex fact of the mother's existence, body and soul. For the infant, the Appearance includes the qualification of cheerfulness. And in this respect it may have —and it often does have—to the contemporary real mother a truth-relation in the fullest sense of the term 'truth' (AI 316, my italics).

Here "fullest" seems to mean "most direct." Thus directness of truth-relation does not require directness of perception, for in this passage indirectness of perception is explicitly asserted.

Even if this passage means there is direct prehension of contemporary mental activity, it does not follow that there is sharing of immediacy. It will be shown below that experiential exclusiveness is entirely compatible with *direct* prehension of the past by the present. But if, as Whitehead generally maintains clearly and emphatically, there is no direct prehension of contemporary occasions, then it would follow a fortiori that there is no sharing of immediacy. In this way an actual occasion transcends its contemporaries. "Thus the occasion of experience is absolute in respect to its immediate self-enjoyment. How it deals with its data is to be understood without reference to any other concurrent occasions. Thus the occasion, in reference to its internal process, requires no contemporary process in order to exist. In fact this mutual independence in the internal process of self-adjustment is the definition of contemporaneousness" (MT 206).

The primary reason for Whitehead's insistence on the mutual independence of contemporaries is the need to leave room for real

individuality. Another reason may be the fact that physical transmission takes time.[3] But the former reason is the more important
one. Why, in Whitehead's system, is the independence of contemporaries necessary for the real individuality of actual occasions?
It is true that each actual entity must have its own perspective.
But this requirement *might* be met by the "principle of intensive
relevance," as Charles Hartshorne has suggested (*Phil. Rev. 48,*
422), without requiring the independence of contemporaries.

The real reason that, in Whitehead's system, the independence
of contemporaries is necessary is the categoreal obligation of internal unity and completeness. If the concrescence is to eventuate
in a complete integration of its feelings, if it is to achieve subjective unity, then there must be a duration in which the concrescence
is closed to further contributions of data from other individual
actual entities. In this duration integration of the primary data
from the initial phase may take place, and the complete feeling of
satisfaction may be attained. If throughout the growth of the concrescence additional data continued to enter the process, the categoreal condition of subjective unity could not be met. This is
the categoreal reason for the causal independence of contemporary
actual occasions.

4. How the present excludes the future

We come to the relation between a present actual occasion and
occasions in its future. Only a brief discussion of this topic is required. Whitehead accepts Alexander's admonition that we "take
time seriously" (TIME 59). And his realistic attitude to time is embodied in his theory of actual occasions.

A present actual occasion stands at the utmost limit of actuality.
Toward the future there is potentiality for what will become, but
no actuality. Nothing in the future beyond the present actual occasion has yet become. "In the present there are no individual occasions belonging to the future. The present contains the utmost
verge of such realized individuality. . . . the future individual
occasions are non-existent. The sole immediate actuality is the

3. In a footnote to a statement of the causal independence of contemporaries Whitehead says, "This principle lies on the surface of the fundamental
Einsteinian formula for the physical continuum" (PR 95, n. 1).

constitution of the present subject . . ." (AI 247-8). That is to say, what the future is for the present does not include any concrete actuality.

The future is something for the present, of course. It has "objective existence." Its objective existence in the present, however, does not involve *even objectively* the individual actuality of any future occasions. "What is objective in the present is the necessity of a future of actual occasions, and the necessity that these actual occasions conform to the conditions inherent in the essence of the present occasion. The future belongs to the essence of present fact, and has no actuality other than the actuality of present fact" (AI 251). This point was discussed in detail in Chapter 2 in connection with anticipatory feeling and need not be labored here. We need only draw some conclusions.

If for the present actual occasion no future occasions exist as individuals, it is an obvious conclusion that no direct prehension can take place between present and future occasions. If A is a present actual occasion and B stands for some future actual occasion, then A can prehend B only as a hypothetical entity, not as an actuality now having subjective immediacy. Also, B cannot prehend A at all, for B has no actuality of its own; it is not a prehending subject.

As in the case of contemporary occasions a further conclusion then follows. If there is no direct prehension there is no sharing of immediacy. A present occasion, existing in its subjective immediacy, excludes the subjective immediacy of any future occasion. There can thus be no mutual enjoyment of feeling.

5. How the present excludes the past

The interpretation we are testing is that no two actual occasions share a common immediacy. We now have to consider the relation between an actual occasion and occasions in its past. Here our problem is not so simple as in the previous cases. For Whitehead says clearly there are direct causal and perceptual relations between the past and the present. So any assertions of experiential transcendence must be qualified with care. Our problem is to see whether some such assertions can be made.

Remembering that "the philosophy of organism is mainly devoted to the task of making clear the notion of 'being present in another entity' " (PR 79–80), we ask in what senses a past occasion is *not* present in an occasion that is actual now. Let A be the present actual occasion, and let X be an occasion in A's past. Now whatever may be the sense in which X is present in A, I shall try to show that in the following senses X is *not* present in A:

a. X is not present in A as "an experiencing subject here-now." For A, X may be 'an experiencing subject there-then," but, for A, X's experience belongs to a center of feeling that is not here-now.

b. Further, X is not present in A as a complete individual. For A feels X from a perspective defined by A's status in the actual world. This means that A feels certain aspects of the experience of X, but not others.

c. No aspect of X prehended by A is present in A with the subjective immediacy it had in X. The subjective immediacy of the feelings in the concrescence and satisfaction of A belongs to A and not to X. This means that A is not a cofeeler with X of any of X's feelings. It also means that none of X's feelings persists with its own immediacy into the concrescence of A. *In this literal sense,* there is no "transfer of feeling" from X to A. "An actual occasion *P*, belonging to *M's causal past,* is objectified for *M* by a perspective representation of its own (i.e. *P's*) qualities of feeling and intensities of feeling. There is a quantitative and qualitative vector flow of feeling from *P* to *M;* and in this way, what *P is* subjectively, belongs to *M* objectively" (PR 486).

I do not intend to deny that there is a "flow of feeling from *P* to *M,"* or in our symbols from X to A. But the expression "flow of feeling" and others like it need not be understood as involving "sharing of immediacy." I suggest that Whitehead's theory of objectification is his more careful and precise description of *how* there is a flow of feeling. So these expressions are to be taken not in a simple and literal sense but only as explained in the theory of objectification. The first step toward understanding the "flow of feeling from *P* to *M"* is to understand how "what *P is* subjectively, belongs to *M* objectively."

Chapters 6 and 7 will give an analysis of causal objectification that is entirely compatible with this suggestion. In this chapter we are concerned with the negative implication (which Whitehead makes explicit) of the theory of objectification, namely that *P* does *not* belong to *M* subjectively, or in its own subjective immediacy.

We have seen that in the present the subjective immediacy of feeling involved in A is confined to A, since there is no sharing of immediacy by contemporary occasions. We have seen also that A does not prehend the immediate feelings of future occasions. If now we can show that this subjective immediacy originates and perishes with A, then it could be said that the subjective immediacy of feeling involved in A originates with, is confined to, and perishes with the concrescence and final satisfaction of A. The experience of A could then be said to be in this sense exclusive of, and thus to transcend, the experiences of all other actual occasions.

a. X is not present in A as "an experiencing subject here-now." For A, X is an "object." Now "Two conditions must be fulfilled in order that an entity may function as an object in a process of experiencing: (1) the entity must be *antecedent,* and (2) the entity must be experienced in virtue of its antecedence; it must be *given*" (AI 229). The location of a past occasion is given for experience more or less vaguely (PR 258). Still, however vaguely the past occasion is given, it is given as a there-then and not as a here-now. The "there" may be "almost here"; the "then" may be "almost now." In human experience, for instance, the immediate past is roughly speaking "that portion of our past lying between a tenth of a second and half a second ago. . . . our immediate past is constituted by that occasion, or by that group of fused occasions, which enters into experience devoid of any perceptible medium intervening between it and the present immediate fact" (AI 233). In spite of the absence of a "perceptible medium" between X and A, X is not given as an experiencing subject here-now. X is there-then, however recent, however near.

Whitehead's realistic interpretation of influence means that what is given as past is also felt as present. Something comes from there-then to here-now. Whatever the nature of the influence from X upon A, however, such influence comes from *there-then.* He says that feelings are "vectors," using the term to mean "definite transmission from elsewhere" (PR 177). A prehension "is referent to an external world, and in this sense will be said to have a 'vector character' " (PR 28). He cites Locke—"the mind, being furnished with a great number of the simple ideas conveyed in by the senses, *as they are found in exterior things*" (as quoted from Essay II, xxiii, 1)—and says that the last phrase, which he has underlined, asserts "the *vector* character of the primary feelings" (PR 86). "Feelings are "vectors'; for they feel what is *there* and transform it into what is *here*" (PR 133). The former part of this last statement must be emphasized at this point: feelings "feel what is *there*." When the feeling in question is of a past occasion, the "there" will be a there-then. A's feelings of X therefore feel what is there-then.

There will thus always be a contrast for A between X, which is there-then, and its own immediate feelings, which are unambiguously here-now. In the analysis of a feeling in the concrescence of A, "whatever presents itself as also *ante rem* is a datum" (PR 355). This contrast is implied by the notion of *perspectives*, under which A feels other occasions (PR 104–5).

Whether or not this contrast is consciously prehended is not essential. The fact remains that a simple physical feeling (i.e. "a feeling for which the initial datum is another single actual entity," PR 361) is a prehension of "a subject diverse from the subject of the feeling which feels it" (PR 362). Nor does this nonpresence of X need to be qualified in respect of past mental activities. The relation of antecedence and consequence applies to mental as well as to physical activity (PR 468–9, AI 318).

This, then, is one sense in which X is not present in A. X is not present in A as an experiencing subject here-now. For A, X is other than the center of feeling which is A itself. It is a center of feeling there-then.

b. X is not present in A in its completeness of internal constitution.

We have seen that A does not feel X as an experiencing subject here-now. There is a further limitation, namely that A does not feel X as a fully complete and concrete experiencing thing. A feels X under an abstraction. That is, A feels certain of X's feelings, certain aspects of X's experience, but not others. Objectification involves abstraction.

It is a categoreal necessity that certain elements in X's real internal constitution be eliminated from A's prehension of X (PR 321). ". . . objectification relegates into irrelevance, or into a subordinate relevance, the full constitution of the objectified entity. Some real component in the objectified entity assumes the rôle of being how that particular entity is a datum in the experience of the subject" (PR 97). Only in this way can the prehending subject achieve its own finite unity of satisfaction. Therefore "the antecedent environment is not wholly efficacious" (AI 255); some elements in the actualities constituting this environment are eliminated. Whitehead seems to say that all actual occasions in the past actual world of the subject are positively prehended (PR 66, 335, 366), but *not all of any actual occasion* is positively prehended, or "felt." A feels some aspect or aspects of X's experience, but not all of X's real internal constitution.

c. No aspect of X prehended by A is present in A with the subjective immediacy it had in X.

We have now to point out, further, that those of X's feelings by which X is objectified for A are not present in A with their own subjective immediacy. The subjective immediacy with which X's feelings are now felt belongs to A and not to X. Since X is any past actual occasion, this means that all the feelings which are subjectively immediate in A originate with the concrescence of A and have A as their subject. X's feelings exist objectively, not as subjectively immediate.

The situation Whitehead describes is that the past actual world, including X, contributes *data* for the new concrescence. These data are objects of which A must take account. They have *objective* existence. Apart from some creative activity which includes them in a novel experiential unity, they would have no share in immediate actuality beyond the experiences of their past subjects. These objects are given a share in the immediacy of present actuality *by the creative activity of the novel concrescence,* which "conforms" to them and absorbs them into its satisfaction.

In themselves, apart from further creative activity, these data are like the dry bones which the word of the prophet Ezekiel reclothed with living flesh (PR 131). An entity which has become objectively immortal, so that it can be given as a datum, is "divested of its own living immediacy" (PR ix). Past actual occasions have perished. They are objectified for the present via abstract characters. And "The mere objectification of actual entities by eternal objects lacks 'immediacy.' It is 'repetition'; and this is a contrary to 'immediacy.' But 'process' is the rush of feelings whereby second-handedness attains subjective immediacy; in this way, subjective form overwhelms repetition, and transforms it into immediately felt satisfaction; objectivity is absorbed into subjectivity" (PR 234–5). The relatedness of actualities "is wholly concerned with the appropriation of the dead by the living" (PR ix).

Feelings are vectors, "But the feeling is subjectively rooted in the immediacy of the present occasion: it is what the occasion feels for itself, as derived from the past and as merging into the future" (PR 247). *What* is felt, the object of the feeling, is felt as derived; but the immediacy of the feeling is not derived. It originates with the present occasion. The tenth category of explanation is "That the first analysis of an actual entity, into its most concrete elements, discloses it to be a concrescence of prehensions, *which have originated in its process of becoming*" (PR 35, my italics). The subjective immediacy of feelings originates with the concrescence whose completion constitutes the full subject of those feelings. A prehension "originates in the process creative of its subject" (PR 41). A feels some aspect of X's experience as there-then, but this feeling of X's past experience originates with and is subjectively rooted in the concrescence and satisfaction of A. It is with this situation in mind that Whitehead says, "All origination is private" (PR 472).

What the new actuality will be is partly determined by antecedent conditions. The activity of the new concrescence must "conform" to these conditions. *That* it is to be actual is wholly determined, so to speak, by the ultimate creativity of which the new occasion is an original embodiment. "Creativity" is the self-causation of the novel occasion (PR 339).

We have now three complementary senses in which a present actual occasion excludes and thus transcends past acts of experience:

i. The experience of the present actual occasion excludes pre-hension of any past occasion as an experiencing subject here-now.

ii. The experience of the present actual occasion excludes all but certain selected factors in the experience of any past actual occasion.

iii. The experience of the present actual occasion excludes any feeling which was a component in a past actual occasion from hav-ing in the present actual occasion the immediate actuality of self-enjoyment which that feeling had in the past actual occasion.

Taken together, these aspects of the exclusiveness of a present occasion amount to a denial of any sharing of immediacy. There is no mutual enjoyment of feeling by a present occasion and a past occasion.

If Whitehead wants to say that a present occasion is influenced by or shares the experience of a past occasion, he must say this so as not to imply the sharing of immediacy, if his theory of actual occasions is to be self-consistent. For instance, it may be said that a present occasion feels a past occasion as being here-now but not as being an experiencing subject here-now. The selected com-ponents of the past occasion may imply or involve or point to the full constitution of the past occasion, but the full constitution is not positively felt in the same sense in which the selected com-ponents are positively felt. Those past feelings which the present occasion feels may be felt as having had immediacy, but not as having *now* the immediacy they had in the past. It is not denied that A immediately feels some feelings which were components in the immediacy of X. What is asserted is that, when A feels these feelings, these feelings are *objectified* for A and hence exist not in the immediacy they formerly had in X, but objectively. "Actual-ity in perishing acquires objectivity, while it loses subjective im-mediacy" (PR 44).

6. Are immediate feelings literally transferred?

Now if the subjective immediacy of A originates with A and perishes with A, then it would seem that A and X do not sub-jectively "enjoy" any feeling *at the same time*. And it would seem,

further, that we must also deny that feelings are *simply* transferred from X to A with retention of subjective immediacy. We
must say that none of X's feelings persists *with its own immediacy*
into the concrescence of A.

This denial, no doubt, sounds very strange when such passages
as the following come to mind:

> There is a flow of feeling (PR 363).

> A simple physical feeling has the dual character of being
> the cause's feeling re-enacted for the effect as subject. But
> this transference of feeling effects a partial identification of
> cause with effect, and not a mere representation of the cause.
> . . . It is a feeling *from* the cause which acquires the sub-
> jectivity of the new effect without loss of its original sub-
> jectivity in the cause (PR 363–4).

> The deterministic efficient causation is the inflow of the
> actual world in its own proper character of its own feelings,
> with their own intensive strength, felt and re-enacted by the
> novel concrescent subject (PR 374).

> The present moment is constituted by the influx of the *other*
> into that self-identity which is the continued life of the im-
> mediate past within the immediacy of the present (AI 233;
> see PR 177).

> There is thus an analogy between the transference of energy
> from particular occasion to particular occasion in physical
> nature and the transference of affective tone, with its emo-
> tional energy, from one occasion to another in any human
> personality (AI 242).

> The direct perception whereby the datum in the immediate
> subject is inherited from the past can thus, under an abstrac-
> tion, be conceived as the transference of throbs of emotional
> energy, clothed in the specific forms provided by sensa (PR
> 178).

> The primitive form of physical experience is emotional—
> blind emotion—received as felt elsewhere in another occasion

and conformally appropriated as a subjective passion. In the language appropriate to the higher stages of experience, the primitive element is *sympathy,* that is, feeling the feeling *in* another and feeling conformally *with* another (PR 246).

These statements seem to suggest a literal transference of immediate feeling from a past occasion to a present occasion. It sounds as though some component feeling in the satisfaction of the past occasion persists with retention of its own immediacy into the concrescence of the new occasion. In this way a "part" of the immediate feeling which constituted the past occasion would seem to "spill over" into the immediate feeling of the present occasion; or to be shot off, like a stone from a meteor, directly into the immediacy of the present occasion; or to be inserted into the immediacy of the present occasion as one organism is inserted *while it is yet alive* into another living organism, as a goldfish into an undergraduate.

Now if these passages are accepted at their face value without careful scrutiny of their contexts, and if "transference of feeling" is taken in a simple and literal sense, then exclusiveness of immediacy would not hold good between a past occasion and a present occasion. Some of the past occasion's feelings would persist with retention of their own immediacy into the concrescence of the present occasion. And to this extent the two occasions would have a common enjoyment of feeling. It would then become very difficult to take seriously Whitehead's doctrine of the perishing and objectification of the past.

In my opinion this interpretation mistakes Whitehead's intention. These passages have a meaning consistent with his theory of objectification. But that meaning is not always clear. To this extent Whitehead himself is responsible for a good deal of confusion.

A more adequate interpretation of these passages will be given in Chapter 7, in connection with an analysis of causal objectification. This interpretation will be compatible with the principle of the exclusiveness of immediacy. For the present I shall point out that the literal meaning of these passages is radically inconsistent with some of the dominating principles of Whitehead's system. These principles, judged by their prominence in the categoreal scheme and by the clear, emphatic, and extended treatment given them elsewhere, seem fundamental to Whitehead's theory of actual occasions. If therefore he intends to say there is transference of feeling in a simple literal sense, then there is a radical inconsistency in his theory.

a. *Creativity*. We have already noticed one of these principles. An actual occasion is a definite embodiment of a primordial and underived activity. It gets its *actuality* at first hand, so to speak, not by derivation from any other entity. It is an instance of creativity.

Now if a fragment or part of the *immediate* actuality of a past occasion *literally* and with retention of its own immediacy passes into the concrescence of a present actual occasion, this principle of the primordial character of creativity would seem to be compromised. For in this case a part of the *immediate* actuality of one actual occasion would be derived from another. And since there are many actual occasions in the immediate past of the present actual occasion, all of which might conceivably be present in it by way of such "simple" transference of feeling, it becomes very difficult to give meaning to the self-causation or self-creativity of the present occasion. "To be *causa sui* means that the process of concrescence is its own reason for the decision in respect to the qualitative clothing of feelings. It is finally responsible for the decision by which any lure for feeling is admitted to efficiency. The freedom inherent in the universe is constituted by this element of self-causation" (PR 135; see RM 101–2, AI 303).

On the literal interpretation of the transference of feeling, not only the objective data for feeling but also the "qualitative clothing" of some feelings in the primary phase would be derived directly and inevitably. This interpretation does scant justice to Whitehead's principle of creative originality. The occasion "conforms" to its past and "anticipates" its future, but within its concrescence there is no activity, in the sense of "immediate functioning," but *its own* self-creative activity.

b. *Time*. Another fundamental principle in Whitehead's philosophy is that time is "epochal." One essential feature of the epochal theory of time is "supersession." An actual occasion perishes, or ceases to exist in the mode of subjective immediacy, and is superseded by another actual occasion (TIME passim; PR 94, 222, 320). It then exists in the mode of objective immortality for those occasions that supersede it. Thus time is constituted by the becoming and perishing of actual occasions in the rhythmic process of creativity. "The ancient doctrine that 'no one crosses the same river twice' is extended. No thinker thinks twice; and, to put the matter more generally, no subject experiences twice. This is what Locke ought to have meant by his doctrine of time as a 'perpetual perishing' " (PR 43).

The process of nature thus consists of many series of discontinuous acts of becoming. Whitehead also has a doctrine of continuity in time, which is expressed in terms of the *potential* divisibility of the acts of becoming. This will be discussed in Chapter 4. What concerns us at the moment is that while there is a becoming of continuity, "there is no continuity of becoming" (TIME 64).

> Supersession is not a continuous process of becoming. If we try to combine the notions of supersession and continuity we are at once entangled in a vicious infinite regress.
>
> For if B supersedes A, then the continuity of B requires that some earlier portion of B has superseded A antecedently to the later portion of B. This argument can be repeated on that earlier portion of B, however you choose that portion. Thus we are involved in an infinite regress. Also the supersession of A has to commence at what should be the infinite end of the regress. But there is no infinite end. Hence supersession cannot be regarded as the continuous unfolding of a continuum. I express this conclusion by the statement that time is *epochal*. The occasion B which acquires concretion so as to supersede A embodies a definite quantum of time which I call the *epochal character* of the concrescence. The epochal theory of time is the foundation of the theory of atomic organisms, and of the modern physical quantum-theory (TIME 63-4).

Now if some feeling which was a component in the immediacy of a past occasion persists *with retention of its own immediacy* into the novel concrescence, could it then be said that the present occasion unambiguously or in all its "portions" supersedes the past occasion? For in this case it would seem that some earlier portion of the present occasion, its primary phase, is contemporary with some portion of the past actual occasion, namely that feeling which has persisted with retention of its own immediacy. To make sense of the epochal theory of time we must suppose that the past, or any part of the past, exists in the present only as objective and not with its own subjective immediacy.

c. *The unity of the subject.* Another fundamental principle that seems to exclude a simple transference of feeling is the unity of the experiencing subject. This is somewhat elliptically stated in the first category of obligation: *"The Category of Subjective Unity.* The many feelings which belong to an incomplete phase in the process of an actual entity, though unintegrated by reason of the incompleteness of the phase, are compatible for integration by reason of the unity of their subject" (PR 39; see 338–44). Any feeling in any phase of A has A as its subject. In any incomplete phase of A, where A has not yet attained its satisfaction, A is nevertheless the subject of the feelings which compose that phase. In that phase A is not yet complete, but the feelings which go to make up that phase of activity already belong to A as their subject.

For just as the internal process of the actual occasion is a process of self-creation or self-production, every feeling in that process is *essentially* "an episode in self-production" (PR 342). "The feelings are what they are in order that their subject may be what it is" (PR 339). This might be rendered: One determinant of the nature of a feeling is the necessity that its incomplete subject become complete.

The mechanism of subjective aim, mutual sensitivity of subjective forms, and "pre-established harmony" of feelings, in terms of which Whitehead tries to make this conception of the subject intelligible, will not concern us here. The notion can best be understood, in terms of human experience, if we concentrate on a phase of experience when there is an intense sense of purposeful activity. In that phase of experience one does not feel oneself to be now complete. Yet one's feelings are felt as essentially belong-

ing to that which one will become in the attainment of the object of the activity.

The implication that interests us here is one which Whitehead
repeatedly makes explicit: "A feeling cannot be abstracted from
the actual entity entertaining it" (PR 338), namely its subject.[4]
That is to say, the notion of a feeling is defined in such a way that
a particular feeling has no existence apart from a specific subject
that "enjoys" or "entertains" it.

It follows as a corollary that the mode of existence of feeling
must correspond to the mode of existence of its subject. A feeling
exists as formally actual only in the immediacy of its subject.
Where its subject has objective existence rather than formal actuality, the feeling also exists objectively. Thus when X has perished
and exists objectively for A, any of X's feelings which are present
in A must be present objectively and not with that immediacy
with which they were enjoyed by X.

It seems clear that this principle entails a denial of literal transference of feeling. For if some feeling which was a component in
the immediate experience of X should persist with retention of
its immediacy into the experience of A, then this feeling would
seem to have been detached from its subject, X. For X is "an experiencing subject there-then," whereas it would seem that a detail
of X's experience is immediate here-now. While the subject of
the feeling has perished, it would seem if there is literal transference of feeling that the feeling lives on. But this, on Whitehead's theory of the unity of the subject, has been shown to be
impossible.

7. The experiential boundaries of an actual occasion

This chapter has shown that an actual occasion as an act of experience transcends other occasions in two ways. Its experience is
both novel and exclusive. No two actual occasions have the same
real internal constitution. And no two actual occasions enjoy the
subjective immediacy of any feeling in common.

The assertion of social transcendence by way of "exclusiveness

4. See also PR 41, where this is pointed out as an implication of categories
of obligation i and vii taken together, and PR 355.

of immediacy" amounts to a denial of "foreign bodies" in the constitution of an actual occasion. An occasion is constituted by feelings some of which have alien entities as their data; but all of the feelings which constitute the occasion have that occasion, and only that occasion, as their subject. They are "subjectively rooted" in that occasion. Conversely, no feeling involved in the concrescence of an actual occasion has immediacy or formal actuality in that occasion if its subject is some other occasion. The subjective immediacy of an actual occasion belongs exclusively to that occasion.

In addition to this general conclusion about experiential exclusiveness we have discovered specific senses in which an actual occasion transcends occasions in its contemporary world, in the future, and in the past respectively.

An actual occasion transcends occasions in its contemporary world in the further sense that there is *no* direct causal or perceptual connection between it and them. This principle of the mutual independence of contemporary occasions leads a fortiori to the conclusion that an occasion does not share the immediacy of feeling enjoyed by any of its contemporaries.

Future occasions do not now have actuality at all. They can, in the nature of the case, only exist for the present actual occasion as possibilities. In the present there is only the necessity that there shall be a future, and that the future must conform to present conditions. No future occasion now exists. Again, a fortiori no present occasion shares the immediacy of feeling to be enjoyed by its successors. The only connection is anticipation.

Past actual occasions are felt by a present occasion as stubborn fact. But they are felt as having been experiencing subjects in the past and not as being experiencing subjects in the present; they are felt under selective abstraction; and those past feelings positively felt are not felt as existing in the present with that immediacy with which they were enjoyed by their past subjects.

The subjective immediacy of a given actual occasion is thus exclusive, in definite senses, of the subjective immediacies of all other actual occasions: "The individual immediacy of an occasion . . . is its moment of sheer individuality, bounded on either side by essential relativity" (AI 227). This last phrase suggests that in the light of the foregoing discussion we may define, after a fashion, the limits or boundaries of the immediate experience of an actual occasion. We may define such boundaries in terms of the experience of the occasion and are not obliged to anticipate the discussion of extension in the next chapter.

One way of defining the experiential boundaries of an actual occasion is suggested by the following passage: ". . . the constitution of any one actual entity is analysable into phases, related as presupposed and presupposing. Eternal objects express *how* the predecessor-phase is absorbed into the successor phase without limitation of itself, but with additions necessary for the determination of an actual unity in the form of individual satisfaction. The *actual entities* enter into each other's constitutions under *limitations* imposed by incompatibilities of feelings" (PR 225). This suggests that the boundaries of the immediate experience of an actual occasion are in general those limits at which, in the creative process, abstractive selection becomes categoreally necessary. Within these limits, i.e. in the internal process constitutive of the occasion, no abstractive selection from predecessor phases for admission into successor phases is involved. In this internal process of feeling, predecessor phases are absorbed into successor phases without limitation. Beyond these limits, abstractive selection from processes of feeling is categoreally necessary. Within the immediate experience of an actual occasion nothing has to be eliminated. But elimination is involved in all prehension of processes of feeling beyond the immediate experience of the given occasion.

Thus the anterior boundary of the immediate experience of an actual occasion would be the limit at which abstractive existence or potentiality ceases and non-eliminative feeling begins. The feelings of antecedent actual occasions are felt under selective abstraction; the feelings of the given actual occasion are felt without elimination of any of their content.

Similarly, the contemporary boundary of the immediate experience of an actual occasion would be the limit beyond which the present exists as passive potentiality. For the presentation of the contemporary world in this mode abstracts from the real individual actualities that compose it. Within this limit, present feeling is felt without elimination.

Again, the posterior boundary of the immediate experience of an actual occasion would be the limit at which the non-eliminative internal process of feeling ceases or perishes. Beyond this limit the actual occasion has ceased to enjoy itself as a concrete unity. It will exist for succeeding processes of feeling only under abstractive selection, that is, in its objective immortality.

In this way the individual immediacy of an actual occasion can be said to be "bounded" by relativity, that is, by objective or abstractive existence. This use of the figurative notion of experiential boundaries may help to make clear the meaning of the experiential exclusiveness of an actual occasion. That such boundaries should be drawn in such a way that they illustrate mutual exclusiveness of immediacy in the case of any two actual occasions is the conclusion this chapter has sought to explain and support.

Finally two relevant points should be mentioned, though neither is essential to the preceding argument:

First, Whitehead's account in his later writings of the spatiotemporal regions of actual occasions is in harmony with the above interpretation of the experiences of actual occasions. The regions of actual occasions, as we shall see, though they may be contiguous, are nonoverlapping and thus mutually exclusive.

Second, I shall argue later that between God and an actual occasion as well as between two occasions there is no sharing of immediacy.

CHAPTER 4

Regions

THE PURPOSE of this chapter is to explain and support an interpretation of the spatiotemporal character of actual occasions. I shall discuss Whitehead's earlier theory of extension, incidentally, because it differs in an important way from his treatment of extension in the later writings.

Since our interest is in actual occasions as socially transcendent individuals, our problem may be suggested by the phrase, "the extensive relations of actual entities mutually external to each other" (PR 440). The question is: In what sense are the spatiotemporal relations between actual occasions "external"? The last chapter dealt with the experiential exclusiveness of actual occasions. This chapter deals with their spatiotemporal exclusiveness.

The interpretation I shall explain and defend is as follows:

1. An actual occasion is extensive.
2. The region of an actual occasion is definite.
3. The regions of actual occasions form an extensive plenum.
4. No two actual occasions have the same region.
5. The regions of any two actual occasions are nonoverlapping.

If these propositions can be adequately explained and supported, then we shall have found a well-defined sense in which actual occasions, in respect to their spatiotemporal characters, are external to one another. This would be another mode of social transcendence. An actual occasion would transcend any other occasion in the sense that they would have no common spatiotemporal parts. We could say that the regions of actual occasions are mutually exclusive.

1. How actual occasions are extensive

It is an important fact that the term "extension" is not used in the categoreal scheme set forth in *Process and Reality* (Pt. I, ch. 2). The first mention of extension in that book occurs in the succeeding chapter titled "Some Derivative Notions." The way extension is introduced corresponds to its place in Whitehead's theory of actual occasions. The extensive character of an actual occasion, its *region,* is derivative from its character as an act of experience.

Whitehead expresses the relation between actual occasions and their regions in various ways. It is true that when attention is on the extended character of nature, a region is sometimes identified with an actual occasion. For example, "both *A* and *B* [i.e. two contemporary actual occasions] are atomic regions in the potential scheme of spatio-temporal extensiveness which is a datum for both *A* and *B*" (PR 188). But this is simply because contemporary occasions are objectified for one another only by way of spatio-temporal relations. In other passages a region is said to be "correlative" to an actual entity (PR 113), and occasions are said to "belong" to regions (PR 190).

When, on the other hand, attention is on the occasion as an act of experience, the region is said to be "the primary real phase" in the concrescence (PR 104) or the creative act is said to "arise from" (PR 522) a region. Again, the occasion is said to be the "enjoyment" of the region or "quantum" (PR 434). From this it should be clear that an occasion is not simply identical with its region. It may be fair to say that the region of an occasion is its extensive character.

In one passage Whitehead explains that "The concrescence presupposes its basic region, and not the region its concrescence." This has two implications. On the one hand it means that an actual occasion is more than its region. The occasion as an act of experience has a unity that its region does not have. "Thus the subjective unity of the concrescence is irrelevant to the divisibility of the region. In dividing the region we are ignoring the subjective unity which is inconsistent with such division"

(PR 434–5. This immediately succeeds the sentence cited above). The region may be abstracted from the occasion and "divided." Thus the region cannot be a "reason" for the subjective unity of the occasion as an act of experience. It is in this sense that the region does not presuppose its concrescence.

On the other hand, an occasion necessarily involves some region. As an act of experience it presupposes some particular region in the sense that *that* act of experience cannot be abstracted from *that* region: "There is nothing self-contradictory in the thought of many actual entities with the same abstract essence; but.there can only be one actual entity with the same real essence. For the real essence indicates 'where' the entity is, that is to say, its status in the real world . . ." (PR 94; see MT 227). The reason why an occasion has a particular region lies in the intrinsic nature of that act of experience. Its extensive character is essential to it, not an accidental fact about it. The region is its "standpoint," the here-now from which it prehends other actual entities.

In passing we should notice that the systematic scheme of extensive relations throughout the actual world, as well as the region of a particular occasion, is interpretable in terms of experience. This systematic scheme, the extensive continuum, is simply an aspect of the systematic interrelations of acts of experience. It is only in this sense that space and time are "abstractions." Space and time are real facts about the world. But categoreally speaking they are derivative from the natures of actual occasions as acts of experience (SMW 101).

Now we can describe the extensive character of an actual occasion more specifically. I suggest two senses in which an occasion is spatiotemporal or extensive:

a. An actual occasion enjoys "extendedness." It is part of the immediate experience of an occasion that it is "here" and "now" (SMW 98). This here-now (SMW 211) is its standpoint (PR 104). It is not a "point" or a "point-instant" but has thickness and spread. This thickness and spread are qualities of the experience of the occasion. Extension gets its fundamental meaning from this thickness and spread of experience. This is the first sense in which an actual occasion is extensive or spatiotemporal in character.

This here-now or standpoint or region is a four-dimensional "volume" (PR 472). The occasion "takes time" and is stretched out in space. Its region is "a volume of space through a duration of time" (SMW 99). But as a feature of the immediate experience of the occasion the region is not divisible into spatial and temporal parts. It is a "quantum" of space-time. Its indivisible unity follows from the indivisibility of the immediate experience of the occasion, which in turn follows from its unity of subjective aim. "The problem dominating the concrescence is the actualization of the quantum *in solido*" (PR 434; see 107). *As a character of the immediate experience of the occasion,* the region is indivisible.

The temporal thickness of the experience of the occasion means it is not a moment but a duration. It is an epoch, or pause, in physical time (SMW 177). Rather, the succession of instantaneous moments making up the time of physics is an abstraction from a succession of real durations. How do the experiences of actual occasions constitute durations?

The internal process of concrescence is a succession of "phases." But

> This genetic passage from phase to phase is not in physical time: the exactly converse point of view expresses the relationship of concrescence to physical time. It can be put shortly by saying, that physical time expresses some features of the growth, but *not* the growth of the features. . . . But the genetic process is not the temporal succession: such a view is exactly what is denied by the epochal theory of time. Each phase in the genetic process presupposes the entire quantum, and so does each feeling in each phase (PR 434).

Here we encounter a notion that is not easy to understand or explain. One phase must be in some way prior to another. What sort of priority is this? Negatively, this genetic priority must be distinguished from other sorts of priority. (i) We are not to think of it as priority in physical time. We are not to think of phase A occurring at time 0100 and phase B occurring at 0100 plus i, however small the increment may be. The internal process is "becoming," not "transition." (ii) Since the concrescence is a creative process in which decision occurs, it would seem that genetic priority is not the logical priority of a premise to a conclusion. (iii) For a similar reason the relation of one phase to another cannot be construed as a whole-part relation. This construction would seem to eliminate the dynamic character of the process. (iv) In an *obiter dictum* Whitehead says of the concrescence, "This development is nothing else than the Hegelian development of an idea" (PR 254). But there is good reason to think this contains considerable exaggeration. Only two pages earlier he had said, "In the place of the Hegelian hierarchy of categories of thought, the philosophy of organism finds a hierarchy of categories of feeling" (PR 252). It seems risky to construe concrescence as a dialectical process in Hegel's sense (see ESP 7, 116, 131).

So it seems that though genetic priority may have analogies with other sorts of priority we must accept it as something of its own kind. The categoreal explanation of concrescence is given in the categoreal scheme. For its applicability Whitehead appeals to our immediate experiences (PR 32).

Now as we saw in Chapter 2 the genetic process is not the whole story of an actual occasion. This process produces a feeling of satisfaction which completes the concrescence. Its feelings have achieved solidarity and it now "takes time." By producing its satisfaction the occasion constitutes one of the durations which make up the temporally extended world. These drops of experience by succeeding one another give rise to the continuity of physical time. But as a feature of the experience of the occasion its duration is "time lived" not "time measured."

The spatial spread of the experience of the occasion is another aspect of its extendedness. The "here" from which it prehends its physical data is not a point. The occasion stretches out in space as well as in time and enjoys feelings of a multiplicity of data (there and there and there) from its "here." Its feelings achieve spatial as well as temporal solidarity. This solidarity means that, as each phase is a phase of one experience "now," so each feeling in each phase is a component of one experience "here." As far as its immediate existence goes, a feeling is "located" not in a subregion of the spatial quantum but in the quantum as a whole. "Each phase in the genetic process presupposes the entire quantum, and so does each feeling in each phase" (PR 434).

b. The second sense in which an actual occasion is extensive is that, as objectified for other actual occasions, it is in principle indefinitely divisible. Whitehead says of the objectified occasion, "This divisibility is what constitutes its extensiveness" (PR 108).

When the satisfaction has completed the concrescence, the occasion becomes an object for succeeding occasions. It is given as an extended fact imposing conformity on its successors. But now it no longer exists as a unified subjective experience. It is an objective fact or datum for analysis and abstraction. The region associated with its satisfaction, therefore, is now divisible spatially and temporally into *partes extra partes*. For "the region is, after all, divisible, although in the genetic growth it is undivided" (PR 435).

From being the thickness and spread of an immediate act of experience, the region has now become a potentiality for division and subdivision by those actual occasions for which it is an object. It is this indefinitely divisible character of the given world which makes it an extensive continuum (PR 103, 434–5).

An actual occasion therefore is extensive in a twofold way, corresponding to its two successive modes of existence; in its subjective immediacy it enjoys extendedness, and in its objective immortality it is divisible. "Thus, an act of experience has an objective scheme of extensive order by reason of the double fact that its own perspective standpoint has extensive content, and that the other actual entities are objectified with the retention of their extensive relationships" (PR 105).

Hereafter in this chapter we shall be concerned with the regions, or extensive characters, of actual occasions.

2. Regions of actual occasions are definite

The region of an actual occasion is in principle precisely definable and in this sense definite. The here-now which is the standpoint for the occasion as an experiencing subject, and which for other actual occasions is a "there" or there-then, has an unambiguous meaning.

The region is definite both in respect to position and in respect to extent. That is to say, it is at some definite place and some definite time in the extensive scheme which characterizes the actual world. And it is definitely limited in its spatiotemporal extent, so that the occasion may be said to occupy a definitely limited amount of space and a definitely limited amount of time. In view of certain confusions these specifications require some explanation and support.

a. *The region of an actual occasion is definite in the sense of having a definite position.* A. O. Lovejoy, in his analysis of the notion of "simple location," against which Whitehead has protested, offers as one possible meaning for the term what he calls "single location." [1] We shall say that an actual occasion has single location. It is at some definite place and time in the extensive scheme. In one sense, "every actual entity in its relationship to other entities is . . . somewhere in the continuum" (PR 104). It has an unambiguous spatiotemporal position in relation to all other occasions.

This is not, as it might seem to be, contradictory of Whitehead's denial of simple location. For his denial has a definite and limited meaning. He is denying that material substances, as traditionally conceived, have concrete actuality.

> To say that a bit of matter has *simple location* means that, in expressing its spatio-temporal relations, it is adequate to state that it is where it is, in a definite finite region of space, and throughout a definite finite region of time, apart from any essential reference of the relations of that bit of matter to other regions of space and other durations of time. . . . I shall argue that among the primary elements of nature as apprehended in our immediate experience, there is no element whatever which possesses this character of simple location" (SMW 81; see 69).

His constructive substitute for this traditional conception is a complex theory, in which two sorts of entities are carefully distinguished, namely objects and events. He undertakes to interpret any "bit of matter," for example a pebble, as the ingredience of

1. *The Revolt against Dualism* (Chicago, Open Court Publishing Co., 1929), p. 165.

certain objects in certain events.[2] Suppose now we ask whether on *his* theory the pebble is *singly* located in Lovejoy's sense. Then, interpreting the pebble as a perceptual object, the answer would be no. For objects are ingredient in other events besides those in which they are "situated." For example, the perceptual object is ingredient in the experience of the percipient as well as in its situation. But if we ask whether, on his theory, *anything* is singly located, the answer is yes. For every event is singly located. This does not contradict Whithead's denial of simple location, because single location does not exhaust the meaning of simple location. Even events (and actual occasions) are not simply located in Whitehead's sense of "simple" because, though they are singly located, they have "essential reference" to other events.

It is true that some of Whitehead's expressions seem to deny that an actual occasion has a definite position. For example:

> . . . in the actual world there are definite atomic actualities determining one coherent system of real divisions throughout the region of actuality. Every actual entity in its relationship to other actual entities is in this sense somewhere in the continuum, and arises out of the data provided by this standpoint. But in another sense *it is everywhere throughout the continuum;* for its constitution includes the objectifications of the actual world and thereby includes the continuum; also the potential objectifications of itself contribute to the real potentialities whose solidarity the continuum expresses. Thus the continuum is present in every actual entity, and each actual entity pervades the continuum (PR 104–5, my italics).

But here it is clear that the actual entity is "in" the past world only in the sense that causal influences from that world have contributed to its nature. As the passage itself hints, it is truer to say the past world is in the new occasion than to say the new occasion is in the past world. Again, the actual entity is in the future world

2. Or, in the language of his later writings, in a historic route of actual occasions. See AI 200–1. See Chs. 5 (on substance) and 10 (on objects and events) below.

only in the sense that upon its completion its satisfaction will be a datum for future actual entities. It is only in respect to the objective existence of other actual entities in it, and in respect to its objective existence in other actual entities, that the occasion is said to be anywhere else than at its basic regional standpoint.

Another instance of this misleading note may be cited: ". . . my theory involves the entire abandonment of the notion that simple location is the primary way in which things are involved in space-time. In a certain sense, everything is everywhere at all times." This certainly sounds as though an actual occasion does not have a single unambiguous position. But in this same passage everything is said to be "everywhere at all times" only in the sense that "every location involves an aspect of itself in every other location. Thus every spatio-temporal standpoint mirrors the world." Just what it may mean to mirror the world we shall try to find out later. We note only that the doctrine is presented as "a mere transcript of the obvious facts," and that among these is the fact that "you are in a certain place perceiving things," and that "your perception takes place where you are" (SMW 128). ". . . each actual entity includes the universe *by reason of its determinate attitude towards* every element in the universe" (PR 71–2, my italics).

In his earlier writings Whitehead clearly attributes single location to events: "The chief confusion between objects and events is conveyed in the prejudice that an object can only be in one place at a time. That is a fundamental property of events; and whenever that property appears axiomatic as holding of some physical entity, that entity is an event" (PNK 65). Lovejoy is correct in pointing out that simple location, in the sense of the single location of *events,* far from being denied by Whitehead, appears in his writings as "the first law of nature" (*The Revolt against Dualism,* p. 167). This statement, it seems, was written without reference to *Process and Reality,* where the distinction between events and actual occasions was made clear. With this distinction, namely that "An actual occasion is the limiting type of an event with only one member" (PR 113), Lovejoy's dictum would apply a fortiori to actual occasions.

Indeed, in *Science and the Modern World* where the distinctive characteristics of actual occasions have already appeared, Whitehead says: "Prehensive unification might be said to have simple location in its volume A. But this would be a mere tautology. For space and time are simple abstractions from the totality of prehensive unifications as mutually patterned in each other" (SMW 101). Since we are concerned with the nature of the region (or volume), not with its derivation, we may provisionally overlook the tautology and regard this as a significant statement.

In *Process and Reality* it is clear that the extensive relations of an actual occasion are essential to it. It cannot be anywhere else, in its formal existence, and be the same occasion: ". . . the actual entity, in virtue of being *what* it is, is also *where* it is. It is somewhere because it is some actual thing with its correlated actual world" (PR 93; see 113). That quantum of the extensive continuum which is the primary phase of an occasion "is constituted by its totality of relationships and cannot move" (PR 124). Thus it is of the essence of an actual occasion to have single location. And since the region of an occasion is simply its extensive character, to say that the occasion has single location means that the region has a definite position.

b. *The region of an actual occasion is definite in the sense of having a definitely limited extent with definable boundaries.* An actual occasion has a definite position in the sense that it is singly located in a particular spatiotemporal region. An occasion is definite also in the further sense that its region is definitely limited in extent, so that in principle its boundaries are precisely definable. It is conceivable that regions might have a definite focus and yet an indefinite extent. May we exclude this possibility?

It will be useful to refer to events in Whitehead's earlier writings before dealing with actual occasions in his later writings. An important passage may be cited in full:

> Thus it is a basal assumption, essential for ratiocination relating to perceptual experience, that there are definite entities which are events; though in practice our experience does not enable us to identify any such subject of thought, as discriminated from analogous subjects slightly more or slightly less.

This assumption must not be construed either as asserting an atomic structure of events, or as a denial of overlapping events. It merely asserts the ideal possibility of perfect definiteness as to what does or does not belong to an event which is the subject of thought, though such definiteness cannot be achieved in human knowledge (PNK 74).

At first sight this gives an ambiguous answer to the question whether events have definite natural boundaries. It suggests that precise definitions of events in spatiotemporal terms are possible by extensive abstraction. Thus, having defined "event-particle" in terms of abstractive sets, Whitehead can say that an event is "uniquely defined by the set of event-particles which form its boundary" (PNK 127). "A boundary can only bound one event and every event has a boundary" (PNK 122). However, the passage above suggests also that such precisely defined events are subjects of *thought*.

Now does this mean that, due to the demand of thought for definite subjects of propositions, such entities are postulated as hypothetical constructions, though they do not exist in nature? On this reading nature would consist of vague and indeterminate wholes in passage, and any precisely definable event would be an abstraction, not a natural fact. This possibility, however, Whitehead seems to repudiate emphatically: "Thus an event has its own substantial unity of being which is not an abstract derivative from logical construction" (PNK 77).

An alternative reading of the passage is that events as natural entities do have definite boundaries, though these boundaries are not precisely discerned in perception. Perceptual experience might, however, *suggest* the boundaries of events, so that the construction of a boundary is in reference to a natural fact. The application of geometrical concepts to the actual world would not then be a matter of assigning conventional limitations where none in fact exist. Geometrical specification would then be in theory capable of referring to spatiotemporal "joints" in the actual world.

This latter reading may be supported by reference to certain passages where the context clearly refers to natural facts and not to abstractions of thought:

. . . a limited event possesses a completely defined limitation of extent which is expressed for us in spatio-temporal terms (CN 74).[3]

A finite event occupies a limited chunk of this manifold . . . (CN 100).[4]

It may be further supported by noticing that when Whitehead refers to the lack of clear demarcations of events as given in perceptual experience, he underlines the *seeming* or *apparent* lack of demarcation, as though sense awareness here did not give a complete account of the natural facts. Finite events "have indistinct demarcations simply owing to lack of perceptive vividness and of discriminative force" (TSM 47). In our experience, "Events appear as indefinite entities without clear demarcations" (PNK 73). Sense awareness is indeterminate (CN 59) and does not enable us to discriminate precisely between events. "Exactness is an ideal of thought, and is only realised in experience by the selection of a route of approximation" (CN 59).

Finally it may be supported by the consideration that the whole process of extensive abstraction, as defined in the earlier writings, seems to presuppose that the events in terms of which extensive relations are described are of limited extent, and that they are natural facts. The difficulties this entailed led Whitehead to give a very different account of extensive relations in *Process and Reality*. But these difficulties are not our immediate concern.

If finite events in the earlier writings have definite spatiotemporal boundaries, there is a strong presumption that the regions of *actual occasions* are of definite spatiotemporal extent also. For an

3. Whitehead's note in CN 197–8, while some of the language is ambiguous, does not seem to invalidate this passage, to which he there refers. He withdraws his previous limitation of infinite events to durations: "There is not only a significance of the discerned events embracing the whole present duration, but there is a significance of a cogredient event involving its extension through a whole time-system backwards and forwards." I interpret this to mean not that the cogredient event extends throughout the time system but that the *significance* of the event extends throughout the time system.

4. That is, the four-dimensional manifold of event-particles. In his ensuing explanation, the relative positions of event-particles are defined in reference to the "given event."

actual occasion is the "limiting type of an event with one member," and an event is "a nexus of actual occasions, inter-related in some determinate fashion in one extensive quantum" (PR 113; see 124).

An examination of *Science and the Modern World* and *Process and Reality* bears out this presumption.[5] The standpoint of a "prehensive unification" is "a volume of space through a duration of time" (SMW 99). The extensive scheme is "atomized" by actual occasions "determining one coherent system of real divisions throughout the region of actuality" (PR 104). An actual occasion involves a definite lapse of time and has a spatial volume for its perspective standpoint (PR 105; see SMW 177, PR 472). The extensive region of an actual occasion is "the determinate basis" presupposed by the concrescence (PR 434; see 124). "In the physical world each epochal occasion is a definite limited physical event, limited both as to space and time, but with time-duration as well as with its full spatial dimensions" (RM 91).

That a region, *conceived as a relatum for extensive connection,* is of definitely limited extent is explicitly asserted. ". . . a certain determinate boundedness is required for the notion of a region—i.e., for the notion of an extensive standpoint in the real potentiality for actualization. The inside of a region, its volume, has a complete boundedness denied to the extensive potentiality external to it. The boundedness applies both to the spatial and the temporal aspects of extension. Wherever there is ambiguity as to the contrast of boundedness between inside and outside, there is no proper region" (PR 547, Corrigenda to p. 459). But not all the regions that are relata for extensive connection, are regions of actual occasions. Some are, as we shall see, "possible" regions. And whether the precise definitions of regions in the theory of extensive connection are applicable to the regions of actual occasions is the question at issue. Hence passages of this latter sort cannot be used as evidence for our proposition.

If the regions of actual occasions are definitely limited in extent then both their positions and their extent are in principle specifi-

5. The regions referred to in *Adventures of Ideas* are in every case types of nexūs, not regions of actual occasions. See AI 254–5, 275–6, 281, 335. In general this is true of the other writings in his later period.

able. That Whitehead takes this possibility seriously is suggested by his treatment of "indicative systems." ". . . a modern traveller sitting on the bank of the Rubicon, and meditating on his direct perceptions of actual occasions can locate, relatively to himself by spatio-temporal specifications, an event [e.g. Caesar crossing the Rubicon] which inferentially and conjecturally he believes to include a portion of the past history of the Rubicon as directly known to him" (PR 298). Every actual occasion has a definite position in the extensive continuum and a definitely limited extent with boundaries which are, at least theoretically, precisely definable.

3. The extensive plenum

Whitehead denies that there is, in a strict sense, any empty space (PNK 36, PR 112, MT 186). Provisionally the earlier writings implement this denial with arguments in support of an ether, filling all space and serving as a medium for physical transmission. In support of the theory of transmission of stress through some medium, and against the theory of action at a distance, Whitehead brings forward considerations based on the wave theory of light, the general character of Maxwell's formulae for stresses, the presupposition by Maxwell's formulae of a physical field, and Maxwell's identification of light with electromagnetic waves. These are cited "in addition to the somewhat vague philosophic preferences, based on the disconnection involved in spatial and temporal separation" (PNK 20). A further argument for the ether is based on the absoluteness of direction, of which the rotation of the earth is given as an illustration (PNK 36–7).

His acceptance of a material ether is only provisional, however. This notion does not really resolve the difficulty in supposing that separated bodies do yet interact (OT 181). It is useful in science only if it is continually supplemented by *ad hoc* hypotheses which make it impossible to test its existence (PNK 37–41, OT 224–5). In fact, all that we know of the ether "is summed up in Maxwell's equations, or in recent adaptations of his equations such as those due to Lorentz" (PNK 22). In itself it is a mere idle concept, a "barren virgin" (CN 78), whose "scientific use is problematical" and whose "philosophical use is *nil*" (OT 225; see ESP 241). It becomes a mere name for the material postulated to underlie electromagnetic occurrences (SMW 139). No scientific facts require the acceptance of a material ether by metaphysical theory. Some medium of transmission is required, but the notion of a material medium is scientifically and philosophically unsatisfactory.

Whitehead would therefore substitute for the material ether an "ether of events" (TSM 55, CN 78), which would serve the scientific purposes for which the material ether was postulated (PNK 41) and avoid its difficulties. "The whole complex of events" (PNK 66), instead of a material ether, would now furnish the continuity required for physical transmission and field theory. The "ether" now becomes an expression for the systematic modification of events throughout space and time (CN 160, PRIN R 37).

In this way he can reject the notion of empty space, and at the same time avoid postulation of a material ether. The result for his theory of actual occasions is that no two regions of actual occasions are separated by "empty space."

In denying empty space he is accepting the Cartesian notion of a spatial plenum. But Descartes's view is modified and generalized in terms of an extensive plenum of *events* in the earlier writings or of *actual occasions* in the later writings (ESP 239, 242). ". . . from the standpoint of any one actual entity, the 'given' actual world is a nexus of actual entities, transforming the potentiality of the extensive scheme into a plenum of actual occasions" (PR 119). Since every event or actual occasion is a process, it may now be said that "something is always going on everywhere, even in so-called empty space" (CN 78).

Whitehead continues to refer to empty space, or to "so-called empty space," but the expression simply means "an environment of faintly co-ordinated achievement" (PR 303), that is to say nexūs of actual occasions with extremely faint intensity and hence of minimum importance. Such occasions are quite as actual as any others and impose conformity on their successors (PR 28, 88). When "occupied" space is distinguished from "unoccupied" space (PR 112, 141), and when in reference to the latter such terms as "unoccupied events" are used (PNK 97, SMW 214), the contrast is simply between nexūs of actual occasions with well-defined characteristics and those with faint coordination among the occasions that compose them.

With this denial of empty space and the corresponding assertion of a plenum of actual occasions, it seems clear that no two occasions can be separated by an interval that is vacant of actual occasions. It is conceivable, however, that such a plenum might be compatible with the occupation by two occasions of an identical standpoint, or with an overlapping of the regions basic to two occasions. We must now consider these possibilities which have been left open.

4. No two occasions have the same region

This proposition might seem so obvious as not to require discussion, since it is a commonplace that each actual occasion is novel. But since occasions are not strictly identified with their standpoints, an occasion being more than its standpoint, this proposition does not follow immediately from the principle of novelty.

It seems that an analogous proposition about *events* would find support in the earlier writings and thus create a presumption in favor of the present proposition. For instance, "The concrete event itself is also defined by (or, analysed by) the event-particles inhering in it, and such a set of event-particles defines only one event" (PNK 127; see 122).

We turn to the later writings and ask whether two *actual occasions* may have the same region. One argument begins with Whitehead's discussion of the "real essence" of an actual occasion. The abstract essence of an occasion is merely a combination of characters, that is to say a complex eternal object. Since an eternal object is a possibility which might be realized in more than one instance, "There is nothing self-contradictory in the thought of many actual entities with the same abstract essence; but there can only be one actual entity with the same real essence. For the real essence indicates 'where' the entity is, that is to say, its status in the real world; the abstract essence omits the particularity of the status" (PR 94). The real essence (to use Locke's term) of an actual occasion involves a particular extensive region. Then, since two actual entities cannot have the same real essence, they cannot have an identical region.

The same conclusion follows from the notion of the actual worlds or given environments of actual occasions. In the categoreal scheme the fifth category of explanation is "that no two actual entities originate from an identical universe" (PR 33–4). More explicitly, "No two occasions can have identical actual worlds" (PR 321), where "the actual world" for a given occasion means "the nexus of actual entities in the universe correlate to" that occasion (PR 34). Now the actual world of a given occasion is relative to (PR 293), or defined by (PR 102), the standpoint or extensive region basic to that occasion (PR 127). The meaning of "actual world" alters according to the standpoint from which it is defined (PR 102). Hence, since no two occasions can have the same actual world, it seems clear that no two occasions can have the same standpoint.

5. Regions of occasions are nonoverlapping

The preceding considerations do not at first sight preclude the possibility that the region of one actual occasion might include or overlap the region of another. Let us take "inclusion" and "overlapping" as defined in *Process and Reality:*

> Definition 2: Region A is said to 'include' region B when every region connected with B is also connected with A.

> Definition 3: Two regions are said to 'overlap' when there is a third region which they both include (PR 452).

According to Assumption 11, inclusion is a case of overlapping.

It must be understood that it is not the usefulness of the definitions of inclusion and overlapping that is under consideration here. Our question is whether the real standpoints of any two actual occasions may be so related. We ask whether two regions basic to different occasions may have extensive parts, spatial or temporal or both, in common.

To see the problem more clearly we should notice that in the earlier writings *events* not only *may* include or extend over other events; they *always do* include some other events and are included by still other events. Also two events may intersect or have parts in common or overlap, these expressions all having the same meaning (PNK 101–2, CN 76, PRIN R 67). Therefore a proposition analogous to proposition 5, framed in terms of *events* as described in the earlier writings, would be clearly false.

These earlier writings also recognize spatiotemporal exclusion as a property of events. That is, two events *may* have no parts in common. Events which do not intersect are said to be "separated." [6] Thus external relations between events in nature are provided for, as well as inclusion and overlapping. In fact every event is spatiotemporally external to *some* other events: ". . . every event is known as being related to other events which it does not include. This fact, that every event is known as possessing the quality of exclusion, shows that exclusion is as positive a relation as inclusion" (CN 186).

In this way between two *events* any of three extensive relationships is possible: (a) inclusion of one event by the other; (b) overlapping or intersection, in which case the two events have spatiotemporal parts in common; and (c) separation (CN 185–6). Event A might include or overlap or exclude event B.

We now ask about relations between *actual occasions*. Do all three of these extensive relationships apply to the regions of actual occasions? Later we shall ask whether Whitehead explicitly denies that relations *a* and *b* apply to the regions of actual occasions. First we ask whether his later theory of extension leaves open the possibility of a denial.

Recurring to the theory of extension in the earlier writings, we note that it is developed in terms of events. In the earlier writings events are the relata involved in the relationship of extension (PNK 61; CN 58, 75). Hence *all* extensive relations have to be stated in terms of events. Inclusion, overlapping, and exclusion are relations between *events*.

6. PNK 61, 102; TSM 50; CN 75–6. All intersecting events are necessarily "joined," but separated events may *also* be joined or, more specifically, "adjoined" (PNK 102–3, CN 101). For an alternative definition of junction see CN 76. Compare the definition of adjunction with that of external connection or contiguity in PR 453, 468.

Now when we come to the later writings we find that the general theory of extension is not developed in terms of actual occasions, nor even in terms of nexūs of occasions (now his interpretation of events), but in terms of regions: "The term 'region' will be used for the relata which are involved in the scheme of 'extensive connection' " (PR 449). This restatement of the theory of extension in terms of regions, and *not* in terms of events or actual occasions, is important for our topic.

In its primary sense a region means the standpoint of an actual occasion. But the term is also used to include in its denotation spatiotemporal quanta which are not *in fact* standpoints of actual occasions, as well as quanta which are real standpoints. In this more general sense a region is not necessarily "basic" to an individual actual occasion. Some regions are hypothetical standpoints. They are regions which *might* be actualized by actual occasions: "When we divide the satisfaction coordinately, we do not find feelings which *are* separate, but feelings which *might be* separate. In the same way, the divisions of the region are not divisions which *are;* they are divisions which *might be.* Each such mode of division yields 'extensive quanta': also an 'extensive quantum' has been termed a 'standpoint' " (PR 435). Using the term in the derivative and more general sense, then not all regions are regions of actual occasions. It is in this more general sense that the term is used in the theory of extensive connection in *Process and Reality,* Part IV.

The notion of a hypothetical standpoint must be made clear. Such standpoints are arrived at in two ways. When the region of an actual occasion is divided, any of the subquanta is a region which "might" be actualized by an actual occasion. Also when the regions of two or more occasions are aggregated, the resultant quantum is a region which "might" be actualized by an actual occasion.

> . . . suppose that *P* is a coordinate division of an actual occasion *A*. Then *P* can be conceived as an actual occasion with its own actual world forming its initial datum in its first phase of genetic origination. In fact, *P* is the hypothetical satisfaction of a hypothetical process of concrescence with this standpoint . . .

Further, in addition to the merely potential subdivision of a satisfaction into coordinate feelings, there is the merely potential aggregation of actual entities into a super-actuality in respect to which the true actualities play the part of co-ordinate subdivisions. In other words, just as for some purposes, one atomic actuality can be treated as though it were many coordinate actualities, in the same way, for other purpose[s], a nexus of many actualities can be treated as though it were one actuality. This is what we habitually do in the case of the span of life of a molecule, or of a piece of rock, or of a human body (PR 439).

Treating these quanta as standpoints, the entities conceived as actualizing them are quasi-actualities (PR 448), *pseudo* sub-organisms or *pseudo* super-organisms (PR 431). They are not actual entities but entities which *might be* actual (PR 435).

The extensive continuum, then, consists of the systematic ordering of (a) the standpoints of actual occasions *and* (b) all hypothetical standpoints arrived at by subdivision or aggregation of actual occasions, on one uniform plan (PR 103–5, 448). Actual occasions are basic to the theory of extension, in its more general form, in the sense that they furnish real standpoints from which hypothetical standpoints may be derived by subdivision and aggregation.

Those regions which are not regions of actual occasions are to be regarded as "hypothetical standpoints," because for Whitehead "vacuous actuality" has no meaning (PR 43, 253, 471). There are no bare stretches of space and time. Space and time have significance only as characteristics of the relations of actual entities. Therefore regions have significance only as actual or hypothetical standpoints for actual entities.

I now suggest that some extensive relations may not apply to the *regions of actual occasions* which are *real* standpoints. Some types of extensive connection apply only to hypothetical standpoints. It is true that *some* types must apply to the regions of actual occasions. But it is not necessary to the theory of extensive connection that all extensive relations should apply to them.

This interpretation of Whitehead's later theory of extension is suggested by the fundamental importance of "potentiality" for that theory. Extension is the complex of events *qua* their potentialities (SMW 179). It is a metaphysical assumption, he says, that "the real potentialities relative to all standpoints are coordinated as diverse determinations of one extensive continuum. This extensive continuum is one relational complex in which all potential objectifications find their niche. . . . This extensive continuum expresses the solidarity of all possible standpoints throughout the whole process of the world." The reality of this continuum "is the reality of what is potential, in its character of a real component of what is actual" (PR 103; see 96, 118, 123, 337).

It seems that this later theory of extension is a theory of possible standpoints. The extensive continuum "expresses the solidarity of all possible standpoints." The theory has reference and applicability to the actual world, because possible standpoints are derived from real standpoints. But in its full generality the theory of extensive connection is an account of relations between possible standpoints.

This interpretation may be stated as follows:

a. All the definitions and assumptions in the general theory of extensive connection are applicable to possible standpoints.

b. Some of the definitions and assumptions apply to real standpoints.

c. Only those definitions and assumptions which are explicitly asserted to do so, or are required to do so by Whitehead's categoreal scheme, apply to real standpoints.

On this view it is not *required* by the general theory of extension that all the relations defined in that theory apply to the regions of actual occasions.

We now ask whether Whitehead explicitly denies that some of these extensive relations apply to pairs of real standpoints. It will be useful to note certain definitions and assumptions that bear directly on this question.

a. *Inclusion*

Definition 2. Region *A* is said to 'include' region *B* when every region connected with *B* is also connected with *A*. As an alternative nomenclature, region *B* will be said to be 'part' of region *A* (PR 452).

Assumption 9. Every region includes other regions; and a pair of regions thus included in one region are not necessarily connected with each other. Such pairs can always be found, included in any given region (PR 452).

b. *Overlapping*

Definition 3. Two regions are said to 'overlap' when there is a third region which they both include (PR 452).

Assumption 11. If one region includes another region, the two regions overlap (PR 452).

c. *Mediate connection*

Definition 1. Two regions are 'mediately' connected when they are both connected with a third region (PR 450).

Assumption 2. No region is connected with all the other regions; and any two regions are mediately connected (PR 451).

d. *External connection*

Definition 7. Two regions are 'externally' connected when (i) they are connected, and (ii) they do not overlap (PR 453; see also 468: Let two actual occasions be termed 'contiguous' when the regions constituting their 'standpoints' are externally connected).

In these definitions and assumptions Whitehead restates the extensive relations which applied to events in the earlier writings. His redefinitions of inclusion and overlapping need not detain us. His reinterpretation of "separation" may be noticed. It will be recalled that separated *events* might also be "joined," and that events which are separated and joined were said to be "adjoined" (PNK 102–3, CN 101). Then "external connection" is a redefinition of the notion formerly expressed by "adjunction." Also not all separated events are joined. By Assumption 2, the analogous case is that of regions which are not connected. But any two regions, including regions that are not connected, are now said to be "mediately connected."

If inclusion and overlapping do not apply to standpoints of actual occasions, then the only types of extensive relations between two real standpoints would be (d) external connection and (c) mediate connection. Further, the scope of mediate connection would have to be narrowed in its application to real standpoints. If no real standpoint includes or overlaps another, then where a mediating region is a real standpoint mediating between other real standpoints, this mediating region is externally connected with the regions it mediately connects.

In support of this interpretation I offer arguments of two kinds. Certain general arguments cover all types of overlapping and inclusion. Certain special arguments have relevance only to specific types of overlapping or inclusion. By the use of several such special arguments all types of inclusion and overlapping may be dealt with, and the general arguments thus reinforced.

In his statement of the theory of extension in *Process and Reality* there is no suggestion that *two regions basic to actual occasions* may overlap. On the contrary, the theory of "coordinate division" seems to exclude this possibility. Coordinate division is division of actual occasions objectified as extended data. A coordinate division yields extensive quanta that are parts of the original region. But the region is not in fact divided into these parts. They are not, in a sense, natural facts. "When we divide the satisfaction coordinately, we do not find feelings which *are* separate, but feelings which *might be* separate. In the same way, the divisions of the region are not divisions which *are;* they are divisions which *might be*" (PR 435). The parts into which a real standpoint is divided are always hypothetical standpoints (regions regarded as standpoints for *hypothetical* actual occasions), and not real standpoints (regions which are standpoints for actual occasions). An indefinite number of modes of dividing the basic region are possible, yielding an indefinite number of corresponding sets of subregions or hypothetical standpoints.

Of his earlier writings Whitehead remarks that there extension was conceived entirely in terms of subdivisions of regions. The notion of extensiveness was conceived "as purely derived from the notion of 'whole and part,' that is to say, 'extensive whole and extensive part' " (PR 439). In *Process and Reality,* he says, another type of extensive relationship is emphasized as well, namely "the merely potential aggregation of actual entities into a super-actuality in respect to which the true actualities play the part of coordinate subdivisions" (PR 439). Thus in the later writings, in order to account adequately for "the extensive relations of actual entities mutually external to each other," "extensive connection" rather than the relation of "extending over" is adopted as the starting point for the theory of extension (PR 440).

In the later theory the "solidarity" of the extensive continuum "embraces not only the coordinate divisions within each atomic actuality, but also exhibits the coordinate divisions of all atomic actualities from each other in one scheme of relationship" (PR 438). Here there seems to be an explicit distinction between (a) the relations of subdivisions of regions basic to actual occasions and (b) the relations between such regions themselves. And the scheme of relations between real standpoints is said to be a "scheme of *external* extensive relationships," in contrast to "the schemes of internal division which are *internal* to the several actual entities" (PR 438). It seems quite clear, therefore, that the extensive relations between regions of actual occasions are always external relations. That is to say, any two such regions are nonoverlapping and have no common parts.

Another argument arises from Whitehead's explanation of physical transmission, which illustrates "the physical importance of 'external connection' " (PR 468). He thinks the prevailing notion of continuous transmission of energy is liable to the difficulties indicated by Zeno's paradoxes [7] and that it "must be replaced by the notion of immediate transmission through a route of successive quanta of extensiveness. These quanta of extensiveness are the basic regions of successive contiguous occasions" (PR 468). Now "contiguity" is defined as follows: "Let two actual occasions be termed 'contiguous' when the regions constituting their 'standpoints' are externally connected" (PR 468). It will be remembered that external connection excludes overlapping. Thus the extensive relations in terms of which physical transmission is explained are

7. See SMW 177–80; PR 53, 105–7, 468. Also quantum theory inclines him to explain physical transmission in some other way. See SMW 190. See in Ch. 9 below on quantum theory in Whitehead's thought.

external connection and mediate connection. Since every route of transmission is a series of externally connected regions, mediating regions are externally connected with the regions which they mediately connect. We have then a denial of overlapping between the regions of actual occasions involved in any route of physical transmission.

In further support of this interpretation of the regions of actual occasions I offer certain special arguments. Since each of these will refer only to certain types of overlapping, a series of diagrams may be useful to illustrate these types:

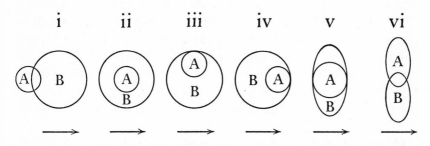

Let A and B represent regions. Then the problem is: May any of the relations indicated in diagrams i–vi hold between regions that are real standpoints? In each case let ⟶ represent the direction of the future from the standpoint of A. Then in types v and vi, A and B will be contemporary regions. In types i–iv A and B will not be contemporary.

In the chapter on "Past, Present, Future" in *Adventures of Ideas* (ch. 12), Whitehead discusses the "mutual immanence" of occasions. The point of interest for us here is that: "Evidently this mutual immanence and constraint of a pair of occasions is not in general a symmetric relation. For, apart from contemporaries, one occasion will be in the future of the other" (AI 254). From this it would seem that the basic regions of the two occasions, *qua* temporal quanta, do not overlap. This is simply an explicit statement of what is implicit in Whitehead's epochal theory of time. "Supersession" of one occasion by another is not a continuous process (TIME 63–4). Therefore types i, ii, iii, and iv would be excluded from the extensive relationships possible between the regions of actual occasions.

Certain of the types indicated above may be eliminated by reference to "durations." A duration is "a locus of actual occasions, such that (a) any two members of the locus are contemporaries, and (β) that any actual occasion, not belonging to the duration, is in the causal past or causal future of some members of the duration" (PR 487). It must be remembered that a duration is not an instantaneous moment but involves a definite lapse of time. A duration is an "epoch" (SMW 177). Since any two members of the duration are contemporaries, that is to say "in unison of becoming" (PR 190), the temporal extent of duration D is identical with the temporal extent of any actual occasion as A, which is a member of D. Now Whitehead says explicitly, "No occasion can be both in the past and in the future, of a duration. Thus a duration forms a barrier in the world between its past and its future" (PR 491). If no occasion can be both in the future and in the past of a given duration D, then it is impossible for any occasion, as B, to be both in the past and in the future of an occasion, as A, which is a member of D.

Of course, as implied in the definition cited above, A lies in more than one duration. In fact, A lies in an infinite number of durations (PR 487-8). No one duration includes all of A's contemporaries. Here is Whitehead's theory of alternative time systems, which he adopts on the ground of relativity physics. This consideration strengthens the argument. For every duration defined by A and some of its contemporaries, according to some definite meaning of unison of becoming, it would hold that no actual occasion can be both in the past and in the future of that duration. Thus it seems that types ii and iii are excluded from the extensive relationships possible between the regions of two occasions. The preceding argument is here reinforced with respect to these types.

Types v and vi, where A and B are contemporary actual occasions, remain to be dealt with. In the chapter on "The Extensive Continuum" in *Process and Reality* (P. II, ch. 2), Whitehead discusses "the contemporary world": "The contemporary world as perceived by the senses is the datum for contemporary actuality, and is therefore continuous—divisible but not divided. The contemporary world is in fact divided and atomic, being a multiplicity of atomic actual entities. These contemporary actual entities are divided from each other, and are not themselves divisible into other contemporary actual entities" (PR 96). The contemporary world appears to be, but in fact is not, continuous, except in the sense of being potentially divisible. To avoid using the argument from actual occasions as acts of experience, another passage should be referred to. In a discussion of presentational immediacy, the perceptive mode in which we apprehend the contemporary world, Whitehead gives a definition of contemporaneousness: ". . . namely, that actual occasions, *A* and *B,* are mutually contemporary, when *A* does not contribute to the datum for *B,* and *B* does not contribute to the datum for *A,* except that both *A* and *B* are atomic regions in the potential scheme of extensiveness which is a datum for both *A* and *B*" (PR 188). The important point is that A and B are atomic regions, and presumably divided regions. This is a real or natural fact *about* A and B, though it is not given directly *for* either one of them. It seems, then, that the regions of contemporary actual occasions are divided from each other and are not divisible into regions of other contemporary actual occasions. If so, then types v and vi are excluded from the extensive relationships possible between regions of actual occasions.

Taken together these special arguments cover all types of overlapping and the more general arguments are reinforced. If these arguments are valid and adequate, then the regions basic to any two actual occasions are nonoverlapping.

This result does *not* imply that regions of actual occasions do not overlap other regions, nor that regions of actual occasions do not include other regions, nor that regions of actual occasions are not included by other regions. This result is entirely compatible with Whitehead's assumption that "every region includes other regions" (PR 452, Assumption 9). What *is* hereby asserted is that those regions which overlap or include or are included by regions of actual occasions are themselves always *possible* standpoints, that is to say standpoints for *hypothetical* actual occasions, and that in no case are those regions *real* standpoints for actual occasions. "Continuity concerns what is potential; whereas actuality is incurably atomic" (PR 95).

Incidentally this interpretation makes more intelligible Whitehead's conception of abstractive sets, in terms of which he defines points, lines, and areas. For an abstractive set is composed of an infinite number of regions (PR 454). And if these regions had to be thought of as real standpoints of actual occasions we should immediately land in confusion. This has indeed been the destination of some interpreters of Whitehead, who incautiously have transferred to actual occasions the extensive characteristics of events as defined in the earlier writings. This is a mistake. The regions that are included by, and in turn include, other regions and thus constitute an indefinitely convergent series (PR 455) are hypothetical entities. They are possible, not real, standpoints.

I am not competent to pronounce on the mathematical adequacy or usefulness of Whitehead's definitions of points, lines, and areas. But the philosophical argument for his theory is not that it refers only to experienced entities, nor even that it employs only "actual entities." Neither of these arguments would be well founded. The philosophical argument for Whitehead's theory of points is only that it employs a term (region) whose general *meaning* can be given by reference to the extended character of occasions of experience.

6. Summary: Spatiotemporal exclusiveness

We have examined Whitehead's theory of extension in his later writings, with a view to understanding the regions of actual occasions and their extensive relations. If the interpretation offered is valid, then his theory of the extended actual world would be as follows: The actual world is a plenum of actual occasions. The region basic to any occasion has definite spatiotemporal position and boundaries, and no two occasions have the same region. The extensive relations between the regions of actual occasions are limited to (a) external connection and (b) mediate connection. Any mediating region which is a real standpoint is externally connected with the real standpoints it mediately connects.

Thus the region of an actual occasion is exclusive of the region of any other occasion. No two actual occasions have any spatiotemporal parts in common. In this sense an actual occasion transcends every other occasion.

CHAPTER 5

Whitehead on Substance

WE HAVE BEEN examining those features of the theory of actual occasions that make up a doctrine of real individuality. As an act of experience an occasion is concrete, novel, unified, and exclusive of the immediacies of other occasions. Derivatively, its spatiotemporal region is definite and exclusive. These features of Whitehead's theory implement his pluralism, his assertion that there are many ultimate matters of fact.

Usually in European philosophy ultimate matters of fact have been called substances, and about certain doctrines of substance Whitehead has had a good deal to say. Some of his historical remarks are perceptive and acute. Others will strike historians as unbalanced and perhaps unjust. Since we are concerned with his own positive view, I shall not attempt to correct his historical judgments. I shall lay his view alongside older ways of thinking as *he* understands them. His attitude to traditional views of substance will serve as a clue to interpret his own scheme. It can help us get his view of "real things" into a certain perspective and see what it amounts to.

It has seemed to some interpreters that Whitehead simply rejects the category of substance. It is true that some expressions in his later writings encourage this opinion.[1] In the light of qualifications he introduces elsewhere, however, and especially in view of the outcome of his own speculation, this opinion cannot be maintained. His treatment of substance taken as a whole amounts to a critique but not a rejection.

We shall ask what he regards as "dead" in traditional interpretations of substance, what he regards as "living," and then sum-

1. For example: ". . . the final contrast between a philosophy of substance and a philosophy of organism" (PR 228). See SMW 74; PR 44, 129, 311; AI 169–70, 356, 361.

marize his treatment of substance. In this way we can bring to-gether and connect up a number of discussions which are scattered through his later writings. Whitehead himself does not systematize these discussions. His main objective is the development of his own categoreal scheme.

1. What is "dead" in the tradition about substance

In Whitehead's judgment a certain doctrine about substance has had an unfortunate influence in Western thought. The root of this doctrine he traces to Aristotle's definition: "A primary sub-stance is 'neither asserted of a subject nor present in a subject' " (PR 79). As a logical derivative of this Aristotelian definition he cites Descartes's definition: "And when we conceive of substance, we merely conceive an existent thing which requires nothing but itself in order to exist" (as quoted from *Principles of Philosophy*, Pt. I, p. 51, in PR 79). The doctrine is that ultimate matters of fact consist in: (a) a substratum that is "vacuous" and static; and (b) accidental qualities and relations external to the substratum. Whitehead scrutinizes this doctrine and rejects it.

Does his rejection of this doctrine amount to a rejection of the category of substance altogether? I shall argue it does not. Cer-tainly he thinks this doctrine has been influential in Western phi-losophy. Indeed he may overestimate its prevalence, if not its im-portance. But, along with this objectionable doctrine, he finds in the philosophical tradition other views of substance which he adopts and absorbs into his own categoreal scheme, as we shall see.[2] The tradition, like an ancient tree, has living branches as well as dead ones.

The reasons why this objectionable doctrine has been important in cosmological theory, Whitehead thinks, are as follows. First, it seems to fit our common-sense experience. Substance and quality so understood are among "the most natural ideas for the human mind. It is the way in which we think of things, and without these ways of thinking we could not get our ideas straight for daily use"

2. For his acceptance of certain elements in Aristotle's and Descartes's doctrines of substance, see on Aristotle PR 45, 81, 209, 319, and on Descartes PR viii–ix, 28, 64, 65, 114, 218–19.

(SMW 74). In practical activities common-sense objects, which are relatively clear and distinct, tend to dominate our interpretation of our experience. When we think of these objects the notion of enduring substances with accidental qualities seems to make sense (SMW 74, PR 119–20, MT 174–7).

Again, common language has been developed out of practical needs to deal with those facts of experience which are relatively clear and distinct (PR 120, AI 209, MT 139). Therefore this doctrine of substance has become embodied in "the common forms of language" (PR 240). In the third place, "The exclusive dominance of the substance-quality metaphysics was enormously promoted by the logical bias of the medieval period" (PR 209). For the traditional Aristotelian analysis of propositions has been exclusively in terms of subject and predicate, and thus has fostered the conception of enduring substances with accidental qualities as a ruling idea in metaphysics (PR 45, 122, 319; AI 356).

Because of these facts about experience, language, and logic, this doctrine of substance has often seemed the most obvious and natural way to conceive ultimate matters of fact. Whitehead does not deny its usefulness for many practical purposes. But he thinks it should not be erected into a metaphysical doctrine. "The simple notion of an enduring substance sustaining persistent qualities, either essentially or accidentally, expresses a useful abstract for many purposes of life. But whenever we try to use it as a fundamental statement of the nature of things, it proves itself mistaken . . . For its employment in language and in logic, there is—as stated above—a sound pragmatic defence. But in metaphysics the concept is sheer error" (PR 122). It is now time to ask why, according to Whitehead, this doctrine is "sheer error" in metaphysics.

a. One element in traditional interpretations of substance which he regards as "dead"—as fundamentally false in metaphysics—is the conception of a vacuous and static substratum. For Whitehead, on the contrary, concrete things are experiencing things. Let us examine his denial of "vacuous actuality," by which he means a real thing devoid of subjectivity.

The bodily substances have, on this theory, a vacuous existence. They are sheer facts, devoid of all intrinsic values. It is

intrinsically impossible to give any reason why they should
come into existence, or should endure, or should cease to
exist . . . This conception of vacuous substantial existence
lacks all explanatory insight . . .

We shall never elaborate an explanatory metaphysics unless we abolish this notion of valueless, vacuous existence.
Vacuity is the character of an abstraction, and is wrongly introduced into the notion of a finally real thing, an actuality
(FR 24).

In this notion of a vacuous substratum Whitehead finds the
germ of materialism which, with Berkeley and Hume, he rejects.
His objection has both a rationalistic and an empirical side. The
rationalistic side is suggested by the foregoing quotation. We cannot form a clear conception of any concrete actuality devoid of
feeling. When the defender of the objectionable doctrine is asked,
"What is it, if not something analogous to our experience, to
which the properties of the thing belong?" he may reply, "Stuff."
In this case the critic asks what is meant by this word, in addition
to such properties as hardness which we experience. And if the defender is driven to Locke's reply, "A something, I know not what,"
then the critic asks, "Why then do you talk about it?" The descent
from "stuff" to "nonsense," the critic will claim, is short and easy.

But this line of objection is valid only if in experience we find
no datum that would justify belief in vacuous actuality. In this
empirical side of his thought Whitehead agrees with Berkeley and
Hume, both in their demand for empirical data [3] and in their
denial that such a datum is found.

The conception of a substratum has often involved the "static
fallacy" also. Whitehead says of his philosophy, "the notion of an
actual entity as the unchanging subject of change is completely
abandoned" (PR 43). There are two grounds on which Whitehead
objects to belief in the existence of static substrata. One is the
evidence of ordinary experience as to the nature of the experiencing subject. Whitehead cites from Descartes the remark, " 'I am,
I exist,' is necessarily true each time that I pronounce it, or that I

3. "The elucidation of immediate experience is the sole justification for
any thought; and the starting point for thought is the analytic observation
of components of this experience" (PR 6; see 253).

mentally conceive it"; and then comments, "Descartes adopts the position that an act of experience is the primary type of actual occasion. But in his subsequent developments he assumes that mental substances endure change. Here he goes beyond his argument. For each time he pronounces 'I am, I exist,' the actual occasion, which is the ego, is different; and the 'he' which is common to the two egos is an eternal object or, alternatively, the nexus of successive occasions" (PR 116). We do not find, as a matter of fact, that the subject of immediate experience has *undifferentiated* endurance. Hence, to conform to our own experience of ourselves, the theory of time as epochal and "perpetually perishing" becomes necessary.

In a subsequent passage another ground for denial of undifferentiated endurance appears. This notion is inapplicable as an ultimate concept in physical analysis. Physical analysis proceeds from common-sense objects to molecules, then to atoms, protons, and electrons. These in turn require analysis into quanta of energy associated with periodic rhythms (PR 121-2). This argument against the notion of undifferentiated endurance is secondary to the argument from immediate experience (see Chapter 9).

For these reasons Whitehead rejects the static fallacy, whether it arises from Aristotle's notion of primary substances "as the static foundations which received the impress of qualification," or from Locke's modern version of this doctrine in his "metaphor of the mind as an 'empty cabinet' receiving the impress of ideas" (AI 355). Neither ordinary experience nor physics gives warrant for belief in unchanging subjects of change. On the contrary, "the very essence of real actuality—that is, of the completely real—is *process*" (AI 354). As we saw in Chapter 2, statements like this last one need careful qualification. None of the needed qualifications, however, reintroduces the static fallacy.

So far we have found that one traditional conception Whitehead rejects is the notion of a static and vacuous substratum, a substratum devoid of internal activity and devoid of internal value.

b. Another traditional conception he rejects is the notion that real things exist in isolation, completely independent of each other. This seems to him a corollary of the notion of "accidental" qualities and relations, taken together with the subject-predicate form of expression. The result is that no "real connections" between real things can be found.

On this view of ultimate matters of fact, "the relations between individual substances constitute metaphysical nuisances" (PR 208). For this doctrine

> entirely leaves out of account the interconnection between real things. Each substantial thing is thus conceived as complete in itself, without any reference to any other substantial thing. Such an account of the ultimate atoms, or of the ultimate monads, or of the ultimate subjects enjoying experience, renders an interconnected world of real individuals unintelligible. The universe is shivered into a multitude of disconnected substantial things, each thing in its own way exemplifying its private bundle of abstract characters which have found a common home in its own substantial individuality. . . . A substantial thing can acquire a quality, a credit—but real landed estate, never. In this way Aristotle's doctrines of Predication and of Primary Substance have issued into a doctrine of the conjunction of attributes and of the disjunction of primary substances (AI 169–70).

Some philosophers, to resolve a gratuitous and insoluble problem, have had recourse to a *deus ex machina* "who was capable of rising superior to the difficulties of metaphysics" (SMW 217), as did Leibniz, or to monism. "Every respectable philosophy of the subject-predicate type is monistic" (PR 208–9). In these ways, and only in these ways, might one explain the solidarity of the world without acknowledging direct connections between real individuals. By postulating his transcendental pre-established harmony Leibniz was able to admit real individuals and deny direct connections among them. Monism resolves the problem more economically by denying real individuals.

Whitehead rejects the first of these views as a bogus solution. Since he himself has been accused of using the notion of God as a catch-all for unsolved problems, we should notice particularly the point of this objection to Leibniz. It is not that Leibniz included a concept of God in his cosmology, but that he gave no reasons why the "windows" of finite monads are open to God though not to other finite monads. Whitehead is objecting to the "arbitrary" introduction of the concept of God into cosmology (AI 171; Chapter 15 below).

He rejects the second view, monism, on the evidence of ordinary experience. Monism is "in defiance of the most obvious deliverances of our intuitive 'prejudices'" (PR 208). On what would commonly be called realistic grounds, he holds there are many ultimate matters of fact, not one only.

Whitehead's denial of the independence and isolation of substances is not based merely on the ground that it forces anyone seeking a coherent view either to a deus ex machina or to monism. He holds that we *do* in fact have direct experience of real connections between real things (PR 10). The interconnectedness of real things is a basic datum in experience. Philosophy must explain it, not explain it away. This is the fundamental reason why Whitehead rejects the doctrine of the mutual independence of real things. Just how he explains real connections between real things will be the topic of Chapters 6–8.

So far we have noticed two elements in traditional interpretations of substance which Whitehead rejects: (a) the conception of a static and vacuous substratum, and (b) the conception that substances are self-sufficient and independent of one another and hence essentially isolated from one another. Now we must ask whether there are not some elements in traditional thought about substance which he accepts as "living" ideas. I suggest that he is really engaged in constructing an alternative doctrine of substance, and that in his reconstruction he has been, as he says, relying on "the positive value of the philosophical tradition" (PR ix). The philosophy of organism, he says, is apt to emphasize just those elements in the writings of earlier philosophers which "subsequent systematizers have put aside" (PR v). But one cannot read Whitehead without noticing his sense of indebtedness to tradition as well as his independence of mind.

2. What is "living" in the tradition about substance

a. One living element, for Whitehead, in the notion of substance is the principle of individuality. He is concerned to maintain the concrete unity and the social transcendence of an ultimate matter of fact. Preceding chapters have explored the way Whitehead formulates this principle. Charles Hartshorne goes so far as to say that "Whitehead is above all the interpreter of individuality . . ." [4] It is not clear that individuality is his supreme concern, but it is clearly one of his major concerns in his later writings. Insofar as he offers a genuine theory of real individuality, he is affirming the validity and importance of a principle which has been, for most philosophers, an element in the notion of substance.

b. Another living element in the notion of substance is the principle of self-existence. Whitehead accepts this principle also and formulates it in his own way. This principle means that the ground or reason for the existence and nature of any real thing lies, in an important sense, in itself. Whitehead's terms are "self-creation," "self-realization," "self-causation," "self-formation," and "self-determination."

He explicitly recognizes that this principle belongs to the philosophical tradition: "Every philosophy recognizes, in some form or other, this factor of self-causation, in what it takes to be ultimate actual fact" (PR 228). He is fond of using Spinoza's phrase, *causa sui*, to denote the self-creativity of every actual entity. He also says that Descartes's argument from the nature of thinking "assumes that this freely determined operation is thereby constitutive of an occasion in the endurance of an actual entity" (PR 228). He thus implies that Descartes's argument logically requires a notion of self-causation similar to his own.

What does Whitehead mean by self-causation or self-creation? Self-causation is not the only kind of causation that is effective in determining the nature of an actual entity. The actual entity is conditioned by the necessity of conforming to the settled past. This is efficient causation. But the way the entity subjectively enjoys and integrates its data is due to its own subjective aim at unity. This is the free "decision" of the concrescence. The concrete actual entity is thus a product of both efficient and final causation. Self-determination is essential to its constitution, and its power of self-determination is not conferred upon it, or de-

4. In *Philosophical Essays for Alfred North Whitehead* (New York, Longmans, Green, 1936), p. 211.

rived by it from some other entity. The uprush of creative feeling is confronted with and conditioned by a given actual world, but is itself original and underived. Actual entities vary in many ways. They vary in intensity, in their subjective patterns, in their effectiveness. But each, in some degree however faint, is an instance of original creative activity and in this sense is self-existent.

The conception of original and originative activity has been familiar in Western philosophy. In our tradition it has been attributed to God, to human wills, or to both. Whitehead's interpretation differs from that of many traditional philosophers at this point. He extends the range of the concept and attributes creativity to all real individuals, whether subhuman, human, or superhuman, though these individuals vary widely in their complexity, intensity, and effectiveness. As a consequence, the conception of substance needs to be revised so as to conform to this principle of the universality of creativity. Later, in Part Three, we shall look at the theological outcome of this principle and see how the divine creativity differs from that of actual occasions.

c. A third living element in the notion of substance that Whitehead accepts and interprets is the principle of permanence.

For Whitehead permanence is one of the fundamental characteristics of the world. Permanence and flux are among the "final opposites," and to ignore either is to distort the evidence of ordinary experience (PR 518). Some philosophers have begun with the intuition of permanence and developed a metaphysics of substance in which change and relations become problematical. Other philosophers have started with the intuition of flux and developed a metaphysics in which the permanent becomes a problem. But, he concludes, the two notions "cannot be torn apart in this way; and we find that a wavering balance between the two is a characteristic of the greater number of philosophers" (PR 318).

There are three ways in which his theory of actual occasions expresses the intuition of permanence: in the doctrine of an actual occasion as epochal, having real duration; in the doctrine of objective immortality; and in the conception of enduring objects.

i. The sense in which an actual occasion has real duration, though not "endurance," has been examined in some detail in Chapters 2 and 4. The question whether actual occasions are genuine *terms* and not mere segments of a flux turns largely on the question whether the satisfaction of an occasion is a process of change. I have suggested that, strictly speaking, the satisfaction is part of neither the process of concrescence nor the process of transition, but is the culmination of the former and the anticipation of the latter. On this view, a complete subject has a real duration and is not merely a flux. That this duration may be very brief is obviously true but does not affect the principle at stake.

ii. As we have seen, objective immortality means, first, that an actual occasion which has perished is still effective in determining the future; and second, that the self-identity of the occasion, though not its immediacy, is retained. In all its objectifications in the future, the occasion will play a self-consistent role. In this doctrine Whitehead expresses two aspects of what the principle of permanence has usually meant, namely that present matters of fact will "matter" or have weight in the future, and that in the future present matters of fact will be themselves and nothing else.

iii. In his conception of enduring objects Whitehead expresses the kind of permanence we ordinarily attribute to common-sense objects like stones, trees, animals, and human beings (PR 50–2, 151–63; AI 258–67). This kind of permanence is important: "Our lives are dominated by enduring things" (AI 361). As one element in traditional philosophical accounts of enduring things, however, he finds the notion of "undifferentiated endurance." For this he can find no warrant in experience, as we have seen. So he thinks a more discriminating and adequate account of enduring things must be given. "The real actual things that endure are all societies. They are not actual occasions. It is the mistake that has thwarted European metaphysics from the time of the Greeks, namely, to confuse societies with the completely real things which are the actual occasions" (AI 262).

Thus electrons and protons (PR 498), chairs, tables, rocks, planets, and animal bodies (PR 98, 166–7) are all "corpuscular societies." Minds, souls, and persons are likewise to be understood as being composed of societies of actual occasions. Our immediate concern is not to decide whether this theory of enduring things is adequate to the facts of experience, but merely to point out one way he gives expression to the principle of permanence in his own systematic terms.

The connection between Whitehead's view and traditional philosophical interpretations of enduring things comes out more clearly when we consider the function of the "defining characteristic" of a historical route of occasions. In a stable environment successive groups of actual occasions will exemplify a common pattern (a complex eternal object), as in the life history of a table or a tree. In this way Whitehead reformulates the traditional contrast between a stable essential character and varying accidental qualities. "A society has an essential character, whereby it is the society that it is, and it has also accidental qualities which vary as circumstances alter. Thus a society, as a complete existence and as retaining the same metaphysical status, enjoys a history expressing its changing reactions to changing circumstances" (AI 262). In a footnote to this passage Whitehead says, "This notion of 'society' has analogies to Descartes' notion of 'substance.'" On this analogy the nonessential or accidental qualities of an enduring thing would be those elements in the individual members of the society which, relative to some subject or other, are negligibly relevant to the defining characteristic. As Whitehead says, "The notion of 'defining characteristic' is allied to the Aristotelian notion 'substantial form'" (PR 51; the text has "nation").

In these ways the principles of real individuality, self-existence, and permanence, which have been elements in traditional interpretations of substance, find expression in Whitehead's philosophy. This reinforces the suggestion that he does not flatly reject the notion of substance but revises it. He dissects it, on the basis of a fresh reading of experience, into those elements which are "dead" and those which are "living." Those elements that he accepts are put in a new perspective and developed in relatively novel ways. Now we are ready to sum up and characterize his treatment of the notion of substance.

3. A reformed doctrine of substance

The "error" in metaphysics to which Whitehead points, in his critique of traditional conceptions, "does not consist in the em-

ployment of the word 'substance'; but in the employment of the
notion of an actual entity which is characterized by essential qualities, and remains numerically one amidst the changes of accidental
relations and of accidental qualities"(PR 122). He has no objection
to using the word if it can be dissociated from this error. Sometimes he does so use it: "An 'actual entity' is a *res vera* in the
Cartesian sense of that term; it is a Cartesian 'substance,' and not
an Aristotelian 'primary substance' " (PR viii–ix. See SMW 174–5;
PR 29, 116, 339). In general he refrains from using it because of
the doctrine it is likely to connote.

His hesitation to use the word "substance" is relatively unimportant. The real question is whether and to what extent he gives
to such terms as "actual entity" meanings which "substance" has
stood for and included. The following passage is explicit and
clear. Referring to Descartes's doctrine of real things and to
Locke's stress on "power," Whitehead says, "The notion of 'substance' is *transformed* into that of 'actual entity'; and the notion
of 'power' is transformed into the principle that the reasons for
things are always to be found in the composite nature of definite
actual entities" (PR 28, my italics). One of his criticisms of Locke
is that "Locke is never tired of disparaging the notion of 'substance'; but he gives no hint of alternative categories which he
would employ to analyse the notion of an 'actual entity' and of
'reality' " (PR 222; the text has "analysis"). This clearly implies
that some of the meanings of "substance" are essential for an
adequate account of reality. If the objectionable doctrine is given
up, as Whitehead thinks it ought to be, then a "reformed" doctrine
of substance must be offered in its place.

This is the point of his criticism of certain philosophers who
eliminate instead of reinterpreting the category of substance. We
need to take account of his criticism of philosophies of pure flux
—and not merely of his criticism of traditional doctrines of substance—in order to put his own view in the right perspective.

On Whitehead's view the world is a process. When we get a
sense of the ongoingness of nature, its restlessness and its production of novelty, continually eluding the conceptual nets we set to
ensnare it, then we have a fundamental clue to the nature of reality. In the present century this view has been made familiar by

Bergson, James, Alexander, and Dewey. Plainly, with these philosophers Whitehead has much in common (SMW xi, 72, 199–200, 205–6; TIME 59; PR vii, 42–3, 319, 489; ESP 116).

It is equally important to notice how, in these and other passages, he diverges from them. His objections to their interpretations of reality, though sometimes implicit rather than explicit, are nevertheless clear. For example:

> The notions of 'process' and 'existence' presuppose each other (MT 131).

> Process and individuality require each other. In separation all meaning evaporates (MT 133).

> Apart from Time there is no meaning for purpose, hope, fear, energy. If there be no historic process, then everything is what it is, namely, a mere fact. Life and motion are lost. Apart from Space, there is no consummation. Space expresses the halt for attainment. It symbolizes the complexity of immediate realization. It is the fact of accomplishment. Time and Space express the universe as including the essence of transition, and the success of achievement. The transition is real, and the achievement is real. The difficulty is for language to express one of them without explaining away the other (MT 139–40).

The implicit criticism is that philosophers of process have left out a doctrine of real individuals. They have not done full justice to our experience of the world. A notion of real individuals, in which ends are not only aimed at but attained, is necessary to make the notion of process itself intelligible.

In Whitehead's philosophy, I suggest, process is not a substitute for the category of substance. Prehensions are not substitutes for subjects which prehend and are prehended. Creativity is not pure flux. It is the originative activity that takes place in the concrescences of concrete and socially transcendent individuals. Nature is the never ending process in which real individual things come into being, attain their satisfactions, perish, and condition the future beyond themselves. They thus constitute those enduring objects which dominate our common experience of the world.

Some interpreters of Whitehead have connected his system so closely with other philosophies of process that the individuality and exclusiveness of actual occasions has been obscured. This study may help to correct this unbalanced estimate of the outcome of his speculation. He differs from these other philosophers precisely because he accepts the necessity of a reformed doctrine of substance.

Finally, he thinks that even the common-sense view of substance must be retained and applied, though with due regard for its limitations. It is an abstraction which, for practical purposes, is not only useful but necessary. The following passage, where this concession is repeated, admirably summarizes Whitehead's attitude to substance:

> I suggest that there can be no doubt, but that this general notion expresses large, all-pervading truths about the world around us. The only question is as to how fundamental these truths may be. In other words, we have to ask what large features of the Universe cannot be expressed in these terms. We have also to ask whether we cannot find some other set of notions which will explain the importance of this common-sense notion, and will also explain its relations to those other features ignored by the commonsense notion (MT 176–7; see Chapter 12 below).

CHAPTER 6

The Problem of Social Immanence

1. Social immanence, weak and strong

WHITEHEAD accepts a problem posed by our experience of the world. The world we experience is a world of many things. And we experience these things not in isolation but in connection with one another. The business of speculative philosophy is to express adequately and systematically such facts of common experience.

He therefore undertakes, in constructing his theory of actual occasions, to state both a doctrine of social transcendence and a doctrine of social immanence. To carry out his intention he needs to show just how "every actual entity, including God, is something individual for its own sake; and thereby transcends the rest of actuality" (PR 135). He also needs to show just how real things are present in, and thus organically related to, other real things.

Preceding chapters have analyzed his doctrine of social transcendence. We now turn to his doctrine of social immanence, his doctrine of the continuity of nature which "balances and limits the doctrine of the absolute individuality of each occasion of experience" (AI 235). His account of how one occasion is present in another is given in terms of "objectification." Objectification is the way an actual occasion transcends itself (PR 347) and enters the experience of other occasions. Thus self-transcendence issues in social immanence.

Because some important categories have already been explained, my comments on Whitehead's doctrine of social immanence need not be as extended as the discussions in the preceding chapters. If the conclusions drawn from those discussions are well founded, then objectification does not in any case involve the sharing of immediacy or the overlapping of regions. One actual occasion is *not* present in another occasion in either of these ways. In addition to this negative result, certain positive meanings for social immanence have already emerged, especially in Chapter 3.

I shall first restate certain weak meanings of "being present in." These weak modes of social immanence characterize the relations of contemporary actual occasions and anticipation of the future by a present occasion. I shall show that these weak meanings of "being present in" depend on a strong meaning given in "causal objectification," the way the past is immanent in the present. Reference to Whitehead's treatment of certain special problems, namely physical transmission, efficient causation, and perception will help to show that causal objectification is the crux of his doctrine of social immanence. In the next chapter I examine in detail the way in which causal objectification takes place.

2. Contemporary occasions

We saw in Chapter 3 that an actual occasion does not prehend its contemporaries in their concrete individual actuality. Contemporary actual occasions are causally independent of one another. This means that one contemporary occasion is not present in another in any strong or primary sense. We discovered two weak senses in which one contemporary occasion is present in another, and I shall now restate and comment on these.

a. A kind of mutual relevance between two contemporary actual occasions is constituted by their participation in a common duration or "locus of becoming." For any occasion there is a "now" beyond its own basic region, which is here-now. This is a "regional feeling" (PR 482) of its contemporary world.

For actual occasions in "empty space," that is occasions of very faintly coordinated intensity, the "now" that is not "here" is defined only negatively and vaguely. It is that region from which there is no causal influence upon the given occasion and to which this occasion will make no causal contribution. There-now is that region which is neither in the causal past nor in the causal future of the occasion. This is "bare" regional feeling (PR 482).

For the occasions that make up enduring physical objects there is more definition of the contemporary world. One part of the causal present of such an occasion (A) is geometrically defined in terms of straight lines projected indefinitely outward from a geo- metrical "seat" in A's basic region. This part of A's causal present is the "spatialized world." It is the region where sense objects are perceived in the mode of presentational immediacy by higher organisms.

The notion of "projection" is explained as follows. A inherits a datum from its past actual world. This datum includes sensa and geometrical relations exemplified in past occasions. A enjoys these sensa and geometrical relations "now." And since the sensa are implicated in the geometrical relations they are enjoyed not merely "now" but "there-now." Thus A experiences a contempo- rary region of spatially related sensa (PR, Pt. IV, chs. 4–5).

The essential fact is that what is projected by the present occa- sion has been derived from its past and modified by the antecedent phases of its experience. There is no need for any direct connec- tion between A and its contemporaries to explain A's experience of a contemporary region. The geometrization of the contem- porary locus, as well as the sensa that illustrate it, depends on the influence of the past and on the creative activity of the present occasion itself. As Whitehead points out, this supposes the possi- bility of defining points and straight lines purely in terms of extensive connection, without reference to physical happenings (PR 194).

Three comments on this account of regional feeling are in order.

i. It gives us a *genuine* sense in which contemporary actual occasions are mutually immanent. The contemporary world is objectified as an extended region, a potentiality for becoming. The datum for this feeling is "becoming going on out there." And there is in fact becoming going on out there. In this sense (and only in this sense) this is a "physical" (PR 482) feeling of the contemporary world.

ii. Though this account yields a genuine sense of immanence, yet it is a *weak* sense. The actual division of the contemporary region into the standpoints occupied by actual occasions is not given in regional feeling. Only possible, or hypothetical, stand- points are given. "Our direct perception of the contemporary world is thus reduced to extension, defining (i) our own geometrical perspectives, and (ii) possibilities of mutual perspectives for other contemporary entities *inter se,* and (iii) possibilities of division" (PR 96). Much less are the actual experiences of contemporary occasions given. Contemporary actual occasions are not directly felt in their concrete actuality. This general regional feeling "is the whole of our *direct* physical feeling of the contemporary world" (PR 482).

iii. Even this weak sense of immanence between contemporaries depends for its meaning on causal objectification. It is therefore a *secondary* mode of social immanence. In the case of "bare" regional feeling, the contemporary world is defined only in relation to the causal past and the causal future. In the case of higher grade occasions, where there are "strain-feelings" (PR 472–99), the sensa and geometrical relations which further define the contemporary world are inherited from the past by causal objectification. So it seems that the objectification of the past in the present must be the primary mode of social immanence.

b. In addition to this direct regional feeling of the contemporary world we found an indirect connection between contemporary occasions by way of common pasts. Contemporary actual occasions have more or less common pasts. The community of their past actual worlds will vary inversely with their remoteness from each other. In many cases this community is negligible. But insofar as they are affected by the same environment they will have similar experiences and characteristics. Therefore, and because of the fortunate structure of the animal body, an occasion's projection of data derived from its own past will often adjust it to important features of the contemporary world.

Here again three comments are in order. (i) This indirect relevance yields a *genuine* sense of social immanence. Indirect relations are not unreal, though they differ from direct relations. (ii) Though a genuine sense this is also a *weak* sense of "being present in." The reason it is weak differs from the reason the sense yielded by regional feeling is weak. In that case contemporary actual occasions were related directly but not as individuals. In this case they are related as individuals but only indirectly.

In neither case are contemporary actual occasions felt directly as individuals. (iii) This indirect relationship between contemporaries is, like regional feeling, a *secondary* mode of social immanence. It depends on the direct objectification of the past in the present.

We have examined two senses in which a contemporary actual occasion is present in another, the only modes of contemporary immanence Whitehead admits. They are genuine modes of immanence. It is untrue that on Whitehead's view contemporaries are completely isolated and thus transcend each other absolutely. It is true however that these are weak senses of "being present in," and that they depend for their intelligibility on causal objectification.

Does Whitehead's account of relations between contemporary actualities do justice to the solidarity of the world as we experience it? This is a question I shall not answer. But I suggest that a certain looseness in the relations of contemporary actualities is required in any philosophical system which stresses both finite individuality and the reality of process.

3. The future in the present

In Chapter 3 we found that future actual occasions are immanent in a present occasion only by way of the "anticipation" of the future by the present. An examination of "anticipation" yielded a dual sense of the immanence of the future in the present. I shall restate and add brief comments on that result.

a. The future is present in the occasion now actual as the object of appetition. An actual occasion embodies a creative urge toward the future beyond itself. This requires that the occasion be transcended by other occasions yet to come and constitutes, one might say, a categoreal reason for the perishing of the present occasion. Yet no future actual occasions are now actual. The ground of this "bare" anticipation of future concrescences lies in the present actual occasion itself.

b. The future is present in the occasion now-actual in a further sense. The character of future actualities is now being partly determined by the activity of the present occasion. Any future actualities must conform to what now becomes actual. The urge to be transcended by future occasions carries with it the urge that the present occasion shall become a potential for these future becomings. The present occasion thus anticipates its own objective immortality and in this sense transcends itself. The ground of this further specification of anticipation lies again in the occasion now actual.

Two brief comments are in order. (i) Anticipation yields only a weak sense of immanence. The future is immanent in the present only as a potentiality for becoming, to which the present activity is contributing limitations. This might well seem an even weaker sense of immanence than the senses in which contemporaries are mutually immanent.

(ii) Explanation of the immanence of the future in the present involves causal objectification, the immanence of the past in the present. Indeed one might prefer to construe anticipation not as a way in which the future is immanent in the present but as a feeling that *in* the future what is now actual will be immanent in what is then actual.

From this rapid survey certain results are clear. *First,* we have not yet found any direct connections between individual actual occasions. In none of these instances does the individual nature of one occasion directly affect, contribute to, or participate in the individual nature of another actual occasion. These relations are not the kind which in an *organic* pluralism must somewhere be found. They give us only weak senses of social immanence.

Second, such connectedness as exists in these cases requires for its intelligibility the immanence of the past in the present. This does not mean that these instances are negligible. They do add something to the doctrine of social immanence. There *is* some direct feeling of the contemporary world. There *are* indirect connections with individual contemporary occasions. And there *is* anticipation of the future. But the "reason" for such connectedness as exists in these cases lies either in the activity of the present occasion itself or in its inheritance from the past. In the relation between past and present occasions therefore lies the crux of the problem of social immanence.

We are thus narrowing the focus of our problem to the question, In what positive sense is a past occasion present in an occasion now actual? Before dealing directly with this I shall show it is crucial not only for social immanence in general but also for certain special problems in Whitehead's philosophy.

4. Physical transmission, efficient causation, and perception

a. When Whitehead interprets *physical transmission* he is applying his philosophical scheme to the facts of experience. In this case the fact is a well-founded scientific concept. The object is to show the adequacy of the scheme. The interpretation turns on the conception of the actual world as a "medium" (PR 176–8, 183–4, 345, 435). There is "mediate objectification" of one occasion in another.

To understand Whitehead's conception of the world as a medium four of his philosophical ideas are important:

i. His rejection of materialism, that is of "vacuous actuality."

ii. His assertion that there is no "empty space." This follows from i and from his rejection of the Newtonian notion of absolute space.

iii. His rejection of a material ether. This follows from i and from the scientific uselessness of the notion.

iv. His assertion that real extensive regions are atomic quanta. Of this, the epochal theory of time is one expression. This follows from the individuality of actual occasions.

It follows from i that physical energy, along with all other physical concepts, is to be interpreted in terms of experience. "Physical energy" becomes then an abstraction from "emotional intensity" (PR 177–9, AI 238, MT 231–2).

It follows from ii that the physical influence of one actual thing on another noncontiguous actual thing must be via a medium.

It follows from iii that this medium must be conceived in terms of experience. Instead of a material ether, the medium for physical transmission is to be conceived as an "ether of events." And events are historic routes of actual occasions, which are acts of experience.

It follows from iv that the flow of energy is not in the strict sense a continuous function, though Whitehead explains how the flow of energy appears as a continuous function, in terms of the potential divisibility of the atomic regions. The medium of transmission is really made up of discontinuous acts of experience located in externally connected (contiguous) spatiotemporal regions. Transmission is therefore via successive and contiguous actual occasions. "Energy passes from particular occasion to particular occasion" (AI 238). Also a definite quantum of energy (emotional intensity) is involved in each instance.

It seems clear that this interpretation of physical transmission involves in a crucial way the objectification of a past actual occasion for a present occasion. The crucial question is how transference of feeling takes place between an immediately past occasion and the present occasion which supersedes it.

b. Whitehead's interpretation of *efficient causation* also involves in a crucial way the immanence of the immediate past in the present. This may be shown by contrasting his interpretation with certain treatments of causation which he opposes.

In the first place he opposes the phenomenalistic view that causation is exhaustively interpretable in terms of mere successions of data. He does not object to this interpretation so far as the purpose of natural science is concerned. For that purpose mathematically correlated successions of data are adequate. If "nature" is taken in abstraction from "life" then we have "merely a formula for succession" (MT 202). Natural science does, and indeed must, make this abstraction. "Science can find no individual enjoyment in nature: Science can find no aim in nature: Science can find no creativity in nature; it finds mere rules of succession. These negations are true of Natural Science. They are inherent in its methodology" (MT 211).

While a phenomenalistic view of causation may be adequate for the purpose of natural science, it is inadequate for an understanding of the concrete processes of the real world. For this purpose one cannot be content with "rules of succession." If one stops here, then "there is an absence of *understandable* causation to give a reason for that formula for that succession. Of course it is always possible to work oneself into a state of complete contentment with an ultimate irrationality. The popular positivistic philosophy adopts this attitude" (MT 202–3, my italics). What is required is a *reason,* in terms of the natures of real things, for the fact that a particular succession of events or data takes place in a particular way. Whitehead therefore undertakes to interpret causation realistically, as involving substantial things dynamically related as "causes" and "effects."

In the second place he opposes an externalistic view of causation. On that view causation is a transference of accidental qualities between things which are *essentially* isolated from each other. On this view there is no reason in the natures of the things for the transfer of the quality. "The mere notion of transferring a quality is entirely unintelligible. Suppose that two occurrences may be in fact detached so that one of them is comprehensible without reference to the other. Then all notion of causation between them, or of conditioning, becomes unintelligible. There is—with this supposition—no reason why the possession of any quality by one of them should in any way influence the possession of that quality, or of any other quality, by the other" (MT 226). Here we are reminded of his polemic against those traditional interpretations of substance which negate the possibility of real connections. If each of two real things can be fully understood apart from the other, then neither can serve as a *vera causa* or "real reason" for the transfer of the quality.

If Whitehead is to be consistent in his rejection of these alternative views of causation, he is obliged to construct a "mechanism" in terms of which causation as a real relation between real things may be made intelligible. And he does in fact hold that the functionings that make up the "real internal constitutions" of occasions constitute such a mechanism. Later we shall examine this mechanism in some detail. We are interested here only in pointing out that by setting out to construct such an explanatory mechanism he differentiates his view of causation from the views he rejects.

He differs from the phenomenalistic view by taking causation as a dynamic process relating real things. He differs from the "externalistic" view by holding that the internal natures of the real things can furnish an intelligible explanation of the process which takes place between them. On the phenomenalistic view no explanatory mechanism in terms of the real functionings of real things *need* be constructed. On the externalistic view no such mechanism *can* be constructed. Whitehead holds that such a mechanism can and must be constructed.

Since efficient causation is in question here, the mechanism must be relational between a past actual occasion and a present actual occasion. For "efficient causation expresses the transition from actual entity to actual entity" (PR 228). It must show how the past actual world is present in, and exerts power on, the present occasion. His account of causal objectification is necessary to his explanation of efficient causation.

c. The objectification of the past in the present is crucial for his treatment of *perception* also.

According to Whitehead perception takes place in two modes. In the mode of presentational immediacy the contemporary world is presented as described above. In the mode of causal efficacy past actual occasions are felt directly as concrete actualities. One way of indicating the importance of this latter mode of perception is to ask, as a hypothetical question, what Whitehead's theory of perception would amount to in its absence.

If presentational immediacy were the only mode of perception, then Whitehead's theory would be purely and simply phenomenalistic. The percipient would be restricted to purely private data. No datum would give information of any concretely actual thing other than the percipient subject itself. In his theory of knowledge Whitehead would then have no cause for quarrel with Hume, as he explicitly recognizes: "Hume's polemic respecting causation is, in fact, one prolonged, *convincing* argument that pure presentational immediacy does not disclose any causal influence . . ." (PR 188, my italics). Actual things other than the subject could be known only by inference. But he finds this sort of inference meaningless apart from some direct perception of an external world. We should therefore be reduced to Santayana's "solipsism of the present moment" (SYMBOLISM 28–9, PR 240).

There can be no doubt that Whitehead rejects this conclusion.

He is logically able to do so because he rejects the view that presentational immediacy is "the primary fact of perception" (PR 263), much less the sole fact of perception. "The confinement of our prehension of other actual entities to the mediation of private sensations is pure myth" (PR 214). On his view causal efficacy is an additional, and even the primary, mode of perception. On this ground he offers a realistic theory of perception.

Now perception in the mode of causal efficacy is but another name for the process by which the past becomes objectified in the present. "A pure physical prehension is how an occasion in its immediacy of being absorbs another occasion which has passed into the objective immortality of its not-being. It is how the past lives in the present. It is causation. It is memory. It is perception of derivation. It is emotional conformation to a given situation, an emotional continuity of past with present" (AI 305. See PR 361, 365; AI 237). Perception in its simplest form, direct physical feeling devoid of consciousness, is not a unique relation in nature. It is identical with the process of efficient causation. Hence the objectification of the past in the present is crucial for Whitehead's theory of perception.

As a result of the foregoing discussion we can now concentrate our inquiry and give it a sharper focus. The validity of Whitehead's account of the immanence of contemporaries and of the future in the present, and his treatment of these special problems, has been shown to depend on a single issue. In what way are past actual occasions present in the experience of a novel concrescence?

CHAPTER 7

Causal Objectification

1. Simple physical feelings

IN THIS DISCUSSION of how objectification of the past in the present takes place, let us take the case of two contiguous occasions. Of these let one be "immediately past" in relation to the other. Let the past occasion be called X, and let the present occasion be called A.

Now the objectification of X in A is effected by a prehension. Let us assume this prehension is a "simple physical feeling" (PR 361–5). For "all our physical relationships [i.e. all our relationships to other actual entities] are made up of such simple physical feelings, as their atomic bricks" (PR 362). So we shall focus our discussion on the simple case in which A prehends X via a simple physical feeling. Whitehead's categoreal analysis of a prehension is: "That every prehension consists of three factors: (a) the 'subject' which is prehending, namely the actual entity in which that prehension is a concrete element; (b) the 'datum' which is prehended; (c) the 'subjective form' which is *how* that subject prehends that datum" (PR 35, category of explanation xi). Let us examine the function of each of these factors in the simple physical feeling in question.

a. *The subject of this feeling* is the present actual occasion, A. A is "the actual entity in which that prehension is a concrete element." The feeling is A's feeling of X. Thus the feeling which effects the objectification of X in A is properly speaking an activity of A. It is in A that this feeling has immediacy or concrete actuality. The fact that the activity which effects the objectification is an activity of A, the subject of the feeling, is important.

Whitehead at times refers to the "activity" of the past. Therefore we must distinguish between the sense in which the past is active in the process of objectification and the sense in which the present is active. The activity of the past can only mean (i) past activity, for example the activity of X before X perished, *or* (ii) the "real conditioning" of the present by the past. The latter sense is the only one in which the past is active *now,* and the only sense which concerns us at this point.

By saying that the past conditions the present, Whitehead means only that as objectively immortal the past is stubborn fact. This is a function of X. But this is not "activity" in the usual meaning of the term. His own term for what we usually call activity is self-functioning, or subjectively immediate activity. And he usually uses the word "activity" to refer to immediate actuality. It is only in order to discriminate the functioning of past actualities (real potentiality) from that of eternal objects (pure potentials) and of the contemporary world (passive potentiality) that Whitehead speaks, for instance, of the function of past actual occasions as "provocation" (AI 226). He means only that there is an effective antecedent limitation on what the present can become. Past actual occasions function only as objects. They have "objective efficacy" (PR 341).

The *immediate* activity involved in objectification is the activity of the subject. It is the subject's feelings which "absorb" (PR 82) or "transform" (PR 235) the object. "The occasion as subject has a 'concern' for the object. And the 'concern' at once *places the object as a component in the experience of the subject,* with an affective tone drawn from this object and directed towards it" (AI 226, my italics). What effects the objectification is the subject's feeling of the object.

b. *The datum of this feeling* is the past actual occasion, X. Now when X functions as a datum or object it is not functioning in the mode of subjective immediacy. Nevertheless this is a function of X. X in this case is not, in any sense of the word, a function of A. "Thus an object must be a thing received, and must not be either a *mode* of reception or a thing *generated* in that occasion" (AI 229).

What Whitehead calls the "initial datum" for A is *that* actual occasion *there-then*. But A's subjective aim requires that some aspects of the initial datum be eliminated by negative prehensions (PR 321). What remains to be positively felt is the "objective datum." In a simple physical feeling the initial datum is positively felt with respect to only one of its feelings. The rest of its feelings are eliminated.

> Thus in a simple physical feeling there are two actual entities concerned. One of them is the subject of that feeling, and the other is the *initial* datum of the feeling. A second feeling is also concerned, namely, the *objective* datum of the simple physical feeling. This second feeling is the 'objectification' of *its* subject for the subject of the simple physical feeling. The initial datum is objectified as being the subject of the feeling which is the objective datum: the objectification is the 'perspective' of the initial datum (PR 361).

Let us say that Xp is the objective datum of the simple physical feeling we are discussing.

It is not the case that A first feels positively the whole content of X's experience, and then eliminates some aspects of X from feeling. Elimination is a primitive and integral factor in the prehension (PR 338, 353). Objectification involves abstraction. The question then arises, Why refer to an initial datum at all? How can this reference be significant?

Whitehead's point is that the objective datum is not an unattached feeling, without a local habitation and a name. What is felt here is one of X's feelings. The fact that it is one of X's feelings is integral to what is felt. No feeling can be abstracted from its subject, and no feeling can be *given* unless its subject is given. The feeling would be meaningless apart from its subject, namely X. Thus for A the objective datum is not some indeterminate p. For A the objective datum is Xp.

It is important to notice that objectification does not affect the content of an objectified entity, save by selective abstraction. The difference between X in its subjective immediacy and X in its objective immortality is not in content but in mode of existence. What X was then, X is now, except that X is now no longer immediate but objective. Thus for A, X is "an experiencing entity there-then but not here-now." It is now experienced as an object. But it is experienced as having been what is was, namely a subject. It is a subject existing objectively. What is felt by A in A's simple physical feeling are "the objectified *experiences* of the past" (PR 176, my italics). "In our experience, as in distinct analysis, physical feelings are always derived from some antecedent experient. Occasion *B* prehends occasion *A* as an antecedent subject experiencing a sensum with emotional intensity" (PR 479).

Likewise, any feeling by which X is objectified for A is given as having been subjectively immediate there-then. Thus X*p* is an objectified *feeling,* and the fact that it is objectified does not derogate from the fact that it is a feeling. The objective datum of the simple physical feeling we are discussing is X-feeling-M-there-then. "The feeling *as enjoyed by the past occasion* is present in the new occasion *as datum felt*" (AI 236, my italics). The point of this discussion is that the two italicized phrases are to be given equal emphasis.

This distinction between the two modes of existence of feelings helps to put in their proper perspective many passages in which a "simple" or literal transference of feeling seems to be asserted. We can now see that while there is "feeling of feeling," the feeling felt exists objectively. It is that feeling subjectively immediate there-then, *not* subjectively immediate here-now.

c. *The subjective form of this feeling* is *how* that subject prehends that datum. It is the *way* A feels X*p*. One might say that the subjective form is the *adverbial* characteristic of a feeling. It is the *how* of feeling. Thus in the feeling A*p*, A may feel X*p* more or less intensely, with "aversion" or "adversion," and so on. More complex feelings in higher organisms may feel their data consciously. Consciousness is a subjective form to be found in some but not all feelings (PR 406).

In our discussion of the individuality of actual occasions we saw how the subjective forms of feelings are partially determined by the subjective aim, the organizing principle of the concrescence. Here as elsewhere social transcendence is balanced by social immanence. The subjective forms of feelings are only partially determined by the subjective aim. The data of feelings also have a part in determining their subjective forms. In the case of the simple physical feeling we are discussing, the subjective form of Ap is determined in part by A's subjective aim and in part by the objective datum Xp.

The categoreal conditions for the subjective form of Ap are then as follows:

i. In the simple physical feeling Ap, A must feel in such a way, or with such a subjective form, that this feeling is compatible for integration with all of A's other feelings, so that the concrescence shall issue in a completely unified feeling of satisfaction.

ii. In the simple physical feeling Ap, A must feel in such a way that Ap is "conformal" to its datum. Ap is a feeling *of* Xp, and this fact must be relevant to the *way* in which Xp is felt. The subjective form must "conform" to the datum.

Thus there are two sets of limitations or determining conditions on the origination of Ap with respect to its subjective form. One set of determining conditions is internal to A; the other set is external to A. The two sets of determinants limit each other. A physical prehension of a datum can modify the subjective aim (PR 416). The subjective aim is the ground for the selection of data to be felt (PR 41). The two sets *together* completely determine (PR 338) the subjective form of Ap. The subjective form of Ap is partly but by no means entirely the result of external compulsion. It is a product of efficient *and* final causation.

2. Conformity of subjective form

Now we are ready to give our enquiry an even sharper focus. We have seen that the crux of the problem of social immanence lies in the meaning of causal objectification. That the notion of conformity of subjective form is the core of Whitehead's theory of causal objectification, and hence the crucial feature of his doctrine of social immanence, is suggested by the following:

> Another point emerges in this explanation, namely, the doctrine of the continuity of nature. This doctrine balances and limits the doctrine of the absolute individuality of each occasion of experience. There is a continuity between the

subjective form of the immediate past occasion and the subjective form of its primary prehension in the origination of
the new occasion. . . . I will term this doctrine of continuity,
the Doctrine of Conformation of Feeling (AI 235).

The point to notice is that Whitehead grounds the continuity
of nature, or social immanence, explicitly and directly on the conformity of subjective form. He illustrates the doctrine by the case
of an angry man, who enjoys the emotion of anger "both objectively, as belonging to the past, and also formally as continued
in the present. This continuation is the continuity of nature"
(AI 236). He is pointing to the conformation of subjective form
to datum as the critical piece of "machinery" by which the past
is objectified in the present. In a discussion of Locke's view of
perception he says, "Locke's principle amounts to this: That there
are many actual existents, and that in some sense one actual
existent repeats itself in another actual existent, so that in the
analysis of the latter existent a component 'determined to' the
former existent is discoverable. The philosophy of organism expresses this principle by its doctrines of 'prehension' and of 'objectification' " (PR 211). I suggest it is A's subjective form which
is the discoverable component "determined to" X. More specifically, it is the subjective form of Ap which is determined to X.

It is therefore of utmost importance to see how the subjective
form of a feeling is determined to or conforms to its datum. First
we ask what it is to which the subjective form of the simple
physical feeling conforms. Then we shall ask what it means to
conform.

a. *What is conformed to?* At times Whitehead seems to say that
what is conformed to is the objective datum as a whole:

> In the conformal feelings the *how* of feeling reproduces
> what is felt (PR 249).

> . . . the subjective form, amid its own original elements,
> always involves reproduction of the pattern of the objective
> datum (PR 357).

In the case we are discussing, the subjective form of Ap would on
this showing conform to Xp.

Some important qualifications, however, must be taken into account:

> This doctrine of conformation only holds for the qualitative side of the content of the objective datum (AI 326).

> Only the qualitative components of an actuality in the datum can pass into the subjective form (AI 327).

Certain elements in the objective datum are not "qualitative" and hence are not conformed to by the subjective form of the subject's feeling. There are "two exceptions" to the doctrine of conformation, and both arise when "abstraction has reached its extreme limit" (AI 326). These are (i) bare mathematical forms, and (ii) the bare notion of an individual actuality "abstracted from the mode of its initial indication" so that it is entertained as a bare "It" (AI 327. See CN 8; PR 295–300, 391–405). These elements can be entertained in thought as objects, but only when abstracted from the qualitative elements in the concrete datum. They cannot therefore function as elements of subjective forms.

Incidentally, Whitehead's explanation of the fallacy in certain traditional doctrines of substance is relevant here. This fallacy consists, as we saw in Chapter 5, in thinking of real individuals as having a substratum devoid of process of any sort (static) and devoid of immediacy (vacuous). This fallacy, Whitehead thinks, is a failure to recognize that these nonqualitative elements in the datum are abstractions. This is what he calls elsewhere the fallacy of "misplaced concreteness" (SMW 72; PR 11, 27). He thinks that two ancient sources of the fallacy are Plato's attribution of real being to ideas, overlooking the abstractness of pure form, and Aristotle's doctrine of primary substance, which overlooked the abstractness of bare individuality (AI 340, 354–6; MT 92–3, 111–13, 126).

What is conformed to, then, is only the *qualitative* element in the objective datum. Now the qualitative element in the objective datum is the subjective form of the feeling felt. In our case the qualitative element in the objective datum of Ap is the subjective form of Xp. What the subjective form of the present feeling conforms to, then, is *the subjective form of the objective datum*. The following passages, where A is a past occasion and B is the present occasion, make this clear:

> In the first stage of B's physical feeling, the subjective form of B's feeling is conformed to the subjective form of A's feeling . . . (PR 446).

> Occasion B prehends occasion A as an antecedent subject experiencing a sensum with emotional intensity. Also B's subjective form of emotion is conformed to A's subjective form. Thus there is a vector transmission of emotional feeling of a sensum from A to B. In this way B feels the sensum as derived from A and feels it with an emotional form also derived from A. This is the most primitive form of the feeling of causal efficacy (PR 479–80).

In our symbols the subjective form of Ap conforms to the subjective form of Xp. This then is a further specification of what is conformed to.

b. *What does it mean to conform?* In a number of passages Whitehead speaks of the "continuity" of the subjective form of the past occasion and the subjective form of the new occasion. The new occasion is said to have the "same" subjective form as the past occasion (AI 236). There is thus an "identity of subjective form inherited conformally from one occasion to the other" (AI 239).

Some caution is needed in interpreting the "identity" of subjective form which "continuity" implies. There is an important sense in which the subjective form of a feeling is peculiar to that feeling. In the "categories of existence" subjective forms are listed as "private matters of fact" (PR 32). This is explained further in a later passage: "The essential novelty of a feeling attaches to its subjective form. The initial data, and even the nexus which is the objective datum, may have served other feelings with other subjects. But the subjective form is the immediate novelty; it is how *that* subject is feeling that objective datum. There is no tearing this subjective form from the novelty of this concrescence" (PR 354; see 356). This clearly implies that no two feelings can have the same subjective form, and that the continuity of subjective form implied in "conformation" cannot be, strictly speaking, an "identity" of subjective form. The subjective form of the past feeling cannot, strictly speaking, be the same as the subjective form of the present feeling.

Suppose then we interpret this continuity as a succession of *similar* subjective forms. Let the subjective form of Ap be denoted by $sf(Ap)$ and the subjective form of Xp by $sf(Xp)$. Then we might say that in the series $sf(Xp)$, $sf(Ap)$ there is continuity in that $sf(Ap)$ is like or similar to $sf(Xp)$.

For example if $sf(Xp)$ is some kind of "redly," then $sf(Ap)$ will be some kind of redly. Just what kind of redly the latter will be depends on both the subjective aim of A and the objective datum of Ap. This initial subjective form will be modified in the supplementary phases of the concrescence, perhaps for example into "angrily." But we are concerned only with the initial phase of the concrescence.

Now it is evident that in this interpretation we have reintroduced the notion of identity. Redly qualifies both the subjective form of the past and the subjective form of the present. In this respect $sf(Ap)$ is "the same as" $sf(Xp)$. Though each of these subjective forms is more than redly, since each is particular to its subject, yet there is an identical element common to both.

If we interpret Whitehead's statements about the "identity" of subjective forms in this way, then we can still do justice to their particularity. If we are to say that one subjective form is "derived from" (PR 479–80) or conforms to another, then they cannot be numerically identical. Their identity must be interpreted as possession of a common character or, in Whitehead's categories, the ingredience of the same eternal object in the subjective forms of both the feelings.

This is indeed Whitehead's explanation. He says, "If we abstract the form from the feeling, we are left with an eternal object as the remnant of subjective form" (PR 354). The "same thing" (SMW 220) which occurs both in X and in A is an eternal object. We are hereby introduced to the important function of eternal objects in objectification. To this topic we turn in the following section, anticipating the more extended discussion of the theory of eternal objects in Part Two.

As we do so it must be kept in mind that we have touched on, and are continuing to deal with, only one part of the meaning of conformation. Another part of its meaning will remain to be dealt with in the next chapter.

3. The function of eternal objects

Some theory of universals seems to be required. The immediate feelings that constitute X do not in their immediacy persist into the concrescence of A. X and A transcend each other in the sense that there is no sharing of immediacy. There is no overlapping of X and A as immediate actualities. The common element required for the significance of Whitehead's theory of conformity, therefore, must be something other than an immediate individual actuality. No actual occasion can happen twice. But this is just what the common element must do. It must happen first in X and again in A. It must be such that it can be a factor in X and also a factor in A, which supersedes and transcends X.

Whitehead calls such elements "eternal objects." Eternal objects are categoreally defined as "Pure Potentials for the Specific Determination of Fact, *or* Forms of Definiteness" (PR 32). The function of eternal objects with which we are concerned is explained as follows:

> A simple physical feeling enjoys a characteristic which has been variously described as 're-enaction,' 'reproduction,' and 'conformation.' This characteristic can be more accurately explained in terms of the eternal objects involved. There are eternal objects determinant of the definiteness of the objective datum which is the 'cause,' and eternal objects determinant of the definiteness of the subjective form belonging to the 'effect.' When there is re-enaction there is one eternal object with two-way functioning, namely, as partial determinant of the objective datum, and as partial determinant of the subjective form. In this two-way role, the eternal object is functioning relationally between the initial data on the one hand and the concrescent subject on the other. It is playing one self-consistent role in obedience to the category of objective identity (PR 364; see 91, 97, 249, 445–6).

Several observations about this "relational function" of eternal objects need to be made. In the first place, eternal objects are not physical causes. They do not add any physical effectiveness to the process of transition. In itself an eternal object "is neutral as to the fact of its physical ingression in any particular actual entity of the temporal world" (PR 70). It is merely a "form of definiteness" of feeling. And according to Whitehead's categories of explanation, a formal description cannot serve as a "reason" for any particular fact in nature. This is required by the ontological principle, which means that "actual entities are the only *reasons*" (PR 37). Only actual entities are physical causes.

Therefore Whitehead's "explanation" of identities, causation, and permanence by reference to eternal objects is not *alternative* to an explanation of these facts by reference to actual entities. He does not in this way have two theories of social immanence. There is a single theory of social immanence, in which both actual occasions and eternal objects have their own functions, neither category being replaceable by the other. Explanation in terms of eternal objects is not something in addition to the theory of objectification. Rather it is a necessary part of that theory. "The organic philosophy does not hold that the 'particular existents' are prehended apart from universals; on the contrary, it holds that they are prehended by the mediation of universals. In other words, each actuality is prehended by means of some element of its own definiteness. This is the doctrine of the 'objectification' of actual entities" (PR 230).

Whitehead needs eternal objects in order to give an account of objectification. Why is this the case? Here we are asking for what we might call a categoreal reason. Why do his principles require him to bring in eternal objects to explain objectification? The basic reason, I suggest, lies in his strong theory of finite individuals. To achieve its concrete unity of satisfaction an actual occasion must exclude the immediacies of other actualities. Therefore "transfer of feeling" cannot be explained as literal persistence of immediate feeling. It must be explained as "repetition" by the present occasion of a subjective form of feeling in the past occasion, the identical element involved being an eternal object.

4. Repetition and the "flow of feeling"

If the account of the conformity of subjective form given above is correct, then what happens in the case of the simple physical feeling Ap is as follows.

The immediately past actual occasion X, as it existed in its own subjective immediacy, included the feeling Xp as a component of its satisfaction. Let the subjective form of Xp be described as "redly." Then the eternal object "red" is a form of the definiteness of $sf(Xp)$. *Now,* that is to say for A, X has perished. X including Xp no longer exists in its subjective immediacy. X is now existing objectively as an initial datum for the new concrescence that is A-in-becoming.

By virtue of the selectivity of the new concrescence, X is objectively given for one of the primary feelings of A, namely Ap, under the aspect of Xp. Thus in Ap, A prehends X-feeling-M-there-then-redly. Xp is the objective datum of Ap.

Now the subjective form of Ap will be like the subjective form of Xp, so that redly is "repeated" or "reproduced" in the new feeling Ap. Since X and A are mutually exclusive in their respective subjective immediacies, repetition cannot mean that $sf(Xp)$ persists into A in a simple or literal sense. Xp with its subjective form cannot be abstracted from its subject X which has perished and is objectively immortal.

Repetition can only mean therefore that a form of definiteness of $sf(Xp)$ now comes to be a form of definiteness of $sf(Ap)$. The eternal object "red" is the element of identity which makes it significant to say that $sf(Ap)$ is like $sf(Xp)$. Strictly speaking, therefore, what is repeated in A is not $sf(Xp)$ but the form of definiteness "red," which was a form of definiteness of $sf(Xp)$ and is now a form of definiteness of $sf(Ap)$. The subjective form of Xp was a redly and the subjective form of Ap is a redly. It is only in this sense that the subjective form of Ap can be said to be "the same as" the subjective form of Xp.

The function of eternal objects in objectification enables us to understand Whitehead's alternative to a *literal* "flow of feeling." We can now understand how causal objectification is more precisely described in terms of "repetition," "reproduction," "re-

enaction," or "re-creation" than in terms which imply some persistence or spilling-over of immediacy from one occasion into
another.

As a matter of fact the former set of terms and equivalent expressions dominates Whitehead's discussions of social immanence.
On this as on other topics his discussions are of two sorts. In some
he develops his categoreal scheme in its own terms, aiming at
logical rigor and discursive clarity. This is especially characteristic
of Parts III and IV of *Process and Reality*. In other discussions he
applies the categoreal scheme to facts of experience in language
that is more vivid and evocative. Thus he is aiming both at rigorous
exposition of the categoreal scheme and at the *use* of this scheme to
interpret our experience. One of the main problems about interpreting Whitehead is to do full justice to both these aims and
modes of expression without confusing them. But I submit that
in his more careful and sustained expositions of the mechanism
of causal objectification he regularly uses the language of "repetition." Some such passages may be cited:

> In the organic philosophy the notion of repetition is funda-
> mental. The doctrine of objectification is an endeavor to ex-
> press how what is settled in actuality is repeated under limita-
> tions, so as to be 'given' for immediacy (PR 208).

> Apart from inhibitions or additions, weakenings or intensifi-
> cations, due to the history of its production, the subjective
> form of a physical feeling is re-enaction of the subjective form
> of the feeling felt. *Thus* the cause passes on its feeling to be
> reproduced by the new subject as its own, and yet as in-
> separable from the cause. There is a flow of feeling. But the
> re-enaction is not perfect . . . The cause is objectively in
> the constitution of the effect, in virtue of being the feeler of
> the feeling reproduced in the effect *with partial equivalence
> of subjective form* (PR 362–3, my italics).

> The deterministic efficient causation is the inflow of the
> actual world in its own proper character of its own feelings,
> with their own intensive strength, felt and re-enacted by

the novel concrescent subject. But this re-enaction has a mere character of conformation to pattern (PR 374).[1]

The subject "reproduces" the objective datum by producing a feeling *of* the datum with a conformal subjective form.

In an earlier discussion of those expressions suggesting a simple flow of feeling, I urged that a literal reading would result in radical inconsistency between Whitehead's theory of objectification and other fundamental principles of his philosophy. An interpretation of causal objectification has now been given which avoids the inconsistency entailed by the literal interpretation. This strengthens the suggestion that these expressions need not be taken in a literal way. Insofar as they suggest that causal objectification takes place by an overlapping of immediacies, they are misleading.

It should be repeated that most expressions like "flow of feeling" do not, when taken in their contexts, make this suggestion at all. Some are describing in vivid and metaphorical language a situation described more precisely elsewhere in systematic terms. Sometimes Whitehead is describing what the fact of inheritance is *felt* to be, the macroscopic fact as there for analysis, not how the situation is to be analyzed in terms of the final realities, actual occasions. Sometimes the difficulty lies in merely verbal confusions. For example, a feeling in the sense of a present immediacy becomes confused with a feeling in the sense of a past immediate feeling existing objectively. What is important is that we can locate such confusions, and that in spite of them a fair account of Whitehead's theory of objectification, consistent with his theory of individuality, can be given.[2]

We can now implement a suggestion made in Chapter 3 about the relations of contemporary mentalities. The question was whether Whitehead means to say there are direct prehensions of contemporary mental activity. It was suggested that he does not. But even if he does it need not compromise the exclusiveness of

1. See SMW 147, 186, 212; PR 196, 202–8, 234–5, 375, 380; AI 248–9.
2. To mention one application, the transmission of physical energy is interpreted in terms of re-enaction of subjective form. "Thus having regard to the 're-enaction' which is characteristic of the subjective form of a simple physical feeling, we have—in the case of the simpler actual entities—an example of the transference of energy in the physical world" (PR 375–6).

contemporary occasions. We have shown that in causal objectification there are "direct" connections that do not involve sharing of
immediacy. Presumably, prehension of the past by the present is
as direct a connection as prehension of contemporary mentality
would be. Hence even *if* there were direct prehensions of contemporary mentalities, no sharing of immediacy need be involved.

The tentative result of our analysis of causal objectification
turns out to be different from, and more complicated than, the
view that an immediate feeling persists as such into a new concrescence. Nevertheless, such metaphorical expressions as "flow of
feeling," "transference of throbs of emotional energy," and the
like contain an important additional truth about objectification.
Our discussion of what it means to conform is not yet complete.

It was suggested above that a part of the meaning of conformal
is "similar to," interpreted as a relation involving partial identity
between its terms. It is obvious that something is yet lacking. To
say that $sf(Ap)$ conforms to $sf(Xp)$ is to say more than that $sf(Ap)$
is like $sf(Xp)$. What has been left out is the element of efficacity
or "power" or "real conditioning," which for Whitehead is intrinsic to the relation between X and A. There is *obligation* that
$sf(Ap)$ shall be like $sf(Xp)$. The past is causally efficacious; it exists
for A not as pure potentiality but as real potentiality. It is this
element in the meaning of conform that the metaphorical expressions cited above add to the mere notion of repetition. The transference of feeling "is the cumulation of the universe and not a
stage-play about it" (PR 363).

There can be no doubt that Whitehead means to say that in a
temporal series there is something more than a succession of occasions with similar characters. He certainly means that similarity
of character is an obligation imposed by antecedent occasions
upon occasions that supersede them. This is precisely the point at
which he takes issue with Hume and phenomenalism generally.
But so far we have not found anything that specifically adds efficacy to the mechanism of repetition described above. It seems
that Whitehead provides no special mechanism for causal obligation in addition to the mechanism of repetition. In what way then
has he an answer to Hume?

CHAPTER 8

Influence

1. Introduction

WE HAVE BEEN examining Whitehead's account of how one actual occasion is "present in" another. This is his doctrine of social immanence, which balances and complements his doctrine of social transcendence. We have seen that causal objectification is crucial for the intelligibility of social immanence, and that the core of the theory of causal objectification is the notion of conformity of subjective form.

As *part* of the meaning of conformation we found an explanatory mechanism describing how a feeling is repeated or reproduced in a subsequent occasion. But there seems to be more to conformation than this mechanism of repetition. It seems to leave out something Whitehead wants to say, namely that the novel feeling *must* repeat its datum. It seems to leave out the power, or influence, or causal efficacy of the past occasion on the new concrescence. The efficacy of the antecedent occasion seems to be put by Whitehead as an *assertion* added to his account of repetition. It does not seem to be a part of the mechanism of repetition itself.

Whitehead takes our common experience of causal efficacy as one of the fundamental facts which philosophy must interpret. "The notion of causation arose because mankind lives amid experiences in the mode of causal efficacy" (PR 266). We influence, and are influenced by, other things. These experiences must be explained, and not explained away. Our next question therefore is, In what sense does Whitehead undertake to explain these experiences of causal efficacy? More particularly, how does he relate the fact of influence to the explanatory mechanism of repetition? Is some additional mechanism necessary for the intelligibility of power or influence? One way we may give this question a sharper

point, and at the same time relate Whitehead's thought to some
of its antecedents, is to ask how he sees the difference between his
treatment of influence and Hume's.

2. The "explanation" of influence

I shall first discuss what I believe to be a mistaken interpretation of Whitehead's reply to Hume. Then I shall state his criticisms of Hume's treatment of causality. It should then be fairly
clear how he explains, and how he does not explain, the fact of
influence.

W. T. Stace in *The Nature of the World* (Princeton University
Press, 1940) takes up Whitehead's example of the man who says,
"The flash made me blink" (PR 266). According to Stace, Whitehead argues against Hume "that there *is* a percept of 'making' in
the mode of causal efficacy" (p. 73). Stace comments, "But in whatever mode, a percept is a percept. It is the perceiving of a datum.
Hence if Hume made any mistake in his analysis of the complex
of data, it was only that he left out one datum, that of *making*.
The principle will in any case be the same. Either on Whitehead's
interpretation or on Hume's what we have is a number of data
following, or accompanying, one another. The flash making the
man blink will be, after all, nothing but a bare succession of data."

This interpretation holds that Whitehead, in order to answer
Hume, attempts to point out an additional datum, namely "making," which is of the same logical order as "flash" and "blink." His
answer to Hume would consist in the addition of another bit of
conceptual mechanism to the mechanism of repetition we examined above.

I think this interpretation is mistaken, but it is a mistake for
which Whitehead is partly to blame. It may well be that in *Symbolism* he did feel that the causal meaning of experience had to
be validated in some such way.[1] Even in some of his writings after
Symbolism there seem to be vestiges of an assumption that power
itself could be caught in a conceptual net. Expressions like "percepta in the mode of causal efficacy" (PR 271) might well suggest

1. See Lowe's remarks on Whitehead's treatment of causal efficacy in
Symbolism (Schilpp 100).

that "in whatever mode, a percept is a percept." Indeed, the notion of two "modes of perception" (presentational immediacy and causal efficacy) has its dangers as well as its good uses.

Stace's interpretation seems to have been encouraged also by those expressions like "flow of feeling" which seem to suggest a literal transference of feeling. I have argued that, taken in this way, these passages would run counter to some of the fundamental principles of the categoreal scheme. And I urge that most of them do not bear this interpretation when examined in their contexts and in the light of Whitehead's more rigorous expositions of causal objectification.

Against Stace's interpretation I call attention to certain features of the following passage:

> The former mode [causal efficacy] produces percepta which are vague, not to be controlled, heavy with emotion: it produces the sense of derivation from an immediate past, and of passage to an immediate future; a sense of emotional feeling, belonging to oneself in the past, passing into oneself in the present, and passing from oneself in the present towards oneself in the future; a sense of influx of influence from other vaguer presences in the past, localized and yet evading local definition, such influence modifying, enhancing, inhibiting, diverting, the stream of feeling which we are receiving, unifying, enjoying, and transmitting. This is our general sense of existence, as one item among others, in an efficacious actual world (PR 271).

In the first place, this is a phenomenological account of experience. This is experience as given for philosophical analysis not experience as interpreted by philosophical analysis. This is what philosophers must "explain." Whitehead does not introduce in this passage his own systematic categories of explanation.

In the second place, notice how the *data* of these feelings are described. They are feelings of "derivation," of "passage," of "influence." These feelings are felt in a certain situation. *What* is felt is an activity going on in that situation, an activity which relates the entities ("items") in the situation in a dynamic way.

These data are not data in the same sense in which clearly and distinctly presented contemporary sensa are data. These are data of a different sort. They are activities, not static entities. This is the important difference between what is felt in presentational immediacy and what is felt in causal efficacy. And if the term "percepta" leads the reader to assimilate the "data" of causal feelings to the data of presentational immediacy, then this term is functioning in a misleading way. It should be understood as implicitly defined in Whitehead's description.

It is true that the activity felt is relational between certain terms. Thus these terms (for example, "oneself in the past" and "oneself in the present") are part of the datum of the feeling. The point to be noticed is that they are felt *as* terms of the relational activity. The important distinction is not between data which are clear and distinct and data which are vague, but between entities given in contemporary space (geometrically related sensa) and the transitional activity apprehended in causal feelings. This activity is not itself an *entity* in the sense in which the data of presentational feelings are entities. The "making" is not a percept in the sense in which the flash and the blink are percepts.

I suggest that Whitehead's reply to Hume does not consist in pointing out a "datum," in the sense of an entitative element in an analytical description, which would validate the causal meaning of our experience. To regard the "making" as an additional component of the same logical order as "flash" and "blink" is to mistake Whitehead's intention.

It is true that he says of the man who blinks, "According to the philosophy of organism, the man also experiences another percept in the mode of causal efficacy" (PR 265). And this lends support to Stace's interpretation if, but only if, "in whatever mode, a percept is a percept." This is precisely the question. The "making" is certainly not a percept in the same sense as the flash of light, the feeling of eye-closure, and the instant of darkness. For when Whitehead in the next sentence goes on to explain the man's "percept in the mode of causal efficacy," he says, "He feels that the experiences of the *eye* in the matter of the flash are causal of the blink. The man himself will have no doubt of it." What the man feels is put as a *proposition* about the flash and the blink, not as an object of the same order as the flash and the blink.

It may well be that Whitehead's language, referring to what is given in the experience of causal efficacy as a "percept," has been misleading. For it seems clear enough that (i) not only does he *agree* with Hume "that in the mode of presentational immediacy there is no percept of the flash *making* the man blink" but also (ii) when he describes the man's experience of causal efficacy, he does not point to anything at all we would ordinarily call a "percept."

A better clue to the relation in his philosophy between power or efficacy on the one hand and the mechanism of repetition on the other is furnished by the following passage from William James, *Some Problems of Philosophy:* [2]

> Our outcome so far seems therefore to be only this, that the attempt to treat 'cause,' for conceptual purposes, as a separable link . . . has led to the denial of efficient causation, and to the substitution for it of the bare descriptive notion of uniform sequence among events. . . . Meanwhile the concrete perceptual flux, taken just as it comes, offers in our own activity-situations perfectly comprehensible instances of causal agency. The transitive causation in them does not, it is true, stick out as a separate piece of fact for conception to fix upon. Rather does a whole subsequent field grow continuously out of a whole antecedent field because it seems to yield new being of the nature called for, while the feeling of causality-at-work flavors the entire concrete sequence as salt flavors the water in which it is dissolved (pp. 217–18).

I suggest that for Whitehead also, "power" is not for conceptual purposes a "separable link." It does not "stick out as a separate piece of fact for conception to fix upon." If so, it would have to be expressed as an additional part of his analytical description. But Whitehead does not do this. It seems rather that he regards "causality-at-work" as "flavoring" the sequence $sf(Xp)$–$sf(Ap)$.

Are we to conclude then that, since in his mature theory of actual occasions Whitehead has provided no special mechanism for

2. New York, Longmans, Green, 1911. Reprinted by permission of Paul R. Reynolds & Son, 599 Fifth Ave., New York 17, N.Y. See Whitehead's comment on James' anti-intellectualism in PR vii.

the fact of efficacy, in addition to the mechanism of repetition, his assertion of causal efficacy has not been made good? In my judgment this would mistake his whole approach to the problem. He is aware of its complexity more than this interpretation would suppose.

Whitehead's account of causal efficacy is not an attempt to demonstrate real connections. It is not his business logically to derive the effect from the cause. It is compatible with his account to say that no explanatory mechanism is adequate to the fact of influence or power. After all has been said about reproduction of feeling, there comes a point where he does not attempt, conceptually, to bridge the gap between cause and effect, between the past subject and the present subject. The obligation to repeat this form of definiteness is simply an empirically acknowledged fact, not an additional bit of explanatory mechanism.

The use of a theoretical explanation of influence, on Whitehead's view, is not to deduce causal efficacy but only to describe a context within which it is logically possible to acknowledge a fact of experience. The explanatory mechanism may describe the *way* in which the influence of one actual occasion on another takes place. Its use is to relate the fact of causal efficacy to other facts such as experiences of subjective unity, purposive action, individuality, and so on. In this sense it defines *how* influence is possible. It is not intended to demonstrate that influence does take place. The *efficacy* of X in the concrescence of A is added not as a part of the explanatory mechanism but as the assertion on empirical grounds that it is *so*.

3. Whitehead on Hume

Whitehead's principal criticism of Hume's treatment of causality is: "Thus Hume's demand that causation be describable as an element in experience is . . . entirely justifiable. The point of the criticisms of Hume's procedure is that we have direct intuition of inheritance and memory: thus the only problem is, so to describe the general character of experience that these intuitions may be included. It is here that Hume fails" (PR 253). Hume fails to do justice to our intuitions because of the implicit cosmology which underlies his description of experience. This cosmology makes it impossible for him to express in theory the fact he accepted in practice. In practice Hume accepted causal efficacy as a fact. But he implicitly regarded the subject of experience as a substance, in the traditional sense, from which view it follows that impressions are "mere private attributes of the mind" (SYM-BOLISM 32). It is then impossible to give theoretical recognition to real connections between the subject and other things in its world. This illustrates the principle that "the relevance of evidence is dictated by theory. For you cannot prove a theory by evidence which that theory dismisses as irrelevant" (AI 284).

This criticism of Hume is double-edged. On one side it recommends that a common fact of experience be taken more seriously. On the other side it recommends a reconstruction of theory. The point of the reconstruction of theory is not to produce a substitute for experience. It is rather to produce a theoretical structure which makes room for all the facts of experience and relates them in a systematic way. Whitehead's own theory of actual occasions, and in particular the mechanism explanatory of causal objectification, is not designed as a substitute for experience. It is designed to make room for the empirically acknowledged fact of influence and to relate it to the general structure of experience.

Whitehead also charges that in his treatment of "memory," "repetition," and "habit" Hume does not abide by his own principles. His discussion of causality is made plausible by his admission of repetition of past impressions. But "At this point of his argument, Hume seems to have overlooked the difficulty that 'repetition' stands with regard to 'impressions' in exactly the same position as does 'cause and effect.' Hume has confused a 'repetition of impressions' with an 'impression of repetitions of impressions'" (PR 204). To justify this use of "repetition" some "impression of repetition" must be found. Hume's answer, that he admits memory, is hardly satisfactory because he interprets memory entirely in terms of "force and vivacity." But this interpretation of memory, says Whitehead, "omits the vital character of memory, namely, that it is *memory*. In fact the whole notion of *repetition* is lost by the 'force and vivacity' doctrine . . . the repetition character, which he ascribes to simple ideas, and which is the whole point of memory, finds no place in his explanation" (PR 205; see AI 236–7). In the same way Whitehead criticizes Hume's employment of the notion of habit. "It is difficult to understand why Hume exempts 'habit' from the same criticism as that applied to the notion of 'cause.' We have no 'impression' of 'habit,' just as we have no 'impression' of 'cause.' Cause, repetition, habit are all in the same boat" (PR 213). For example, in the case of the man who says the flash made him blink, one of Hume's explanations, according to Whitehead, is that "what the man really felt was his *habit* of blinking after flashes. The word 'association' explains it all according to Hume. But how can a 'habit' be felt, when a 'cause' cannot be felt? Is there any presentational immediacy in the feeling of a 'habit'? Hume by a sleight of hand confuses a 'habit of feeling blinks after flashes' with a *'feeling of the habit* of feeling blinks after flashes' " (PR 266).

This criticism of the self-consistency of Hume's analysis of experience does not in itself constitute an answer to Hume's skeptical query about causation. Whitehead's answer to this query consists in an appeal to experience. Do we not experience real transitions from past to present? And should we not find some way to give an adequate account of this experience?

At this point it becomes a fair question whether Whitehead's answer to Hume, since he does not implement transfer of feeling with any specific mechanism other than repetition, does not itself amount to an "appeal to practice" (PR 203). The answer is yes, if an appeal to practice is simply a recognition that causal connection is not formally demonstrated or deduced. The answer is no, however, if an appeal to practice means either (i) "appealing to 'practice' away from the critical examination of our sources of information" (PR 231) or (ii) refusal to give recognition in metaphysics to what is acknowledged in practice. Whitehead's mechanism of repetition is the way he gives critical recognition in metaphysics to what is acknowledged as a stubborn fact. "Whatever is found in 'practice' must lie within the scope of the metaphysical description. When the description fails to include the 'practice,' the metaphysics is inadequate and requires revision. There can be no appeal to practice to supplement metaphysics, so long as we remain contented with our metaphysical doctrines.

Metaphysics is nothing but the description of the generalities which apply to all the details of practice" (PR 19).

In what sense, then, is belief in causality "rational"? It is *not* rational, we conclude, if rationality means conceptual demonstration, or complete analytical description, of causal efficacy. To this extent Whitehead agrees with Hume. Whether causal efficacy is real is a question of empirical fact not of logical demonstration. Whitehead says Hume is justified in asking for evidence, evidence in immediate experience. On the other hand, belief in causality *is* rational in the sense that we have an explanatory mechanism which makes room for the empirically acknowledged fact of causal efficacy and which serves to relate this fact, so acknowledged, to the general structure of the subject-object situation. Influence is thus related to individuality; the basis of social immanence is related to the basis of social transcendence in an intelligible way; and a generally coherent and self-consistent, and in this sense "rational," description of the world of experience is arrived at. But the problem of rationality in this instance is not logically to deduce causal efficacy. It is rather "so to describe the general character of experience" that the "direct intuition of inheritance and memory . . . may be included" (PR 253).

This concludes our examination of the *structure* of Whitehead's doctrine of social immanence within the immediate context of his theory of actual occasions. In Parts Two and Three we shall enlarge our perspective on this topic.

There is an important point at which our account of the structure of the doctrine must remain incomplete until Part Three. The problem left over is as follows. Whitehead takes it as a fact of common experience that the past is given for the present as a real condition imposing the obligation of conformity. But how is it possible, categoreally speaking, that the past, which has perished, is given for the present? In an answer to this question I shall suggest a "reason" for causal efficacy. But it will not be a reason in the sense of a logical demonstration that causal efficacy does in fact take place, and in this respect it will not qualify the main conclusion of this chapter.

In the next chapter, within a larger framework, I shall sum-marize the doctrine of social immanence and consider some of its *consequences*. I shall ask how Whitehead's account of immanence affects the shape of his theory of actual occasions as a whole. For example, in the light of our conclusions about objectification, in what sense is Whitehead's philosophy a "philosophy of organism"? More particularly, in what sense are the connections among actual occasions "organic" connections?

CHAPTER 9

Pluralism and Organism

1. Are actual occasions genuine individuals?

HOW WELL does the theory of actual occasions express the fact that there are many real things? Does Whitehead's cosmology amount to a genuine pluralism? It asserts a multiplicity of actual occasions. So the crucial question is how well an actual occasion qualifies as a real individual thing, transcending all other such things. This calls for a recapitulation of the conclusions of Chapters 2–5.

The conclusions supported by the arguments of those chapters are as follows:

a. An actual occasion is concrete. It is more than a collection of abstract characters. It has significance for itself. It is *actual*.

b. An actual occasion has unity and completeness. It is more than a flux of experience. It has a structure and a consummation. There is a completeness of internal unity, aimed at in the concrescence and achieved in the satisfaction. In this sense an actual occasion is *individuum*.

c. An actual occasion is socially transcendent, that is to say:

i. As an act of experience, an actual occasion is a *novel* unity, not repeated in the advance of nature. Every actual occasion is unique in character.

Also, as an act of experience an actual occasion is *exclusive* of any other occasion in the fundamental sense that no two occasions have any immediacy of feeling in common. No occasion includes, as a functioning part of its own immediacy, any other experiencing subject or any feeling belonging to another subject in the latter's own subjective immediacy. "Feeling of feeling" does not involve any common immediacy, because the feeling felt is objectified. The feeling felt exists, for the feeler, not in the mode of subjective immediacy but in the mode of objective immortality. There is no sharing of immediacy. In addition to this general exclusiveness of immediacy, contemporary occasions are causally independent, and for any present occasion future occasions are hypothetical only. In these ways an occasion excludes, or leaves out of its constitution, all other occasions.

ii. As extended, an actual occasion occupies a novel spatio-temporal region. The regions of occasions are nonoverlapping and thus mutually exclusive. The only types of extensive connection that are possible between two regions of actual occasions are external and mediate connection. And real mediating regions are externally connected with the real regions they mediately connect.

The novelty and exclusiveness of the region of an actual occasion reflect its novelty and exclusiveness as an act of experience. The experiential boundaries of an occasion are reflected in the definiteness of regions in position and extent. The mutual exclusiveness of immediate unities of experience is reflected in the mutual exclusiveness of regions. For we do not have here two coordinate types of actuality, namely feelings and regions, which condition one another. Rather we have a single basic type of actuality, namely relational feelings. Extension, and with it the notions of space, time, and regions, is derivative by abstraction from the nature of feelings. Therefore the novelty and exclusiveness of an actual occasion as an act of experience is the basic fact on which the social transcendence of occasions depends. The value of the conclusions of Chapter 4 about Whitehead's theory of extension is that they are what, on his theory of actual occasions, one would expect them to be. Thus they give some support, indirectly, to the conclusions of Chapters 2 and 3.[1]

I suggest that these conclusions, if they are well founded, justify our saying that an actual occasion is a real individual. If we add to these the conclusions of Chapter 5, then it is reasonable to say that an actual occasion is a substantial individual, if the proper qualifications are understood. But other questions have to be raised.

1. As a matter of fact, as this study proceeded I arrived at the conclusions about the nonoverlapping of regions and the exclusiveness of immediacies more or less independently.

We have seen that it is by virtue of their subjective aims that actual occasions have subjective unity. So the conception of a subjective aim is essential to, and indeed crucial for, Whitehead's account of real individuals. Its importance in his system can hardly be overestimated.

Some interpreters have objected to his theory of the unity of the subject. They have argued that an explanation of subjective unity in terms of aim at satisfaction is insufficient. They urge that his theory of feeling is itself unintelligible except on a more orthodox conception of the subject of experience, namely "the assumption of a subject or experient as condition of its experiences and self-identical throughout the concrescent process." [2]

Whitehead could, in fact, give an interpretation of this predicate. For Whitehead the subject *is* a "condition of its experiences," as defined in categoreal obligations i and vii (PR 39, 40–1). And the subject *is* "self-identical throughout the concrescent process," in the sense that *what* is aimed at in the initial phase of the internal process is fully realized in the satisfaction. Another important consideration is that the internal process is epochal, so that there is no "transition" *within* the subject. But these critics seem to mean something else. They seem to mean that the subject must exist before it has its experiences and that it must be unaffected by its experiences. And it is certainly true that Whitehead does not accept this theory of the subject of experience.

But there is an important question about the *ground* of the internal unity of an actual occasion: How does the subjective aim originate? Whence comes the original idea which the concrescence adopts as its ideal? Since it is a novel idea, it cannot come from the past actual world. Nor can it come from the contemporary world, because the concrescence is independent of its contemporaries. It cannot come from the future, which is not actual. Yet a prehension of this idea is basic to the process of concrescence.

At this point it becomes evident that Whitehead's theory of actual occasions, the temporal actualities which make up the world, leads us beyond itself. We have already seen that eternal objects are necessary to explain the *datum* of the novel subjective

2. David L. Miller and George V. Gentry, *The Philosophy of A. N. Whitehead* (Minneapolis, Burgess Publishing Co., 1938), p. 128.

aim of an actual occasion. And we shall see that Whitehead's explanation of the *ground* of the subjective aim requires a reference to God, the nontemporal actual entity. Since he aims at coherence, which means that "fundamental notions shall not seem capable of abstraction from each other" (PR 5), this is as it should be. But we must ask in Part Three whether, by the functions he assigns to God, he compromises the real individuality of actual occasions and thereby the genuineness of his pluralism. Will it turn out in the end that actual occasions have the status of "appearances" rather than "realities"? This is a question for which we are not yet ready.

2. Are there organic relations among actual occasions?

We might agree, provisionally, that Whitehead's claim to be a pluralist has been made good in his theory of actual occasions. Now we look at another side of that theory. Is it a fair conclusion that there are real connections among actual occasions? Does Whitehead's theory of actual occasions express a genuinely *organic* pluralism? This requires a summary and interpretation of the conclusions of Chapters 6–8.

First we ought to see that this is a question about the relations *between* actual occasions, not about the internal constitution of an occasion. Thinking of the internal unities of actual occasions we might well agree that on Whitehead's showing the world is "a system of organisms" (TIME 60). But this does not imply that the world is an organism. Are the internally organic actual occasions organically related to one another? Is the immanence of one occasion in another an organic relation?

Some analysis of Whitehead's use of the term "organism" is plainly needed. In the first place it is remarkable that, though he usually speaks of his philosophy as "the philosophy of organism" (e.g. PR v), he makes little use of the term otherwise. Elsewhere it occurs mainly in allusions to biological organisms and is used in a presystematic way. It does not appear in the index of either *Process and Reality* or *Adventures of Ideas*.

In the categoreal scheme itself the term "organism" occurs only once, and then only incidentally in the phrase "the philosophy of organism" (PR 37). Properly speaking therefore it is not a category of explanation. In relation to the categoreal scheme it is an *explicandum*. But it is employed in a few passages in *Process and Reality* with the purpose of interpreting the outcome of the scheme, and in these passages it takes on a relatively systematic meaning. These passages belong to a level of discourse, in contrast with more precise and rigorous expositions of his categories, where Whitehead is building bridges between the language of the categoreal scheme and ordinary language.

The principal point of these passages is to make a distinction among "the organisms of the world."

> These organisms are of two types: one type consists of the individual actual entities; the other type consists of nexūs of actual entities (PR 439).

> In the philosophy of organism . . . the notion of 'organism' has two meanings . . . namely, the microscopic meaning and the macroscopic meaning. The microscopic meaning is concerned with the formal constitution of an actual occasion, considered as a process of realizing an individual unity of experience. The macroscopic meaning is concerned with the givenness of the actual world, considered as the stubborn fact which at once limits and provides opportunity for the actual occasion (PR 196–7).

This distinction is correlated with the distinction between the internal process of concrescence and the external process of transition (PR 326–7).

The importance of this distinction is that it yields two meanings of "organic relations," which we should not confuse. In the microscopic meaning of organism, organic relations are *within* a concrescence among prehensions which have the same subject. In the macroscopic meaning of organism, organic relations are between different actual entities. We are concerned with relations of the latter sort and therefore with the kind of organism that is a nexus. When Whitehead says that "the community of actual things is an organism" (PR 327) he is saying only that the world is a nexus of actual entities.

Now a nexus is categoreally explained as "a set of actual entities in the unity of the relatedness constituted by their prehensions of each other, or—what is the same thing conversely expressed—constituted by their objectifications in each other" (PR 35, category of explanation xiv). All the things which ordinary experience finds in nature, and the world itself in any stage of its process, are nexūs. Now the sense in which a nexus is a unity can only be discovered by analysis of the relations among its members, "their objectifications in each other." And this bring us back to the problem of social immanence. Thus it is clear that the term "organism" in its macroscopic meaning is an *explicandum*.

This does not mean that Whitehead's use of the term is pointless. It only means that his point is carried by a metaphor, to emphasize the real connections among the things which make up the world. One way of putting his general point is in terms of the contrast between internal and external relations. With Bradley he would deny that there are any *absolutely* external relations. This denial is embodied in the principle of relativity. At the same time he urges against Bradley that just as relations modify the relata so also the relata modify the relations (AI 201). Also he avoids Bradley's conclusion that even internal relations are "not true in the end" (*Essays in Truth and Reality*, p. 312). He avoids this conclusion by embodying in his theories of actual occasions, of eternal objects, and of God and the world, a doctrine of transcendence as well as a doctrine of immanence.

To explain how "the community of actual things is an organism" we should develop in summary fashion an account of the modes of immanence of actual occasions. Then we can ask how these relations resemble "organic" relations in the ordinary sense of the word.

a. *The primary mode of social immanence: Causal objectification.* The immanence of a past actual occasion in its immediate successor yields the strongest sense of "being present in" to be found in Whitehead's theory of actual occasions. It is also the primary mode of social immanence, since the other modes depend on it for their intelligibility. Let A be a present actual occasion and X an immediately past actual occasion. Then A prehends X by the physical feeling A*p*X. Conversely expressed, in A*p*X the past occasion X is objectified for A. Then in this mode of immanence X is present in A *objectively* and *effectively*.

i. X is present in A *objectively*. The past occasion, which existed "then" in its subjective immediacy, "now" exists in its objective immortality. It has perished subjectively. It exists for A as the datum of the physical feeling A*p*X. It is *that* actual occasion subjectively immediate there-then. But it is not subjectively immediate here-now.

ii. X is present in A *effectively*. X makes a difference to A. An explanation of how X is effective by way of A*p*X may be given in the following stages:

(a) A*p*X makes a difference to A. A's experience is other than it would have been had there been no such past occasion as X, or if X had been different in some respect from what it was.

(b) A*p*X makes an essential, not an "accidental," difference to A. This is to be understood in the context of Whitehead's critique of the traditional doctrine of substance. It is a consequence of his denial of an "unchanging subject of change," a substratum unaffected by particular experiences. An actual occasion is *constituted by* its concrescence, so that A*p*X is a component in A's "real internal constitution." There is a "mutual sensitivity of feelings" (PR 338) so that A*p*X will affect and be affected by all the other feelings that compose the concrescence of A. Subjective unity is a categoreal condition of concrescence.

(c) A*p*X makes an essential difference to A more specifically by making A in some respect like X. The subjective form of A*p*X will conform to the subjective form of one of X's feelings. The same form of definiteness which was immediately actualized in the subjective form of X's feeling will now be immediately actualized in the subjective form of A*p*X. There is thus repetition, or re-enaction, or reproduction, or re-creation, of X's feeling in the concrescence of A. In this way A becomes like X. This is the essential difference A*p*X makes to A.

(d) X is the *reason* for the difference A*p*X makes to A. X's achievement of satisfaction, its "absoluteness" of attainment, determines what the future must conform to. The new concrescence cannot choose whether or not it shall conform to X. A has to deal with X as a stubborn fact, given for its experience. Just *how* it shall conform to X is not completely determined. But in some way or other it must conform to X. Also the importance of X for A will vary according to the intensity of X's satisfaction and the general nature of A's environment. In some degree and in some way X is efficacious for A.

(e) Expressions like "flow of feeling" and "transference of feeling" may now be used to describe this relation between X and A. They are not to be understood in a simple or literal way as meaning that X shares the immediacy of A or that A shares the immediacy of X. They are not substitutes for the explanatory mechanism of conformity of subjective form. They belong to a mode of discourse in which Whitehead is interpreting his scheme, not to his more precise and rigorous explication of the scheme. Yet they add something to a statement of causal objectification. They properly convey, in an imaginative mode, the quality and the over-all effect of the process of transition.

The mutual immanence of contemporary occasions, and the immanence of future occasions in the present, yield senses of "being present in" which are relatively weak compared with causal objectification. In these cases an actual occasion is present objectively, but not effectively, in another. Also these are secondary modes of immanence, not in the sense that they are entirely derivative from causal objectification but in the sense that they are dependent on it.

b. *Secondary modes of social immanence: Presentational objectification.* Let A and B be two actual occasions in "unison of becoming." Since they are causally independent B is *not effectively* present in A. Further, since A does not prehend B directly as a concrete individual, *a fortiori* A does not share B's immediacy. Hence B is present in A only *objectively*. The problem is to give some meaning to the objective existence of B in A.

In presentational objectification (PR 91) the feeling in A which enacts the objectification is a transmuted feeling (PR 355). Its datum is a nexus of contemporary occasions. This nexus, of which B is a member, is directly given only as an extended region. The conditions of concrescence require elimination of all other features of the nexus. On this region A projects sensa derived from its past. Thus B is directly present in A only as an undiscriminated component of the region there-now. It is given for A only in the mode of "passive potentiality" (PR 96). Only in this way does it enter directly into the concrescence of A. This is indeed a weak sense of immanence.

Since A and B have more or less common pasts, there is an indirect relevance between them. This again yields only a weak sense in which B is present in A.

c. *Secondary modes of social immanence: Anticipation.* Since future occasions are not now actual they can*not* be *effectively* present in A. Also there can be no question of sharing immediacy. A cannot now share the immediacy of M which is not yet actual. The question is, again, how to give meaning to the *objective* reality of M in A.

Among the feelings which compose A's satisfaction are anticipatory feelings. A anticipates that *some* actual occasions will supersede it and that these occasions will conform to it when they become actual. M is present in A only as a possible value for this variable. Only in this weak sense is the future immanent in the present.

We have been summarizing Whitehead's doctrine of social immanence in preparation for asking how the relations between actual occasions are organic. Our next step is to think of some relations which might be called organic, and ask whether the relations between actual occasions approximate or resemble these in any way. At least three biological analogies might be considered.

i. Two actual occasions are related to each other as two parts of a cell are related to each other.

ii. One actual occasion is related to another as a cell is related to the larger organism in which it functions.

iii. Two actual occasions are related to each other as two cells in a larger organism are related to each other.

Here we have three natural senses in which things might be said to be organically related. In the light of Whitehead's doctrine of social immanence are actual occasions related in any of these ways?

i. We ordinarily suppose that among the parts of a cell there are real and effective connections within any duration which forms a cross-section of its history, as well as between the successive durations which make up that history. Now it is clearly Whitehead's view that the experience of an actual occasion is a functional unity within a given duration. Because of the subjective aim there are real and effective connections among the prehensions which compose the concrescence. So this analogy with the parts of a cell would hold for the prehensions which make up an individual actual occasion.

The relations *between* actual occasions, however, are certainly not organic in this sense. The only effective connections between occasions occur in causal objectification. This mode of immanence, since it involves the perishing of the past and the exclusiveness of immediacies, cannot be thought of as a functional unity of parts within a single duration. The relation is temporal and asymmetrical. Therefore if relations between actual occasions are organic they must be so in some other sense.

ii. We ask then whether two actual occasions are organically related as a part of a cell is related to the cell as a whole. Again it seems clear that this is not the case. Analysis of an actual occasion cannot reveal any other actual occasion, functioning in its own subjective immediacy, as a part of the given occasion. This is precluded by the exclusiveness of the immediacies of actual occasions, reflected in the exclusiveness of their regions. Yet if the whole-part analogy in sense ii were applied to relations between actual occasions, this is just what we should find. Hence it seems that relations between actual occasions are not organic in this sense. One actual occasion is not related to another as a part of a cell is related to the cell as a whole. Whitehead makes this clear in the following passage: "The philosophy of organism is a cell-theory of actuality. Each ultimate unit of fact is a cell-complex, not analysable into components with equivalent completeness of actuality" (PR 334).

iii. Finally we ask whether the relation between two actual occasions is like the relation between two cells which function as parts of a multicellular organism. Two interpretations of this analogy are possible. One is that God is the "organism" of which actual occasions are the cell-like parts. Consideration of this interpretation will be left until Part Three.

The other interpretation of this biological analogy is that the world is the "organism" of which actual occasions are cell-like parts. As we have seen, Whitehead does say "The community of actual things is an organism." He immediately adds, "but it is not a static organism. It is an incompletion in process of production" (PR 327). This qualification is crucial. For it reintroduces the consideration which ruled out the first of our biological analogies. The force of this qualification is not simply a reminder that organisms are living and growing things and hence not static. For sometimes we think of a living body as functioning as a whole in each of its durations. If we think of a multicellular organism in this way, then the world as Whitehead construes it would lack something which ordinary organisms would have. Since contemporary actual occasions are causally independent, the world does not function as a whole *within* the durations that make up its history. Contemporary actual occasions are not related to each other as two cells that function in a larger living body. The world is not an "organism" in this sense. Influence occurs only in "temporal strings."

In a somewhat weaker sense, however, this last biological analogy does have an application to Whitehead's view of the world as a nexus. Influence occurs only in temporal strings, but the different strings, that is to say historical routes of occasions, interact with one another. This may be explained as follows:

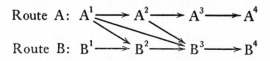

Let the A's and B's stand for actual occasions, and let the movement of time be from left to right. Then there is no direct influence between A^1 and B^1, or between A^2 and B^2, and so on. But any occasion, for example B^3, is conditioned directly or indirectly by all of the occasions in its past actual world. Thus B^3 is influenced by B^1 and by B^2. But it is also influenced by A^1 and A^2. This will be true for any actual occasion. It grows out of a past composed of many interconnected historical routes. *Any* actual occasion in the past actual world of a concrescence directly or indirectly, or both (PR 435), influences and is thus immanent in that concrescence (PR 345–7, 468–70). This interconnectedness of historical routes of actual occasions makes the world a nexus and, in a weak sense, an "organism."

This analogy between the world as a nexus and an ordinary organism is enfeebled even further by two other considerations. First, ordinarily speaking an organism has an environment, from which it is distinguished by spatiotemporal boundaries and with which it interacts. By definition the world has no environment in this sense. Second, ordinarily speaking an organism has a unifying structure which persists throughout its history. But the world as a nexus, on Whitehead's view, has no such structure so far as we know. His doctrine of "cosmic epochs" leaves open the possibility that no single dominant society persists through all epochs as *the* order of nature (PR 128, 139, 146, 171).

We may conclude that Whitehead's name for his system, "the philosophy of organism," is by no means inappropriate, since an actual occasion is an "organism" in a strong sense of the word and since, in various intelligible senses, actual occasions are "organically" related to other occasions. But it would be a mistake to infer from his use of the name that the *world* is conceived as an organism except in the weak sense explained above. The statement that an actual entity is in a sense "everywhere" throughout the extensive continuum (PR 104) is an assertion of universal social immanence. But when distinctions between strong and weak senses of social immanence are taken into account, this assertion becomes considerably less impressive. The reason is that in Whitehead's theory of actual occasions the themes of individuality, transcendence, and plurality are in fact as important as the themes of influence, immanence, and organism.

3. Social transcendence and social immanence: The question of coherence

Whitehead's doctrines of social transcendence and social immanence, if they are understood in the senses defined in this study, are self-consistent and compatible with each other. But if his writings have to be interpreted in other ways, then problems about the consistency and compatibility of these doctrines would arise.

For example, if the satisfaction of an actual occasion has to be interpreted in such a way that it is not a concrete, immediate, complete feeling having a real duration, then the theory of real individuals, on which social transcendence depends, would break down. Again, if causal objectification has to be interpreted so that it involves transference of feelings from one occasion to another in a simple or literal sense, then the crucial mode of social transcendence, namely experiential exclusiveness, would be ruled out. Insofar as his writings encourage these interpretations, then *either* what Whitehead says is in this respect misleading *or* his theory of actual occasions does not fulfill his promise of doing justice to the experience of many real things.

These alternative interpretations have been critically examined. Reasons have been given for believing they are not justified. If they are not, then Whitehead's doctrines of social transcendence and social immanence are essentially compatible with each other as aspects of an organic pluralism.

We may go further. Not only are these doctrines compatible with each other; they require each other in certain ways. The satisfaction of an actual occasion points to its origins and to its results. *Now,* as subjectively immediate, it is neither its origins nor its results. It is itself, concrete and complete. But it points to its past and to its future effectiveness. Its transcendence of past individuals must issue in self-transcendence, which is its immanence in future individuals. In these ways an account of the individuality of an occasion, from which its social transcendence follows, requires an account of the immanence of other occasions in it, and its own immanence in its successors.

On the other hand, the process of causal objectification requires reference to socially transcendent individuals. On one side, the conformal feeling points to its object which is a past individual, objectified. On the other side the conformal feeling points to the individuality of the prehending subject. In these ways the individual subject of the feeling and the individual object of the feeling are involved in the conformal feeling itself.

Thus the fact of social transcendence points to the fact of social immanence. The fact of social immanence points to the fact of social transcendence. This "pointing" is what Whitehead means by "significance." And significance is grounded in the process by which many individuals contribute to the becoming of a new individual in the course of nature. Then this new individual in turn passes on its contribution to its successors. This is the rhythm of creativity, which Whitehead intends his theory of actual occasions to analyze.

4. The question of evidence

On what facts, as evidence, does Whitehead base his theory of actual occasions? Speculative philosophy, he says, is like the flight of an airplane. It leaves the ground for its flight of conceptual construction and then returns to the ground for application of its constructions. We ask, From what field of facts does Whitehead logically "take off"?

Two possibilities suggest themselves: scientific facts and facts of immediate experience. It is clear that Whitehead appeals to facts of both sorts, for example to quantum phenomena and to our experience of, in William James' phrase, "drops of perception" (PR 105). But it is very doubtful whether these two sorts of facts have for Whitehead equal evidential value. On the contrary, quantum phenomena seem to be on a level distinctly secondary to the facts of immediate experience.

This is the inference to be drawn from his general view of the relation of physics to concrete experience. In one of the earliest of his philosophical writings he strikes a characteristic note: ". . . both science and metaphysics start from the same given groundwork of immediate experience, and in the main proceed in opposite directions on their diverse tasks" (OT 113–14). Throughout his writings the ultimate facts appealed to are the concrete experiences from which the abstractions of physics are derived. No doubt the well-founded generalizations of physics point to important facts about nature. Any cosmological theory must take account of such facts and must be capable of interpreting any particular physical theory, such as the quantum theory, which seems to be well founded. But cosmological theory is to be based on concrete experience rather than on the abstractions of physics, and it is to the "given groundwork of immediate experience" that a cosmological theory must refer for its final evidence.

Whitehead has offered an interpretation of quantum phenomena in his theory of "primates" in *Science and the Modern World*. But the general facts about nature to which both the field theory and the quantum theory point, namely the continuity and the atomicity of nature, are not themselves new discoveries: "These contrasted aspects of nature, continuity and atomicity, have a long history in European thought, reaching back to the origin of science among the Greeks" (AI 238). This suggests that these general facts about nature emerge at a prescientific or at least a pretechnical level of experience. Whitehead's attitude to the phenomena specifically referred to in quantum theory is paralleled by his attitude to the phenomena on which biological theories are based. Both quantum phenomena and biological phenomena seem to point to more or less discrete unities in nature. Any adequate cosmology must be capable of interpreting these physical and biological facts.[3] But he does not seem to offer these scientific facts as direct evidence for the cosmology in terms of which he interprets them.

This does not exclude the possibility that physical theories may have suggested to Whitehead some of the outlines of his philosophy. In one passage, after a discussion of the bearing of psychological and physiological facts on his philosophy, he says it is equally possible to arrive at the organic conception of nature from the fundamental notions of modern physics. And "by reason of my own studies in mathematics and mathematical physics, I did in fact arrive at my convictions in this way" (SMW 213). But we are not asking how, in the course of his intellectual history, he happened to arrive at his theories.[4] We are asking on what facts as evidence he logically bases his theory of individuality. I suggest

3. "This quantum-theory also has analogues in recent neurology" (PR 365). He may have had in mind the "all-or-none" law of nerve impulse.

4. Victor Lowe remarks: "It is natural to include the quantum theory among influences on him; I think, however, that in fact this was to him a supporting illustration rather than a formative influence in the creation of his atomic pluralism" (Schilpp 90).

that quantum phenomena in physics are not of primary importance in this connection.

Indeed, one might make out a case for the view that his dissatisfaction with traditional scientific interpretations of space and time is at least as important as quantum theory in shaping his theory of actual occasions (SMW 90, PR 105–8). Certainly this dissatisfaction was one of the main motives for his earlier philosophy of nature. The deficiencies of traditional theories of space and time, and quantum theory, both lead him in the same direction. But he does not seem to offer either as direct evidence for the existence of actual occasions as the final individual realities.

In fact he recognizes very clearly that there is no physical evidence that quanta of energy are irreducible. He describes the increasing abstractness of the basic concepts of physics. Successively, the locus of concrete substantiality has been removed from the common-sense object (as the stone) to the molecule, then to the atom, then to the protons and electrons, then to "the mysterious quanta of energy." Further, "these quanta seem to dissolve into the vibrations of light" (PR 121–2). His own conclusion from this gradual attenuation of concreteness in the history of modern physics is that "In physics, there is an abstraction. The science ignores what anything is in itself" (SMW 213). Now "The mere phrase that 'physical science is an abstraction,' is a confession of philosophic failure. It is the business of rational thought *to describe the more concrete fact from which that abstraction is derivable*" (AI 239, my italics). The moral is that Whitehead does not offer the concepts of modern physics as direct evidence for his own theory of concrete individuals.

This result increases the evidential burden which his appeal to immediate human experience must bear. But this is clearly where he lays the burden. His doctrines of individuality and of influence are both generalizations from human experience. Whitehead has said this so clearly and so frequently that there seems no reasonable excuse for announcing it as a skeleton discovered in his closet. This sort of generalization is of the essence of his philosophical procedure. "In describing the capacities, realized or unrealized, of an actual occasion, we have, with Locke, tacitly taken human experience as an example upon which to found the generalized description required for metaphysics" (PR 172).[5]

Is this burden of evidence too heavy for human experience to bear? A critical treatment of this question would take us much too far afield. One basic consideration is whether and to what extent there is continuity between the structure of nature and the structure of human experience. Whitehead himself sees the alternatives for speculative philosophy in the following way:

> An occasion of experience which includes a human mentality is an extreme instance, at one end of the scale, of those happenings which constitute nature. As yet this discussion has fixed attention upon this extreme. But any doctrine which refuses to place human experience outside nature, must find in descriptions of human experience factors which also enter into the descriptions of less specialized natural occurrences. If there be no such factors, then the doctrine of human experience as a fact within nature is mere bluff, founded upon vague phrases whose sole merit is a comforting familiarity. We should either admit dualism, at least as a provisional doctrine, or we should point out the identical elements connecting human experience with physical science (AI 237).

In addition to these questions about the evidence on which Whitehead bases his theory of actual occasions, other questions need to be asked, though they take us beyond the limits of this study. They concern the adequacy of the theory of actual occasions. Is it capable of interpreting all the kinds of real things we encounter in experience? Does it do justice to all the facts?

For example is the theory *too* strong for what we encounter in our experience of sticks and stones? Are these things really made up of units of experience?

Again, is it strong *enough* to do justice to our own existence as conscious persons? Do we have more unity and continuity of experience than Whitehead's categories allow? Do we have a capacity for summing up our experience which we cannot in-

5. See SMW 123–31, 156–7, 220; PR 105, 266–8, 310–11; AI 99, 237, 239, 242, 284; MT 231–2.

terpret in his systematic terms? Is there a kind of self-transcendence *within* immediate experience, as well as self-transcendence by way of objective immortality? Is there within our experience a literal flow of feeling? Are we individuals in a way which his theory does not enable us to express clearly and adequately?

A reasoned answer would require both a phenomenology of human self-consciousness and an analysis of Whitehead's discussions of personal existence including his theory of "societies." It would also require consideration of what *might* be said about personal existence in the language of the categoreal scheme, consistent with Whitehead's principles, going beyond what he has said in his writings.

PART TWO

Eternal Objects

CHAPTER 10

Objects and Events

1. The earlier philosophy of nature

BEFORE EXAMINING the theory of eternal objects in Whitehead's later writings, let us look at an earlier stage of his thought for the sake of historical perspective. In his writings on the philosophy of nature between 1915 and 1925 his basic constructive categories were "objects" and "events." Since "objects" are the ancestors of eternal objects and "events" are the ancestors of actual entities, some attention to these earlier notions will help us to understand the later ones.

In the earlier writings Whitehead set out to give an account of "the data of science." He thought the traditional categories for describing nature, namely the concepts of "Time (flowing equably in measurable lapses) and of Space (timeless, void of activity, euclidean), and of Material in space (such as matter, ether, or electricity)" (PNK 1) did not fit the facts. So he began, in his reconstruction, with the concept of *events*. He thought that in terms of events, extended unities, he could do justice to the connectedness of nature, to which the traditional concepts were inadequate.

The notion of an event as an extended unity was probably suggested to Whitehead by biological organisms. But it is important to notice that his argument against the traditional concepts is not a vitalistic argument. He argues that these concepts are inadequate to the facts *physics* deals with. This argument, which originates as early as his essay, "La théorie relationniste de l'espace" (completed in 1914), and continues throughout the earlier writings, is that "The concept of unities, functioning and with spatio-temporal extensions, cannot be extruded from *physical* concepts" (PNK 3, my italics; see 66).

The corresponding concept of *objects* is first introduced in a discussion of congruence. Measurements require judgments of constancy, and "a judgment of constancy is recognition" (PNK 56). An object is what is recognized in recognition. Objects are "recognita." "Objects convey the permanences recognized in events, and are recognized as self-identical amid different circumstances; that is to say, the same object is recognized as related to diverse events" (PNK 62–3). The main types of objects Whitehead discusses are (a) sense objects, for example "the colour red of a definite shade" (PNK 83); (b) perceptual objects, for example a chair; and (c) scientific objects, for example electrons.

It is not necessary to recapitulate Whitehead's early philosophy of nature. To lay a foundation for understanding his theory of eternal objects we confine ourselves to the main differences between objects and events and to the "ingression" of objects in events. We may speak of the differences between objects and events as modes of transcendence and ask first how objects transcend events. Then we can discuss ingression as the way objects are immanent in events.

2. How objects transcend events

The most important ways in which objects transcend events are in respect to space and time. Before stating these a note of caution is needed. It would not be true to say simply that events are in space and time and objects are not. This would be misleading about both events and objects.

It would be wrong to think of events as "in" space and time if this meant that space and time have some kind of existence antecedent to and independent of events. For space and time are not containers into which events fit. On the contrary, "Events (in a sense) are space and time, namely, space and time are abstractions from events" (PNK 63).

Likewise it would be wrong to think of objects as simply "out" of space and time. On this point some of Whitehead's own statements are liable to be misleading, as he acknowledges (PNK 202). For example he says that objects "are only derivatively in space and time by reason of their relations to events" (PNK 63; see TSM 56). Again, he says that "strictly speaking" objects are "without space and time" and that "primarily an object is not in space or in time" (PNK 63, 65). These strong statements need to be qualified, as we shall see later. We shall find it is more accurate to say an object is "in a sense" (CN 78) out of space and time than to say an object is "strictly speaking" out of space and time.

For the objects dealt with in the earlier writings ("natural objects") are also, in a sense, *in* space and time. They "require" space and time (PNK 202). Therefore a better way of putting the difference between objects and events is to say they differ in the *kinds* of relations they have to space and time (SMW 121). With this preliminary warning we can go on to some specific ways in which objects transcend events.

a. *Events are extended; objects are not extended.* An event has temporal thickness (duration) and spatial spread. Within its unity are temporal and spatial "parts." It takes up space, and it is in "passage." Objects on the contrary do not take up space and they do not pass.

Here we should pause to consider the notion of passage in Whitehead's early writings. Let us discriminate two possible senses of passage: (i) an entity passes when it ceases to be or, in his later terminology, "perishes"; and (ii) an entity passes when it changes or undergoes alteration.

Now in sense i events pass and objects do not. But the contrast in respect to sense ii is not so clear, and that on two counts. In the first place "events never change" (PNK 62). Though events happen, nothing happens within an event except other events, which themselves become and cease to be but do not change. In these earlier writings Whitehead has no adequate way of distinguishing between "external process" and "internal process."

In the second place, objects of a certain peculiar sort, namely rhythms (for example a tune), require minimum durations and seem to have a kind of internal process (PNK, ch. 18). Thus we have the paradox that though no event has inner change yet some objects do. It is for this reason that Whitehead is so plainly unhappy about calling rhythms objects.

This suggests a question. How, without some conception of internal process, can he explicate the temporal thickness which distinguishes a real duration from an instantaneous moment?

When he says that events are "lived through" (PNK 63), is he still consistently maintaining his program of excluding "mind" from nature? Or is he implicitly projecting into the experienced event the internal process that really belongs to the "percipient object" which is outside nature?

Does not Whitehead need, even within the limited inquiry undertaken in the early writings, some conception of internal process with which to explicate "becomingness"? (See PNK 202.) Later when he introduces the conception of internal process in nature, namely the concrescence of actual occasions, a theory of enduring objects can be developed. Then a more subtle and satisfactory account of ryhthms can be given. Then it is possible to distinguish among: (i) entities which begin, develop internally, and pass but do not change (actual occasions); (ii) entities which do not begin, develop, change, or pass (eternal objects); and (iii) entities which begin, change, and pass (enduring objects).

It is true that Whitehead's introduction of new categories, as he moves from the earlier to the later writings, results from an extension of the scope of his inquiry. He moves from a philosophy of nature, concerned only with the data of science, to construction of a scheme which can be used to interpret *all* the items and modes of experience. It seems true also that obscurities and deficiencies in his philosophy of nature were a stimulus to extending the scope of his inquiry.

Returning to the immediate question, we notice that objects have no spatial or temporal parts.[1] They are not extended. Whitehead acknowledges it is more difficult to think of an object (for example a chair) as not having spatial parts than to think of it as not having temporal parts. This is because ordinary language obscures the distinction between the chair as an object and the events in which it is situated. The event in which the leg of the chair is situated is a part of the event in which the chair is situated. But the leg is one object and the chair is another object.

b. *Events have single location; objects have multiple location.* Here I am using "location" in a more ordinary sense than Whitehead does (PNK ch. 14, CN 160–3), and as in Chapter 4 above I take the expression "single location" from Lovejoy. An event oc-

1. See PNK 65–6, 91–2; TSM 56; CN 125; PRIN R 37.

curs once and only once. It occurs at some place and only at that place. An object, for example a stone or redness, can on the contrary be at more than one time and at more than one place at the same time. The "permanence" conveyed by objects is not endurance or continuation but repetition. "Here it is again." [2]

c. *No two events coincide; objects coincide.* Every event has one and only one location in space and time. Also no two events have the same location. It would be a contradiction to speak of two events with the same spatiotemporal boundaries. But two or more objects may exist at the same time and place. This is to say, as we shall see, that two or more objects may be ingredient in the same event. "For example, for any one percipient event, the situation of a sense-object of sight is apt also to be the situations of [other] sense-objects of sight, of touch, of smell, and of sound" (CN 154).

In the above ways objects differ from events in relation to space and time. Objects are nonextended, have multiple location, and coincide. Events on the contrary are extended, have single location, and do not coincide. Now we move on to other ways in which objects differ from or transcend events.

d. *Events are "lived through"; objects are recognized.* Entities of the two types enter experience in different ways. Experience of events involves a sense of passage. Events are the "development" (PNK 63) of our physical experience. On the other hand, "Objects enter into experience by way of the intellectuality of recognition" (PNK 64). In this distinction between living through events and recognizing objects lies the germ of the later distinction between physical and conceptual prehensions. Recognition is awareness of something which has recurred or might recur. Objects are recognized, not lived through (PNK 63).

e. *Objects are comparable; events are incomparable.* It is true that we speak of the comparison of events. "But it is not the events which are compared. For each event is essentially unique and incomparable. What are compared are the objects and relations of objects situated in events" (CN 125. See TSM 51; CN 144, 189). For example, when we note "red there-now and red there-then," we are noting two different sets of spatiotemporal relations of the

2. See PNK 62–3, 65, 82; CN 125, 143–5, 169.

same object. The spatiotemporal relations are external to the essence of the object (PNK 64), for the same object can be situated in many events. There is a sense in which we are comparing two events (PNK 64). But they are then events which have lost their quality of passage (CN 125). They are not being lived through. Properly speaking it is not events we are then comparing but different sets of relations of an object.

In his later writings Whitehead can speak of "objectified" events. But the notion of objectification has not yet been developed, because the events which are the data of science have no experiential content (subjective immediacy) to become objectified.

f. *Events are continuous; objects are "atomic."* There are three senses in which events are continuous. Events and transitions between events are experienced as continuous (PNK 74, CN 59). There are no minimal events: "The continuity of nature arises from extension. Every event extends over other events, and every event is extended over by other events" (CN 59; see TSM 55). And finally there are no empty spaces or times (see Chapter 4).

The "atomicity" of objects is not the kind of concrete unity that is later attributed to actual occasions. Nor does it mean that objects are separated from each other in space and time. It means rather that they are recognized according to an "all-or-none" law. An object "is always wholly itself" (PNK 91). An object has no parts. This property follows directly and simply from the fact that "the essence of an object does not depend on its relations" (PNK 64), that is, its spatiotemporal relations in any particular situation.

g. *"Actuality" applies to events; "possibility" applies to objects.* In the early writings "actuality" means determinateness of spatiotemporal relations. The relations of an event belong to the essence of the event. An event is "that happening there-then," and the particular there-then is essential to the event. "An actual event is thus divested of all possibility" (PNK 61).[3]

3. The implied contrast is with "imaginary events" or "imaginations of events." These would be objects or, in terms of the later writings, propositions. On the actuality of events in the early writings see also PRIN R 63, ESP (1923) 134–8. In the later writings he adds "subjective immediacy" to the meaning of "actuality."

On the other hand, the spatiotemporal relations of an object are indeterminate as far as its essence is concerned. "Whenever the concept of possibility can apply to a natural element, that element is an object . . . It has in fact certain relations to other natural elements; but it might (being the same object) have had other relations" (PNK 64). In the later writings, as we shall see, the scope of "possibility" will be widened to include "ideality," that is to say the objects of "logical, emotional, aesthetic and moral apprehensions" (PRIN R 20) as well as the "natural objects" (PNK 202) with which the early writings are concerned.

h. *Events are concrete; objects are abstract.* First we must notice some qualifications on the "concreteness" of events in the early writings:

i. What is fully or unqualifiedly concrete is "fact" or "factuality." This is not one fact among others, nor even the sum of "factors"; "it is rather the concreteness (or, embeddedness) of factors, and the concreteness of an inexhaustible relatedness among inexhaustible relata" (PRIN R 15; see IDIN 133, CN ch. 1).

ii. Nature, with which science is concerned, is not identical with fact or factuality. Science makes an abstraction when it restricts its attention to nature. "Nature is an abstraction from something more concrete than itself which must also include imagination, thought, and emotion" (PRIN R 63; see PNK 201, PRIN R 21, CN 66). The contrast between events and objects is a contrast *within nature.* Hence the paradoxical expression, "our lowest, most concrete, type of abstractions whereby we express the diversification of fact must be regarded as 'events,' meaning thereby a partial factor of fact which retains process" (PA 223). Events are "the concrete facts of *nature*" (CN 167, my italics. See PNK 4; PRIN R 21, 63).

In experience we do not begin with isolated and detached entities. The factors we experience in sense awareness and thought [4] are "embedded." They belong to contexts. It would follow that an entity is concrete to the degree that, when it is experienced, its embeddedness is experienced. Those factors which can be entertained apart from their embeddedness in fact are in that degree abstract.

Objects, then, are the "abstract elements of the world . . .

4. Thought is "the refinement of awareness" (PRIN R 15).

which are devoid of becomingness and extension," in contrast with the "more concrete elements (events) which retain becomingness and extension" (PRIN R 37). Objects are detachable from the contexts in which they are found. They are not embedded the way events are. They can be considered apart from the events in which we find them. Thus "red," "three," "the Tower of London" (PRIN R 17), and "the sun, the earth, Cleopatra's Needle, or a human body," and molecules and electrons are all abstractions. "The concrete facts are the events themselves" (CN 171).

A warning about "abstraction" is in order. It would be a mistake to think of abstractions, in Whitehead's early writings, as entities having no existence, or having their existence only "in the mind" or in a realm apart from nature. An abstract entity is rather something discriminated or "prescinded from" its background of fact (PRIN R 14). We are, for the purposes of thinking, taking that factor out of its real context in fact. The entity is really *in* nature.

> I have already explained to you that to be an abstraction does not mean that an entity is nothing. It merely means that its existence is only one factor of a more concrete element of nature. So an electron is abstract because you cannot wipe out the whole structure of events and yet retain the electron in existence. In the same way the grin on the cat is abstract; and the molecule is really in the event in the same sense as the grin is really on the cat's face (CN 171; see 173).

To summarize, objects transcend events primarily by having different relations to space and time. Events are extended processes; objects are unextended. An event is only at a single place and time; an object may be at more than one place and time. No two events can be at the same place and time; two or more objects may be at the same place and time. In other words objects are not space-bound and time-bound the way events are. Objects are externally related (but not *un*related) to space and time. This is the primary way in which they transcend events, for events are internally related to space and time.

The other ways in which objects transcend events can be related to this primary mode. Recognition is awareness of what is not tied to some one place and time. The comparability of objects depends on their multiple location and on their coincidence. The atomicity of objects means that being unextended they have no parts. The category of possibility has already been introduced in defining the spatiotemporal relations of objects. And the abstractness of objects means that they can be considered apart from their embeddedness in some particular spatiotemporal context.

Finally we should notice some senses of "out of space and time" which Whitehead has *not* asserted of objects.

a. An entity might be said to be out of space and time if there is no place and time at which it exists. Whitehead has not said that objects are out of space and time in this sense. Events are singly located and objects are multiply located, but he has not said that objects are *unlocated*.

b. An entity might be said to be out of space and time if it exists at all times and places in the same way. As we shall see when we come to discuss ingression and situation, Whitehead certainly does not mean that objects exist at all times and places in the same way in which they exist at *some* times and places. An object is not *omnipresent* in this absolute sense.

c. An entity might be said to be out of space and time if it could be understood without any reference to space and time. In this case we might say that its essence does not involve any reference to space and time. Whitehead does not say that objects are out of space and time in this sense. On the contrary, though the essence of an object does not involve a reference to this or that place or time, yet it does involve reference to space and time in a general way. An object is not absolutely *independent* of space and time.

Objects thus are in a sense out of space and time, but only *in a sense*. We have not found that objects are absolutely, or even "strictly speaking," out of space and time. We have found that objects have other relations to the extended and passing realm of nature than do events. Indeed, as Whitehead says in one of his later (1925) notes in *The Principles of Natural Knowledge*, "natural objects *require* space and time, so that space and time belong to their relational essence without which they cannot be themselves" (PNK 202, my italics). The distinction between "individual essence" and "relational essence" alluded to here (SMW 222–3) was not made explicit in the earlier writings. But it is implicit throughout, and it underlies the doctrine of the *ingression* of objects in events, to which we now turn. This is Whitehead's explanation of how objects are immanent in events.

3. How objects are immanent in events: Ingression

When Whitehead speaks of "the ingression of an object into an event" (CN 144), the "plain" meaning of his language is that an object enters an event from somewhere outside that event. "Ingression" suggests (a) that objects *move,* and (b) that an object comes *from somewhere,* from some antecedent locus, perhaps from outside the whole flux of events, but at least from outside the particular event into which it "ingresses."

By this time we should have been well warned that the "plain" meanings of Whitehead's terms are not always his meanings. So we should examine ingression with some care. Let us look first at the way the term is introduced in his writings.

As far as I can tell, this term is first used in *The Concept of Nature* and is introduced in the following manner. In the first chapter Whitehead refers to "entities which are not parts of fact [i.e. not events] though they are *ingredients* in it" (CN 14, my italics). Similarly he speaks of "ingredient characters" of events (CN 82). Finally in the chapter on "Objects" he introduces ingression more formally: "An object is an ingredient in the character of some event. In fact the character of an event is nothing but the objects which are ingredient in it and the ways in which those objects make their ingression into the event" (CN 143–4).

Does it not appear that "being an ingredient" is a more accurate expression of Whitehead's meaning than "ingression"? But if we interpret these as equivalent expressions, as they seem to be, then we must take "ingression" not as the name of an *action* (like "journey") but as the name of a timeless *relation,* namely "being an ingredient."

This suggestion finds support in other passages where ingression is discussed. For example, later in the same chapter of *The Concept of Nature* Whitehead is discussing the relations between a sense object (blue) and events. He says, "I will use the term 'ingression into nature' for this systematic correlation of the blue with nature" (CN 152). It appears again that ingression is a name for a relationship, not for an action. Similarly, and perhaps more clearly, "The apparent world discloses itself to us as the ingression of sense-objects amid events. In this statement the term 'ingression' is used for the complex relationship of those abstract elements of the world, such as sense-objects, which are devoid of becomingness and extension, to those other more concrete elements (events) which retain becomingness and extension" (PRIN R 37). Again, of the relation of sense objects to events he says, "I have suggested the term 'ingression' for this many-termed relation" (ESP [1923] 139). He speaks of "the ingression of sense-objects amid events" as "a character of nature" (ESP 142; see 144–5). Finally, nowhere does Whitehead say that an object "ingresses" into an event. Indeed, he nowhere uses the word "ingress" either as a verb or as a noun. These facts about his usage are evidence that ingression means a relation, not an action, and that the term is generated not from a verb but from the relational adjective "ingredient." He adopts "ingression" simply as a more economical way of saying "being an ingredient in." Insofar as ingression suggests entry from an antecedent locus, Whitehead has made trouble for his readers.

Before he introduced the term "ingression" he had referred to objects as "characteristics" of events: "A reference to objects is only a way of specifying the character of an event" (PNK 73); "An object is a characteristic of an event" (PNK 195). Now he says, "An object is an ingredient in the character of some event. In fact the character of an event is nothing but the objects which are ingredient in it and the ways in which these objects make their ingression into the event" (CN 143–4. See PNK 189; CN 80; 189). We might think of an event as a "that" happening there-then. The "that" is a complex of objects. An object belonging to this complex is thus an ingredient in the character of the event, and in this sense an ingredient in the event.

This sort of language needs to be guarded. It is natural to name events after the objects prominently situated in them. It is also misleading to do so. The trouble is that we then have no way of distinguishing the objects from the event. And Whitehead thinks that an adequate interpretation of nature requires this distinction.

His problem is to distinguish the spatiotemporal "parts" of the event from the components of its character. The green of the leaf is not related to the shape of the leaf, or to the leaf itself, in the same way as one spatial part of the leaf is related to another part, or as the existence of the leaf during one half-second is related to its existence during the next half-second. Different *sorts* of relations are involved. The problem is how to make this clear. "Ingredient" and "ingression" are used to distinguish (a) the relation of objects to the event as a whole from (b) the relations of its spatiotemporal parts to each other.

Whitehead's earliest account of the relation of objects to events is in terms of "situation." He says, "The notion of the situation of an object is logically indefinable being one of the ultimate data of science . . ." (PNK 165). In *The Concept of Nature* he formally introduces "situation" in the following way:

> . . . ingression takes a peculiar form in the case of some events; in a sense, it is a more concentrated form. For example, the electron has a certain position in space and a certain shape. . . . and the cook is in the kitchen. I will call this special form of ingression the 'relation of situation'; also, by a double use of the word 'situation,' I will call the event in which an object is situated 'the situation of the object' (CN 146–7).

Thus, situation is treated as a special form of the relation of ingression.

According to this usage an object is ingredient in events in which it is not situated. Indeed every object seems to be ingredient in every event, though in many events its ingredience will be very unimportant:

> An object is ingredient throughout its neighborhood, and its neighborhood is indefinite. Also the modification of events by ingression is susceptible of quantitative differences. Finally therefore we are driven to admit that each object is in some

sense ingredient throughout nature; though its ingression may be quantitatively irrelevant in the expression of our individual experiences (CN 145).

For example, the electron has a "field." Indeed, "the object in its completeness [in the case of scientific objects] may be conceived as a specific set of correlated modifications of the characters of all events, with the property that these modifications attain to a certain focal property for those events which belong to the stream of its situations" (CN 190). Similarly, "The waves as they roll on to the Cornish coast tell us of a gale in mid-Atlantic; and our dinner witnesses to the ingression of the cook into the dining room" (CN 146).

It is clear that the cook is not in the dining room in the same way she is in the kitchen. Another way of putting the point is in terms of the "significance" of events and objects. The dinner here *signifies* the cook there.

Now we may ask whether being an ingredient in events is an essential property of objects. It would seem so: "Nature is such that there can be no events and no objects without the ingression of objects into events" (CN 144; see PNK 202). And we may ask further whether all objects are situated? In addition to the general relation of ingression, does *every* object have the relation of situation (which relates the object in a special way to *some* events)?

In general Whitehead's discussions clearly suggest that all objects are situated. It seems that it is of the essence of an object to be situated *somewhere*. For example, "The connexion of objects with space requires elucidation. Objects are situated in events" (CN 160). It is entirely clear that all *sense objects* are situated. "When we perceive green, it is not green in isolation, it is green somewhere at some time. . . . it is essential that we see it somewhere in space related to our eyes at a certain epoch of our bodily life" (PRIN R 24–5; see CN 15). And in the accounts of *perceptual objects* it is constantly implied that they have situations. For example, "A perceptual object is a physical object when (i) its situation is an active conditioning event for the ingression of any of its component sense-objects, and (ii) the same event can be the situation of the perceptual object for an indefinite number of possible percipient events" (CN 156). Indeed in *The Principle of Relativity* and in "Uniformity and Contingency" the relation of a perceptual object to its situation is a "stronger" relation than that of sense objects to their situations. "A perceptual object is a true Aristotelian adjective of some event which is its situation" (ESP [1923] 145). *Scientific objects* are also situated. For example, "The situation of an electron in any small duration may be defined as that event which has the quantitative character which is the charge of the electron" (CN 159). Put another way, the field of an electron is divisible into the "occupied events" and the "unoccupied events." And "The occupied event corresponds to the situation of a physical object" (PNK 96). Thus it seems clear that sense objects, perceptual objects, and scientific objects are all situated. It is not essential that an object be situated in *this* event or in *that* event. It is essential that it be situated in some event or other.[5]

It would be possible to look at objects generally as "qualities" of events instead of as "ingredient in" events, but this would suggest that an object has no reference to entities other than the event it qualifies. Whitehead wishes to avoid this suggestion and therefore prefers to speak of ingression instead of qualification. The relation between an object and events is not a simple two-termed relation, as of quality to substance, but a many-termed relation. "The oversimplification involved in the Aristotelian concept of 'quality-subject' has obscured the analysis of ingression" (PNK 204. See PNK 60, 84; CN 151; PA 219; TSM 52; and Chapter 12 below).

Thus Whitehead is willing to use conventional language in-

5. Figures, patterns, and rhythms (PNK 190–200) all seem to be situated, though in different modes. On different modes of situation, see CN 160. The following passage needs comment: "The things recognised are what I call 'objects.' In this general sense of the term the relation of extension is itself an object. In practice however I restrict the term to those objects which can in some sense or other be said to have a situation in an event; namely, in the phrase 'There it is again' I restrict the 'there' to be the indication of a special event which is the situation of the object" (CN 189). Here extension is said to be an "object" in a more general sense of the term. It is ingredient in nature but not situated "in an event." There is no instance in which it appears in a more *concentrated* form.

cluding terms like "character," "quality," and "adjective" to describe the way objects are immanent in events. Indeed he *needs*
to use them, in order to introduce "ingression," because they are
familiar and—up to a point—enable us to analyze what we experience. But he thinks these terms get us into difficulties when
we try to give a clear and systematic account of nature. Therefore he elects to substitute "objects ingredient in events" for
"qualities [or characters] of events" as his basic concept.

As we have noticed, however, his new terminology is not itself
faultless. It brings its own misleading connotations, particularly
the phrase "ingression into events." [6] It is misleading insofar as it
suggests that objects enter an event from an antecedent locus. This
particular connotation of "ingression" has to be corrected by
reference to the more conventional terminology of "characteristic," and so on. No terms are proof against misleading suggestions.

There is a sense in which objects do "enter" into nature though
not, strictly speaking, into *events*. In nature new events become.[7]
In a new event certain objects will be ingredient. In this derivative
sense, objects might be said to "enter" nature. I now see blue,
though I did not see blue a moment ago. Blue has entered nature.
An event in which blue is ingredient has become. But blue has
not "entered" the event, because the event did not exist before
the blue, nor did the blue exist before the event. The blue is in
and with the event. "Thus nature is always a newness relating
objects which are neither new nor old" (PNK 98).

The notion of "entry" might also be defended on the score that
objects are transmitted from the past to the present. The blue I
did see a moment ago I now see again. Thus one might say the
blue has come into the present event from the past event. But
plainly this will not cover all cases of ingression. Sometimes I see
blue when I did not see blue a moment before. These suggestions
therefore do not free Whitehead's terminology from the taint of
being misleading, though he has certainly made a considerable
effort to be clear.

6. Note in the passage from CN 143-4 above: ". . . the ways in which
these objects make their ingression into the event."

7. But in his early writings Whitehead does not have a developed doctrine of novelty, because he has no developed doctrine of individuality.

4. Summary

It is now time to summarize Whitehead's doctrines, in the early writings, of how objects are immanent in events and how they transcend events.

Where do objects exist? The right answer is not "nowhere." Objects are not "out of space and time" in the sense that they exist nowhere. The right answer is "in events." Objects exist nowhere but in events, and there are no objects which are not ingredient in events. Indeed, by significance, every object exists in every event. Against the idealists Whitehead insists that objects are "there" to be recognized. Objects are really in events. Nor is the right answer "everywhere." This is too simple. An object is not ingredient in all events in the same sense and in the same way. The significance of an object will not be the same for all events and will differ in importance according to the event considered. Further, in addition to its varying significance throughout nature, the object is "situated" in some events and not in others.

Indeed, when we ask, where do objects exist? we are likely to mean, Where are objects situated? And the answer to this more specific question is not "nowhere" or "everywhere" nor simply "in events" but rather "here and there." Any object will exist in this sense at *some* wheres and not at others. Objects are situated in certain events, where they happen to be found, and not in others.

Similarly we ask, *When* do objects exist? In general the answer is not "never." Nor is the right answer "always." The general answer, again, is "in events." And when we ask more specifically, When are objects situated? the answer is clearly "now and then." Objects exist in events when they happen to be found. Thus objects are ingredient in, and in this sense present at, particular where-whens. This is one sense in which objects are *in* space and time.

Now we ask, *How* are objects in events? One relevant answer would be "as a whole." Objects do not have spatiotemporal "parts" and are not *included* (in a spatiotemporal sense) in events. An object is ingredient "as a whole" in an event. It cannot be ingredient "in part" for it has no spatiotemporal parts. This is the "atomic" property of objects which contrasts with the continuity of events. An object is either situated in an event or it is not. It is either there-then or not there-then for any finite there-then. In a given event the object is either situated "as a whole," in this non-spatial sense of "whole," or it is not situated in that event.

Now we ask, Can any object be anywhere at any time? Here we move from the immanence of objects to the transcendence of objects. The answer is "yes, as far as objects themselves are concerned." Objects *are* at certain times and places. But their natures do not require that they be at any of those times and places at which they are. An object must be *somewhere*, but there is no particular event where the object must be, as far as the object itself is concerned. An object is relatively (though not absolutely) independent of events.

This Whitehead would say is the foundation of empiricism. "Red" or "chair" is just where and only where we find it, and we find it not by inspecting "red" or "chair" but only by looking around us. It is the business of science to discover and describe precisely the conditions under which objects of various sorts are found.

But there is no "realm" of objects, in the sense of some extra-natural locus outside space and time, from which objects might be said to "enter" events. There is no "where," other than events, and there is no "when," other than events, in which objects exist. So objects transcend events, not by having a different "where" and a different "when" from those of events, and not by having a different *kind* of "where" and "when," but rather by having a different set of relations to "wheres" and "whens."

Anyone who comes to Whitehead's early writings expecting a Platonic philosophy of science is likely to invest his objects with ideal and ethereal qualities. On closer inspection they lose these qualities and are seen as natural entities. There is no doubt that objects transcend events. But "transcendence" here does not mean either "unrelatedness" or "absence." Objects are not only related to events but present in events in specifiable ways:

a. Objects are not "nowhere." They are present at particular where-whens, though unlike events they are multiply located and may be at other where-whens as well.

b. Objects "pervade" the events in which they are present, though unlike events they do not exclude other objects from being present in these events.

c. Objects have spatiotemporal relations with one another, though only mediately or derivatively by way of their situations in events.

The immanence of objects in events in these ways balances and complements the way in which objects transcend events.

CHAPTER 11

Eternal Objects and Actual Entities

To be abstract is to transcend particular concrete occasions of actual
happening. But to transcend an actual occasion does not mean being
disconnected from it (SMW 221).

1. Introduction

As WE MOVE from Whitehead's earlier writings to the later ones
we find that while he does not withdraw from his major positions,
he goes beyond them. He is now painting on a larger canvas. He is
devising a system of concepts to interpret all of the items of experience, no longer restricting himself to "the data of science."
It will not be a surprise to find that in the larger setting eternal
objects have functions which objects did not have. We shall also
find continuity between the earlier and the later theories.

Whitehead's formal or categoreal definitions of eternal objects
are:

> [Category of existence v] Eternal Objects, *or* Pure Potentials
> for the Specific Determination of Fact, *or* Forms of Definite-
> ness (PR 32).

> [Category of explanation vii] That an eternal object can be
> described only in terms of its potentiality for 'ingression' into
> the becoming of actual entities; and that its analysis only
> discloses other eternal objects. It is a pure potential. The
> term 'ingression' refers to the particular mode in which the
> potentiality of an eternal object is realized in a particular
> actual entity, contributing to the definiteness of that actual
> entity (PR 34).

Whitehead coins the term "eternal object" to avoid certain connotations attached to terms in current usage. One such term is

"universal" (SMW 221). Chapters 12 and 13 will examine the ways in which Whitehead's theory of eternal objects diverges from what he takes to be the traditional theory of universals. "Form," "idea," and "essence" ("as used by the Critical Realists"), all suggest meanings different from what he intends. "Accordingly, by way of employing a term devoid of misleading suggestions, I use the phrase 'eternal object' for what in the preceding paragraph of this section I have termed a 'Platonic form' " (PR 70).

The choice of the term is not haphazard, for eternal objects are clearly lineal descendants of *objects* as conceived in the earlier writings. Eternal objects are abstract and unextended, have multiple ingression, and coincide, contrasting with the concreteness, extendedness, single location, and noncoincidence of actual entities, as objects contrasted in these ways with events.[1] Furthermore, just as objects and events were Whitehead's fundamental constructive categories in his earlier philosophy of science, so eternal objects and actual entities are the "fundamental types of entities" in his later cosmology (PR 37).[2]

In the later writings the unqualified term "object" takes on a more general meaning. It is no longer the name for entities of a single categoreal type, as it was earlier. Even then Whitehead had found it difficult to manage objects of all sorts within a single category. Now it becomes a functional term. In general anything is an object when it is the datum of a prehension (PR 89, 327). Thus entities of various categoreal types may and do function as objects. "There are four main types of objects, namely 'eternal objects,' 'propositions,' 'objectified' actual entities and nexūs" (PR 82). An "enduring object" is a nexus with a certain complicated sort of structure (PR 50).

In Whitehead's earliest use of "eternal object" (SMW 122) he explains the sense of "eternal." In order to analyze nature, he says, we have to take account of *change,* and we have to take account of *endurance.* In addition, we have to take account of a

1. Unlike events, however, actual entities can be compared. For actual entities are real individuals, as events are not, and retain their identity even in objectification. Also actual entities are "atomic," as events are not. They are minimal events; no actual entity includes another.

2. See PR 33, 239, 287, but notice a qualification in MT 95–6.

third fact, namely *eternality*, which is different from both change and endurance. "The mountain endures. . . . A colour is eternal. It haunts time like a spirit. It comes and it goes. But where it comes, it is the same colour. It neither survives nor does it live" (SMW 121). Eternal objects, then, are objects which neither change nor endure.

Some observations about Whitehead's usage of the phrase "eternal objects" and its equivalents will prepare the way for further explanation of his meaning. In *Science and the Modern World* (1925) and in *Time* (1926), "eternal objects" is used systematically. In *Religion in the Making* (1926) "eternal objects" does not occur. Some equivalent expressions used there are: forms, ideal forms, abstract forms, ideal forms of possibility, ideals, possibilities. In *Symbolism* (1927) "eternal objects" does not occur and exact equivalents are rare. They include: abstractions, abstract attributes, qualities and relations, forms. In *The Function of Reason* (1929) "eternal objects" does not occur. Equivalents, rarely used, are: forms, forms of experience, forms of realization, forms of definiteness. In *Process and Reality* (1929) "eternal objects" is used systematically and is always the *standard* term. In those parts of the book which apply the categoreal scheme to special problems and relate it to other philosophical systems, equivalents occur. Some of these (in addition to those contained in the categoreal definitions) are: forms, abstract forms, possibilities, potentialities of definiteness, abstract potentialities. Such equivalents occur more frequently in Part II than elsewhere. In those parts of the book where Whitehead is rigorously developing and explaining his scheme, equivalents occur rarely, for example chapter 9 in Part II, and Part III generally.

In *Adventures of Ideas* (1933) "eternal objects" occurs only a half dozen times, all but one of these occurrences being concentrated in three pages (312–14). Equivalents are: ideas, ideals, ideal possibilities, abstractions, abstract possibilities, modes of possibility. In *Modes of Thought* (1938) "eternal objects" does not occur. Equivalents are: forms, forms of potentiality, forms of composition (of transition, etc.), eternal forms, possibilities, abstractions, potential forms, and other variants. In the last lectures ("Mathematics and the Good" and "Immortality"), and in the essays published in *Essays in Science and Philosophy*, "eternal objects" does not occur. Equivalents such as "forms" and "possibilities" are rare.

In summary:

a. "Eternal objects" is *standard* usage in, but only in, *Science and the Modern World, Time,* and *Process and Reality.*

b. "Eternal objects" *occurs* elsewhere only in *Adventures of Ideas.*

c. Whitehead has no *standard* equivalent for "eternal objects," though many equivalents occur.

d. "Eternal objects" supplants all equivalents in the more rigorous [3] statements of Whitehead's scheme.

2. Whitehead's criticism of Platonic forms

The categoreal definitions of eternal objects suggest that, at least as a first approach, they can be understood as *possibilities* (PR 226). So understood, the contrast between actual entities and eternal objects is a restatement of a contrast which had occupied Whitehead's mind throughout his philosophical reflections, namely the contrast between actuality and possibility.[4]

His main intention is to keep a firm contrast between actuality and possibility, and to maintain both as fundamental and final categories of thought. He is resistant therefore to any philosophical tendency to absorb either of these categories in the other. It is in connection with this philosophical resolution that his criticism of the Platonic theory of forms is best understood.

Whitehead's admiration for Plato's imaginative power, his faith in rational harmony, and his speculative boldness is plain enough (PR 63, 142–7; FR 7, 29; AI 187–98). And he is aware of the difference between the Plato of the *Phaedo* and the *Republic* and the Plato of the *Philebus* and the *Sophist* (AI 354; MT 126, 132–3; DIAL 217). He says he is indebted to the writings of A. E. Taylor (PR ix, 68; AI viii) for his interpretation of Plato. So he knows, as he often

3. What Whitehead says of *Modes of Thought* applies to most of his writing after *Process and Reality* except a few chapters in *Adventures of Ideas:* "In these lectures I have not entered upon systematic metaphysical cosmology" (MT 231).

4. For a very early expression of this contrast see OT 188. For late expressions see MT 95–6, 136.

says, that the view he selects for criticism is not the whole Plato. Our own concern is not with the historical adequacy of Whitehead's remarks but with the light they throw on his theory of eternal objects.

His criticism centers on the view, which does in fact appear in the dialogues and by a long tradition has been identified with Plato, that the forms are perfect and self-sustaining. According to this view forms exist in a realm separate from the realm of things and are independent of the things that become and perish. They have real being, exempt from becoming. They are therefore "perfect." They have no necessary reference beyond themselves. They are the standard of being, to which things in the world of becoming may approximate in greater or lesser degree. Things are real to the degree that they imitate the changelessness and self-sufficient perfection of forms. Things are thus shadows of forms. This ascription of "perfection" to forms is, in Whitehead's judgment, the "error" which "haunted Plato in respect to his Ideas" (IMM 696. See PR 318–19; AI 354; MT 92–5, 109–13, 126, 138).

One way of putting Whitehead's objection is to say that this Platonic view absorbs actuality into possibility. Actuality evaporates from the world of things. This world becomes infected with unreality. Whitehead holds on the contrary that nothing is more real than temporal individuals. The ontological principle and the principle of process run counter to the Platonic view. For this view the locus of being is "there." For Whitehead the locus of being is "here." Therefore he rejects "the feeble Platonic doctrine of 'imitation'" (IMM 686). It leads to a "vicious separation" of permanence from flux. "Such philosophies must include the notion of 'illusion' as a fundamental principle—the notion of '*mere* appearance.' This is the final platonic problem" (PR 526).

Whitehead blames this otherworldliness of Plato, as we might call it, on his fascination with mathematical ideas. "Plato in the earlier period of his thought, deceived by the beauty of mathematics intelligible in unchanging perfection, conceived of a super-world of ideas, forever perfect and forever interwoven" (AI 354). Whitehead's own view of mathematics is "that mathematics is concerned with certain forms of process issuing into forms which are components for further process." So he offers "a belated reminder to Plato that his eternal mathematical forms are essentially referent to process" (MT 126).

Whatever the cause, the result was unfortunate for both cosmology and theology:

> When Plato is faced with the problem of expressing the relationship of God to the World, and of the relation to the World of those Ideas which it is in God's nature to contemplate, Plato's answer is invariably framed in terms of mere dramatic imitation. When Plato turns to the World, after considering God as giving life and motion to the ideas by the inclusion of them in the divine nature, he can find only second-rate substitutes and never the originals. For Plato there is a derivative second-rate God of the World, who is a mere Icon, that is to say an image. Also when he looks for the ideas, he can only find, in the World, imitations. Thus the World, for Plato, includes only the image of God, and imitations of his ideas, and never God and his ideas (AI 215).

For Whitehead has committed himself to a realistic view of the world of process. He refuses therefore to identify permanence with reality and process with unreality. Instead he holds, as we saw in Part One, that particular processes of concrescence and satisfaction are reality. This is clearly Whitehead's platform and program. On this basis he must regard the outcome of Plato's theory of forms as an unfortunate and erroneous theory of reality.[5]

We might therefore construe Whitehead's contrast between actuality and possibility as a correction of Plato's contrast between things and forms, and as a substitute for the contrast between Being and becoming. This construction may be developed in the following way:

a. Forms are possibilities. A form defines how something might be actual. It is a form of definiteness of actuality. Thus its very meaning contains an essential reference to actuality, though to actuality generally. An eternal object is "a *form for* realization" (FR 26).

5. We must ask, in Part Three, whether Whitehead's theory of God and the world reintroduces the notion of an "eminent reality," which he here rejects.

b. Things are actualities. The particular things which exist in space and time are the final realities. They are real individuals. Their involvement in process, both in the internal process of concrescence and in the external process of transition, does not mean involvement in unreality. They are not mere imitations of forms.

c. Thus it is truer to say that forms participate in (are ingredient in) things (PR 30, 63, 481), than to say that things participate in forms.

d. In a sense therefore actuality is primary over possibility. This may be illustrated from the following passage: "The explanatory purpose of philosophy is often misunderstood. Its business is to explain the emergence of the more abstract things from the more concrete things. . . . In other words, philosophy is explanatory of abstraction, and not of concreteness. It is by reason of their instinctive grasp of this ultimate truth that, in spite of much association with arbitrary fancifulness and atavistic mysticism, types of Platonic philosophy retain their abiding appeal; they seek the forms in the facts" (PR 30). We begin with the concrete, with actuality (PR 223, 321). Possibilities are abstractions from actuality. The correction of the Platonic view of forms would consist, we might say, of underlining "in the facts" in the last sentence of the above passage. Where Plato made forms primary over things, Whitehead makes actuality primary over possibility.

e. Yet, in participating in things, forms do not lose their character as potentials. They continue to transcend things by their suggestions of alternatives avoided (PR 225–6). This thing might have had other forms. What is red might have been green. And other things may have *this* form. Other things may also be red. Thus actuality does not "absorb" possibility. Possibility still transcends actuality. For any situation there are possibilities which are not actual. There are always unactualized possibilities.

f. Neither forms nor things have Being, in the sense of self-sufficient perfection. Whitehead's principle of relativity [6] is a clear rejection of this concept of Being. Instead, "it belongs to the nature of a 'being' that it is a potential for every 'becoming' " (PR 33). Every possibility is a possibility of actualization. Every ac-

6. Which Whitehead himself connects with the Plato of the *Sophist* (see AI 230, 254).

tuality is a concrescence of many other entities into a novel unity and in turn becomes an element in other actualities.

In this way, for Whitehead, the contrast between actuality and possibility supplants the Platonic contrast between Being and becoming, and corrects the Platonic contrast between forms and things. (i) Forms are possibilities, not Being. (ii) Actuality is process, not Being. Thus he avoids not only Plato's attribution of perfection to form, and the consequent absorption of actuality into possibility, but also Spinoza's absorption of possibility into actuality. Actuality is ever incomplete and beyond it are unrealized possibilities. In one way or in the other, in Plato's way or Spinoza's, the contrast between actuality and possibility would be weakened or destroyed. This contrast Whitehead means to maintain and strengthen. There are always unactualized possibilities. And actuality—temporal, finite, concrete, individual being—is real being, not a mere imitation or reflection of pure form.[7]

3. Pure possibility

I suggested that the notion of possibility is the key to an understanding of Whitehead's theory of eternal objects (PR 226). But here as elsewhere he finds current usage inadequate for his purposes. It would be misleading to translate "an eternal object" simply as "a possibility."

This is because the latter term is vague, and "the vagueness of philosophical terminology" (AI 294) is why Whitehead develops his own categoreal scheme. "A possibility" might mean (a) a general or abstract form. For example, "red" or "four" or "being first in a series." Or it might mean (b) a hypothetical state of affairs, that is, the possibility that some form is or will be realized in a particular time and place. For example, "The Red Sox will win the pennant this year," or "The Orioles will win the pennant this year." Both statements describe possible states of affairs. Here a distinction is necessary. We say, "It is *really* possible that the Red

7. Whitehead's theory of actuality and possibility, as here construed, is a rejection of "the principle of plenitude" as interpreted by Arthur O. Lovejoy. See *The Great Chain of Being* (Harvard University Press, 1953), p. 54.

Sox will win the pennant this year. But it is not *really* possible for
the Orioles to win the pennant. For even if they won all their remaining games, and their leading opponents lost all theirs, still
the Orioles would not win the pennant." Thus "a possibility"
might mean (c) a *real* possibility in contrast with a hypothetical
possibility, that is, a state of affairs which the circumstances *permit*.
It is a real possibility that the Red Sox will win the pennant this
year. It is not a real possibility, under the circumstances, that the
Orioles will win the pennant this year.

Now Whitehead wants to distinguish among these various meanings of possibility so as to avoid confusions. He does so as follows:

a. *Eternal objects* are "pure potentials." They are "pure" possibilities in that they do not refer to or describe any particular
state of affairs, actual or hypothetical. An eternal object is a
"mere" potentiality (PR 280). They are completely "indeterminate"
as to their realization in some state of affairs or other. They express a "general potentiality" (PR 101–2) unrestricted by any particular state of affairs. There is no reference to any particular
actuality, though they contain a reference to actuality in general.
They are "possibles."

b. *Propositions* are "impure potentials" (PR 33). They describe
hypothetical states of affairs. They are thus not "pure" possibilities. Nor are they "pure" actualities. They are "hybrid" or "impure" entities, for the statement of a proposition involves reference both to particular actualities and to pure possibilities (PR
35, ch. 9 in Pt. II, and ch. 4 in Pt. III).

c. *Real potentiality* is the limited, "natural" (SYMBOLISM 36)
potentiality, relative to some particular state of affairs or actual
world, which is permitted by the circumstances of that actual
world. The hypothetical state of affairs expressed in a proposition
is *really* possible if, relative to a given subject which entertains it,
this state of affairs is compatible with the subject's past actual
world (PR 34, 101–2, 340). The past actual world of a concrescent
subject determines what is really possible, relative to that subject.
Thus, under the circumstances, the proposition expressed in the
statement that the Orioles will win the pennant this year is not
a real possibility.

At present we are particularly concerned with pure potentials, and that is to say with eternal objects. To throw light on White-head's theory of pure possibility I shall first cite some examples of eternal objects mentioned in his writings. Then I shall discuss how eternal objects transcend and are immanent in, actual entities.

4. Examples of eternal objects

Whitehead does not give a comprehensive and exhaustive clas-sification of eternal objects anywhere in his later writings. The distinction he makes most use of is between eternal objects of the subjective species and eternal objects of the objective species (PR 445–8). But while no doubt any eternal object belongs to one or the other of these classes, his writings suggest, but do not develop, other modes of classification. I shall not myself attempt to give a firm and clear classification of all the types of eternal objects. But we may notice a passage in which several examples of eternal ob-jects are suggested: "These 'eternal objects' are Locke's ideas as explained in his *Essay* (I, I, 1), where he writes: '. . . men have in their mind several ideas, such as those expressed by the words, "whiteness, hardness, sweetness, thinking, motion, man, elephant, army, drunkenness," and others' " (PR 82). Whitehead adds that in other passages Locke mentions "ideas" of a quite different sort, not to be interpreted as eternal objects.

Next I present a very roughly ordered inventory of those types of eternal objects which Whitehead explicitly mentions as such. I list them without attempting to decide at every point how they are to be related to one another.

a. "Sensa" (PR 100, 174), for example green and blue (SMW 36, 233; AI 322) and definite shades of colors (SMW 232; PR 132–3, 202).

b. Eternal objects of the subjective species (PR 445–8), that is, universals of quality (Chapter 12 below). Sensa functioning as qualities of emotion, for example redness (PR 447). Qualities of shapes (AI 49, 326), of intensity (PR 446). Belief-character (PR 408), "loved" and "coldly esteemed" (PR 226), bad temper (PR 100), happiness (AI 50). A subjective form in abstraction from its feel-ing is a complex eternal object (PR 356).

c. Eternal objects of the objective species, that is mathematical forms in the strict modern sense of mathematics (PR 445–8; AI 326), for example triplicity (AI 322).

d. The "eternal objects designated by the words 'any' and 'just that' " (PR 245).

e. Patterns (PR 175, 356–8) and relations (PR 295, MT 100, Chapter 12 below).

f. The abstract essence of an actual occasion (PR 93).

g. General principles, as color (PR 295).

h. Forms of imperfection. Speaking of the notion of perfection he says, "its naive attachment to the realm of forms is entirely without justification. How about the form of mud, and the forms of evil, and other forms of imperfection? In the house of forms, there are many mansions" (MT 94). (I do not think this echo of the *Parmenides* is to be taken as ironical. His main point is that a form is not more "perfect" than a thing.)

i. Grades of generic abstraction, for example: scarlet, red, color, sense datum, manner of connectedness of diverse sense data (PR 202).

This list, I repeat, is not a systematic account of the realm of eternal objects. Indeed, in Chapters 13 and 14 we shall explore a reason why a systematization of types of eternal objects would be impossible. As we shall see, "the variation in the grades of ideas is endless" (IMM 692). Nor is it a comprehensive account. A more comprehensive account might be constructed by adding entities which Whitehead would no doubt call eternal objects but are not explicitly so called in his writings, for example Truth, Beauty, Adventure, Art, and Peace as discussed in the last part of *Adventures of Ideas,* which are there called qualities (AI 367). But "in the house of forms, there are many mansions," and it would be impossible to give a completely comprehensive list of types of eternal objects. My object is only to mention *some* of the entities Whitehead explicitly calls eternal objects, so the reader may have some examples in mind, and to indicate roughly the range of the term.

5. How eternal objects transcend actual entities

Three preliminary considerations are in order. The first is that the kind of transcendence we are now considering is a relation between entities of different categoreal *types.* In this way it is unlike the transcendence of one actual occasion by another, and unlike the transcendence of actual occasions by God. In those cases transcendence is a relation between entities of the same categoreal type. Here, on the contrary, as with objects and events in Chapter 10, we are concerned with entities of different categoreal types. We ask how any and every entity of one type transcends any and every entity of the other categoreal type.

Second, "actual entities" refers to God as well as to actual occasions. For it is clear that eternal objects are categoreally transcendent of God as well as of actual occasions. Whitehead says,

> The forms belong no more to God than to any one actual occasion (RM 157).

> Now an eternal object, in itself, abstracts from all determinate actual entities, including even God (PR 392).

He says "even God" because, while any actual occasion will prehend only some, not all, eternal objects (PR 69, 335), God prehends all eternal objects in his primordial nature. Even so, the *being* of eternal objects does not depend on the existence of God.

In the third place, we must remember that for Whitehead there is no absolute transcendence. The various modes of reality, or categories of existence, require each other (MT 95–6). There is no absolutely independent existence (IMM 696). In the next section we shall see how eternal objects are immanent in actual entities. Here and throughout Whitehead's system transcendence and immanence are not mutually exclusive categories. If M transcends N, it does not follow that M is not immanent in N. Instead, in any of their applications one of these relations limits and balances the other.

There are three ways in which eternal objects transcend actual entities. Eternal objects are timeless, indeterminate as to their realization, and abstract. Actual entities are temporal, determinate, and concrete.

a. *Eternal objects are timeless; actual entities are temporal.* "Eternality," as we have seen, does not mean endurance (SMW 121, 147–8). Though eternal objects express a kind of "permanence" (PR 44), the kind of permanence they express is not persistence through a duration of time, but timelessness (PR 64, 514; MT 64; IMM 688). What does this mean?

i. This is to say, for one thing, that eternal objects do not come into being or pass out of being. "The eternal objects are the same for all actual entities" (PR 34). Throughout the course of nature there are no changes in the membership of the multiplicity of eternal objects. No new members of the multiplicity are gained, and none are lost. A "novel form" (PR 356) would mean a form hitherto *unrealized* in actuality, not a novel possibility *added* to the infinite multiplicity of eternal objects. It is "an old form in a new function" (PR 284). "There are no novel eternal objects" (PR 33).

ii. In the second place this means that any eternal object is unaffected, in itself, by its "adventures" (PR 92) in the actual world. Eternal objects have their being *as* possibilities for realization in the world of passage (MT 95). But the "individual essence" (SMW 222, PR 251) of an eternal object is not affected by its realization, or lack of realization, in any particular actual entity.

In these senses eternal objects are timeless. Actual entities, on the contrary, are temporal in both of these senses. New actual entities are always coming into being.[8] In the second place, every actual entity (including God) is affected by the passage of nature (transition), and its being is *constituted* by its becoming (concrescence) (PR 34–5). Thus process is external to eternal objects but internal to actual entities.

In a striking sentence Whitehead says, "Every actual entity is 'in time' so far as its physical pole is concerned, and is 'out of time' so far as its mental pole is concerned. It is the union of two worlds, namely the temporal world, and the world of autonomous valuation" (PR 380). This "out of time" is misleading unless it is qualified. For the valuations of the mental pole of an actual occasion occur at a certain time and place. They are the conceptual feelings of that subject there-then. These valuations are "out of time" only in the sense that the *data* of these feelings, eternal objects, are timeless in the ways explained above. God's conceptual prehensions are timeless in a stronger sense, as we shall see in Part Three.

8. There is one actual entity which is always in being, namely God, by virtue of his primordial nature. Yet God is always in process of concrescence, by virtue of his consequent nature. In this way God "combines the actuality of what is temporal with the timelessness of what is potential" (PR 64).

b. *Eternal objects are indeterminate; actual entities are determinate.* Here the indetermination of an eternal object means indetermination as to its ingressions. "In the essence of each eternal object there stands an indeterminateness which expresses its indifferent patience for any mode of ingression into any actual occasion" (SMW 240). It does not mean indeterminateness of its "individual essence." For an eternal object does have a "definite self-identity" (PR 251). What is indeterminate about an eternal object is not its "individual essence" but its realization in the actual world. In this respect an eternal object is wholly indeterminate. "An eternal object is always a potentiality for actual entities; but in itself, as conceptually felt, it is neutral as to the fact of its physical ingression in any particular actual entity of the temporal world" (PR 70). This is to say that, given any actual entity A and any eternal object R, there is no necessity in the nature of R that it should be a form of definiteness of the physical actuality of A, and there is no necessity in the nature of R that it should *not* be a form of definiteness of the physical actuality of A. An eternal object is a *capacity* for being realized in *any* actual entity. In this its transcendence of actuality, as a pure potential, consists (PR 366–7). "Its analysis only discloses other eternal objects" (PR 34). ". . . an eternal object refers only to the purely general *any* among the undetermined actual entities. In itself an eternal object evades any selection among actualities or epochs. You cannot know what is red by merely thinking of redness. You can only find red things by adventuring amid physical experiences in *this* actual world. This doctrine is the ultimate ground of empiricism; namely, that eternal objects tell no tales as to their ingressions" (PR 391; see 174–5, 392–3, 444).

In contrast, actual entities are determinate. As we have seen, the result of the process of concrescence is a fully determinate satisfaction. Determinateness is of the essence of actuality; indeterminateness as to physical realization is of the essence of pure potentiality.

c. *Eternal objects are abstract; actual entities are concrete.* We saw in Chapter 2 how actual entities are concrete. Eternal objects on the contrary are abstract. "Abstraction" is the title of the chapter on eternal objects in *Science and the Modern World* (see

RM 156; PR 48, 300, 392, 421; AI 49; MT 91, 135–6). Thus Whitehead continues and develops a theme introduced in his earlier writings, where the abstractness of objects is contrasted with the concreteness of events.

Abstraction, as a process of thought, is a disjoining (MT 171) of entities which are in fact joined. It thus contrasts with the process of concrescence, in which entities are brought into a novel togetherness and become *concrete* (SMW 244, AI 303). An abstraction is an entity considered apart from some of the roles or functions it has in the actual world. Since it is not possible, in a finite and conditioned act of experience, to prehend *all* of the functions of any entity in nature, thought essentially involves abstraction.

Now as soon as we abstract we "necessarily introduce the notion of potentiality" (MT 136). We are considering what *might* be apart and what *might* be together. A *pure* potential, an eternal object, is an entity reached at a certain extreme of abstraction, namely abstraction from its realization in *any* particular actual entity. Even so, this is not *complete* abstraction (PR 392).

A complete abstraction would be an entity considered apart from *all* of the functions it has in the actual world. Complete abstraction would mean ignoring *all* of the relations of the entity to other entities. Thus a completely abstract entity, in this sense, would be an entity existing in absolute independence of any other entity. If the possibility of complete abstraction is admitted, then absolute transcendence is asserted. An entity which could be considered apart from any relation to any other entity or entities would be absolutely transcendent.

But Whitehead denies the possibility of complete abstraction and of absolute transcendence: "It follows from the fourth category of explanation [i.e. the principle of relativity] that the notion of 'complete abstraction' is self-contradictory. For you cannot abstract the universe from any entity, actual or non-actual, so as to consider that entity in complete isolation" (PR 42. See PR 321; MT 90–7, 168–70; IMM 685). How then is it possible to consider eternal objects "in themselves"? It is possible because, while the notion of an eternal object abstracts from the ingression of the eternal object in particular actual entities, it does not abstract from its general relation to actual entities. It is a possible form of definiteness of actuality. This *is* the eternal object as a pure potential. Consideration of an eternal object in itself therefore is not a complete abstraction but an incomplete one, and is thus in harmony with Whitehead's principle of relativity.

In these ways eternal objects transcend actual entities. These are ways of describing the fundamental contrast between actuality and pure potentiality in Whitehead's metaphysics. Now we turn to the complementary relationship of immanence and ask how eternal objects are immanent in actual entities. This is the "ingression" or "realization" of eternal objects.

6. How eternal objects are immanent in actual entities: Ingression

One point Whitehead wishes to make against the Platonic theory of forms is that eternal objects are really immanent in the temporal world, as well as transcendent of it. When Plato "looks for the ideas, he can only find, in the World, imitations" (AI 215). Whitehead's alternative principle is the Translucency of Realization. "By this I mean that any eternal object is just itself in whatever mode of realisation it is involved. There can be no distortion of the individual essence without thereby producing a different eternal object" (SMW 240). Therefore it is better to say that eternal objects "participate" in actual entities than that actual entities participate in eternal objects (PR 63, 481, 496). The "exemplification" of an eternal object in an actual entity needs to be understood with this translucency of realization in mind.[9] He does not mean that something *like* the eternal object is in the actual entity. And he does not mean that the actual entity is *like* the eternal object. He means that the eternal object itself, just itself, is in the actual entity as a "form of definiteness."

For this relation "ingression" is the standard term. It applies to the immanence of eternal objects in actual entities, as in the earlier writings it applied to the immanence of objects in events. The dynamic connotation of pre-existence and entry still needs

9. See PR 63, 444, 472; AI 313; MT 94. See also, on the "illustration" of eternal objects by actual entities, PR 38, 284, 295; AI 269. For the odd reverse expression, an actuality illustrated by eternal objects, see PR 447, AI 313, MT 75.

correction.[10] This correction is facilitated by Whitehead's frequent use of equivalents which do not carry these connotations. The most important of these are "realization" and "functioning." [11] These terms are employed more systematically than other equivalents in rigorous expositions of the categories.

Recurring to category of explanation vii, for example, "The term 'ingression' refers to the particular mode in which the potentiality of an eternal object is *realized* in a particular actual entity, contributing to the definiteness of that actual entity" (PR 34, my italics. See SMW 240, 246–7; AI 312; MT 122, 138, 229). Thus the ingression of an eternal object is its realization in some actual entity or entities. It is the realization of a pure potential. Similarly, from category of explanation xxiv, "The functioning of an eternal object in the self-creation of an actual entity is the 'ingression' of the eternal object in the actual entity" (PR 38). This needs to be taken in conjunction with category of explanation xx, as follows: "That to 'function' means to contribute determination to the actual entities in the nexus of some actual world" (PR 38). The "functioning" of an eternal object and its "ingression" are equivalent expressions (PR 249, 251, 445).

"Ingression" is Whitehead's way of saying that eternal objects are immanent in or present in or elements in (SMW 100) actual entities. The complete analysis of an actual entity would reveal eternal objects among the entities of various types that are present in its real internal constitution. This is the general meaning of "ingression." But there are different *modes* of ingression,[12] and to these we now turn.

10. A few other expressions with dynamic connotations occur in the later writings. For example: an eternal object is "a determinant of the datum" of a physical feeling (PR 249; see 364). "Determinant" here clearly means no more than "being a form of definiteness of," as the latter passage and categoreal obligation iv (PR 39–40) suggest. The expression that a form has an "activity" (MT 138) is to be understood in the same way. See below on the "functioning" of an eternal object.

11. For other equivalents see the references above on "participation," "exemplification," and "illustration." See also on "inclusion" SMW 238–9. An eternal object is "included" as an element in an actual entity. This is close to saying it is an ingredient in the actual entity.

12. Or modes of inclusion (SMW 238–9), modes of realization (SMW 240, 246–7), modes of functioning (PR 249, 445).

7. Modes of ingression

Whitehead gives two lists of modes of ingression. The earlier one is: "Hence, to sum up, there are four modes of functioning whereby an eternal object has ingression into the constitution of an actual entity: (i) as dative ingression, (ii) in conformal physical feeling, (iii) in conceptual feeling, (iv) in comparative feeling" (PR 249). The later one is simpler: "An eternal object can only function in the concrescence of an actual entity in one of three ways: (i) it can be an element in the definiteness of some objectified nexus, or of some single actual entity, which is the datum of a feeling; (ii) it can be an element in the definiteness of the subjective form of some feeling; or (iii) it can be an element in the datum of a conceptual, or propositional, feeling. All other modes of ingression arise from integrations which presuppose these modes" (PR 445).

The later list is simpler and clearer for two reasons. In the first place, ingression "in conformal feeling" (249 ii) simply means that one and the same eternal object is ingredient both in the datum of a physical feeling (as 249 i or 445 i) *and* in the subjective form of that feeling. Thus 249 i and 249 ii overlap. With this "relational" functioning in mind, the sentence introducing the later list should say: "in one *or more* of three ways." In the second place, the distinction between 249 iii and 249 iv is not needed. The distinction between conceptual feelings and comparative feelings (for example, feelings of propositions) is important in a genetic analysis of the concrescence. But the eternal objects that are felt function in the same mode, and for this 445 iii is sufficient.

Let us then take the later list of modes and adopt a more economical set of terms to express them. We might speak of: (i) dative ingression, (ii) subjective ingression,[13] and (iii) conceptual ingression. Eternal objects of the subjective species may have ingression in any of these three modes. Eternal objects of the ob-

---

13. In PR 249 "subjective ingression" includes 249 ii, 249 iii, and 249 iv. But there is something to be said for using it to mean ingression in the subjective forms of feelings in contrast to ingression in the data of feelings, whether the data be of physical or conceptual feelings. Whitehead himself does not use the phrase systematically.

jective species may have dative ingression or conceptual ingression but not subjective ingression (PR 445–8).

Do we need to add to this list another mode of ingression, namely "negative ingression"? Certainly there are negative prehensions of eternal objects. Indeed every actual occasion (though not God) has some negative prehensions of eternal objects. Do these prehensions constitute another *mode* in which eternal objects have ingression in actual entities? Speaking generally of an eternal object, Whitehead says, "Its own nature as an entity requires ingression—positive or negative—in every detailed actuality; but its nature does not disclose the private details of any actuality" (PR 444). He does not develop this incidental suggestion of an additional mode of ingression. And the suggestion is weakened by the point of the following passage: "Only a selection of eternal objects are 'felt' by a given subject, and these eternal objects are then said to have 'ingression' in that subject." This seems to imply that negatively prehended eternal objects do not have ingression. He adds, "those eternal objects which are not felt are not therefore negligible." The importance of negatively prehended eternal objects consists in the fact that "each negative prehension has its own subjective form, however trivial and faint" (PR 66; see 35).

Formally speaking, it is possible to regard a negatively prehended eternal object as having conceptual ingression. It is the datum of a conceptual feeling. The difficulty is that this datum has a very peculiar status. Hence there is justification for either treating negative prehensions of eternal objects as instances of ingression, or not. In either case there seems no good reason for introducing into our list a fourth *mode* of ingression.

8. Conceptual prehensions

The major contrast among the modes of ingression is between the two modes of physical ingression (dative ingression and subjective ingression) on the one hand, and conceptual ingression on the other. In this section we consider eternal objects as data of conceptual prehensions. In the next chapter we study the physical ingression of eternal objects.

Pure conceptual prehensions (PR 280; see 49) are the simplest forms of mental experience. We leave to one side the "higher phases of experience," including propositional feelings, physical purposes, intellectual feelings, conscious perceptions, and judgments (PR 391–428). These are phases by which the physical experience and the conceptual experience of an actual entity are synthesized into its satisfaction. Whitehead's treatment of these topics is extremely subtle and suggestive. But our attention must be focused on his theory of eternal objects more directly and more strictly. We limit ourselves to those instances of mentality where the data are eternal objects, that is to pure conceptual prehensions. These prehensions are so simple that consciousness is not necessarily involved in their subjective forms (PR 35).

The first point to notice is the origination of these prehensions in the process of concrescence. We begin with categories of obligation iv and v:

> (iv) *The Category of Conceptual Valuation.* From each physical feeling there is the derivation of a purely conceptual feeling whose datum is the eternal object determinant of the definiteness of the actual entity, or of the nexus, physically felt.

> (v) *The Category of Conceptual Reversion.* There is secondary origination of conceptual feelings with data which are partially identical with, and partially diverse from, the eternal objects forming the data in the first phase of the mental pole. The diversity is a relevant diversity determined by the subjective aim (PR 39–40; see 378–82).

These categories define the two "phases of conceptual origination" (PR 378) in the concrescence of an actual entity. In these ways "physical feelings give rise to conceptual feelings, and conceptual feelings give rise to other conceptual feelings" (PR 376). There are two sorts of physical prehensions from which conceptual prehensions are derived: pure physical feelings and hybrid physical feelings. "In a 'pure physical feeling' the actual entity which is the datum is objectified by one of its own physical feelings. . . . In a 'hybrid physical feeling' the actual entity forming the datum is objectified by one of its own conceptual feelings" (PR 375–6). Now from a hybrid physical feeling there will arise, in accord with the category of conceptual valuation, a pure conceptual feeling having as its datum the eternal object which was the datum of the objectified conceptual feeling. "A hybrid physical feeling originates for its subject a conceptual feeling with the same datum as that of the conceptual feeling of the antecedent subject" (PR 377). In this way eternal objects which had only conceptual ingression in the past, and not physical ingression, may enter the new concrescence by way of its mental pole.

Conceptual reversion is important because "novelty in the physical world, and error in authentic perceptive feeling, arise by conceptual functioning, according to the category of reversion" (PR 410). It is by reversion that the subject prehends eternal objects which have neither physical nor conceptual ingression in its past actual world. But it turns out that reversion is only a provisional explanation of the origination of novelty. Whitehead's fuller explanation of novelty requires his conception of God, which we study in Part Three.

According to this more complete explanation, pure conceptual prehensions originate in every case from prehensions of actual entities. But they are by no means simply faint copies of physical feelings. Mentality does not merely record or reflect what has been physically realized. On the contrary, mentality prehends possibilities which in the past actual world had been only conceptually entertained. Further, by way of hybrid physical feelings of God, mentality introduces possibilities which were neither physically realized nor conceptually entertained in the past actual world. Mentality is in this way the "organ of novelty" (FR 26).

We should now look more closely at the way eternal objects function as data of pure conceptual prehensions. This should make it clearer how mental operations—even in their simplest forms—differ from the operations which constitute physical experience. The contrast before us is between "unrestricted" (physical) ingression and "restricted" (conceptual) ingression (PR 445). Otherwise expressed it is between the "complete ingredience" or "complete inclusion" (SMW 237) and the "abrupt realisation" (SMW 246) of eternal objects in actual entities. In unrestricted ingression eternal objects are functioning as forms of definiteness of data of physical feelings (dative ingression), *or* as forms of definiteness of subjective forms of feeling (subjective ingression). Unrestricted ingression is the full physical realization of eternal objects, objectively or subjectively.

Restricted or conceptual ingression, on the other hand, is ingression "with mere potentiality withholding the immediate realization of its function of conferring definiteness" (PR 445). Restricted ingression therefore involves a kind of negation. "Conceptual feeling is the feeling of an unqualified negation; that is to say, it is the feeling of a definite eternal object with the definite extrusion of any particular realization" (PR 372). The eternal object is felt as *not* physically realized, that is to say as a pure potentiality. It is felt as a potentiality *for* realization. It is something which *might be* a form of definiteness of the datum of a physical prehension or of the subjective form of a prehension. But in conceptual ingression it is felt in the generality of its potentiality and as *not* physically realized.

As a datum of a conceptual prehension then, an eternal object has a role different from that of an eternal object prehended, in a "physical purpose" (PR 406), *as* physically realized in a given actual entity. This role also contrasts with that of an eternal object in a "proposition," where it is a potential form of definiteness of some particular nexus of actual entities. A proposition is an "impure potential" (PR 32, 287). A pure conceptual prehension might have as its datum, for example, "red nowhere in particular." A propositional feeling might have as its datum, for example, *"that might be red."* Thus, while conceptual feeling is the feeling of an "unqualified" negation, a propositional feeling "involves (as one side of a contrast) a qualified negative determined to some definite situation" (PR 372).

The negation involved in conceptual feelings must not be confused with the negation involved in negative prehensions. A negative prehension "holds its datum as inoperative" in the concrescence in which the prehension occurs (PR 35). The datum of a conceptual feeling (a positive conceptual prehension) is not "withheld" but has a positive function in the concrescence. The negation involved in conceptual feelings is not a negation of the *function* of the datum in the concrescence. Negation enters into feeling as a property of the datum itself. The datum of a negative conceptual prehension is *not* "felt." The datum of a conceptual feeling is positively felt as *not* physically realized. Mental experience is "the experience of forms of definiteness in respect to their disconnection from any particular physical experience, but with abstract evaluation of what they *can* contribute to such experience" (FR 26).

9. Why eternal objects are needed

This becomes two questions, to be answered in succession: (a) How do Whitehead's other categories require eternal objects? (b) Why does he adopt a set of categories which includes eternal objects? The first question has to do with the coherence of Whitehead's system; the second with the facts which his categories are devised to interpret. The first question calls for reasons internal to the categoreal scheme; the second for reasons external to the categoreal scheme.

a. The fundamental categories of the scheme are actual entities and eternal objects. It will be sufficient therefore to show how actual entities require eternal objects. To begin with, how do actual occasions require eternal objects? In two ways, I suggest. Eternal objects are required to explain (i) the novelty and individuality of actual occasions, and (ii) the influence of actual occasions.

i. In Part One we saw how the subjective aim of an occasion is essential for its real individuality. The aim at a unity of experience, which informs each concrescence, might be called Whitehead's principle of individuation. It is the necessary and sufficient condition of the emergence of a novel real individual out of a given world of settled facts.

The subjective aim grows out of the initial conceptual aim, which has as its datum a possibility not realized in the actual world. The presentation of this novel possibility might be called the formal condition of individuality. The appetition of the concrescence for its realization might be called the material condition of individuality.

Every actual occasion is self-creative. Its appetition for some novel realization is an instance of creativity. It must conform to a given world, but it must do so in its own way. It determines itself internally. The novel possibility becomes the focus of this internal activity of the concrescence. Responded to with creative appetition, it catalyzes the many feelings of the concrescence into a unity of experience.

Now this possibility, as we shall see in detail in Part Three, is "derived" from God. In God's conceptual experience it is envisaged with his own subjective form of appetition. But if the new occasion is to be a real individual, the possibility must be capable of being prehended with a novel subjective form, particular to the new concrescence itself. For if it could be prehended *only* with the divine subjective form of appetition, then no room would remain for the self-creative activity of the concrescence. The occasion would then sink to the status of a mode of infinite Being.

This means that to maintain the principle of creativity, the datum of the initial aim must be something objective to God as well as to the concrescence.[14] In other words, there must be the possibility of disconnection between the datum and any subjective form of feeling, including the subjective form of God's primordial appetition. Now this is to say precisely that the datum of the initial aim must be a pure potential, indeterminate as to its realization. This is why Whitehead says that eternal objects "belong no more to God than to any one occasion" (RM 157).

God does not create eternal objects any more than he creates actual occasions—and for the same reason, namely the principle of creativity. There must be room in every concrescence for the self-creativity of the actual entity, however faint in intensity, however negligible in importance that actual entity may be. And creativity requires a multiplicity of pure potentials, indeterminate as to the subjective forms with which they are prehended.

In this way the theory of actual occasions as real, socially transcendent individuals requires the existence of entities of another sort, namely pure potentials or eternal objects.

14. This is the point at which Platonic realism diverges from Platonic (I should say neoplatonic) idealism. The former leaves open the possibility of pluralism. The latter tends to monism.

ii. We saw in Part One that the crucial explanatory mechanism in Whitehead's theory of influence was conformity of subjective form. It was argued that, on his principles, transition from the past to the present has to be interpreted in terms of the repetition or reproduction of subjective forms of feeling. Some form of definiteness of feeling in the antecedent is repeated, or a feeling having this form of definiteness is reproduced, in the consequent actual occasion. In this way Whitehead's theory of influence requires the existence of entities which can be multiply located, as actual occasions cannot. Their function, as he puts it, is relational. Further, since there are no *a priori* restrictions on the influence one actual occasion may have on another, any such entity must be such that it *might,* abstractly speaking, be realized in *any* instance of transition. Such entities therefore must be timeless in their mode of existence and indeterminate as to their physical realization. That is to say they must be pure potentials.

We have seen, still further, that Whitehead's claim to real connections among his real individuals rests crucially on his theory of influence. On his own showing, the mutual immanence of contemporaries and the immanence of the present in the future require the influence of the past on the present. Thus we might generalize and say that his theory of social immanence, as well as his theory of social transcendence, requires for its intelligibility the existence of eternal objects.

Some philosophers have suggested that Whitehead's system might be reformed in such a way as to make eternal objects unnecessary. This proposal is no doubt generated by the feeling that eternal objects are more "strange" or "queer" than Whitehead's other categories of existence. It is felt, perhaps, that it is more difficult to identify eternal objects in experience than to identify actual occasions and nexūs, for example. Thus if eternal objects could be eliminated the system would be more plausible.

We do not need to examine the objections to eternal objects that underlie this proposal. It is by no means clear that eternal objects are more strange to common experience than, for example, actual occasions are. It might also be remarked that Whitehead's speculative system is designed not as a simple description of common experience but as an instrument for analyzing it. But the main point which follows from the preceding discussion is that, if it is thought possible to eliminate eternal objects from White-head's system, then what he means by actual occasions has not been understood. Now why is it that he adopts a system of concepts to which the category of eternal objects is necessary, in the ways we have seen?

b. As Whitehead develops, explains, and defends his system he appeals at a number of points to direct experience. This appeal reflects his conception of speculative philosophy. Its function is to frame a set of ideas "in terms of which every element of our experience can be interpreted" (PR 4). So the "ultimate appeal" of any speculative system must be "to the general consciousness of what in practice we experience" (PR 25). The reasons external to his system by which it would have to be justified are simply the features of experience.

Whitehead does not claim that his system can be validated by appeal to some one crucial set of facts. On the contrary, "the relevance of evidence is dictated by theory. For you cannot prove a theory by evidence which that theory dismisses as irrelevant" (AI 284). Much less would it be reasonable to suppose that the theory of eternal objects, abstracted from its place in Whitehead's system, could be proved or disproved in this manner.

It would be impossible to list all those features of experience to which Whitehead appeals in his writings. It is possible to select certain "facts" to which he appeals more often than to others, generally because he thinks they are slighted or explained away by other philosophers, and to suggest some connections between these facts of experience and the theory of eternal objects. I offer four such facts:

i. There are many real things.

Monism is "in defiance of the most obvious deliverance of our intuitive 'prejudices' " (PR 208).

ii. These many real things are really connected with one an-other.

The point of Whitehead's criticisms of Hume was "that we have direct intuition of inheritance and memory: thus the only problem is, so to describe the general character of experience that these intuitions may be included" (PR 253).

iii. Process is real.

If "changeless order is conceived as the final perfection," so that "the historic universe is degraded to a status of partial reality, issuing into the notion of mere appearance," then "the most evident characteristic of our experience has been dismissed into a subordinate role in metaphysical construction" (MT 109).

iv. Aims are effective.

"The conduct of human affairs is entirely dominated by our recognition of foresight determining purpose, and purpose issuing in conduct . . . The evidence is so overwhelming, the belief so unquestioning, the evidence of language so decisive, that it is difficult to know where to begin in demonstrating it" (FR 9–10).

Things, connections, process, and aims are among the most familiar and important features of the world we experience. Whitehead's purpose is to devise a system of categories which will do justice to these and other facts of experience.

It is possible to trace from each of these "facts" a thread of Whitehead's thought leading toward the theory of eternal objects. These threads of thought become interwoven with many others into the fabric of his system. Short of a justification of the system as a whole, tracing these connections will take us as far as we can expect to go toward identifying some external reasons why eternal objects are needed.

i. To express in a metaphysical system the fact of a multiplicity of things, categories of definiteness and distinctness are required. A thing is *this* and not *that*. It is distinct from another thing in this or that respect. Thus there are forms or characters or qualities in respect to which things differ from each other. This line of thought leads toward the conception of eternal objects as forms of definiteness.

ii. To express real connections between real things mediating entities are required. To think of these mediating entities as being themselves "things" would lead to a fruitless regress of relations. They must not take the place of the influence or power one thing exerts on another, or the presence of one thing in another. This is the very fact which needs to be explained, not explained away. They must rather characterize the continuity which the influence effects. They must be forms of definiteness both of the cause and of the effect. Thus we would be led toward the conception of eternal objects as relational.

iii. Process requires novelty. Something becomes which did not exist before. If this fact of novelty is subject to rational analysis,[15] then the form of definiteness of the novel thing cannot be an isolated and unrelated "meaning." Though previously unrealized, it must be capable of determinate relations with other forms. This line of thought leads toward the conception of eternal objects as pure potentials.

iv. If aims are effective, then something not yet actual, an envisaged possibility, has a function in the present. There is final causation. To explain final causation mental operations of some sort are required. Thus we might be led to a doctrine of conceptual prehensions, with pure potentials as their data.

In such ways it is possible to see how Whitehead might appeal to facts external to his system to support the theory of eternal objects. Our main concern has been with those internal reasons in terms of which the coherence of his system would have to be defended.

In the two succeeding chapters we shall again take Whitehead's own advice as we did in Part One, "laying the new ideas alongside of our pre-existing trains of thought" (PRIN R vii). In these chapters we shall lay his theory of eternal objects alongside the traditional theory of universals, as he understands it. This will enable us to see how he interprets qualities, relations, and the principle of classification.

15. See Whitehead's remarks on Bergson in PR vii, AI 287, ESP 116.

CHAPTER 12

Qualities and Relations

1. Whitehead on universals

SCATTERED through Whitehead's later writings are many critical remarks about traditional views of universals. From these remarks I propose to reconstruct the theory of universals he has in mind and is opposing, in order to bring out more clearly his own alternative.

First I shall cite a passage which sets forth in a clear way his general approach to the traditional theory. Then I shall state the main doctrines which compose that theory, together with his alternative doctrines. This will give us a framework within which we may discuss, in the rest of this chapter, his treatment of qualities and relations. First, then, the general point of view:

> The antithetical terms 'universals' and 'particulars' are the usual words employed to denote respectively entities which nearly, though not quite [Note 9: "For example, prehensions and subjective forms are also 'particulars' "], correspond to the entities here termed 'eternal objects,' and 'actual entities.' . . . The notion of a universal is of that which can enter into the description of many particulars; whereas the notion of a particular is that it is described by universals, and does not itself enter into the description of any other particular. According to the doctrine of relativity which is the basis of the metaphysical system of the present lectures, both these notions involve a misconception. An actual entity cannot be described, even inadequately, by universals; because other actual entities do enter into the description of any one actual entity. Thus every so-called 'universal' is particular in the sense of being just what it is, diverse from everything else; and every so-called 'particular' is universal in the sense of

entering into the constitutions of other actual entities (PR 76; see PNK 201, PR 239).

I take the main doctrines of the traditional theory of universals, of which Whitehead is critical, to be the following:

a. Universals and particulars are entities of different categoreal types.

b. Universals do not determine their instances in particulars.

These two doctrines do not require extended explanation. Whitehead does not disagree with them, and his own way of stating them will be explained briefly below.

c. No other particulars enter into the description of a given particular. Hence qualities and relations are universals, predicated of particulars as their logical subjects.

Whitehead's criticisms of the traditional theory center on this doctrine. Most of this chapter will be devoted to these criticisms and to his alternative doctrine.

d. The main use of universals is to classify particulars into genera and species.

This doctrine and Whitehead's criticisms of it will be discussed in Chapter 13.

I take the main doctrines of the theory of eternal objects, Whitehead's alternative to the traditional theory, to be the following:

a. Eternal objects and actual entities belong to different categories of existence.

Whitehead makes it clear that among the categories of existence the fundamental contrast is between eternal objects and actual entities: "Among these eight categories of existence, actual entities and eternal objects stand out with a certain extreme finality" (PR 33). These are two mutually exclusive classes of entities (PR 239). In this respect his own theory parallels the traditional view.

b. Eternal objects do not determine their ingressions in actual entities.

Here again Whitehead does not disagree with the theory of universals. Like universals, eternal objects are "abstract." "These transcendent entities have been termed 'universals.' I prefer to use the term 'eternal objects,' in order to disengage myself from presuppositions which cling to the former term owing to its prolonged philosophical history. Eternal objects are thus, in their nature, abstract. By 'abstract' I mean that what an eternal object is in itself—that is to say, its essence—is comprehensible without reference to some one particular occasion of experience" (SMW 221).

c. Eternal objects are forms of definiteness of particular facts of qualitative experience and of particular facts of relatedness. Their functions are modal and relational.

Whitehead's view will be explained in detail in this chapter.

d. The multiplicity of eternal objects includes mathematical ideas as well as qualitative predicates, and permits the "mingling" of forms in novel real individuals.

This doctrine will be explained in Chapter 13.

Within this framework we can turn our attention to doctrine c of the traditional view of universals. A close connection with the topic of Chapter 5 will be apparent. We shall center on the view of qualities and relations Whitehead is opposing, and on his own interpretation of the facts to which the traditional view refers.

2. Criticism of qualification

Whitehead's criticism of the traditional view of qualities begins in his earlier writings. On that view qualities are solely or primarily predicates of substances, as their logical subjects. Predication is thus a simple two-termed relation between a primary substance and a universal quality. For example, "The grass is green" predicates a universal quality of a particular substance. In the traditional theory of substance this two-termed relation of predication is taken as the standard relationship between universals and particulars.

We may remember that in his earlier writings Whitehead took "objects" and "events" as entities of fundamentally different types, because if objects were regarded as qualities of events, he said, one got into difficulties. The standard theory was not adequate to describe "the apparent world," that is to say "nature," with which he was concerned in those writings.

He held that a full account of the appearance of green in a particular situation would refer not only to the green and to its situation but also to the percipient event (i.e. "the bodily life of the observer") and to the whole of nature in that duration. "Under the obsession of the logical theory of universals and concrete particulars the percipient event was suppressed, and the relation of green to its situation represented as universal qualifying particular" (PRIN R 27). This traditional theory therefore oversimplifies a complex situation. ". . . in the apparent world, that is to say, in the world of nature disclosed by sense-awareness, no example of the simple two-termed relationship of a universal signifying its particular is to be found" (PRIN R 26). There are multiple relations in nature, of which the relation of situation between sense objects and events is one example, which the standard interpretation of qualities obscured (CN 18 [cp. PR 20], 150–1; PA 217). This criticism was closely connected with what he had to say about the "simple-minded theory that an object is at one place at any definite time, and is in no sense anywhere else" (CN 145). This is the fallacy which he calls, in *Science and the Modern World*, "simple location." For "simple location" is also a simple two-termed relation between a universal and a particular. In this case the particular is not a substance but a place.

For this reason Whitehead decides not to describe objects as qualities of events. This language, because of its association with the traditional theory of universals, would suggest that an object has no inherent reference to entities other than the event it is qualifying. Whitehead on the contrary wants to say that a sense object situated in an event is significant of other objects, for example the "conveyance" of perceptual objects by sense objects (PNK 88), and significant of events other than its situation, for example the percipient event.

Then he moves from his earlier concern with "nature," as the subject matter of science, to "reality" as the subject matter of metaphysics, and in the later writings his criticism of qualification is continued, with an important difference. Now he has developed a doctrine of real individuals, in his theory of actual occasions. It is no longer enough to admit multiple relations. These relations must be construed now as real connections between real individuals.

It is not enough to admit that in our experience of nature there are many-termed relations, if these relations are then thought of merely as qualities of a subject. Leibniz, for example, retained the Cartesian view "that the final real entities are substances supporting qualities." Thus, while he admitted many-termed relations, his "perspectives," he did so "only on the condition that they are purely qualities of the organising monads." Hence for Leibniz "there was no concrete reality of internal relations" *among* concrete individuals (SMW 216–17). The result of "describing the world in terms of subject and predicate, substance and quality, particular and universal . . . always does violence to that immediate experience which we express in our actions, our hopes, our sympathies, our purposes, and which we enjoy in spite of our lack of phrases for its verbal analysis. We find ourselves in a buzzing world, amid a democracy of fellow creatures; whereas, under some disguise or other, orthodox philosophy can only introduce us to solitary substances, each enjoying an illusory experience: 'O Bottom, thou art changed! what do I see on thee?' " (PR 78–9). This criticism runs throughout the later writings (AI 169–70, 355–6, 361; MT 101; MG 678).

3. Restricted applications of qualification

If Whitehead thinks the traditional notion of qualification is too simple, he should give some account in his own terms of those "abstract" features of experience to which this notion *does* apply. He does so in two ways. The first is his doctrine of "Aristotelian adjectives," later developed into the Category of Transmutation. The second is his doctrine of the privacy of enjoyment.

a. The doctrine of Aristotelian adjectives in the earlier writings is Whitehead's way of recognizing that "after all the search for universals to qualify events in the simple two-termed manner does represent a justifiable demand. We want to know what any particular event A is in itself apart from its reference to other events" (PRIN R 28). Those characters which function as Aristotelian adjectives are perceptual objects, like a man or a chair. These objects are "signified" by sense objects. They are the "controls of ingression."

> The grass exhibits itself as green, the bell exhibits itself as tolling, the sugar as tasting, the stone as touchable (ESP [1923] 146).

> Now an Aristotelian adjective marks a breakdown of the reign of relativity; it is just an adjective of the event which it qualifies. And this relation of adjective to subject requires no reference to anything else. Accordingly, a perceptual object is neutral as regards events, other than those which it qualifies. It is thus sharply distinguished from a sense-object, whose ingression involves all sorts of events in all sorts of ways (ESP 147).

Two comments need to be made on this doctrine of perceptual objects as Aristotelian adjectives. First we should notice it is the *object,* not the event, which is "neutral" as regards other events. Whitehead is not contradicting his doctrine that any *event* requires reference to other events. His point is that perceptual objects have another kind of relation to events than sense objects do. Whereas sense objects in their ingression involve not only the situation event and the percipient event but all the events which make up the whole of nature in that duration, perceptual objects have a simpler relation to their situations.

Second, he does not suggest that perceptual objects and their relations to events be taken as fundamental either for the philosophy of science or for metaphysics. Physical objects (i.e. nondelusive perceptual objects) are important because of their "high perceptive power," and attention to them "is the first condition for the survival of complex living organisms." But "the scholastic philosophy of nature" makes the mistake of looking on sense objects "as mere attributes of the physical objects" (CN 156). That is to say, it is a mistake to regard the two-termed relation of perceptual objects to their situation events as the standard relation of objects to events.

In Whitehead's later writings this doctrine of perceptual objects as "adjectives" is developed into the Category of Transmutation. His formal statement is:

> When . . . one and the same conceptual feeling is derived impartially by a prehending subject from its analogous, simple, physical feelings of various actual entities in its actual world, then, in a subsequent phase . . . the prehending subject may transmute the *datum* of this conceptual feeling into a characteristic of some *nexus* containing those prehended actual entities among its members, or of some part of that nexus. . . .
>
> It is evident that the complete datum of the transmuted feeling is a contrast, namely, 'the nexus, as one, in contrast with the eternal object.' This type of contrast is one of the meanings of the notion 'qualification of physical substance by quality' (PR 40).

As in the earlier writings his theory of perceptual objects was his explanation of our common-sense experience of "things," so here "Our usual way of consciously prehending the world is by these transmuted physical feelings" (PR 387).

His explanation amounts to saying that some organisms sum up and "transmute" their feelings of many actual entities into a feeling of one actuality qualified by a universal (eternal object). He compares transmutation with Leibniz' doctrine of "confused" perception (PR 40, 384). The point of interest is that this summing up involves an abstraction "from the multiplicity of members" of the nexus (PR 98). There is here "the merely potential aggregation of actual entities into a super-actuality in respect to which the true actualities play the part of coordinate subdivision." For some purposes "a nexus of many actualities can be treated as though it were one actuality. This is what we habitually do in the case of the span of life of a molecule, or of a piece of rock, or of a human body" (PR 439).

This is a "simplification" (AI 273) of experience. The fact that it takes place is "a real fact of nature" (AI 272). But what is qualified, when we say "The stone is gray," is not a real individual but an aggregate of real individuals. And while the grayness of the stone appears as a simple qualification, complete analysis of the fact would require reference to the individual actual occasions which compose the nexus, and their objectifications in one another.

b. The second restricted application Whitehead gives the traditional notion of qualification is in his doctrine of the private enjoyment of qualities. Subjective forms are "private matters of fact" (PR 32). Now if the subjective form of a feeling is taken in abstraction from its objective datum (PR 356–8), then an eternal object which is an element in the definiteness of that subjective form can be regarded as a "quality" of the subject which enjoys that feeling.

> The fundamental example of the notion 'quality inhering in particular substance' is afforded by 'subjective form inhering in feeling' (PR 354; the text reads "is particular substance").

> An eternal object considered in reference to the privacy of things is a 'quality' or 'characteristic'; namely, in its own nature, as exemplified in any actuality, it constitutes an element in the private definiteness of that actuality. It refers itself publicly; but it is enjoyed privately (PR 444; see 480).

Here again we are dealing with an abstraction from fact. The feeling has been abstracted from its objective datum in the actual world beyond the subject. And the subjective form has itself been conditioned by this actual world, to which the subject has had to conform. "The theory of prehensions is founded upon the doctrine that there are no concrete facts which are merely public, or merely private" (PR 444).

In these two ways Whitehead recognizes and gives an account of the practical importance of the substance-quality theory. At the same time he rejects the notion of a quality simply inhering in a particular substance as a fundamental category in science and metaphysics.

4. Are qualities universals?

Like "substance," "causality," and "organism," the term "quality" is for Whitehead an *explicandum*. It is not one of his own systematic categories of explanation. It needs interpretation, or rather reinterpretation, in terms of his categoreal scheme, because of the traditional doctrine with which it has been associated in philosophical discourse.

On the traditional view qualities may be attached to a particular substance without affecting its substratum. Qualities are thus *adjectival,* and their attachments to particular substances are *accidental.* Since their attachments to particulars are accidental, a quality cannot connect one particular with another. Thus on the traditional view qualities are nonrelational.

In contrast, for Whitehead qualities are *modal* and *relational.* In his system actual entities are the ultimate particulars which have qualities. And since actual entities are acts of experience, qualities must be interpreted as modes of feeling. Qualities are actual or possible "hows" of feeling. "It is held that every qualitative factor in the Universe is primarily a qualification of subjective form, so that the infinite variety of qualities involves the possibility of an infinite variety of subjective forms exemplifying those qualities" (AI 325).

As modes of feeling, qualities are relational in two ways. In the first place the subjective form of a feeling enters the real internal constitution of the subject. A quality in this sense has an internal relation to the subject of the feeling. In the second place the subjective form of a physical feeling conforms to its datum. Thus the quality expresses a real connection between the subject and its actual world. In my feeling of the datum which includes "angry feeling there," the quality of anger mediates to me the angry man I confront and introduces him as a concrete actuality into my experience. Thus on Whitehead's view qualities are relational as well as modal.

One way of *construing* the main intent of his criticism of the traditional doctrine is to take it as a denial that qualities are universals. The "blues," the "sweets," the "joys" we experience are subjective forms of feeling in particular subjects, ourselves or others. Now the subjective form of a feeling is not a universal. It is how *that* subject feels *that* datum. No two feelings can have the same subjective form. The primary point about qualities is that they are qualifications of subjective forms of feelings.

But if we construe Whitehead's treatment of quality in this way we must add that while qualities are not universals there are universals of quality. Otherwise this construction would be very misleading. There are forms of definiteness of subjective forms of feeling. In this secondary and derivative sense a quality is not a subjective form but an eternal object. Two feelings cannot have the same subjective form. But their subjective forms may include some common form of definiteness. In this sense two subjects can feel in the same way. Two feelings can have the same universal of quality.

Indeed insofar as Whitehead gives to "quality" any standard meaning in his exposition of the categoreal scheme, a quality is an eternal object (PR 444; AI 325, 327; MT 231). More specifically, a quality is an eternal object of the "subjective species": "A member of the subjective species is, in its primary character, an element in the definiteness of the subjective form of a feeling. It is a determinate way in which a feeling can feel. It is an emotion, or an intensity, or an adversion, or an aversion, or a pleasure, or a pain" (PR 446). A quality in this sense is something abstracted from subjective forms of feeling. It is a "form of quality" (MT 100). In this derivative sense qualities are possible forms of feeling. This is Whitehead's reinterpretation of the notion that qualities are universals.

But even in this secondary sense qualities are not adjectival and accidental in relation to the actual entities they qualify. These universals of quality are still not universals in the traditional sense. They are *ingredient* in the actual entities they qualify and characterize their operations, their processes of feeling. They are thus adverbial or modal, not adjectival, in their functions, except in the restricted applications of the traditional doctrine explained above. And since the operations of actual entities include real connections with other actual entities, namely physical prehensions, these universals of quality function relationally as well as modally. Eternal objects of the subjective species reflect, in their functions, the functions of the subjective forms from which they are abstracted. They are possible forms of modal and relational feeling.

Thus in order to remedy the deficiencies of the traditional theory Whitehead offers a choice of categories for the interpretation of a quality. (a) Feelings have subjective forms, and we experience the subjective forms of feelings in other subjects as well as our own. (b) There are forms of definiteness ingredient in the subjective forms of feelings. These are eternal objects.

Though this choice is open there is still an advantage, in construing the main intent of Whitehead's treatment of universals, to saying that qualities are not universals though there are universals of quality. This brings out more sharply his basic criticism that in the traditional theory universals of quality tend to supplant those particular and relational qualitative experiences that are the most insistent and stubborn facts of life.

5. Relations and universals

Similarly we might *construe* Whitehead's treatment of relations as a denial that relations are universals (see AI 201). Again this is only a way of interpreting the main intent of his criticism of the traditional theory. He is not denying there are universals of relation any more than he denies there are universals of quality. His main protest is that, just as universals of quality were allowed to supplant or obscure particular facts of qualitative feeling, so universals of relation have been allowed to replace or to obscure particular facts of relatedness. In both cases he is protesting against a confusion of fact with form.

From doctrine c of the traditional theory of universals, namely that no other particular enters into the constitution of any given particular, it would follow that all relations are universals. For on that theory a particular may be understood without reference to any other particular. "The 'particular' is thus conceived as being just its individual self with no necessary relevance to any other particular" (PR 79). Then each of two related particulars can be understood apart from the other, and the relation between them can be understood apart from both. A relation which can be understood without reference to certain particulars is a universal. Thus the traditional theory implies that all relations are universals. This consequence illustrates Whitehead's view that with the doctrine of "the individual independence of real facts," "the relations between individual substances constitute metaphysical nuisances" (PR 208).

One result is to assimilate relations to qualities. "Being the friend of John," to the extent that this can be understood apart from the character of John, approximates the meaning of "being friendly" (cf. MT 81). And this is in fact one of Whitehead's charges against the traditional view. In the preface to *Process and Reality* he says, "Descartes retained in his metaphysical doctrine the Aristotelian dominance of the category of 'quality' over that of 'relatedness.'" Whereas, Whitehead says, "In these lectures 'relatedness' is dominant over 'quality'" (PR ix). This does not mean a rejection of the category of quality. It means, as we have seen, that qualities are relational. And it means that relations are not qualities in the sense in which, on the traditional view, they tend to be.

Whitehead's clearest discussion of the traditional view of relations is found in *Adventures of Ideas,* in a passage discussing "the vagueness of philosophical terminology" (AI 294). As one example of this vagueness he takes "the terms expressive of the connectedness of things": "For this topic, the reigning philosophical term is the word Relation. . . . It is generally held that relations are universals, so that A can have the same relation to B as C has to D. For example 'loving,' 'believing,' 'between,' 'greater than,' are relations. There can be no objection to this doctrine. For it is a mere definition. Universals which require two or more particulars for their illustration need some term to indicate them, and Relation is the word chosen" (AI 295–6). Thus it is clear that he is not denying that there are universals of relation. He continues, "But with this meaning to the term, a relation cannot signify the actual connectedness of the actual individual things which constitute the actual course of history. For example, New York lies between Boston and Philadelphia. But the connectedness of the three towns is a real particular fact on the earth's surface involving a particular part of the eastern seaboard of the United States. It is not the universal 'between.' It is a complex actual fact which, among other things, exemplifies the abstract universal 'between-ness' " (AI 296).

We noticed how in his treatment of quality Whitehead offers two categories, "subjective form" and "eternal object," in order to avoid confusing facts and forms. Here again, in his treatment of relation, the categoreal scheme offers a way of saying what "the vagueness of philosophical terminology" has made it impossible to say clearly. The traditional theory has obscured the real connections between real individuals. Several categories are expressly designed to refer to particular facts of relatedness of various kinds.

6. Particular facts of relatedness

Prehensions are of fundamental importance. They are "Concrete Facts of Relatedness" (PR 32). Actual entities prehend entities of all the categoreal types. And all prehensions are "real, individual, and particular" (PR 30). They constitute a network of real connectedness between an actual entity and all other entities. They cannot be abstracted from their subjects or from their data. A prehension is *this* actual entity feeling *that* entity. In a primary way, prehensions are the particular facts of relatedness which give unity and continuity to the world.

Nexus is the term for a set of actual entities with a complex pattern of relatedness. Category of explanation xiv is: "That a nexus is a set of actual entities in the unity of the relatedness constituted by their prehensions of each other, or—what is the same thing conversely expressed—constituted by their objectifications in each other" (PR 35; see 350–3). Since a nexus is defined in terms of prehensions, nexūs are "real individual facts of the togetherness of actual entities which are real, individual, and particular, in the same sense in which actual entities and the prehensions are real, individual, and particular" (PR 29–30). It is worth noting further that "The ultimate facts of immediate actual experience are actual entities, prehensions, and nexūs. All else is, for our experience, derivative abstraction" (PR 30).

Contrasts are "Modes of Synthesis of Entities in one Prehension" (PR 33). Contrasts are particular facts of relatedness. But they are of a less primary sort than prehensions, or even than nexūs. In general, a "real synthesis of two component elements in the objective datum of a feeling must be infected with the individual particularities of each of the relata. . . . A contrast cannot be abstracted from the contrasted relata" (PR 348–9). For example take a contrast of two eternal objects, that is to say a synthesis of two eternal objects in one prehension: "The contrast between blue and red cannot be repeated as *that* contrast between any other pair of colours, or any pair of sounds, or between a colour and a sound. . . . Certain abstractions from that contrast, certain values inherent in it, can also be got from other contrasts. But they are *other* contrasts, and not *that* contrast; and the abstractions are not 'contrasts' of the same categoreal type" (PR 349). In other words, a contrast has a unity of its own, an "individual definiteness," and in this sense it is "particular," a particular fact of relatedness. This is as true of multiple contrasts as of dual contrasts: "A multiple contrast is analysable into component dual contrasts. But a multiple contrast is not a mere aggregation of dual contrasts. It is one contrast, over and above its component contrasts" (PR 349). A contrast is a "mode of synthesis," and any contrast is just *that* mode of synthesis and not another. There is a further sense in which a contrast is a *particular* fact of relatedness. A "realized contrast" (PR 352) is particular with the particularity of the prehension to whose datum the contrast belongs.

We might say that a contrast between actual occasions, realized in some prehension, would be particular in a stronger sense than a contrast between eternal objects. It would be "infected" with the *concrete* particularity of its relata, namely the contrasted actual occasions. It would be the contrast of those occasions *there* and *there*. But this would be a nexus, and while in one sense a nexus is a contrast Whitehead says he will avoid this application of the term (PR 349).

In summary, there are prehensions by actual entities of other entities; there are sets of actual entities which prehend one another (nexūs); and there are syntheses of entities in the data of prehensions (contrasts). In these ways Whitehead would describe the particular facts of relatedness we find in experience. It is these particular facts of relatedness, he thinks, which the traditional theory of relations has obscured. It has tended to resolve particular facts of relatedness into universals of relation.

7. Universals of relation

Whitehead's aim is not to rule out universals of relation but only to distinguish them clearly from particular facts of relatedness. Here again he wishes to avoid confusing forms with facts. As with "quality," so also "relation" is not a term he employs in the construction of his metaphysical scheme. It requires interpretation in terms of that scheme.

His own account of what I have been calling universals of relation is as follows:

> A relation is a genus of contrasts (PR 350).

> What are ordinarily termed 'relations' are abstractions from contrasts. A relation can be found in many contrasts; and when it is so found, it is said to relate the things contrasted (PR 349).

For example "between" is a relation in this sense. When "between" is abstracted from the real connectedness of Boston, New York, and Philadelphia (AI 295–6), it applies also to the real connectedness of Boston, Springfield, and Albany. It is a genus of contrasts or, to put it another way, an abstraction from contrasts.[1] The relation is not itself a contrast. Hence it is not particular in the sense in which contrasts are particular. Nor is it a nexus. It is not the real connectedness of Boston, New York, and Philadelphia. It is a universal or, in Whitehead's terms, an eternal object (PR 295).

Whitehead fully agrees with Bradley that relations, so con-

---

1. A "genus of contrasts" is to be distinguished from a "generic contrast." The latter is a contrast and hence particular, as explained above for all contrasts. A generic contrast is a contrast between entities of different categoreal types, as for example between a nexus and a proposition (as in "intellectual feeling," PR 407), between a nexus and an eternal object (as in a "physical purpose," PR 421), or between an actual entity and a proposition (as in a "coordinate division," PR 437). The data of comparative feelings are generic contrasts (PR 406). Generic contrasts, unlike other sorts of contrasts, are "proper entities." Other sorts of contrasts, and "multiplicities," are *not* proper entities (PR 45).

sidered, do not relate. Bradley saw the consequences of the traditional theory of substance, for on that theory "the relations between individual substances constitute metaphysical nuisances: there is no place for them. Accordingly—in defiance of the most obvious deliverance of our intuitive 'prejudices'—every respectable philosophy of the subject-predicate type is monistic" (PR 208–9). Bradley was right in asking for "an underlying unity and an inclusive whole" (AI 296). Unlike Bradley Whitehead holds that there are real facts of relatedness which connect real individuals, and he undertakes to give an account of them. He thinks the "underlying unity," which Bradley rightly asked for, does not have to be the Absolute. The trouble with Bradley was that in describing internal relations he used language shaped by the traditional categories and hence appropriate to external relations (AI 201).

> Bradley's discussions of relations are confused by his failure to distinguish between relations and contrasts. A relation is a genus of contrasts. He is then distressed—or would have been distressed if he had not been consoled by the notion of 'mereness' as in 'mere appearance'—to find that a relation will not do the work of a contrast. It fails to contrast. Thus Bradley's argument proves that relations, among other things, are 'mere'; that is to say, are indiscretions of the absolute, apings of reality without self-consistency (PR 349–50; see 69).

In this way Whitehead gives an account, in his own categories, of universals of relation. His main concern however is to point out that a relation, in this sense, will not do the work of a contrast or of any other particular fact of relatedness.

8. The relational function of eternal objects

Although eternal objects cannot do the work of actual entities or prehensions or nexūs or contrasts, yet they have their own work to do, work which cannot be done by entities of other categoreal types. One function of eternal objects is their "relational" function in objectification. This doctrine is a development from the doctrine of the "significance" of objects in the earlier writings, where the ingression of objects is said to "signify" events (ESP [1923] 144–6).

In his later writings Whitehead describes this function in various ways. Eternal objects are said to "interpret" (SMW 210) events to other events. They "convey" other subjects. "They are here in the perceiver; but, as perceived by him, they convey for him something of the total flux which lies beyond himself" (SMW 210). They "introduce" (PR 93) one actual entity into another. They "connect" (PR 97) different actual entities. An eternal object can "effect" (TIME 60), or be an "agent" in (PR 445–7), the objectification of one actual entity for another. All these terms—mediate, interpret, convey, introduce, connect, agent—are used to describe the relational function of eternal objects.

It should be noticed at once that the suggestion of activity in the connotations of these terms is misleading and needs correction. According to the ontological principle, "actual entities are the only *reasons*" (PR 37). This means that actual entities are the only agents. It would be contrary to this principle to suggest that eternal objects are the *reasons* why actual entities are mediated, interpreted, conveyed, introduced, or connected with each other.

Here as elsewhere, though by no means everywhere, Whitehead's language is concrete and vivid, metaphorical rather than abstract. He wishes to convey the sense of activity and concreteness. So he sacrifices exactness for suggestiveness. Part of the justification for this is that elsewhere he has said what he means in other ways, and that no one way of saying it is perfectly adequate to the facts. Nevertheless it is important to notice that, as in the case of expressions like "flow of feeling," some of his ways of stating a doctrine are less metaphorical, more rigorous and precise, than others. He is not content with being suggestive, as a poet might be. His is a philosophical aim, and we are justified in holding him to it. His more exact descriptions of the "function" of eternal objects are in terms of "ingression," "abstraction," and "possibility." The immediate point is that expressions imputing activity to eternal objects must be corrected by the principle that the *agent* in objectification is the subject of the feeling, the feeler of the datum.

It is important to distinguish two senses, a weak and a strong, in which an eternal object may function relationally. Whitehead does not make this distinction explicit, though it lies immediately beneath the surface of what he says. An eternal object has dative ingression (PR 249) when it is "an element in the definiteness of some objectified nexus, or of some single actual entity, which is the datum of a feeling" (PR 445). I shall say that an eternal object which has *only* dative ingression in some feeling is relational in a weak sense. When the same eternal object is also an element in the definiteness of the subjective form of a conformal feeling, then I shall say it is relational in a strong sense.

The eternal object which has only dative ingression is an ingredient in the new concrescence only as a form of definiteness of the datum. This is an essential function in objectification, where the problem is to make some abstraction from the totality of the given world. Otherwise the new concrescence would be overwhelmed by this totality and no new instance of creativity could occur. Unless there were forms of definiteness of the datum, abstraction would not be possible. Eternal objects define the joints in the given world along which it may be cut into manageable sizes and shapes for the construction of a new actuality. They "constitute the forms of the objectifications of actual entities for each other" (PR 91). But if they have only this function, then they relate the subject to the object in only a weak sense.

Some eternal objects function relationally *only* in this weak sense.[2] These are eternal objects of the "objective species." An eternal object of this species is a "bare mathematical form." "Such forms by their very natures cannot qualify subjective form. For example, there is not a square-ness of emotion. Thus, except in an indirect fashion—such as the qualitative feelings of smoothness of a sphere, of spikeyness of a square, of amplitude of a volume—, the doctrine of conformation does not apply to mathematical pattern. Here pure mathematics in its strictest modern sense is in question" (AI 326. See PR 97, 445–6; AI 322).

An eternal object is relational in the *strong* sense when it func-

2. The relational functioning of eternal objects in transmuted feelings and presentational immediacy (SYMBOLISM 22, 50; PR 97–8, 446–7; AI 314–23) might be treated as a still weaker sense of "relational." But it has been explained in Part One how contemporary actual occasions are and are not "related."

tions in conformal physical feeling. In this case the eternal object has dative ingression and subjective ingression in the same feeling. "In the conformal feelings the *how* of feeling reproduces what is felt. Some conformation is necessary as a basis of vector transition, whereby the past is synthesized with the present. The one eternal object in its two-way function, as a determinant of the datum and as a determinant of the subjective form, is thus relational" (PR 249; see 446–7, 479–80; AI 314–16, 326–7). For example, a feeling in the initial phase of a concrescence has for its datum an angry feeling in some other subject, *and* it feels this angry feeling angrily. Thus the eternal object defines, or partially defines, both the subjective form of the past feeling, which is now a datum, and the subjective form of the present feeling, which feels that datum. Only eternal objects of the subjective species may have this two-way function.

The conclusion from this discussion is that, whether in the weak or the strong sense, the relational functioning of eternal objects does not supplant the functions of prehensions, nexūs, and contrasts. Eternal objects do not take the place of particular facts of relatedness. On the contrary they are relational only by way of being abstract forms of definiteness of the data and subjective forms of concrete and particular physical feelings. The primary facts of relatedness are prehensions by actual entities of other actual entities.

9. Summary and conclusions

Whitehead's constructive proposals about qualities and relations may be summed up in the following way:

a. Qualities are modal and relational.

i. An actual entity is a unity of qualitative feelings (prehensions) subjectively enjoyed. The subjective forms of these feelings are affected by the other actual entities which the subject feels. In turn these feelings, with their subjective forms, are felt by and affect other actual entities.

ii. Some eternal objects (those of the subjective species) are forms of definiteness of the subjective forms of feeling and hence may be said to be "qualities," or universals of quality, meaning that they are forms of qualitative feeling.

b. Relations are particular and real.

i. There are particular facts of relatedness, namely prehensions, nexūs, and contrasts, which connect actual entities with other entities.

ii. Some eternal objects (genera of contrasts) may be said to be "relations," or universals of relation, meaning that they are forms of definiteness of particular facts of relatedness.

One of Whitehead's intentions, in his theory of qualities and relations, is to avoid confusing forms with facts. What do we mean by "quality"? by "relation"? Do we mean something concrete? something abstract? Do we mean by "a quality" a particular fact? Do we mean a universal? Do we mean by "a relation" a particular fact of relatedness? Or do we mean an abstract form which may be exemplified in many concrete facts of relatedness? We ought to be able to say what we mean without ambiguity and confusion. A better set of categories is needed than the traditional ones, a scheme by means of which clearer distinctions can be made.

Even more fundamental than this proposal for avoiding ambiguity is an appeal for what we might call the primacy of actuality. The traditional theory of universals has not done justice to concrete facts. It has allowed abstractions to supplant them. Instead we must begin with concrete experiences. And if we cannot describe these experiences adequately in traditional language then we must reshape language as an instrument for our purpose. This is the major movement of Whitehead's thought as he reflects on traditional ways of thinking about qualities and relations.

Certainly there are universals, implicit in experience and suggested by experience. But these universals are themselves possible forms of experience. Universals of quality are adverbial forms of feeling. Universals of relation are forms of syntheses in the data of feelings. The kind of *being* universals have is potentiality. They are possible forms of definiteness of actual entities. Certainly universals transcend actuality. But they transcend actuality *as* possibility, not as some more perfect kind of being.

Running through Whitehead's distinctions and underlined in his emphases, the main thrust and weight of his thought on this topic is toward the primacy of actuality, concreteness, and concrete experience. The central theme is a protest that the metaphysical assumptions of the traditional theory lead to the substitution of universals for particular qualitative facts and particular facts of relatedness.

Finally let us recur to one of Whitehead's epigrammatic remarks for a closing comment: "Descartes retained in his metaphysical doctrine the Aristotelian dominance of the category of 'quality' over that of 'relatedness.' In these lectures 'relatedness' is dominant over 'quality' (PR ix). On the traditional theory qualities tend to be regarded as "inhering" in substances or as being privately enjoyed by substances, without any relational function. Relations on the other hand tend to be construed as universals. They then cease to relate particulars to other particulars and tend to function as qualities. Thus there is dominance of quality over relatedness.

On Whitehead's theory, since qualities have a relational function and since relations are more rigorously distinguished from private qualities, relatedness is dominant over quality. This latter dominance, however, does not mean that qualities are *merely* relational. Along with their relational character, namely their function in objectification, qualities are privately enjoyed in the experiences of actual entities. Therefore Whitehead might well have added that the meaning of "dominance" in the first sentence is not the same as in the second sentence. For the traditional categories exclude real relatedness of individual things, whereas his categories do not exclude private and subjective enjoyment of qualitative experience.

CHAPTER 13

Classification

1. Introduction

WE HAVE BEEN reconstructing a theory of universals which, in Whitehead's judgment, has been both historically important and philosophically inadequate. Now we examine another part of his critique of that theory. One of its doctrines is that the main use of universals is to classify particulars into species and genera. In this chapter we study Whitehead's criticisms of this doctrine and the alternative he proposes in his theory of eternal objects.

In his later writings we find many critical remarks about the place of classification in Aristotelian logic. For example: "The logical instrument which Aristotle used for the analysis of actual fact into more abstract elements was that of classification into species and genera. This instrument has its overwhelmingly important application for science in its preparatory stages. But its use in metaphysical description distorts the true vision of the metaphysical situation." The passage continues: "The use of the term 'universal' is intimately connected with this Aristotelian analysis: the term has been broadened of late; but still it suggests that classificatory analysis. For this reason I have avoided it" (SMW 236–7). So his criticism of classificatory analysis is part of his critique of the traditional theory of universals. The connection is that the traditional theory tends to treat all universals as "qualitative predicates" (AI 196), and this naturally suggests a classificatory analysis.

Whitehead does not deny that classification is necessary for practical purposes and for the early stages of scientific inquiry (SMW 236–7, AI 183–4, MT 215, IMM 691). His point is rather that classification results in an incomplete analysis and hence is misleading as a fundamental metaphysical principle. It obscures and leads to neglect of certain features of the world which require other modes of analysis. This criticism parallels his treatment of traditional doctrines of substance, quality, and relation. They express important features of the world we experience but are misleading if taken as guiding principles in metaphysics. They are incapable of adequate generality.

2. Science and mathematics

For one thing, the principle of classification obscures the importance of applying mathematical ideas to the facts of nature:

> Classification is a halfway house between the immediate concreteness of the individual thing and the complete abstraction of mathematical notions. . . . Classification is necessary. But unless you can progress from classification to mathematics, your reasoning will not take you very far (SMW 41–2).

> Aristotelian Logic, by its neglect of mathematical notions, has done almost as much harm as good for the advancement of science. We can never get away from the questions: —How much,—In what proportions,—and In what pattern of arrangement with other things (AI 196; see 150, 191, 194, and MT 193–4).

From the history of science Whitehead concludes that as mathematics has become more abstract it has become more useful for analyzing nature (SMW 46). Indeed, he says, "The paradox is now fully established that the utmost abstractions are the true weapons with which to control our thought of concrete fact" (SMW 47).

Among the mathematical ideas that the principle of classification has overshadowed are "the complex possibilities of multiple relationship within a system" (AI 150). Here we have to do not with mathematical ideas in the narrower sense such as number and quantity but with "patterns of connectedness," which "the general science of mathematics" investigates (AI 196–7). To understand some particular thing we must ask about it, "In what pattern of arrangement with other things?"

The importance of pattern is stressed in a passage where Whitehead marks four stages in the development of a science. The first

is the choice of the types of things composing its subject matter.
The second is the stage of classification. It is an essential stage.
"But every science strives to get beyond it." The third stage introduces questions of "number, quantity, and measurement." The
fourth stage "is the introduction of the notion of pattern" (MT
194). For example, to know the properties of a mixture of carbon
atoms and hydrogen atoms, we want to know not only the number of atoms of each sort but also how much free oxygen, how much
free carbon, how much carbon monoxide, and how much carbon
dioxide. And there will be "an enormous number" of alternative
chemical patterns. Further, "there are an indefinite number of
regional patterns for the distribution of the chemical substances.
. . . Thus beyond all questions of quantity, there lie questions
of pattern, which are essential for the understanding of nature.
. . . Indeed quantity itself is nothing other than analogy of functions within analogous patterns" (MT 195). Now mathematics is
"the most powerful technique for the understanding of patterns"
(MG 678). And analysis of types of pattern is becoming the central
function of mathematics. Thus, in urging that a science must
pass on from the "halfway house" of classification to the "complete
abstraction of mathematical notions" (SMW 41), Whitehead is em-
phasizing the importance of pattern for the understanding of
nature.

A pattern is a "mode of togetherness" (MT 196). A science concerned with patterns is thus in contrast with Aristotle's science of
"mutually exclusive classification" (AI 176). Then we might say
that on Whitehead's view it is more important to find out how
things are together than to find out how they are separate. For the
pattern of their relations will *include* the differences of status and
function which suggest classifications.

The principle of exclusive classification, "the fixity of species
and genera" and "the unqualified definiteness of their distinction
from each other," is an implicit presupposition in much of the
"learned literature" of science (IMM 691). But it results in an
oversimplified view of nature. It is certainly true that there are
"gaps" in nature. Nature has its "surprises" (PR 145). But it is
also true that there are unsuspected continuities in nature: "Nature suggests for our observation gaps, and then as it were with-

draws them upon challenge. For example, ordinary physical bodies suggest solidity. But solids turn into liquids, and liquids into gases. And from the gas the solid can again be recovered" (AI 265). Sharp-cut scientific classification "hides the truth that the different modes of natural existence shade off into each other" (MT 215). It obscures "the aspect of continuity between these different modes. There are border-line cases, which bridge the gaps. Often the border-line cases are unstable, and pass quickly. But span of existence is merely relative to our habits of human life" (MT 216). A science which hopes to be adequate to nature cannot afford to make the principle of classification its final method of analysis. It must become mathematical by concerning itself with exact measurement and with patterns.

3. The function of philosophy

Philosophy even more than science must avoid making classification its fundamental mode of analysis. The reason is that philosophy seeks larger generalizations than science does. It constructs schemes in terms of which *all* the items of experience can be interpreted. It aims at "full comprehensiveness" (AI 184). "The emphasis of philosophy is upon generalizations which almost fail to classify by reason of their universal application" (AI 183). In this way the subject matter of metaphysics lends itself to treatment by the principle of classification even less than the subject matter of science does.

In an important passage Whitehead speaks of the method of philosophy as descriptive generalization, "an ascent from a particular fact, or from a species, to the genus exemplified" (AI 301). The converse process, he goes on to say, is impossible. It is not possible to descend from a genus to a species or to a particular fact. His reason is that "facts and species are the product of the mingling of genera."

> No genus in its own essence indicates the other genera with which it is compatible. For example, the notion of a backbone does not indicate the notions of suckling the young or of swimming in water. . . . A species is a potential mingling of genera, and an individual instance involves, among other

things, an actual mingling of many species. A syllogism is a scheme for demonstrating ways of mingling.

Thus the business of Logic is not the analysis of generalities but their mingling.

The point to notice is that philosophy is concerned with generalities *in a certain way*. It ascends to the genus. But it is not content to contemplate the genus, or to analyze it in and for itself. "Philosophy is the ascent to the generalities *with the view of understanding their possibilities of combination*. The discovery of new generalities thus adds to the fruitfulness of those already known. It lifts into view new possibilities of combination" (AI 302, my italics). This is another way of saying that philosophy must be concerned with patterns or "modes of togetherness."

In his reply to John Dewey (ESP 129) Whitehead quotes the following passage from Plato's *Sophist* (252D, 253):

> *Stranger*. Now since we have agreed that the classes or genera also commingle with one another, or do not commingle, in the same way, must he not possess some science and proceed by the processes of reason [he] who is to show correctly which of the classes harmonize with which, and which reject one another, and also if he is to show whether there are *some elements extending through all and holding them together so that they can mingle, and again, when they separate, whether there are other universal causes of separation*.

> *Theaetetus*. Certainly he needs science, and perhaps the greatest of sciences (brackets and italics are Whitehead's).

With this belongs a sentence from "Indication, Classes, Numbers, Validation": "This memoir illustrates a conception of the scope of Logic which was obscured by the dominant Aristotelian theory. The concept was adumbrated by Plato, when in *The Sophist* (252D, 253) he points out the importance of a science of the mingling of forms" (ESP [1934] 328).

Now for Whitehead all "mingling" or "real togetherness" is togetherness in the formal constitutions of actual entities. The concrete things in which abstract generalities are combined are experiencing individuals. Here is a reason more specific to Whitehead's own outlook why philosophy cannot be content with classification. Science can limit itself to abstractions, whereas philosophy is the criticism of abstractions by reference to the total concrete situation. Science does not and indeed cannot give an adequate account of real individuality. Philosophy can and must. In order to do so it must find more ample and adequate methods of analysis than the principle of classification.

4. The class theory of particulars

There is, indeed, a philosophical theory which purports to dispense with real individuals and claims to be content with classes of universal qualities. Rejecting—Whitehead would say correctly —the notion of a substratum, a "something-I-know-not-what" in which qualities inhere, it proposes that a particular is a class of qualities and nothing else. According to Hume, "We have therefore no idea of substance, distinct from that of a collection of particular qualities" (*Treatise,* Selby-Bigge ed., p. 16). Whitehead thinks that this proposal cannot be carried out and that its failure is further evidence of the limitations of the principle of classification.

We may notice in passing that Whitehead himself, in his earliest writings about science and nature, had a theory of "perceptual objects" which was similar in some respects to the class theory of particulars. For example, "Three simultaneous sense-objects [of sight, of sound, and of touch] which are also spatially coincident, are combined by thought into the perception of one cat." (OT 142; see 129, TSM 53, PNK 88). Fairly soon, however, he gave up this theory. In a note added in the second edition (1925) of *The Principles of Natural Knowledge* he says that his discussion in the first edition (1919) "is confused by a wavering between the 'class-theory' of perceptual objects and the 'control-theory' of physical objects, and by the confusion between perceptual and physical objects. I do not hold the class-theory now in any form, and was endeavouring in this book to get away from it" (PNK 204; see CN 153–8, ESP [1923] 146–7).

This early theory of perceptual objects, later rejected, was not itself a strict equivalent of the " 'class theory' of particular substances" (PR 348). For in his early writings all objects are abstract in distinction from events which are concrete. Hence a class theory of perceptual *objects* would not function as a theory of concrete particulars. In the second place, his earlier writings propose a theory about "nature," not about reality. He offers there a philosophy of science, not a metaphysics, whereas the class theory of particular substances is sometimes *employed* as (though not generally proposed as) a metaphysical theory.

Whitehead thinks this is an illegitimate use of the notion of a class. He objects that a class cannot be employed as a substitute for a particular, for example as the subject of a proposition. For this purpose it would be necessary to attribute to a class a kind of unity it does not have.

This objection is introduced in a discussion of the category of objective diversity, namely that "there can be no 'coalescence' of diverse elements in the objective datum of an actual entity, so far as concerns the functions of those elements in that satisfaction" (PR 344). The real individuals which are prehended in the satisfaction of an actual entity have "real diversity of status," for "each particular component imposes its own particularity on its status." In a real unity, that is to say in the unified experience of some actual entity, every component has its own place and function, a place and function duplicated by no other component. "A real unity cannot provide sham diversities of status for its diverse components" (PR 348).

The very mark of a class or collection, in contrast with a concrete particular, is the absence of diversity of status on the part of its components. The members of a class are all members in the same sense and in the same way. This is to say that a class is not a concrete but an abstract unity.

> The prohibition of sham diversities of status sweeps away the 'class theory' of particular substances, which was waveringly suggested by Locke (II, XXIII, 1), was more emphatically endorsed by Hume (*Treatise*, Part I, Sect. 6), and has been adopted by Hume's followers. For the essence of a class is that it assigns no diversity of function to the members of its extension. The members of a class are diverse members

in virtue of mere logical disjunction. The 'class,' thus appealed to, is a mere multiplicity. But in the prevalent discussion of classes, there are illegitimate transitions to the notions of a 'nexus' and of a 'proposition.' The appeal to a class to perform the services of a proper entity is exactly analogous to an appeal to an imaginary terrier to kill a real rat (PR 348).

An abstract unity cannot serve the purposes for which a concrete unity is required.

Here as at other points there is confusion because of "the vagueness of philosophical terminology" (AI 294). The notion of a class is employed in an ambiguous way. Therefore "illegitimate transitions" occur. To clear up the ambiguity Whitehead offers a choice of categories: There are multiplicities; there are nexūs; there are propositions.

Whitehead supposes that ordinarily in current philosophical discussion a class is a *multiplicity*, that is, no diversity of status is assigned to its members. His categoreal explanation is: "Every statement about a particular multiplicity can be expressed as a statement referent either (a) to *all* its members severally, or (b) to an indefinite *some* of its members severally, or (c) as a denial of one of these statements" (PR 36). But a multiplicity is not a "proper entity" (PR 45). It cannot serve as the subject of a proposition. But this is what a particular, on the traditional theory, must do. Hence the proposal to treat a particular substance as a multiplicity would defeat itself.

Now there are other types of entities, *nexūs* and *propositions*, which need to be distinguished from multiplicities. A nexus or a proposition may be "closely allied to some multiplicity, i.e., systematically allied to each member of some multiplicity" (PR 36). Therefore unless these different types of entities are clearly distinguished there is danger of overlooking the differences and attributing to a multiplicity some of the properties of a nexus or a proposition. The main difference is that nexūs and propositions have a unity that multiplicities do not have. A nexus "is a set of actual entities in the unity of the relatedness constituted by their prehensions of each other." And a proposition "is the unity of certain actual entities in their potentiality for forming a nexus, with its potential relatedness partially defined by certain eternal objects which have the unity of one complex eternal object" (PR 35–6). In either case particular actual entities are presupposed in certain systematic relationships, actual or potential, to each other. This means that the components of a nexus or of a proposition have diverse functions in the unity of the entity.

Whitehead's point, then, is that a class, understood as a multiplicity, cannot perform the function of a nexus or a proposition. A similar point is made in a discussion of "multiple contrasts": "This doctrine that a multiple contrast cannot be conceived as a mere disjunction of dual contrasts is the basis of the doctrine of emergent evolution. It is the doctrine of real unities being more than a mere collective disjunction of component elements. This doctrine has the same ground as the objection to the class-theory of particular substances. The doctrine is a commonplace of art" (PR 349). A fortiori a multiplicity cannot take the place of a particular substance, that is to say a concrete individual. The proposal to treat particular things as classes of qualities cannot be carried out, since it is necessary to attribute to a particular thing a kind of unity which a class does not have. For example, Hume's own acknowledgment of a "principle of union" among ideas "is inconsistent with the phrase 'nothing but a collection,' which at the beginning of the quotation settles so simply the notion of 'substance' " (PR 201).

Therefore when a particular is said to be nothing but a class of qualities it may be asked what is meant by a class. For example suppose that the particular denoted by "that man" is said to consist of a class of perceived qualities (color, shape, texture, etc.). Then if a class is construed as a multiplicity the theory is implausible. For the qualities plainly have diversities of status and function within a unity. Some account of the unity should be produced. Whitehead's categories offer the possibility of describing this macroscopic particular as a nexus of individual actual occasions.

5. The concreteness and novelty of real individuals

Whitehead objects to construing particular substances as classes of qualities. He also holds that real individuals cannot be adequately described as *members* of classes or instances of kinds. An individual is something more than a member of a species. The principle of classification is inadequate to account for real individuals. A principle of synthesis is needed.

This principle is "creativity." Creativity "is that ultimate principle by which the many, which are the universe disjunctively, become the one actual occasion, which is the universe conjunctively" (PR 31). In the concrescence of an actual entity there is a grasping of many diverse entities into a real togetherness. There is a concretion of forms of definiteness. "The organism is a unit of emergent value, a real fusion of the characters of eternal objects, emerging for its own sake" (SMW 152). In a real individual there is a mingling of forms, a fusion of diverse eternal objects.

The mingling of forms in the concrete unity of real individuals supersedes the exclusiveness of forms suggested by classification. The question is what mode of analysis brings us nearest to concrete reality. On Whitehead's view the fundamental way to explain the difference between individuals is not to say that they exemplify mutually exclusive forms, but that the same forms have different modes of ingression in the concrete individuals. In metaphysics particulars are not to be taken as members of different species but as concrete individuals. They present different *syntheses* of the relevant forms. The fundamental principle is the existence of a creative process by which the "many" become "one."

If this is true there must be a sense in which each individual is unique, and we have seen in Part One how this is the case. Every actual occasion is a *novel* unity. It has a unique spatiotemporal region, and its region is an abstraction from its character as an act of experience. In its experience it aims at a unique possibility. This possibility is not a class or a species or a genus. It is the ideal for *that* concrescence and determines *how* actual entities and eternal objects may mingle in its experience. That is to say the subjective aim of an occasion is a "form of composition" (MT 129). It defines a pattern, or mode of togetherness, relevant to the situation in which the concrescence arises. It defines *how* the concrescence may become *concrete*. This principle of individuality, in Whitehead's metaphysics, supersedes in importance the principle of classification.

6. The infinitude of possibility

Now we are ready to approach the theory of eternal objects more directly. We have been examining his criticisms of the principle of classification as a mode of analysis in metaphysics. He thinks it is inadequate to express concrete unities. In recurring to his own theory of concrete unity and real individuals we have touched on a feature of eternal objects at which we need to look more directly.

Let us begin with those lines from Plato's *Sophist* which Whitehead italicizes for emphasis. The philosopher should show whether there are "some elements extending through all and holding them together so that they can mingle, and again, when they separate, whether there are other universal causes of separation." This suggests that if we take "the classes or genera" in themselves, they are neither mingled nor separated. They may mingle, or they may separate. Their mingling depends on "some elements extending through all and holding them together." At least this is a possibility the philosopher is to explore and decide. Again, he is to decide whether their separation depends on "other universal causes." Whitehead seems to be impressed with the suggestion that the forms in themselves are neither mingled nor separated but are capable of either mingling or separating.

In the next chapter I shall argue in detail that Whitehead has adopted this suggestion and embodied it in his theory of eternal objects. Here I want to show its bearing on classification. Eternal objects taken in themselves are in "isolation" (smw 230). As far as they themselves are concerned they *may* be together in any way at all or in no way. They *may* exclude each other in any way at all or in no way. This is to say they are "pure" possibilities. We should notice an implication of this view, namely the boundless and unstructured infinity of the "realm" of eternal objects, and the relation of this feature of eternal objects to the principle of creativity.

Whitehead is deeply impressed with what we might call the immensity of the domain of possibility. For example, he speaks of the inadequate grasp in "medieval philosophy, and indeed modern philosophy" of "the fecundity of nature and of the corresponding fecundity of thought" (FR 35), and says, "There are more ideas in heaven and on earth than were thought of in their philosophy" (FR 36). In another place where he is discussing the gradations of generality of ideas he says, "Thus the variation in the grades of ideas is endless, and it is not to be understood as a single line of increasing generality. This variation may be conceived as a spread involving an infinitude of dimensions. We can only conceive a finite fragment of this spread of grades" (IMM 692). Particularly interesting in this connection is an incident related by Lucien Price and dated in 1939: "Suddenly he stood and spoke with passionate intensity, 'Here we are with our finite beings and physical senses in the presence of a universe whose possibilities are infinite, and even though we may not apprehend them, those infinite possibilities are actualities.' He remained standing a moment, absorbed in his own thought . . ." (DIAL 133–4).

It is because of "the infinitude of possibility" (IMM 691) that forms are, we might say, always "patient" of new facts. For any situation in the course of nature, a novel "form of composition" is available. Something new can always come out of past achievements. Yet no new possibilities need to come into being *as possibilities*. "There are no novel eternal objects" (PR 33). New situations affect the relevance but not the being of eternal objects. There are and always will be enough ideas to go around. This infinitude of possibility is required by the principle of creativity.

Because the domain of eternal objects is all-inclusive it has no fixed order or structure. It is the entire multiplicity of possibilities including all possible orders or structures. " 'Order' is a mere generic term: there can only be some definite specific 'order,' not merely 'order' in the vague. . . . There is not just one ideal 'order' which all actual entities should attain and fail to attain" (PR 128). In this way also the domain of eternal objects is "patient" of creativity. Cosmic epochs with various types of order come into existence and pass out of existence. There can be no "final order" such that "beyond it there can be no progress" (PR 169). Thus the infinitude of possibility in both senses of infinitude, in boundlessness of extent and in absence of fixed order, is the counterpart or, one might better say, the expression of the principle of creativity. In contrast with the mutual exclusiveness of forms presupposed by classification, eternal objects may mingle, in infinitely many ways, in novel occasions of experience.

7. Incompatibility

This does not mean that there are no incompatibilities among forms. On the contrary, "Considering the Ideas by themselves, Plato points out that any selections are either compatible for joint exemplification, or are incompatible. It thus follows, as he notes, that the determinations of compatibilities and incompatibilities are the key to coherent thought, and to the understanding of the world. . . . The Aristotelian Logic is only a specialized derivative from this general notion" (AI 188). But this passage is misleading if it suggests that the incompatibilities are decided by eternal objects themselves. The phrase "for joint exemplification" needs strengthening by reference to other passages; for example: "Whatever is realized in any one occasion of experience necessarily excludes the unbounded welter of contrary possibilities. There are always 'others' which might have been and are not" (AI 356; see 334, MT 72, ESP [1932] 118). Note the phrase "in any one occasion of experience." There *are* incompatibilities and exclusions. An entity cannot both "be" and "not be." The point to notice is that the incompatibilities and exclusions of forms are not laid up in heaven:

> In the nature of things there are no ultimate exclusions, expressive in logical terms. For if we extend the stretch of our attention throughout the passage of time, two entities which are inconsistent for occurrence on this planet during a certain day in the long past and are inconsistent during another day in more recent past—these two entities may be consistent when we embrace the whole period involved, one

entity occurring during the earlier day, and the other during the later day. Thus inconsistency is relative to the abstraction involved (MT 76).

Exclusions of possibilities are decided by the natures of actualities. "Such exclusions belong to the finitude of circumstance" (MT 75).

Whitehead's point is that a mutually exclusive classification, for example that no elephants have wings, refers to a certain state of the world. It *happens* that there are no winged elephants. With the creative advance of nature new combinations become real possibilities. Exclusiveness among forms must be stated by contradictory propositions, and a proposition, in Whitehead's system, has for its logical subjects some set of actual entities (PR 35–6). If a proposition p predicates some eternal object of a certain set of actual entities, then the negation of p is an assertion that *those* actual entities do not have that form of definiteness. This is another way of saying that "In the nature of things there are no ultimate exclusions, expressive in logical terms."

The categoreal basis for the mutual exclusiveness of forms lies in the categoreal obligations of objective identity and objective diversity, which govern the concrescences of actual entities (PR 344–5). Real individuals are possible only if out of the concrescence there comes unambiguous character. A real individual must be *this* and not *that*. All contrasts must be decided. "For every actuality is devoid of a shadow of ambiguity" (PR 340). This intolerance of ambiguity, as an obligation within each individual concrescence, determines *that* forms are compatible or incompatible. The given situation, in conjunction with the subjective aim of the concrescence, determines *what* is compatible or incompatible for that concrescence. The subjective aim in response to the actual world determines how, in a given actuality, forms may mingle and how they may not. We might say it is a matter of fact, rather than a matter of logic, which determines both the necessity for and the nature of exclusions. "In the nature of things there are no ultimate exclusions expressive in logical terms" (MT 76).

It follows that incompatibilities of forms are relative to actual entities. It follows further that an adequate theory of forms must allow for new combinations of forms, in novel individuals which "escape" from the exclusions relative to their past actual worlds. "Now process is the way by which the universe escapes from the exclusions of inconsistency" (MT 75; see ESP 118). An adequate theory of forms must recognize the mingling of forms as well as their exclusiveness. And it follows that the principle of classification is subordinate to the principle of individuality, since classes are derivative from individual decisions.

In Part One we saw how the real individuality of an actual occasion, as a novel concretion of experience, required exclusiveness. Its subjective aim excludes alternate possibilities. Its experience excludes the subjective immediacies of other actual occasions. Derivatively, its spatiotemporal region excludes the regions of other actual occasions. We might now say that Whitehead points to the existence of mutually exclusive individuals, not to an exclusiveness intrinsic to forms themselves, as the real principle of "division." The exclusiveness of forms is required by, derivative from, and relative to the exclusiveness of real individuals. Instead of a fixed order of mutually exclusive forms, Whitehead's theory of eternal objects proposes an infinitude of possibility, patient of creative acts of becoming in which novel patterns of inclusion and exclusion are realized. Thus " 'order' in the actual world introduces a derivative 'order' among eternal objects" (PR 132). This, according to the ontological principle "that actual entities are the only *reasons*" (PR 37), is what should be expected.

8. Conclusion

We have examined Whitehead's criticism of the doctrine of classification which belongs to the traditional theory of universals. That doctrine is that universals are qualitative predicates, the chief use of which is to classify particulars into species and genera. Whitehead grants the importance and the necessity of classification for practical purposes and for science. We have explored his reasons for rejecting this doctrine as a sufficient principle of logic and as a fundamental principle in metaphysics.

In the course of his criticism certain features of his alternative view have emerged to be laid alongside the traditional one. These features of the theory of eternal objects may be restated as follows:

a. The domain of eternal objects includes mathematical ideas as well as universals of quality.

b. Among these mathematical ideas are patterns or "forms of composition." Thus there can be mingling of forms in novel individuals.

c. The exclusiveness of forms reflects and is relative to the exclusiveness of real individual actualities.

d. The domain of eternal objects is infinite, being all-inclusive and in itself unordered, so that it is open to, or patient of, creativity.

This final proposition needs to be substantiated, explored, and related to other features of Whitehead's system. This will be the aim of the following chapter.

CHAPTER 14

Is There a Realm of Eternal Objects?

1. Is there a consistent doctrine?

IN *Science and the Modern World* (1925) Whitehead speaks often of "the realm of eternal objects" or "the realm of possibilities" (chs. 10–11 passim, esp. 224). In *Religion in the Making* (1926) he continues to use equivalent expressions such as "realm of forms" (90, 98, 119, 154, 160), though the term "eternal objects" does not itself occur.

In *Symbolism* (1927) and *The Function of Reason* (1929) there is no reference to a "realm" of forms or ideas or eternal objects. This is not very significant, since in neither of these two small books does Whitehead introduce his own categories of existence in a systematic way. It is more significant that nowhere in *Process and Reality* (1929) does he speak of a "realm" of eternal objects or forms. Where he might have been expected to refer to the "realm" of eternal objects, he refers to the "multiplicity" of eternal objects (e.g. PR 46) or to "all" eternal objects (e.g. PR 48). Finally in *Adventure of Ideas* (1933), *Modes of Thought* (1938), and the last lectures ("Mathematics and the Good" and "Immortality") he mentions a "realm" of forms mainly as a doctrine of Plato requiring criticism and revision (MT 93–5, 138).

It seems clear that after 1926 Whitehead was reluctant, to say the least, to give the notion of a *realm* of eternal objects any important constructive function in his system. It would not be fair to conclude that there is *no* sense in which eternal objects are a realm. For in the course of his criticism of Plato he says, "We must admit that in some sense or other, we inevitably presuppose this realm of forms, in abstraction from passage, loss, and gain" (MT 93). But he would revise the Platonic conception. The realm of forms is not the realm of *being*, in some eminent sense of "being."

On the contrary, "The realm of forms is the realm of potentiality" (MT 95). But it does seem clear that he became discontented with this term. And this must mean there is some important sense in which eternal objects are *not* a realm.

The term "realm" might suggest: (a) a collection of entities severally different from the entities belonging to comparable collections; and (b) some fixed and necessary order among the members of the collection, so that these entities could not exist except in this order. Since the latter of these senses presupposes the former, whereas the former does not require the latter, we may call the former the weak sense and the latter the strong sense of the term.

Now from chapter 10 of *Science and the Modern World* it would appear that eternal objects *are* a realm in sense b, the stronger sense of the term. Whitehead says there: "Accordingly there is a general fact of systematic mutual relatedness which is inherent in the character of possibility. The realm of eternal objects is properly described as a 'realm,' because each eternal object has its status in this general systematic complex of mutual relatedness" (SMW 224). But in *Process and Reality* he says quite clearly that eternal objects do *not* have any "systematic mutual relatedness," and thus are *not* a realm in the strong sense of the term. They are a "multiplicity" (PR 46, 69). And according to category of existence vii multiplicities are "Pure Disjunctions of Diverse Entities" (PR 33).

Category of explanation xvi is:

> That a multiplicity consists of many entities, and its unity is constituted by the fact that all its constituent entities severally satisfy at least one condition which no other entity satisfies.
>
> Every statement about a particular multiplicity can be expressed as a statement referent either (a) to *all* its members severally, or (b) to an indefinite *some* of its members severally, or (c) as a denial of one of these statements (PR 36; see 44, 348).

Eternal objects, considered in themselves, are a "barren, inefficient disjunction of abstract potentialities" (PR 64). "There is not, however, one entity which is merely the *class* of all eternal objects. For if we conceive any class of eternal objects, there are additional eternal objects which presuppose that class but do not belong to it. . . . A multiplicity is a type of complex thing which has the unity derivative from some qualification which participates in each of its components severally; but a multiplicity has no unity derivative *merely* from its various components" (PR 73).[1] Another way of putting the point is to say that if we take eternal objects apart from the actual entities in which they are ingredient, they have no real togetherness. "The ontological principle can be expressed as: All real togetherness is togetherness in the formal constitution of an actuality" (PR 48; see 288). Eternal objects taken in themselves are a multiplicity.

The same doctrine is found in *Adventures of Ideas* and *Modes of Thought*. Whitehead speaks of an "unbounded welter" of possibilities (AI 356). His treatment of the notion of inconsistency makes the point particularly clear. Speaking of "the exclusions of inconsistency" he says, "Such exclusions belong to the finitude of circumstance" (MT 75). "In the nature of things there are no ultimate exclusions, expressive [i.e. expressible] in logical terms. . . . Thus inconsistency is relative to the abstraction involved" (MT 76). That is to say exclusion is a function of fact not of potentiality. And this implies the absence, from the welter of possibilities, of a general fixed structure intrinsic to the possibilities themselves. For if there were some such order in which every possibility had its status, then any *other* such order would be excluded. Some

1. In *Process and Reality* two different uses of "class" must be noted. (a) In this passage Whitehead means by a class something different from a multiplicity. He means a "complex thing" with an inner structure intrinsic to its components. Thus it would be possible to talk about the thing as a whole, or about some part of the thing, meaning by "whole" and "part" something more than all or some of the components of the thing taken severally. Here he is making a concession to current usage. For this sense of "class" he would substitute "nexus."

(b) A very different meaning of class appears later in *Process and Reality*. Here Whitehead *identifies* a class with a multiplicity: "For the essence of a class is that it assigns no diversity of function to the members of its extension. The members of a class are diverse members in virtue of mere logical disjunction. The 'class,' thus appealed to, is a mere multiplicity" (PR 348; see 137, ESP [1934] 314–16, *Principia Mathematica* I 62–3, 187).

"possibilities" would not then be possible. The realm of possibility would then itself determine what might or might not be actual. And it is just this that Whitehead is denying in *Modes of Thought*. He is in effect asserting that pure possibilities are *not* a realm in the strong sense of that term, but a multiplicity.[2]

How then can we explain the apparent conflict between *Science and the Modern World*, which asserts eternal objects *are* a realm in the strong sense of the term, and the later assertions that they are *not?* Two considerations about *Science and the Modern World* are in order. The first is that Whitehead does not give there a comprehensive exposition of his cosmology. There he is presenting for the first time, and only one at a time, some of his novel philosophical categories. Everything cannot be explained at once. The second consideration is that even in *Science and the Modern World* there are clear indications that the doctrine of a realm of eternal objects requires qualification. These indications occur at two points. One is the principle of the "isolation" of eternal objects. The other concerns the relation of eternal objects to God.

The relationships which form the structure of the realm of possibility "do not involve the individual essences of the eternal objects; they involve *any* eternal objects as relata, subject to the proviso that these relata have the requisite relational essences. . . . This principle is the principle of the *Isolation of Eternal Objects* in the realm of possibility. The eternal objects are isolated, because their relationships as possibilities are expressible without reference to their respective individual essences" (SMW 230). I take this to mean that the realm of eternal objects is a scheme of possible orders of eternal objects, not a single fixed order of eternal objects. As far as its "individual essence" is concerned, an eternal object does not imply or require any other eternal object. It has no single fixed place in the realm of possibility. It exists in isolation.

2. Compare George Santayana in *The Realm of Essence:* "No essence, accordingly, can imply any other in the sense of excluding from the realm of essence the opposite of the essence implied, or any different complement. From itself an essence may exclude anything; in fact it excludes everything not itself; but when a thing or a thought is said to preclude another, this happens only by virtue of adventitious laws of nature" (New York, Charles Scribner's Sons, 1927, p. 82).

Whitehead's very first reference to the conception of God he will later elaborate and defend is to "an underlying eternal energy in whose nature there stands an envisagement of the realm of all eternal objects" (SMW 148). But the passage most relevant to the issue at hand comes in chapter 11, where he is presenting an argument for the existence of God. He begins with the fact that there are particular, finite, ordered actualities. To explain this some limitation on possibility, not supplied by "the general metaphysical situation," is needed. That is to say neither the "general activity" (i.e. creativity) nor "the realm of eternal objects" nor both together could by themselves explain this fact. "So far as the general metaphysical situation is concerned, there might have been an indiscriminate modal pluralism apart from logical or other limitation." To explain the fact we must suppose "a limitation of antecedent selection" (SMW 248). Hence he introduces the conception of God as the principle of limitation.

This clearly implies that apart from God an "indiscriminate modal pluralism" is possible. Apart from the existence of God there would be no *order* of possibilities, and thus no *realm* of eternal objects in the strong sense of the term. Just as, without a principle of limitation, there could be no finite and ordered actualities, so also without such a principle there could be no value. Therefore there is a "second way of limitation," namely "an antecedent limitation among values, introducing contraries, grades, and oppositions" (SMW 249). The ordering of possibilities of actuality and value depends on the principle of limitation. If we consider eternal objects in themselves, apart from God, they have no logical order and no "contraries, grades, and oppositions." They are a realm only in the weak sense of that term.

Now this is the same doctrine we find in *Process and Reality*, namely that it is "the divine element in the world, by which the barren inefficient disjunction of abstract potentialities obtains primordially the efficient conjunction of ideal realization" (PR 64). If therefore we suppose that chapter 10 of *Science and the Modern World* should be taken with the qualification made explicit in chapter 11, it describes eternal objects as they exist in the primordial vision of God. It is then possible to resolve the apparent conflict between its doctrine and the clear teaching of

Process and Reality. The "general systematic complex of mutual relatedness," in which each eternal object has its status, is a limitation on the realm of eternal objects and is not intrinsic to it. Insofar as eternal objects have any order, this order is not intrinsic to them. It is derivative from and dependent on God. Later we shall find reason to question whether, even in the primordial vision, eternal objects have a *fixed* and *necessary* order. But first we should explore Whitehead's theory of eternal objects in themselves.

2. Eternal objects in themselves

Considered in themselves, eternal objects constitute a realm only in the weak sense. They are a multiplicity. There is some property common to eternal objects which no members of comparable multiplicities have. It is simply that an eternal object is an instance of a certain mode of existence. It is not an actual entity, or a prehension, or a nexus, or a subjective form, or a proposition, or a multiplicity, or a contrast. It belongs to a different "category of existence."

So the realm of eternal objects is distinct from comparable realms only in the way one category of existence is distinct from others. The separation between two such realms is not a separation between two actualities, like the separation between the United States and Canada. It is a distinction between two modes of existence (see AI 314).

At this point some brief remarks about Whitehead's ontology are in order. (a) He makes no systematic distinctions between "existence" and "being." All entities exist, and anything we think of is an entity (PR 206). The specific functions of entities of different categoreal kinds, including actual entities, are indicated in the eight categories of existence (PR 32–3) and explained in the categories of explanation. (b) Existence is not itself the ultimate category or, as Whitehead puts it, the Category of the Ultimate. Existence has to be explained:

> 'Creativity,' 'many,' 'one,' are the ultimate notions involved in the meaning of the synonomous terms 'thing,' 'being,' 'entity.' These three notions complete the Category of the

Ultimate and are presupposed in all the more special categories (PR 31).

. . . 'potentiality for process' is the meaning of the more
general [i.e. more general than "actuality"] term 'entity' or
'thing' . . . (PR 68; see 33, 43, 321, and AI 304).

This is why, in the categoreal scheme, there are categories of existence but existence is not a category of explanation.

Now we ask how it is possible to consider eternal objects in
themselves, that is to say in abstraction from actual entities. The
following passages pose a problem.

The ontological principle declares that every decision is re-
ferable to one or more actual entities, because in separation
from actual entities there is nothing, merely nonentity—
'The rest is silence' (PR 68).

Finally, the reformed subjectivist principle must be repeated:
that apart from the experiences of subjects there is nothing,
nothing, nothing, bare nothingness (PR 254).

'Actuality' means nothing else than this ultimate entry into
the concrete, in abstraction from which there is mere nonentity. In other words, abstraction from the notion of 'entry
into the concrete' is a self-contradictory notion, since it asks
us to conceive a thing as not a thing (PR 321; see 42, AI 254).

In these passages the insistence on concreteness is so strong that
it seems to rule out abstraction altogether. If we took them literally
we might reject the possibility of saying anything at all about
eternal objects in themselves. But this rejection would plainly
run counter to Whitehead's own practice. How then should "separation," "apart from," and "abstraction" be understood in these
passages?

Whitehead is saying, I suggest, that there cannot be anything
absolutely separated from actual entities, *totally* apart from the
experiences of subjects, in *complete* abstraction from "entry into
the concrete." He is ruling out discourse about entities which
have *no* relation to the actual world. *Complete* abstraction would
mean leaving out *all* relations to the actual world. And, he says,

"the notion of 'complete abstraction' is self-contradictory" (PR 42).

But he is not ruling out discourse which omits only *some* relations to the actual world. We might call this sort of discourse *relative* abstraction. In the following passage this distinction between complete and relative abstraction is made reasonably clear, and is applied to eternal objects: "Now an eternal object, in itself, abstracts from all determinate actual entities, including even God. It is merely referent to *any* such entities, in the absolutely general sense of *any*. . . . Thus the endeavour to understand eternal objects in complete abstraction from the actual world results in reducing them to mere undifferentiated nonentities" (PR 392).

This passage says (a) that it is meaningful to speak of eternal objects in themselves, and (b) that to do so is to abstract from all particular actual entities but not from actual entities in general. Legitimate abstraction leaves out some of the relations of eternal objects to actual entities, namely those relations which connect them with particular actual entities. But it does not leave out *all* of the relations of eternal objects to actual entities. Even at the extreme of abstraction the reference of eternal objects to "any such entities" is retained.

In *Modes of Thought* Whitehead says that in those lectures "The very notion of 'multiplicity' itself has been construed as abstraction from the forms of process whereby data acquire a unity of issue into a novel datum" (MT 133). This tells us how it is possible to think of eternal objects as a multiplicity. It is possible because the notion of a multiplicity is itself suggested by, and is an abstraction from, the actual world. There are many things around us. As we experience them, they function in a complicated network of relations, and they are of different kinds. Suppose now, selecting some one of the kinds, we ignore the network of relations among the things of this kind. We would then be contemplating a multiplicity. "The very diversity of eternal objects has for its reason their diversity of functioning in *this* actual world" (PR 392).

We have not yet done justice to a note which recurs in Whitehead's treatment of this subject, namely his hesitation at including multiplicities in the categories of existence. For example,

"Thus the many eternal objects conceived in their bare isolated multiplicity *lack any existent character*" (PR 530, my italics; see 392). Here is a paradox: Though multiplicities are one of the categories of existence they do not really exist. We may suppose Whitehead's difficulty runs as follows: All statements about a multiplicity can be expressed as statements about the members of the multiplicity severally. *Are* these statements then really *about* the multiplicity? Do we really have an *entity*, if all we can say about it must be said about its members? This ambiguity is the reason he says that multiplicities are not "proper entities." "Whenever the word 'entity' is used, it is to be assumed, unless otherwise stated, that it refers to an entity of one of the six kinds [i.e. the first six categories of existence: actual entities, prehensions, nexūs, subjective forms, eternal objects, propositions], and *not* to a multiplicity. . . . Entities of the first six kinds, and generic contrasts, will be called 'proper entities' " (PR 45; see 342).

This is an awkward expedient, because the statement of the categories of existence seems to presuppose a univocal meaning for "existence" and for "entity." It reflects, however, Whitehead's state of mind about multiplicities, including the multiplicity of eternal objects. Can it be thought of? The diversity of its members still reflects the diversity of the characteristics of actual entities. It is not a complete abstraction. But it is an extreme abstraction. Beyond this abstraction cannot go. Beyond this lies nonentity.

The question is, Can abstraction go this far? Does diversity have any meaning without some pattern of interrelations among the diverse entities? This is the question that troubles Whitehead and leads him to say that multiplicities are not proper entities. Certainly the attempt to think of eternal objects as a mere multiplicity takes us to a certain limit of thought.

3. How eternal objects are ordered by actual entities

Turning from consideration of eternal objects in themselves, transcendent of actual entities, we now consider the immanence of eternal objects in actualities. Still asking if there is a realm of eternal objects, we think of them less abstractly and ask about the ordering of them when they are ingredient in actual entities.

The general principle which applies here is that " 'order' in the actual world introduces a derivative 'order' among eternal objects" (PR 132). First consider how actual occasions introduce order among eternal objects. Guided by its subjective aim, an actual occasion achieves a certain order among its feelings as it proceeds toward satisfaction. In the feeling of satisfaction this order has become completely determinate. Certain aspects of its actual world will be included and other aspects excluded from the synthesis of feelings. Hence some eternal objects will become more important than others in the concrescence and satisfaction. Some will be subordinate to others. Some will be of negligible importance. Thus there will be a certain ordering of eternal objects, reflecting the pattern of feelings in the concrescence and satisfaction of the occasion (PR 69).

Now this ordering of eternal objects is an actual occasion's contribution to its future. Together with other actual occasions, X constitutes the actual world for some future concrescence M. Let us consider the totality of the orderings of eternal objects derivative from the occasions of M's actual world. Does this totality of orderings transform the multiplicity of eternal objects into a realm in the strong sense? Has the multiplicity of eternal objects taken on a single fixed order of relationships?

In two ways the orderings of eternal objects derivative from actual occasions fall short of transforming the multiplicity of eternal objects into a realm. In the first place, these orderings are *incomplete*. In any actual occasion "All the [already constituted] actual entities are positively prehended, but only a selection of the eternal objects" (PR 335). Again, at the end of a passage stressing the connection between "decision" and "givenness" Whitehead adds, "Conversely, where there is no decision involving exclusion, there is no givenness. For example, the total multiplicity of Platonic forms is not 'given.' But in respect of each actual entity, there is givenness of such forms" (PR 69; see 46). In X only a selection of eternal objects was positively prehended. Therefore the entire multiplicity of eternal objects will not be ordered for M by the satisfaction of X. And even if we add those orderings derivative from all the other actual occasions in M's actual world, some eternal objects will not be included. For some eternal objects will not have been realized anywhere in M's actual world. In this way the ordering of eternal objects by the decisions of actual occasions falls short of transforming the multiplicity of eternal objects into a realm. Any such ordering is incomplete because some eternal objects are not included in that order.

In the second place, the orderings of eternal objects derivative from actual occasions are *relative*. This is another way in which these orderings fall short of transforming the multiplicity of eternal objects into a realm. The order among eternal objects derivative from X is relative to X in the sense that it is effectively (PR 64) or positively (IMM 685) relevant only for those other occasions for which X is given. Thus it would not be effectively relevant for X's antecedents, and it would be effectively relevant for X's contemporaries only indirectly.

This relativity of the orderings derivative from actual occasions has been implicit in our discussion of the previous point. For the meaning of "actual world" is relative to particular concrescences (PR 34). Hence it was necessary to speak of M's actual world. The totality of orderings of eternal objects derivative from the occasions of M's actual world is relative to M. Only M has precisely *that* actual world. Hence only for M is the ordering of eternal objects derivative from that actual world effectively relevant.

In these two ways the orderings of eternal objects derivative from the decisions of actual occasions fall short of organizing eternal objects into a realm with a single determinate order of relationships. These orderings are incomplete, and they are relative.

Whitehead calls the order of eternal objects derivative from an actual world the "objective lure" for the concrescence arising from that actual world. "The 'objective lure' is that discrimination among eternal objects introduced into the universe by the real internal constitutions of the actual occasions forming the datum of the concrescence under review" (PR 281). The objective lure for a particular concrescence is "the gradation of eternal objects" in relevance to the data for that concrescence. It is a particular ordering of eternal objects. Eternal objects are "constituents" of the objective lure when they are "germane to the data" (PR 131). The objective lure includes eternal objects not physically realized

in the datum, as well as those which are. As an example Whitehead cites Hume's admission of an exception to the derivation of
"simple ideas" from "simple impressions," namely the possibility
of imagining a particular shade of blue one has never seen (PR
132–3). Again, he suggests that the possibility of a victory by
Napoleon at Waterloo, though excluded by actuality, is yet relevant to our actual world (PR 282).

Though some eternal objects are neither physically nor conceptually realized in the past actual world of a new concrescence,
all eternal objects *are* effectively relevant to the concrescence.
Whitehead's proximate explanation of this is the category of
"conceptual reversion" (PR 40). His ultimate explanation is that
each concrescence in its initial phase prehends God as well as
the occasions composing its past actual world. And God's nature
includes as its mental pole an envisagement of the entire multiplicity of eternal objects. "The primordial created fact is the
unconditioned conceptual valuation of the entire multiplicity of
eternal objects. This is the 'primordial nature of God' " (PR 46;
see 48, 248). So we have to consider the consequences of this
divine envisagement, as well as the orderings of eternal objects
derivative from the decisions of actual occasions.

This divine envisagement of the entire multiplicity of eternal
objects transforms this multiplicity into something more like a
realm in the strong sense of the term.

> This is the ultimate, basic, adjustment of the togetherness of
> eternal objects on which creative order depends (PR 48).

> This final entity is the divine element in the world, by which
> the barren inefficient disjunction of abstract potentialities ob-
> tains primordially the efficient conjunction of ideal realiza-
> tion. . . . By reason of the actuality of this primordial valua-
> tion of pure potentials, each eternal object has a definite,
> effective relevance to each concrescent process. Apart from
> such orderings, there would be a complete disjunction of
> eternal objects unrealized in the temporal world (PR 64; see
> 73, 392, 522).

Unlike the orderings derivative from actual occasions, the togetherness of eternal objects derivative from God's primordial vision is

absolute and complete. It is absolute in the sense that it is not relative only to some actual occasions but is effectively relevant to all
actual occasions. It is complete in the sense that no eternal objects
are omitted.

Furthermore the orderings of eternal objects derivative from
actual occasions depend on the order derivative from God. For
the ordering of the feelings of an actual occasion, from which the
ordering of eternal objects is derivative, is itself a function of the
subjective aim of the occasion, which is in turn dependent on God.
Thus the ordering of eternal objects derivative from God is not
only absolute and complete but primordial.

Though the temporal orderings of eternal objects depend indirectly on God, they nevertheless add something to the order of
eternal objects derivative from God. "There will be additional
ground of relevance for select eternal objects by reason of their
ingression into derivate actual entities belonging to the actual
world of the concrescent occasion in question" (PR 46). These
temporal orderings do not alter or negate the timeless togetherness
of eternal objects in the primordial nature of God. Whitehead
speaks of "the inevitable ordering of things, conceptually realized
in the nature of God" and says, "This function of God is analogous
to the remorseless working of things in Greek and in Buddhist
thought" (PR 373). If God's valuation of eternal objects is timeless, it cannot be affected by what occurs in time. But clearly these
temporal orderings must make some difference.

The way they make a difference is by adding to the relevance of
certain possibilities for succeeding occasions. Thus the eternal
object "blue" would have *some* relevance for any actual occasion,
by virtue of its inclusion in God's primordial vision. But it would
have *added* relevance for an actual occasion in whose actual world
blue things were important. The general relevance of all eternal
objects to a concrescence depends on the primordial nature of
God. A special relevance of some eternal objects is added by the
character of the actual world. In this way the pattern of relevance
of eternal objects changes with the creative advance of nature, although the timeless ordering of eternal objects in God's primordial
vision does not change.

Since the actual worlds of different concrescences differ in the
degree of order they have achieved, the orderings of eternal ob-

jects derivative from these actual worlds will differ in "richness" as well as in pattern: "The degree of order in the datum is measured by the degree of richness of the objective lure" (PR 136). The order of possibilities constituted by the actual world of one concrescence will include more eternal objects, more subtly related to each other in many complex ways, than the order relevant to another concrescence.

In the creative advance of nature, new "possibilities" are opened up. A form of definiteness prehended timelessly by God has a general relevance to actuality. It exists as a pure possibility. At some time and place, that is for some actual occasion, it may become a real possibility. The added relevance of eternal objects for a concrescence resulting from the decisions of past occasions makes the difference between pure possibility and real possibility. The emergence of new actualities makes some pure possibilities "really" possible. Thus actual occasions, as they lay down conditions for their successors, add their orderings of eternal objects to the timeless ordering of eternal objects in the primordial nature of God. This brings us to the heart of our problem.

4. Is there one ideal order of possibilities?

If the ordering of eternal objects is relative to individual actual occasions, so that the order of eternal objects relevant to M is different from that relevant to N, where M and N are any two actual occasions, then how can we speak of *an* order of eternal objects? We would seem to have, rather, as many orderings of eternal objects as there are actual occasions. This, indeed, is the case. " 'Order' is a mere generic term: there can only be some definite specific 'order,' not merely 'order' in the vague. . . . There is not just one ideal 'order' which all actual entities should attain and fail to attain. In each case there is an ideal peculiar to each particular actual entity, and arising from the dominant components in its phase of 'givenness' " (PR 128; see 64). There is not just one ideal order of possibilities which all actual entities approximate. Does this require us to rethink the significance of the primordial nature of God? It calls into question, it seems, the sense in which this primordial envisagement transforms the multiplicity of eternal objects into a *realm*.

Whitehead tells us that "eternal objects, as in God's primordial nature, constitute the Platonic world of ideas." But in what sense is this a "world"? Immediately after this sentence he adds, "There is not, however, one entity which is merely the *class* of all eternal objects. For if we conceive any class of eternal objects, there are additional eternal objects which presuppose that class but do not belong to it" (PR 73). And this suggests that, even as envisaged in the primordial nature of God, there is not one final and necessary order of eternal objects. For if there were such an order, then this would itself be a complex eternal object, and then there would be an eternal object which included all other eternal objects. Just this, it seems, Whitehead is denying. Some passages from *Adventures of Ideas* will help to make this clear:

> There are perfections beyond perfections. All realization is finite, and there is no perfection which is the infinitude of all perfections (AI 330).

> There is no totality which is the harmony of all perfections. Whatever is realized in any one occasion of experience necessarily excludes the unbounded welter of contrary possibilities. There are always 'others,' which might have been and are not (AI 356).

> This principle of intrinsic incompatibility has an important bearing upon our conception of the nature of God. The concept of impossibility such that God himself cannot surmount it, has been for centuries quite familiar to theologians. Indeed, apart from it there would be difficulty in conceiving any determinate divine nature. But curiously enough, so far as I know, this notion of incompatibility has never been applied to ideals in the Divine realization. We must conceive the Divine Eros as the active entertainment of all ideals, with the urge to their finite realization, each in its due season. Thus a process must be inherent in God's nature, whereby his infinity is acquiring realization (AI 357).

Particularly in the last of these passages he seems to be saying that, not only in themselves but also as objects of the divine envisagement, eternal objects have no final and necessary order.

All the ideal opposites are envisaged in the primordial nature of God. He includes in his primordial vision all possibilities. He envisages the entire multiplicity of eternal objects. His conceptual experience is "infinite, devoid of all negative prehensions" (PR 524). He does not choose between incompatible ideals but entertains them all. His primordial nature is the urge to the realization of *all* possibilities. "It has within it no components which are standards of comparison" (PR 75).

If, in the primordial nature of God, there were some eternal object which included all others and thus defined an ideal order of possibilities, then this eternal object would have been created by God. For among eternal objects in themselves there is no such entity, as we have seen. Eternal objects in themselves are a multiplicity. Hence this peculiar eternal object would have come into existence only by virtue of God's primordial vision. But this is impossible. "He does not create eternal objects; for his nature requires them in the same degree that they require him" (PR 392; see RM 157).

Thus there are no possibilities in the vision of God which are not members of the multiplicity of eternal objects taken in themselves. No eternal object escapes the status of membership in the multiplicity. Hence there is no eternal object which sums up or dominates the possibilities envisioned in the primordial nature of God. *Within* this realm of eternal objects, we might say, there is no sovereign.

Consequently even in the divine envisagement eternal objects are not a realm in the stronger sense of the term. There is not one fixed and necessary order of eternal objects. There is not one and only one way in which all things *must* happen. There is not even a pre-existing concept in the mind of God of how all things *will* happen. There is not even an ideal pattern of how all things *may* happen.[3] There is not as it were a heavenly city, an ideal cosmos conceptually realized in the mind of God, which the earthly city, the totality of temporal events, approximates. The

3. Does it follow that, in the absence of any such ideal order, God cannot be said to be disappointed by the particular order in which things *do* happen? Certainly Whitehead would say that God is not *defeated* by any particular order of happenings. To this point we return in Part Three.

realm of eternal objects is not a model, which the actual world might imitate or resemble. In short, "There is not just one ideal 'order' which all actual entities should attain and fail to attain" (PR 128).

But certainly there is some sense in which the primordial envisagement of God orders eternal objects. Eternal objects as envisaged by God certainly have a status and function which in themselves they do not have. I suggest that the primordial nature of God orders eternal objects in the sense, and only in the sense, that in God's envisagement eternal objects are *together*. "In what sense can unrealized abstract form be relevant? . . . 'Relevance' must express some real fact of togetherness among forms. The ontological principle can be expressed as: All real togetherness is togetherness in the formal constitution of an actuality. . . . Such a primordial superject of creativity achieves, in its unity of satisfaction, the complete conceptual valuation of all eternal objects. This is the ultimate, basic adjustment of the togetherness of eternal objects on which creative order depends" (PR 48). Because God values (i.e. has appetition for the realization of) *each* possibility in the multiplicity of eternal objects, all eternal objects become relevant to each other. Thus we have the "general scheme of relatedness of eternal objects" described in chapter 10 of *Science and the Modern World*.

This general scheme of relatedness is not, in one sense, an *order* of eternal objects. It is not a teleological arrangement of eternal objects into a single hierarchy. It is rather a matrix for those orderings effected by particular actual occasions in the course of nature. To say that there is a general scheme of relatedness among eternal objects is only to say that all relations are possible (SMW 229–30). If some certain eternal object were actualized, then all other eternal objects would be relevant in *some* way or other. It does *not* mean that if some certain eternal object were actualized, then there is some *particular* way in which it would be necessary for all other eternal objects to be relevant. The primordial nature of God is not an organizing principle in the sense of instituting an ideal order among possibilities. It is rather "the reservoir of potentiality" (MT 128).

In this light we should understand Whitehead's references to "the eternal order which is the final absolute wisdom" (PR 527), to "the unity of ideal inherent in the universe" (MT 39; see 142), and such passages as: "The basic elements in the World of Fact are finite activities; the basic character of the World of Value is its timeless coordination of the infinitude of possibility for realization" (IMM 695–6; see 686–7, 692–3). Though the overtones of these passages suggest the concrete unity of God's nature, primordial and consequent, their main point of reference is God's primordial appetition for the realization of *all* possibilities and in consequence the togetherness of eternal objects. Because of this togetherness "there is an order in the relevance of eternal objects to the process of creation" (PR 522; see 425). What needs to be kept in mind is that "order" in this sentence is a relative term. For *any* particular instance of becoming, all eternal objects are ordered in relevance to *that* concrescence, because all are together in the primordial vision of God. Likewise when Whitehead speaks of "the graduated order of appetitions constituting the primordial nature of God" (PR 315), this should not be understood as a single fixed and necessary order of eternal objects.

For *any* novel occasion, the whole multiplicity of eternal objects will be graded in relevance. They will be graded because the environment of the occasion has laid down basic conditions to which its concrescence must conform. These conditions pose real alternatives, and the necessity of decision and exclusion. Real possibility thus limits pure possibility and determines conditions of relevance. For *that* occasion the divine appetitions, by which unrealized possibilities become relevant for it, will have a certain graded order of relevance. For any other actual occasion, the divine appetitions will have a different order of relevance. Any particular ordering of primordial appetitions in God is relative to a particular instance of becoming. God in his primordial nature excludes *no* possibilities and for this very reason does not *order* possibilities, in the strong sense of "order." But he presents the entire multiplicity of eternal objects together, so that for any particular instance of becoming *all* pure possibilities will be ordered. In the primordial nature of God, taken in abstraction from acts of becoming, and hence in abstraction also from his consequent nature, eternal objects have togetherness but not gradations of importance.

Therefore it is truer to say that God envisages possibilities of order than that God envisages an order of possibilities. For his aim is not at some one order of things but at maximum intensity of feeling. " 'Order' and 'novelty' are but the instruments of his subjective aim which is the intensification of 'formal immediacy' " (PR 135). Whitehead's God, like Leibniz', envisages all possible worlds. Unlike the God of Leibniz' system, Whitehead's God does not choose *any* of the possible worlds. Rather, he values them *all*, even though they are not compossible. Thus God's primordial vision does not determine what world there shall be. God is not antecedent to nature, or before all creation. He is *with* all creation (PR 521). The function of his primordial nature is to hold the possible worlds together by his appetition for them all, so that all are relevant, in one way or another, to any particular actual world which occurs in the course of nature.

From the lack of a final and necessary order of eternal objects in the primordial nature of God it follows that there is no final order of nature.

> The immanence of God gives reason for the belief that pure chaos is intrinsically impossible. At the other end of the scale, the immensity of the world negatives the belief that any state of order can be so established that beyond it there can be no progress. This belief in a final order, popular in religious and philosophical thought, seems to be due to the prevalent fallacy that all types of seriality necessarily involve terminal instances. It follows that Tennyson's phrase, '. . . that far-off divine event To which the whole creation moves,' presents a fallacious conception of the universe (PR 169; see 139, AI 375).

Beyond any state of things there are unrealized possibilities with a claim on realization. No set of actualities can so exhaust the realm of possibility that nothing new could become. Creativity transcends any (though not all) of its instances.

A recapitulation of the interpretation of eternal objects this chapter has explained and supported is now in order:

a. In themselves, eternal objects have no fixed order. They do not constitute a realm in the strong sense of the term. They are a multiplicity.

b. As envisaged in the primordial nature of God, eternal objects are still not a realm in the strong sense of the word. Even as data for God's conceptual prehensions, eternal objects are not related in any single fixed order. In the primordial vision they are a realm only in the sense that they have a general togetherness; their individual essences are only externally related. In the divine vision there is no dominant or all-inclusive eternal object to which God subordinates all others. It follows that there is no one fixed order of possibilities in relation to which the ordering of all actualities could be determined.

c. Relative to any particular instance of becoming there is an ordering of eternal objects into degrees and modes of relevance. In the past actual world of the new concrescence certain possibilities have been realized. Others have not. This matter of fact determines an order of real possibility for the new concrescence, within the domain of possibility in general. The actual world has given an added relevance to certain eternal objects, which would otherwise have only the general relevance derivative from the primordial nature of God. To this order of real possibility the new concrescence must conform. In turn, by its integration of feeling in its satisfaction, it bequeaths to the future its own ordering of possibility.

We shall see in Part Three how God, in his consequent nature, prehends and coordinates into his own satisfaction the orderings of possibility achieved by actual occasions. But these orderings of eternal objects are relative and temporal—not necessary and eternal. It is still the case that there is no one fixed order of eternal objects. It is still true that in *this* sense eternal objects are not a realm.

5. Eternal objects and creativity

Now we are in position to ask another question about the coherence of Whitehead's system. Toward the end of Chapter 11 we considered how the theory of eternal objects is required by the theory of actual occasions. Now we can ask how the theory of an infinite and unordered multiplicity of eternal objects on the one hand, and the principle of creativity on the other, require each other.

First we ask how the theory of an infinite and unordered multiplicity of eternal objects logically requires the principle of creativity. Since according to the ontological principle actual entities are the only reasons, we must rephrase our question. How does the primordial appetition for the actualization of all eternal objects require creativity? A further refinement is necessary. For creativity is not an entity. Creativity is the unending production of finite and novel actual entities. So the question becomes: How does this primordial appetition require an infinite multiplicity of finite and novel actual entities?

If there is to be actualization of an infinite and unordered realm of possibilities, as envisaged in the primordial nature of God, then:

a. There must be an infinite multiplicity of actualities. This can be shown as follows. Any finite actuality orders possibility in its own constitution. And any finite set of actualities, taken together as a nexus, constitutes a more complex ordering of the realm of possibility. But no order of possibilities exhausts the realm of eternal objects, for it is an unordered realm. Hence, for the actualization of eternal objects an infinite multiplicity of actualities is required. Also:

b. There must be unending production of novel actualities. For this infinite multiplicity of actualities cannot exist at once. In that case the realm of possibilities would be exhausted and no unactualized possibilities would remain. But this would be contrary to the theory of eternal objects as an inexhaustible domain of possibility.

In this way Whitehead's theory of eternal objects requires creativity. The entertainment in the primordial nature of God of *all* possibilities with appetition for their realization requires a theory of actuality which has room for the unending creative activity of novel becomings.

Second we ask how, conversely, the principle of creativity requires the theory of eternal objects. Unending production of novel actualities by radical self-causation is logically possible only if the realm of eternal objects is inexhaustible and intrinsically unordered. Suppose on the contrary a single fixed order of possibilities. Then actuality would have to be construed in one of the following ways: (a) The necessary order of possibility is eternally and exhaustively actualized in an order constituted by one or many actualities, so that there are no unactualized possibilities and no actualities ever come into being; *or* (b) some actualities come into being, but they do so in accord with the eternally fixed order of possibilities which eternally determines what actualities shall become.

The first of these theories, like the systems of Spinoza and Mc-Taggart, construes actuality as necessary existence. The realm of possibility, one might say, is exhausted. The second, like the metaphysics of Leibniz, admits a certain kind of contingency of existence. The realm of possibility is ordered, prior to any actualization, but not exhausted. But it is a very mild kind of contingency indeed.

In either of these cases the principle of creativity is rejected. For creativity means the unending production of novel actualities by a process of self-creation. Against (a) the principle of creativity requires a theory of unactualized possibilities, so as to give meaning to novelty. Against both (a) and (b) the principle of creativity requires a looseness of relationship within possibility, the absence of a single fixed order of possibilities, so as to give meaning to the radical contingency involved in self-creation.

It appears then that the theory of a single fixed order of possibilities makes the principle of creativity logically impossible. For it leads to a theory of actuality which excludes novelty or self-creation or both. From this it then follows that the principle of creativity requires that possibilities be inexhaustible and unordered. This is to say that the principle of creativity requires the theory of eternal objects.

Therefore it seems that the theory of eternal objects and the principle of creativity require each other and that in this respect Whitehead's system is coherent. It would follow that, to the extent that the theory of actual occasions (as examined in Part One) requires and is required by the principle of creativity, that theory is coherent with the theory of eternal objects.

PART THREE

God and the World

CHAPTER 15

God and the Categories

1. Introduction

IN WHITEHEAD'S writings before 1925 I find only two remarks which might contain anticipations of his theory of God and the world. The first comes in the conclusion of his presidential address to the Mathematical Association in 1916. The essence of education, he says, is that it be religious. This means it should inculcate duty and reverence. And, he continues, "the foundation of reverence is this perception, that the present holds within itself the complete sum of existence, backwards and forwards, that whole amplitude of time, which is eternity" (OT 28; see 6). This might suggest that even at this stage his relational theory of space and time had for him an overtone of religious significance.

The second remark occurs at a point in *The Concept of Nature* where he is discussing the relation of mind to space and time. In the context he is directly concerned only with finite minds. But to make his point about finite awareness he introduces the idea of an "imaginary being," "whose awareness, conceived as his private possession, suffers no transition, although the terminus of his awareness is our own transient nature." Such a being might contemplate "all nature as an immediate fact" (CN 67, 69; see PA 221, ESP 135). He makes it clear that he is introducing a purely hypothetical idea merely for the sake of throwing light on our finite awareness of nature. This imaginary being has no function in his early philosophy of nature.

Whitehead's first explicit proposal of a doctrine of God comes in *Science and the Modern World,* in the chapter so titled. In *Religion in the Making* he relates his conception to some historical alternatives in religious thought. In the first four parts of *Process and Reality* his discussion of God is concerned primarily though not exclusively with the primordial nature of God (PR 47, 523), and for the most part is incidental to the development of his theory of actual occasions. In Part V the conception of God is discussed briefly though more directly. *The Function of Reason* has little to contribute to Whitehead's doctrine of God. Though *Adventures of Ideas* and *Modes of Thought* contain no extended systematic discussions of the subject, there are important passages in both. This is also true of the lecture on "Immortality" and the *Dialogues*.

As this brief survey might suggest, Whitehead's theory of God and the world is stated much less fully and systematically than his theory of actual occasions, and somewhat less so than his theory of eternal objects. The incompleteness of the theory and the location of the principal lacunae will appear as we proceed. Its main outlines are reasonably clear, but at several points we have to consider what formulations Whitehead's general principles suggest. In this respect Part Three is more interpretative than Parts One and Two, which were not altogether free from this necessity. Even so, my object is to make clear what Whitehead's principles require, not to construct an alternative theory.

Whitehead's language poses another problem of interpretation. Sometimes when we hope for rigorous statements of his theory of God and the world we find, as we have found elsewhere in his writings, metaphors and cryptic sayings. This reliance on concrete and evocative language is not a lapse from philosophy. As Whitehead sees it, speculative philosophy must (a) evoke the concrete experiences with which it begins, (b) construct a logical and coherent categoreal scheme, and (c) use the abstract categories to interpret the concrete experiences. Part of the philosopher's responsibility is to bridge the gap between his own systematic terms and those more familiar terms in which concrete experiences are ordinarily expressed. Also he ought to relate his terms to traditional philosophical language. On this view of philosophy we cannot expect a simple use of language. The problem is to know just how Whitehead is using language in a given passage. This sort of problem is somewhat more acute when we come to his doctrine of God because his systematic formulation is less complete.

With this conception of philosophy in mind, four brief remarks are in order on the relation of religious intuitions to White-head's systematic categories.

a. His system has no doubt been shaped in some degree by his own religious background and experience. But an adequate treat-ment of this genetic question would require a more intimate and extensive knowledge of his personal history than his writings af-ford us.

b. He accepts religious intuitions as part of the evidence to be considered in constructing a metaphysical system (RM 58–67, PR 23). They are by no means the whole evidence. Aesthetic, scien-tific, and practical experiences have to be interpreted also. Indeed religious and moral intuitions are "somewhat exceptional ele-ments in our conscious experience" (PR 521).

c. Metaphysics cannot be content with those imaginative repre-sentations which directly reflect religious intuitions. These ideas play an essential part in religious life. "But if we attend to the general principles which regulate all endeavours after clear state-ment of truth, we must be prepared to amplify, recast, generalize, and adapt, so as to absorb into one system all sources of experi-ence" (RM 149). Speculative philosophy must construct a scheme of ideas which transcends ordinary formulations of experience in logical rigor, coherence, and generality. It must absorb into the system whatever truths about experience religious intuitions may apprehend. Most of Part Three will be occupied with Whitehead's doctrine of God and the world as a feature of his metaphysical scheme.

d. It is then possible to apply this system of general concepts to the problems of religious thought. For example, in Part V of *Process and Reality* he says, "Apart from reference to existing reli-gions as they are, or as they ought to be, we must investigate dis-passionately what the metaphysical principles, here developed, require on these points [i.e. the points at which the historic reli-gious conceptions conflict with one another], as to the nature of God" (PR 521).

It remains to indicate the topics of the succeeding chapters in Part Three. In the present chapter I examine the relation of Whitehead's conception of God to the basic categories of his sys-tem. Chapter 16 asks how God affects the actual occasions which make up the world. Chapter 17 asks the opposite question, how the world affects God. Chapter 18 sums up Whitehead's theory of God and the world, employing for this purpose the categories of transcendence and immanence. Finally Chapter 19 presents his critique of traditional theology and comments on its significance.

2. God as an actual entity

The first though not the only philosophical question about Whitehead's conception of God is whether it is consistent and coherent with the first principles of his system. He invites this question when he charges Descartes and Leibniz with introducing the concept of God in arbitrary ways. For example, referring to Descartes's conception of bodily substances, he says, "Descartes tells us that they are sustained by God, but fails to give any reason why God should care to do so" (FR 24). Again, he criticizes the artificial way in which Descartes made God a requirement of his theory of knowledge (PR 78, 219). Similarly, Leibniz mitigated the mutual isolation of the monads by introducing the concept of God: "But no reason can be given why the supreme monad, God, is exempted for [from] the common fate of isolation. Monads, according to this doctrine, are windowless for each other. Why have they windows toward God, and Why has God windows toward them?" (AI 171). Of this use of the concept of God Whitehead says, "It is a device very repugnant to a consistent rationality. The very possibility of knowledge should not be an accident of God's goodness; it should depend on the interwoven natures of things. After all, God's knowledge has equally to be explained" (PR 289; see SMW 217, PR 78). His objection is not to making God necessary for knowledge. It is rather that Descartes and Leibniz have not shown *how* the nature of God is interwoven with the natures of other beings.

At the beginning of his discussion of God in the final part of *Process and Reality* he says, "In the first place, God is not to be treated as an exception to all metaphysical principles, invoked to save their collapse. He is their chief exemplification" (PR 521; see SMW 130, AI 216). Here he points to the root of the errors he has been indicating and resolves to avoid them. The root of these errors consists in making God an exception to the fundamental principles of the system. In effect, if not in the intention of those philosophers, their categories fail to apply to God. Whitehead, on the contrary, proposes to treat the concept of God as the chief exemplification of the categories of his system. We must ask whether he has carried out this intention successfully.

One way of putting the question is to ask whether God "exists" in a categoreally different sense from that in which finite actualities exist. Whitehead holds, contrary to Descartes, that "God's existence is not generically different from that of other actual entities, except that he is 'primordial' in a sense to be gradually explained" (PR 116). God and actual occasions are alike actual entities. Actual entities

> differ among themselves: God is an actual entity, and so is the most trivial puff of existence in far-off empty space. But, though there are gradations of importance, and diversities of function, yet in the principles which actuality exemplifies all are on the same level (PR 28).

> The presumption that there is only one genus of actual entities constitutes an ideal of cosmological theory to which the philosophy of organism endeavours to conform. The description of the generic character of an actual entity should include God, as well as the lowliest actual occasion, though there is a specific difference between the nature of God and that of any occasion (PR 168; see 135).

We may ask therefore whether in effect as well as in Whitehead's intention all that is said about actual entities generally in the categoreal scheme does apply to God as well as to actual occasions.

Whitehead certainly applies to God many of the categories that apply to actual occasions. God is a unity of conceptual and physical experience (PR 54). He is concrescence (PR 47, 54, 134), satisfaction (PR 48, 135), and superject (PR 135, 532; MT 128). He has subjective aim (RM 100; PR 134–5, 522, 524) and subjective forms of feeling (PR 50, 134, 522). He exists formally, as an immediate actuality, and he exists objectively for other actual entities (PR 47, 377–8). In all these ways God appears to be an exemplification of the categories defining actual entities.

It is equally certain that there are important differences be-

tween God and actual occasions. The fundamental difference is
that God is primordial (PR 116). Every other actual entity originates at some time and emerges into being from some definite
past actual world. God originates at no time. In the concrescence
of other actual entities, physical experience is genetically prior to
conceptual experience. Actual occasions originate from the physical pole of their experience (but see PR 343). In the concrescence
of God conceptual experience is genetically prior to physical experience. Thus God "originates" from the mental pole of his
experience (PR 54). God's prehensions of the multiplicity of eternal objects are not conditioned by his prehensions of actual entities. This envisagement of pure possibilities is nontemporal and
thus primordial. "The given course of history presupposes his
primordial nature, but his primordial nature does not presuppose it" (PR 70; see 11, 134).

From this fundamental difference between God and actual occasions it follows that (a) his conceptual experience is unlimited,
as we saw in Chapters 13 and 14, since it is not restricted by the
exclusions of actuality. (b) It follows also that God is everlasting.
He does not perish, as all other actual entities do. For primordial
means "not *before* all creation, but *with* all creation" (PR 521).
In his "consequent" nature he prehends every other actual entity
throughout the course of nature.

The difference between God and actual occasions does not
amount to a categoreal difference, however, and this explains why
there is no explicit reference to God in the categoreal scheme.
God is not specifically mentioned in any of the categories of existence, the categories of explanation, or the categoreal obligations.
Instead, the conception of God is systematically introduced in the
following chapter titled "Some Derivative Notions," along with
the conceptions of personal and social order and the extensive
continuum. The reason for omitting mention of God from the
categoreal scheme is that the scheme gives a rigorous statement of
the generic traits of actual entities. And in Whitehead's intention
God is an actual entity, not a being outside the range of the
categoreal scheme. Categoreally speaking, the conception of God
like the conception of the extensive continuum is a "derivative
notion." The existence of a primordial and everlasting actual en-

tity follows not from the categoreal scheme but from the nature of the world.

Now we are ready to examine Whitehead's claim. As we survey the categoreal scheme two major problems arise about the application of the categories to God. They concern conceptual valuation and the satisfaction of an actual entity.

3. Conceptual valuation

Categoreal obligation iv, the category of conceptual valuation, is as follows: "From each physical feeling there is the derivation of a purely conceptual feeling whose datum is the eternal object determinant of the definiteness of the actual entity, or of the nexus, physically felt" (PR 39–40; see 379–80). It seems that this category does not apply to God in the same way as to actual occasions. For God's conceptual prehensions do not originate from his physical experience. They are primordial and timeless. Therefore, "God differs from other actual entities in the fact that Hume's principle, of the derivate character of conceptual feelings, does not hold for him" (PR 134; see 378). But might not God have *both* underived and derived conceptual feelings, while actual occasions have *only* derived conceptual feelings? In this way the category of conceptual valuation might still apply. I do not believe this is a fair reading of Whitehead's intention. But it deserves some attention for the sake of making his theory clearer.

Applied to God, categoreal obligation iv would mean that from each of God's physical feelings some purely conceptual feeling is derived. Now since God prehends every actual occasion, new physical prehensions continually enter his concrescence. It would follow that new conceptual feelings, derived from these physical feelings, arise in his experience. But how is this possible, if God's primordial conceptual experience is complete? In his primordial nature there are prehensions of all eternal objects. No new eternal objects can arise in the course of nature. Then how is it possible for God to have new conceptual prehensions?

The difficulty may be put as follows. Suppose some actual occasion A in which an eternal object R is ingredient. Then from his prehension of A, God would derive a pure conceptual prehension of R. But God has a primordial prehension of R. So God would have at least two pure conceptual prehensions of R.

This result conflicts with a principle of economy that is implicit in the conception of organic unity. This Whiteheadian version of Occam's Razor lies just below the surface of the categoreal scheme and becomes explicit at several points. It is most explicit in categoreal obligation ii, the category of objective identity: "There can be no duplication of any element in the objective datum of the 'satisfaction' of an actual entity, so far as concerns the function of that element in the 'satisfaction' " (PR 39; see also categories of explanation vi and xxvi). This principle of economy would seem to apply also to the case we are considering. For it is not clear how the function of the derived feeling of R would differ from the function of the underived feeling of R in the divine experience. They would seem to have only a sham diversity (PR 348).

Certainly God must have conceptual valuations, and there must be a conceptual valuation relevant to the ingredience of R in A. To this extent the category of conceptual valuation applies to God as well as to actual occasions. But this is provided for without any derivation of conceptual feelings from physical feelings. When God prehends A, his aim at unity produces a propositional feeling to integrate his prehension of A and his primordial prehension of R. The proposition felt has A as its logical subject and R as its predicative pattern (PR 393). Later genetic phases in the divine concrescence integrate this propositional feeling with others into the divine satisfaction. But in this process there seems no need for a derived conceptual feeling of R. Since God timelessly envisages all pure possibilities he does not need to derive any purely conceptual feelings from his physical experience.

To bring out the features of Whitehead's theory more distinctly let us consider some alternative views. Suppose that God's conceptual experience, as well as his physical experience, were always incomplete. On this theory God's pure conceptual experience could be affected by his physical experience. Two versions of this theory might be distinguished.

a. We might hold with Whitehead (and Santayana) that there are specific, or "particular," pure potentials. "Thus every so-called 'universal' is particular in the sense of being just what it is, diverse from everything else" (PR 76; see SMW 222). But we might also hold, against Whitehead, that novel pure potentials come into *being* in the course of nature. These novel potentials would be apprehended by God when and only when novel actual situations occur. The domain of pure possibility, for God, would be a growing domain. Thus his conceptual experience would be always incomplete.

The contrast with Whitehead's view would be as follows. He holds that in the advance of nature some pure possibilities become effectively *relevant* which were only barely relevant before. Pure possibilities become real possibilities. But pure possibilities do not come into being. They are *eternal* objects. On the alternative view pure possibilities come into *being* which were not in being before.

b. Another version of the theory that God's conceptual experience is incomplete is suggested by Charles Hartshorne. On this view there are no specific pure possibilities. There are only dimensions of potentiality. Possibility is not a multiplicity but a continuum. Actualization is the specification of what is unspecific, the determination of what is indeterminate. On this version God's conceptual experience is always incomplete in the sense that its data are always incompletely specified, though always becoming more specific in the course of nature.

It is true that on Whitehead's view the process of actualization *includes* a kind of specification, as we shall see in the next chapter. But in any particular process of actualization what becomes more specific is not a pure possibility but a real possibility or, more exactly, a proposition. Eternal objects are timelessly specific. An eternal object is "just what it is, diverse from everything else" (PR 76). Thus the data of God's *pure* conceptual experience do not become more specific and therefore his conceptual experience is not in this sense incomplete.

On either of these versions of the theory that God's conceptual experience is essentially incomplete, God's physical experience would affect his pure conceptual experience. On the first version his physical experiences *produce* new data for his pure conceptual feelings. On the second version his physical experiences *specify* what was unspecific in the data (or perhaps we should say the datum) of his pure conceptual experience. But neither of these views would be consistent with Whitehead's theory of eternal objects and his conception of God.

The completeness of God's primordial nature seems to prevent the category of conceptual valuation from applying to God in the way it applies to actual occasions. For the same reason categoreal obligation v, the category of conceptual reversion, is inapplicable to God. This states: "There is secondary origination of conceptual feelings with data which are partially identical with, and partially diverse from, the eternal objects forming the data in the first phase of the mental pole. The diversity is a relevant diversity determined by the subjective aim" (PR 40). This explains how an actual occasion can prehend eternal objects that are not ingredient in its actual world. Clearly it is not designed to apply to God. Later, when he has introduced hybrid physical feelings of God, it turns out that even as applied to actual occasions it was only a provisional explanation. "Thus, a more fundamental account must ascribe the reverted conceptual feeling in a temporal subject to its conceptual feeling derived, according to Category IV, from the hybrid physical feeling of the relevancies conceptually ordered in God's experience. In this way . . . a more complete rational explanation is attained. The category of reversion is then abolished" (PR 382). If this category is not even a necessary condition of finite concrescences, its inapplicability to God raises no problem.

A more important consequence concerns categoreal obligation vi, the category of transmutation, which presupposes categoreal obligation iv (PR 40). This is designed to explain how finite mentalities simplify physical experience. "The irrelevant multiplicity of detail is eliminated, and emphasis is laid on the elements of systematic order in the actual world" (PR 388; see 382-9, AI 273-8). God does prehend all patterns of order in the actual world. But we shall see in Chapter 17 how he does not need to eliminate from his data in order to prehend the actual world into a unity of experience. So here too, as in the case of the category of conceptual valuation, God is exempt from some of the conditions that limit finite experiences, and for the same reason.

If categoreal obligations iv and vi do not apply fully to God, how are we to reconcile this fact with the claim that God is the "chief exemplification" of "metaphysical principles" (PR 521)? One might say that these categories are not meant to be statements of metaphysical principles in a strict sense of "metaphysical." The inclusion of the category of conceptual reversion in the scheme would count in favor of this suggestion. On this view God does not need to exemplify all the categories in order to exemplify metaphysical principles. Indeed sometimes it seems that Whitehead does not object to exempting God from *some* "metaphysical principles" (in a weaker sense of "metaphysical") but only to exempting him "from *all* the metaphysical categories which applied to the individual things in this temporal world" (AI 216, my italics).

Another suggestion is to apply the category of conceptual valuation to God by construing "derivation" ambiguously. We might say that in actual occasions the concrescence *produces* a pure conceptual feeling by abstraction from the physical datum, and that in God the concrescence *connects* a (primordial) conceptual feeling *with* the physical datum. In all cases the concrescence then proceeds by producing propositional feelings to integrate conceptual and physical feelings. With this interpretation of derivation, the category of transmutation might also be applied to God as an account of how he prehends all the patterns of order in the actual world, but without the suppression of individual particularities that attends transmutation in actual occasions. But this construction of derivation is certainly not suggested by the category as stated.

A better suggestion is that categoreal obligation iv might be restated. It might say *there is* conceptual valuation of every physical feeling. Then it might be a consequence or "derivative notion" (PR 46 title) that actual occasions *derive* purely conceptual feelings from physical feelings. This would leave the way open for saying that, as a consequence of his complete primordial valuation, God does *not* derive purely conceptual feelings from physical feelings.

It is plain that the pure conceptual feelings of actual occasions have to be "explained" in a sense in which God's pure conceptual feelings do not. God's conceptual feelings have no "origin" in the sense that those of actual occasions do. This difference between "the primordial actual entity" and "the temporal actual entities" (PR 102) is repeatedly emphasized in Whitehead's discussions of actual entities. The categoreal scheme ought to allow for this difference more carefully than it does. The line between those statements that properly apply to all actual entities without exception, and those statements that apply only to actual occasions or only to God, needs to be drawn more clearly and firmly. But this could be done without altering the basic structure of the system.

4. Satisfaction

The second major problem about the application of the categories to God concerns the feeling of satisfaction. The problem about God's conceptual valuations arose because of the completeness of his primordial experience. This problem arises because of the incompleteness of his consequent experience.

Category of explanation xxv is as follows: "The final phase in the process of concrescence, constituting an actual entity, is one complex, fully determinate feeling. This final phase is termed the 'satisfaction.' It is fully determinate (a) as to its genesis, (b) as to its objective character for the transcendent creativity, and (c) as to its prehension—positive or negative—of every item in its universe" (PR 38). Does this category properly apply to God as well as to actual occasions? Whitehead certainly means to say God has a satisfaction (PR 48, 134, 135). But at least three questions naturally arise.

One question is about (a) the *unity* of God's satisfaction. The satisfaction is a unified feeling. God's satisfaction would be a unification of his primordial nature and his consequent nature. But since God is always in concrescence, how can his experience have such a unity? Another question is about (b) the *determinateness* of God's satisfaction. How can God's satisfaction be "fully determinate" as to its data, since his physical experience is of a changing world? A third question is about (c) the *finality* of God's satisfaction. The satisfaction is the "final phase" in the process of concrescence. But if God is everlasting, how can he have a final phase? It is easy to see that these questions are closely related, but they must be dealt with one at a time.

a. *The unity of God's satisfaction.* The satisfaction of an actual entity is the realization of its subjective aim at unity of experience. The feeling of satisfaction unifies the many feelings which have arisen in the concrescence. It is an integral feeling. How can God have such a unified feeling when novel physical prehensions are continually being added to his experience?

To this, as to some other problems about the significance of God in his system, Whitehead has not given much explicit attention. An answer might be constructed in somewhat the following way:

i. Suppose as God's satisfaction a single continuous feeling. It has no temporal origination, nor does it ever cease. It continues throughout the course of nature.

ii. The data of this feeling, "at any time," are (a) the entire multiplicity of eternal objects and (b) all those actual occasions which, at that time, have come into being.

iii. The subjective form of this feeling is derived uniformly, though not exclusively, from God's timeless and unchangeable subjective aim.

The divine satisfaction would then be a continuous feeling with a constant subjective form and changing data, though not all the data change. It would be one complex integral feeling. We could say that God is *always* satisfied, meaning "at any time," or "relative to any finite standpoint." His physical prehensions would contribute their subjective forms as well as their data to his satisfaction (PR 39). But since these subjective forms are unified by God's unconditioned subjective aim (PR 49–50, 523), there would be no disharmonies to mar the unity of the divine satisfaction.

b. *The determinateness of God's satisfaction.* In the feeling of satisfaction all indetermination has "evaporated" (PR 71). The relation of the subject to every other entity is entirely determinate. But how is this possible in the case of God? If the data of his physical prehensions are always changing, how can his satisfaction be fully determinate?

The satisfaction of an actual occasion can be determinate because the actual occasion is in the strict sense unchanging. It perishes but does not change. During its internal process it is closed against further additions to its data, so that its experience may become unified and determinate. It is for this reason that contemporary actual occasions must be causally independent. At the end of this definite duration it must perish. This is the essence of the epochal theory of time.

In the case of God this condition for determinateness of experience does not hold. Actual occasions perish but do not change. God changes but does not perish. Thus we confront a challenging question. Unlike that provoked by traditional theology, which forces us to ask: How can an utterly unchanging being have any real knowledge of the changing world?, the question Whitehead's view provokes is: How can a constantly changing being have a fully determinate experience of the changing world?

The answer to this question begins to appear when we consider the categoreal explanation of determinateness of satisfaction. The feeling of satisfaction is fully determinate as to its prehension of every item "in its universe" (PR 38). Now if we understood by "universe" a static totality of actual things, and if we asked how a changing being could have a determinate experience of the universe so understood, we should indeed have an insoluble puzzle on our hands. But this interpretation of "universe" is precisely what Whitehead's principle of process excludes (PR 327). It denies the existence of a fully *actual* totality. The existence of unactualized possibilities and the becoming of novel actualities is a categoreal necessity. "Universe" like "actual world" has meaning relative to finite standpoints in the creative advance of nature (PR 42, 354). The universe now, for any meaning of "now," is not what it was and not what it will be.

We can then say that God's prehension of every item in the universe, relative to any finite standpoint, is fully determinate. Relative to any standpoint, he prehends possibilities as possibilities and actualities as actualities. It is true that God apprehends an indeterminate, because unactualized, future. But so do actual occasions, and in both cases there is prehension of determinate possibilities for that future. It is further true that God, unlike actual occasions, is everlasting so that he is continually prehending new actualizations. But it remains true that, whether for God or for an actual occasion, only those entities can be physically prehended which, relative to a finite standpoint, are *then* actual.

We may say then that God's satisfaction is always incomplete in two senses. It is incomplete in that it always includes appetitions for unrealized possibilities. And it is incomplete in that new data are ever being prehended into it, with the creative advance of nature. In this way we might say that God is always incompletely actualized. Nevertheless his prehensions of actual occasions, as well as his prehensions of eternal objects, are at all times fully determinate. In this sense his satisfaction is always complete.

This interpretation reconciles internal process in God with determinateness of satisfaction by assuming a *systematic* relationship between God's experience and the changing world. And this implies that there is a reflection within his own experience of the epochal character of actual occasions. It means, to appropriate from another context some words of James which Whitehead quotes with approval, that God's experience of the changing world "grows literally by buds or drops of perception" (PR 105).

c. *The finality of God's satisfaction.* How can we say that God's satisfaction is the "final phase" of his concrescence? God aims not at some finite objective but at the realization of all possibilities whatever. So it would seem that, since there will always be unrealized possibilities, God must be always unsatisfied. How can there be any final phase in his experience?

This question must be answered in two stages. First let us recur to the distinction between the two kinds of process (PR 320, 326–7), for they suggest two different senses of "finality." The process of concrescence goes on within the immediacy of the actual entity. It is internal process. In the process of transition the influence of the actual entity passes beyond itself and affects other actual entities. The actual entity becomes objectively immortal in another.

Consider first the process of transition. In the case of actual occasions, transition requires perishing. The satisfaction must be final in the sense that the occasion has no immediate experience after its own satisfaction. Becoming objectively immortal means ceasing to have subjective immediacy. The satisfaction must be the end or terminus of the internal process of the occasion. Considering the process of transition, then, we may say that the satisfaction of an actual occasion is temporally final. With the satisfaction the occasion comes to an end in time.

Now it is clear that God's satisfaction cannot be final in this sense. In his case, and in his case alone, objectification does not require perishing. Is God in this respect an exception to Whitehead's categories as stated in the categoreal scheme? Does the categoreal scheme require that all actual entities perish?

The only explicit assertion about perishing in the categoreal scheme occurs in a subordinate sentence in category of explanation xxii, which is: "That an actual entity by functioning in respect to itself plays diverse roles in self-formation without losing its self-identity. It is self-creative; and in its process of creation transforms its diversity of roles into one coherent role. Thus 'becoming' is the transformation of incoherence into coherence, and in each particular instance ceases with this attainment" (PR 38; see 517). Two alternative interpretations, each consistent with Whitehead's doctrine of God, are possible: (i) The phrase "in each particular instance" might be taken as restricting the final clause of the last sentence to actual occasions. Thus "becoming" applies to God and to actual occasions; "cessation" applies only to "particular instances," that is to actual occasions. (ii) The consequent nature of God is made up of many particular instances of becoming, since every actual occasion makes a particular contribution to God's unending satisfaction. The reaction of God to an actual occasion is thus a particular instance of God's continual becoming. Each of these internal processes (particular instances) of becoming begins with God's prehension of an actual occasion and ceases with the absorption of this datum into his satisfaction.

Either interpretation is consistent with Whitehead's doctrine that God does not perish as actual occasions do. Unlike the satisfactions of actual occasions, God's satisfaction cannot be temporally final, for God does not come to an end in time. It can be final only in some other sense.

Another sense of finality becomes prominent as we turn from the process of transition to the process of concrescence. This is a process of growth. Many prehensions, physical and conceptual, are shaped by the immanent teleology of the subjective aim into a unity of experience. This process begins with an initial phase of conformation to the given world. It continues, through intermediate phases of conceptual elaboration including comparative feelings, until all these feelings are brought together in the feeling of satisfaction.

When we consider the satisfaction from within the concrescence, its primary significance is teleological. It is the goal and the achievement of subjective aim. In the case of actual occasions the satisfaction is also a terminus. This is because the subjective aim is at intensity in both the immediate subject and the relevant future (PR 41), and because the perishing of an actual occasion is a condition of the becoming of future occasions. Therefore the satisfaction is the temporal end or *finis* of the occasion. Its terminal character is entailed by the finiteness of actual occasions. But from the standpoint of the internal process the satisfaction is primarily the internal end or *telos* of the concrescence.

Now we can explain how God's satisfaction is the "final phase" of his concrescence. In an actual occasion the satisfaction is both the telos and the finis of the concrescence. It is the goal achieved by the concrescence and it is also the temporal end of the concrescence. In God on the contrary the satisfaction is telos but not finis. God aims at and achieves satisfaction but he does not perish. Only in this way can God's concrescence have a final phase.

We now have to ask, as a second stage in dealing with our question, how God can achieve a telos. The problem is not how appetition for unrealized possibilities can be a component in a satisfaction. Such appetition is not distinctive of God. An actual occasion also includes such appetition, as anticipatory feeling, in its satisfaction. Every actual entity, whether God or an actual occasion, must synthesize given facts and unrealized possibilities.

The problem is rather how, in relation to the multiplicity of actual situations in nature, God has *a* satisfaction. It is possible to think of God as having specific satisfactions corresponding to these actual situations. But then God would have as many satisfactions as there are actual occasions. We return thus to our earlier question about the unity of God's satisfaction.

In the course of nature the data of God's physical prehensions vary. Later we shall see how the subjective forms of these prehensions also vary, in conformity with their data. Now these subjective forms are conditioned not only by their data but also by God's subjective aim which arises from his primordial appetition and therefore is always the same throughout the course of nature (PR 523). Thus while the data of his physical prehensions vary discontinuously, as novel epochal acts of experience come into being, the subjective forms of these feelings vary continuously. Moreover, relative to any finite standpoint his physical prehensions are synthesized with his primordial conceptual prehensions into his satisfaction. Thus God's experience has a constant aim and structure which gives it unity and continuity through time.

For this reason the satisfaction into which God absorbs his prehensions of the multiplicity of actual occasions is not itself a multiplicity but a unity of feeling. It is one continuous satisfaction. It is not a timeless feeling, as pure abstract forms are "timeless." It is not *timelessly* one, determinate, and final. It is a living experience. But it is *always* one, determinate, and final. It is indeed *unchangeably* one, determinate, and final. The changing course of nature, though it affects God's experience in ways we shall examine in Chapter 17, cannot change the categoreal structure of God's satisfaction.

5. Conclusion

A careful inspection of the categoreal scheme fails to reveal other problems about its application to Whitehead's conception of God. In the first category of existence and in the first category of explanation "actual entity" and "actual occasion" are used as though they were interchangeable, contrary to later rules of usage. But this is only an inelegance in use of terms. I conclude that Whitehead's attempt to state a set of first principles which apply both to God and to actual occasions has been reasonably successful. Further support for this conclusion and further discussion of its implications will be forthcoming in later chapters.

It is not enough to see whether all that is said of actual entities in the categoreal scheme can be reasonably interpreted as applying to God as well as to actual occasions. As we trace Whitehead's elaboration of the categoreal scheme and reflect on the outcome in his theory of God and the world, two important questions about the coherence of his system need to be raised.

The first is whether his conception of God is a decorative but dispensable addition to his cosmology. Is it a burden of which the system might well be relieved without essential damage to its structure? Do Whitehead's principles require his conception of God? More specifically, do any of the functions of actual occasions supplant or supersede or render superfluous, instead of supplementing, any of the essential functions of God?

The second of these questions is whether Whitehead's system leads to an absorption of the world in God. By being the chief exemplification of the categories, does God's existence reduce the existence of actual occasions to virtual unimportance and ineffectiveness? Does Whitehead's system in effect amount to a doctrine of realities and Reality, even if not a doctrine of Appearance and Reality? More specifically, do any of the specific functions of God supplant or supersede, instead of supplementing, any of the essential functions of actual occasions?

The next step toward finding some answers to these questions is to see in what ways, on Whitehead's principles, God affects the world.

CHAPTER 16

How God Affects the World

IN THIS CHAPTER I propose to discuss three questions about the influence of God in the formation of actual occasions. These questions concern the influence of God on: (A) the subjective aim of an actual occasion; (B) the data of its physical feelings; and (C) the relation between contemporary actual occasions.

A. GOD AND SUBJECTIVE AIM

1. The function of subjective aim

Before we look at the influence of God on the subjective aim of an actual occasion we ought to recall the function of the subjective aim in the formation of an occasion. We may say that the subjective aim is the immanent ground of final causation. "In its self-creation the actual entity is guided by its ideal of itself as individual satisfaction and as transcendent creator. The enjoyment of this ideal is the 'subjective aim,' by reason of which the actual entity is a determinate process" (PR 130).

To explain how a subjective aim functions, let us begin with the first categoreal obligation: "*The Category of Subjective Unity.* The many feelings which belong to an incomplete phase in the process of an actual entity, though unintegrated by reason of the incompleteness of the phase, are compatible for integration by reason of the unity of their subject" (PR 39). In any incomplete phase the concrescence has not yet attained the unity of satisfaction. Yet in such a phase, for example the initial one, the feelings are compatible for integration. Those initial data that are not compatible are eliminated by negative prehensions.

Further, the data that are positively prehended are felt in such a way that they can become components of the satisfaction. Conceptual feelings of eternal objects and propositions arise, enabling the physical data to be felt in patterns and converting oppositions into contrasts. Furthermore the subjective forms of these conceptual feelings are congruent with one another, in accord with categoreal obligation vii: *"The Category of Subjective Harmony*. The valuations of conceptual feelings are mutually determined by the adaptation of those feelings to be contrasted elements congruent with the subjective aim" (PR 40–1).

Thus there is a "pre-established harmony" among the data and subjective forms of the feelings in an incomplete phase of the genetic process (PR 41, 338, 342, 353, 389). But "pre-established" is misleading. The harmony is not established before the concrescence begins. It is due to the activity of the concrescence itself. For this reason Whitehead's adoption of this phrase from Leibniz, for whom it meant an eternally established harmony of external relations, is unfortunate.

The explanation of this harmony is that throughout the concrescence the subject is at work, interpreting its data so as to achieve final satisfaction. Now obviously this subject at work in the incomplete phases is itself incomplete. The subject is completed only in its satisfaction. How then is the subject "inherent" in "the process of its production" (PR 342)? Whitehead's answer is that from the very beginning of the concrescence there is a feeling with a unique and crucial function. This feeling is the subjective aim.

This aim at subjective intensity provokes, so to speak, the origination of conceptual feelings (PR 41), it determines the subjective forms of conceptual feelings, and it conditions the subjective forms of conformal physical feelings. Thus it functions as the ontological ground or "reason" for the harmony of feelings in incomplete phases of the concrescence (PR 36–7, 373). Since unity is a condition of intensity, the subjective aim is an appetition for unity of satisfaction. It thus gives a dynamic, teleological unity to the whole process which constitutes an actual occasion.

Here we should pause to reflect on the importance of this notion in the theory of actual occasions. The subjective aim is the ground of the internal unity of an occasion. Further, the internal unity of an occasion is essential to its being a complete and concrete thing, that is to say a real individual. Internal unity is essential also to the novelty and exclusiveness of an occasion and hence to its social transcendence. Thus Whitehead's pluralism, his doctrine that there are many individual and socially transcendent things, logically depends on the notion of the subjective aim of an actual occasion.

2. The derivation of subjective aim

Now we are ready to ask whether the subjective aim of an occasion is itself subject to explanation. Would it be reasonable to ask how an actual occasion comes to have a subjective aim? Here we must recur to the ontological principle, which is stated in category of explanation xviii: "That every condition to which the process of becoming conforms in any particular instance, has its reason *either* in the character of some actual entity in the actual world of that concrescence, *or* in the character of the subject which is in process of concrescence. . . . It follows that any condition to be satisfied by one actual entity in its process expresses a fact either about the 'real internal constitutions' of some other actual entities, or about the 'subjective aim' conditioning that process" (PR 36–7). We ask, Can this principle be applied to the subjective aim itself? The subjective aim is a ground. Is it also grounded? Whitehead's answer is that: "This subjective aim is both an example and a limitation of the ontological principle. It is an example, in that the principle is here applied to the immediacy of concrescent fact. The subject completes itself during the process of concrescence by a self-criticism of its own incomplete phases. In another sense the subjective aim limits the ontological principle by its own autonomy" (PR 373). The subjective aim is an example of the ontological principle in the sense that it is the reason for the internal unity of the concrescence, as we have seen. But it is a limiting case of the ontological principle. For the self-creative activity of the concrescence is an expression of the ultimate creativity of the universe, for which no explanation can be given. In the former sense we can answer the question, Why are there actual occasions? In the latter sense we cannot.

But suppose we ask a more restricted question about subjective aims. What is the "reason" why *this* subjective aim is operative in the process of *this* concrescence? On Whitehead's principles this is a reasonable question. Although the creativity of a concrescence can have no reason other than itself, the specific fact that *this* ideal not *that* is aimed at is a condition for which a reason may be asked.

Let us consider "the initial phase of the 'subjective aim'" (PR 104), also called "the basic conceptual aim" (PR 343), the "initial subjective aim" (PR 164, 375), and the "initial aim" (PR 374). This is a conceptual feeling of some eternal object with a subjective form of appetition. What Whitehead says of propositional feelings in another context may be applied to this eternal object: "this particular possibility has been picked out, held up, and clothed with emotion" (PR 428). It is the origin of this particular datum that is not self-explanatory. Speaking of the initial aim Whitehead says, "But the origination of the novel conceptual prehension has, more especially, to be accounted for" (PR 48).

Accounting for the origination of the initial aim means finding some actual entity which has suggested, so to speak, the novel possibility. Whitehead denies that ideas float into actuality from a realm of pure being. On the contrary, in the ontological principle he is "extending and rigidly applying Hume's principle, that ideas of reflection are derived from actual facts" (PR 64). Thus the datum of the initial aim must be "somewhere." "Everything must be somewhere; and here 'somewhere' means 'some actual entity'" (PR 73). So our question becomes, From what actual entity is this novel possibility derived?

Clearly this datum cannot be derived from any contemporary or future actual occasion. Nor can it be derived from any antecedent occasion. The new concrescence must conform to its past actual world. But it must do so in its own way. It must determine its perspective on the past and it must respond with its own subjective forms of feelings. Now it is precisely the subjective aim of the concrescence that so determines its objectifications of the past and confers novelty on its subjective forms of feeling (AI 327–8). Hence it would seem that the datum of its initial aim cannot itself be derived from the past. The problem of the concrescence is to produce a *novel* actuality.

It seems that to explain the origination of the initial aim there

must be an actual entity which is not an actual occasion. In fact
Whitehead answers our question in the only way his principles
permit. He says:

> . . . the initial stage of its aim is an endowment which the
> subject inherits from the inevitable ordering of things, con-
> ceptually realized in the nature of God. The immediacy of
> the concrescent subject is constituted by its living aim at its
> own self-constitution. Thus the initial stage of the aim is
> rooted in the nature of God, and its completion depends on
> the self-causation of the subject-superject (PR 373).

> In this sense God is the principle of concretion; namely, he
> is that actual entity from which each temporal concrescence
> receives that initial aim from which its self-causation starts
> (PR 374; see 104, 164, 434, 527).

The derivation of the initial aim from God takes place in the
following way. In its initial phase the concrescence includes a
"hybrid physical prehension" of God, which means that God is
objectified for the concrescence by one of his conceptual feelings
(PR 376–7). That is, the objective datum of this hybrid prehension
is God's prehension of some eternal object. Now "A hybrid physical prehension originates for its subject a conceptual feeling with
the same datum as that of the conceptual feeling of the antecedent
subject" (PR 377). This derivation of a pure conceptual feeling
from the hybrid physical feeling is in accord with the category
of conceptual valuation (PR 39–40). The derived conceptual feeling is the initial aim of the new concrescence. It sets the pattern
for the unification of the concrescence.

Now the occasion's hybrid physical feeling of God, like all
physical feelings, is a conformal feeling. Its subjective form conforms to and "reproduces" God's own subjective form of feeling.
So the initial aim derived from this conformal hybrid prehension
"reproduces" not only the datum but also the valuation of God's
conceptual feeling (PR 343, 377). In this way God not only makes
a novel possibility theoretically available but also evokes appetition for that possibility in the new concrescence. This evocation
by God of the novel appetition is "the supreme Eros incarnating

itself as the first phase of the individual subjective aim in the new process of actuality" (AI 256; see PR 522, AI 270). This is what Whitehead means by the divine "persuasion."

Though we have found how the datum of the initial aim is derived, we have not yet found out how it is determined. How is it that the concrescence derives *this* possibility and not *that* from its prehension of God? Construing the datum of the initial aim as an objective datum abstracted from an initial datum, namely God's conceptual experience as a whole, what determines the particular abstraction that occurs?

Certainly the primordial nature of God cannot be a sufficient reason for a finite aim at *this* possibility and not *that*. In his primordial nature God does not envisage any particular actual occasions, and he does not exclude any possibilities from his timeless envisagement. Nor is the past actual world sufficient reason for the aim at *this* possibility. Though the actual world narrows the range of real possibility, it does not completely specify what shall come out of the situation it poses.

So we are tempted to think of the occasion as selecting or picking out the datum of its initial aim from among the possibilities envisaged by God. The determination would be made by the novel concrescence itself. But this cannot be the case. We shall see how the concrescence does have self-determination in certain ways, but this cannot be one of those ways. For any selection from among God's feelings by decision of the concrescence itself would presuppose its initial aim. The datum of the initial aim is its principle of selection. Therefore it would not make sense, on Whitehead's principles, to say that the concrescence has any *real* alternatives to the possibility which becomes the datum of its initial aim. At this point there seems to be no room for freedom on the part of the concrescence. We have to look further for a sufficient reason why *this* possibility becomes the datum of the initial aim.

So far we have left something out of account, namely the consequent nature of God. The concrete existence of God includes not only his conceptual prehensions of eternal objects but also his physical prehensions of actual occasions. In the case of any novel concrescence God has prehended the actual occasions which compose its past actual world. Now God's aim is at maximum intensity of experience for himself and for the world. So the reaction of the world upon God results in an ordering of possibilities in the divine experience in relevance to the novel concrescence. And it seems that for any given set of conditions there will be a particular possibility which if actualized would produce maximum intensity of satisfaction. If the past had been other than it was, then some other initial aim would have been "supplied" (PR 164) by God. As things are, this is the possibility with which the subjective aim of the concrescence must begin. Only this possibility can be the datum of the initial aim. This interpretation seems called for by the following passages:

> The initial stage of its aim is an endowment which the subject inherits from the inevitable ordering of things, conceptually realized in the nature of God. . . . This function of God is analogous to the remorseless working of things in Greek and in Buddhist thought. The initial aim is the best for that *impasse*. But if the best be bad, then the ruthlessness of God can be personified as Atè, the goddess of mischief. The chaff is burnt (PR 373).

> . . . God and the actual world jointly constitute the character of the creativity for the initial phase of the novel concrescence. The subject, *thus constituted,* is the autonomous master of its own concrescence into subject-superject (PR 374, my italics; see 104, 164, 434).

It is important to notice that the datum of the initial aim is not *pre*determined, either from eternity or from a previous time. There is no one fixed order of eternal objects. Therefore no eternal object is eternally destined to be the datum of the initial aim of this novel concrescence. Nor is the course of nature a necessary order of things. As we have seen, the datum of the initial aim of a new concrescence is conditioned but not sufficiently determined by the past actual world. Therefore we might well say that the completion of the determination of this datum is effected *at* the concrescence of the novel occasion, though not *by* it. It is effected jointly by the creative self-determinations of immediately past actual occasions and by the creative self-determination of God in reaction to that temporal situation. In this way there is a kind of contingency in the determination of the datum of the initial aim, though the new concrescence itself does not contribute to that determination.

A further question about the derivation of the datum of the initial aim is, In what sense is this datum novel? On this question the relevant texts are not very explicit. It seems clear enough that the datum must be novel in some sense. Whitehead speaks of "conceptual novelties" (PR 245) and seems to refer to the *data* of certain conceptual prehensions and not merely to novel *prehensions*. These are "new forms" (PR 387, 427), or rather "old" (eternal?) forms in new functions (PR 284). So we may ask of the function of an eternal object as datum of an initial aim, In what sense is this a new function? Must this datum be an eternal object that has not been realized in the past actual world?

Passages like the following have to be taken into account: "Thus a single occasion is alive when the subjective aim which determines its process of concrescence has introduced a novelty of definiteness not to be found in the inherited data of its primary phase. The novelty is introduced conceptually and disturbs the inherited 'responsive' adjustment of subjective forms. It alters the 'values,' in the artist's sense of that term" (PR 159; see 245, 280, 284). Now it might be argued that this passage implies some occasions are *not* "alive" in this particular sense. This interpretation might find support from another context where he seems to say that ideas introduced into an occasion by "novel conceptual prehensions" may be "old or new" (AI 249). I do not think this interpretation is warranted. In the context of the passage quoted Whitehead is describing various types of "societies" in the order of nature. In particular he is distinguishing between living and nonliving societies (PR 154–64). His general point is that life consists in originality, and that in some societies the originality of their component actual occasions is macroscopically negligible. In this passage he is explaining *how* an occasion has originality. So I do not think he means to say that some occasions are *not* alive. If this is a fair reading of the passage, then the subjective aim of every occasion introduces an eternal object "not to be found in the inherited data of its primary phase."

There are four ways in which the eternal object might have been realized in the past actual world: (a) as the datum of the initial aim of some past actual occasion; (b) as the datum of a supplementary conceptual feeling; (c) as a form of definiteness of the datum of a physical feeling; (d) as a form of definiteness of a subjective form of feeling. Might the datum of the initial aim of the new concrescence have functioned in one or more of these ways in the past actual world?

It would certainly seem that the first of these functions is excluded by Whitehead's theory of actual occasions. It seems that the eternal object which is the datum of an initial aim must not have functioned as the datum of an initial aim in the past. The novelty of the datum in this sense of novelty seems necessary for the novelty of an actual occasion. At least it is difficult to see how the subjective aim of an occasion can be novel unless the datum of its initial aim is novel in *this* sense. And the novelty of an actual occasion as a concrete existent depends on the novelty of its subjective aim, as we have seen.

It is not altogether clear whether Whitehead's theory of actual occasions excludes (b), (c), and (d) as well as (a). If his principles do require that the eternal object must not have functioned in the past world in *any* of these ways, then the datum of the initial aim would have to be novel in a radical sense. It could have functioned in the experiences of past occasions only as a datum of negative conceptual prehensions. Considering the complexity and multiplicity of past occasions, and hence the vast number of realized eternal objects that would no longer qualify as data of initial aims, an inexhaustible infinity of potential data would have to be available. But this is precisely the case, since the multiplicity of eternal objects is inexhaustibly infinite. So the demand for radical novelty in the data of initial aims would be consistent with Whitehead's theory of eternal objects. And since God envisages the entire multiplicity of eternal objects, the derivation of radically novel initial aims would be consistent with Whitehead's theory of God. The source of supply would be more than adequate to the demand.

An important general conclusion about Whitehead's philosophy follows from the foregoing discussion. It is that his theory of actual occasions logically requires his doctrine of God. The subjective aim of an occasion, on which its unity, its individuality, and its social transcendence all depend, requires an explanation. And the only explanation available on Whitehead's principles is one requiring his doctrine of God. His doctrine of God is in this way required by the theory of actual occasions, and is not a merely decorative addition to that theory.

3. The freedom of an actual occasion

Now we must ask some questions about other logical consequences of this derivation of subjective aim from God. Do its implications undermine Whitehead's pluralism? Does this function of God supplant or supersede the self-creative activity of the finite actual entity? Is there still room for freedom in the formation of the actual occasion?

Certainly God "qualifies" (PR 344) an actual occasion in a radical way. In an important passage Whitehead speaks of actual occasions as "derivative" actualities (PR 46) in contrast with God, who is the only "non-derivative actuality" (PR 48). He even goes so far as to say, referring to the derivation of subjective aim, "In this sense, God can be termed the creator of each temporal actual entity." It is true that he immediately adds "But the phrase is apt to be misleading by its suggestion that the ultimate creativity of the universe is to be ascribed to God's volition" (PR 343–4; see 519, AI 303). But considering how the internal unity of an occasion is dependent on God, we ought to re-examine his emphatic denials that God has "eminent reality" (PR 11, 116).

The need for this re-examination is enforced by his remark about the last part of *Process and Reality:* "In this part, the approximation to Bradley is evident. Indeed, if this cosmology be deemed successful, it becomes natural at this point to ask whether the type of thought involved be not a transformation of some main doctrines of Absolute Idealism onto a realistic basis" (PR viii). It is not clear just what "main doctrines" of absolute idealism Whitehead had in mind. Also he is not always the best judge of the relation of his philosophy to other systems. But we certainly want to know how the relation of God to actual occasions is like the relation of the Absolute to "finite centres" of experience. It becomes natural to ask whether the doctrine of God compromises the real individuality of actual occasions, and in particular whether the derivation of subjective aim from God has this effect.

The principle of creativity means that no actual entity is completely determined by other actual entities. Other actual entities condition but do not completely determine what shall become in a new concrescence. "The creativity is not an external agency with its own ulterior purposes. All actual entities share with God this characteristic of self-causation. For this reason every actual entity also shares with God the characteristic of transcending all other actual entities, including God" (PR 339). According to this principle even God does not completely determine the concrescence of an actual occasion, though he is "the aboriginal condition which qualifies its action" (PR 344). We are asking whether the derivation of subjective aim is consistent with this principle of creativity. Hence we need to know how the self-causation of an actual occasion affects its subjective aim.

I suggest that the novel concrescence acts with creative freedom or self-determination in three ways: (a) in the autonomy of the subjective form of its initial aim; (b) in its specification of its subjective aim; and (c) in its concrete actualization of its aim. Thanks to God, the concrescence includes a possibility which may give unity to its experience of many data. The valuation of this relevant possibility, the progressive clarification of the ideal aim, and the realization of this aim in a concrete feeling of satisfaction—all this belongs not to God but to the self-creative activity of the novel occasion. "Thus an originality in the temporal world is conditioned, though not determined, by an initial subjective aim supplied by the ground of all order and of all originality" (PR 164).

a. *Autonomy of subjective form*. It seems clear enough, in general, that Whitehead's categories require autonomy in the subjective forms of feelings. The category of subjective harmony posits a "mutual sensitivity of feelings," so that the "subjective form of a feeling is affected by the totality of the actual occasion" (PR 292; see 40–1, 359, 420). It follows that the subjective form of a feeling is novel, since the occasion is novel (PR 354). The degree of originality in the subjective forms of feelings will vary (PR 374–5). But in no case is there bare conformity. In every case there is some originality. The subjective form of a feeling reflects the creative self-causation of the concrescence.

This general principle applies to the conceptual feelings derived from hybrid feelings, and by clear implication to the initial aim derived from the hybrid physical feeling of God.

> A hybrid physical feeling originates for its subject a conceptual feeling with the same datum as that of the conceptual feeling of the antecedent subject. But the two conceptual feelings in the two subjects respectively may have different subjective forms.
>
> There is an autonomy in the formation of the subjective forms of conceptual feelings, conditioned only by the unity of the subject as expressed in categoreal conditions I, VII, and VIII. These conditions for unity correlate the sympathetic subjective form of the hybrid feeling with the autonomous subjective form of the derivative conceptual feeling with the same subject (PR 377).

In other words the conceptual aim in the new concrescence (the "derivative conceptual feeling") will not have the same subjective form as God's conceptual feeling. The specific difference between the two subjective forms will be due to the freedom of the novel concrescence. The subjective form of the initial aim is not a *mere* reproduction of the subjective form of God's conceptual feeling. Though it is *"partly* dictated by the qualitative element in the objective content" (AI 326, my italics), it is partly determined also by the actual occasion itself.

The only problem about this application of the principle of autonomy of subjective form is: How can the subjective form of the initial aim be conditioned by the subject when no prior unity of the subject exists? Whitehead says that "self-determination is always imaginative in its origin" (PR 374). But the initial aim is the origin of imagination. How can the subject affect the subjective form of that feeling which is itself the basis of the unity of the subject?

This difficulty arises from construing the initial aim as though it were genetically prior to the other feelings in the primary phase of the concrescence. This is not the case. It arises *with* the other feelings in the primary phase of the concrescence. In this phase the initial aim both influences and is influenced by other feelings. Its datum determines the abstractions of objective data from the initial datum. On the other hand its own subjective form is influenced by the other feelings, so that its datum is felt in a way appropriate to *that* concrescence. Thus there is a mutual conditioning of feelings.

Of course there is a more general problem about Whitehead's notion of genetic priority. A genetically earlier phase is not temporally prior to a later phase in the concrescence. Considered in reference to physical time we would have to say that though the concrescence "takes time" it takes place "at once." In putting forward a notion of priority different from logical priority and also different from priority in physical time, Whitehead has to appeal to our immediate intuitions. But the intelligibility of this notion of genetic priority is a larger problem. The autonomy of the subjective form of the initial aim is a feature of Whitehead's general theory of experiencing subjects.

b. *Specification of subjective aim.* The second way an actual occasion has freedom vis-à-vis God is by what I shall call its specification of its subjective aim. The datum of the initial aim is derived from God's primordial envisagement and becomes the ideal for the concrescent subject. As the concrescence proceeds its ideal of itself becomes, in a certain sense, more specific. Some passages indicating this function of the concrescence are in order:

> Process is the growth and attainment of a final end. The progressive definition of the final end is the efficacious condition for its attainment. The determinate unity of an actual entity is bound together by the final causation towards an ideal progressively defined by its progressive relation to the determinations and indeterminations of the datum (PR 227–8).

> This basic conceptual feeling [i.e. the conceptual aim] suffers simplification in the successive phases of the concrescence.

It starts with conditioned alternatives, and by successive decisions is reduced to coherence. The doctrine of responsibility is entirely concerned with this modification (PR 342).

It [i.e. the temporal entity] derives from God its basic conceptual aim, relevant to its actual world, yet with indeterminations awaiting its own decisions (PR 343; see 373, 375, 390, 416).

Here is another way in which the complete actual occasion is a result of self-causation. It arises with a relevant ideal. It remains for the concrescence to decide what, more specifically, this ideal means in the particular context of its physical experience here-now. This is the "immanent decision" of the concrescence.

The initial aim is vague in the sense that the relations of its datum to other possibilities and to the physical data are not completely determinate. It includes indeterminations which the concrescence must determine. The concrescence aims at "that sort of thing." As the process goes on the aim becomes more specific so that it is finally "this thing and no other." It is as though someone started out to be a doctor, then had to decide what sort of doctor he would be, and ended up being just this sort of doctor and no other.

An interpretation of this process of "progressive definition" should begin by distinguishing (i) the pure conceptual feeling with which the subjective aim begins from (ii) the subjective aim proper. The pure conceptual feelings is derived, in accord with the category of conceptual valuation, from the hybrid physical feeling of God. Its datum is an eternal object, a pure potential. In the first phase of the subjective aim, namely the initial aim, this pure potential is felt as an ideal for *that* concrescence. So the datum of the subjective aim proper is a proposition, an impure potential felt as a real possibility for actualization. The idea becomes an effectively relevant ideal. Since the subjective aim is thus a propositional feeling we should look at certain general features of such feelings.

A propositional feeling results from integration of a physical feeling with a conceptual feeling. The physical feeling is indicative of the logical subject (or subjects) of the proposition felt.

The datum of the conceptual feeling becomes the predicate of this proposition and is called the "predicative pattern" of the propositional feeling. If the predicative pattern is derived from the indicative feeling, then the resulting propositional feeling is a "perceptive feeling." If on the contrary the predicative pattern is derived from some other physical feeling, then the resulting propositional feeling is an "imaginative feeling." In an imaginative feeling the relevant eternal object is predicated of an actual entity from which it has not been derived (PR 391–405).

Now we can interpret the subjective aim as a propositional feeling. In this case the indicative feeling is the self-feeling (PR 38, AI 248) of the immediate concrescence. Thus the logical subject of the proposition felt is the concrescent subject itself. The predicate of this proposition is initially the datum of the initial aim. And since this eternal object is not derived from the indicative feeling, the subjective aim is an imaginative feeling, not a perceptive feeling. So the subjective aim is an imaginative propositional feeling. Its datum is a proposition whose logical subject is the concrescent subject itself and whose predicate is, initially, the eternal object derived from God as explained above.

Now the subjective aim undergoes development (PR 254, 287) and has "phases" (PR 75), as does the concrescence as a whole. In any phase the proposition felt functions as a "lure for feeling" (PR 427). Thus the subjective aim initiates and sustains the final causation immanent in the concrescence. "Each new phase in the concrescence means the retreat of mere propositional unity before the growing grasp of real unity of feeling. Each successive propositional phase is a lure to the creation of feelings which promote its realization" (PR 343). Finally the concrescence achieves its satisfaction, which completes the internal process.

Let us ask how the predicative pattern of the subjective aim in a genetically later phase ($ppII$) differs from the predicative pattern in the initial phase (ppI). In this way we can discover how the subjective aim is progressively defined as the concrescence proceeds. The basic difference between these two eternal objects is that $ppII$ includes ppI in a pattern of relatedness. In $ppII$ some relations between ppI and other eternal objects are articulated and made determinate. *How ppI is related to other possibilities* is now part of the new predicative pattern. In a still later phase this new predicative pattern will have its own relations to other possibilities spelled out.

In this way the predicative pattern of the subjective aim becomes both more complex and more specific. This modification (PR 343, 416) of the subjective aim may also be regarded as a "simplification" (PR 342) of the initial aim. It is an *ordering* of relevant possibilities by way of subordinations, contrasts, and eliminations of alternatives (MT 207–8). But ppII is not a simpler eternal object than ppI. On the contrary the predicative pattern of the "subjective end" (PR 342) of a genetically later phase is more complex than that of an earlier one. It represents a higher mode of abstraction from possibility (SMW 233–4).

This process of specification of the initial conceptual datum is an activity of the concrescence itself. The concrescent subject works out (or we might say *elaborates*) the meaning of its own idea. It progressively decides (PR 423) what it would mean to realize that ideal in its physical situation. The eternal object does not logically require the particular elaboration it receives or, indeed, any elaboration at all. ppI does not entail ppII, and ppII does not entail ppIII. This is because eternal objects in themselves are a multiplicity, as we have seen, and have no single fixed pattern of relatedness. They have modes of togetherness only when ingredient in actual entities. The actual occasion works out its own (relative and incomplete) ordering of the multiplicity of eternal objects. In doing so it is conditioned but not completely determined by the past actual world, to which it must conform, and by God, who supplies the datum of its initial aim. In the determination of a subjective aim the spontaneity of self-causation is involved (AI 328).

c. *Actualization of subjective aim.* An actual occasion's valuation and specification of its aim do not exhaust the meaning of its freedom. It also actualizes its aim. Indeed we should look at valuation and specification as features of a more inclusive process of actualization. The valuation of the initial aim in an appetition for enjoyment of satisfaction, and specification of the aim is instrumental to attaining this enjoyment.

So far in this discussion of the freedom of an occasion we have been concerned primarily with its conceptual experience. We should remember that actualization involves physical experience also. The datum of an occasion's initial aim is relevant to its physical situation. It elaborates this aim under the stimulus and control of its physical experience of other actual entities. And it realizes this aim by producing a concrete unity of physical and conceptual feelings.

Indeed if, as I suggest, the subjective aim is a propositional feeling, then the aim itself has a physical component (the indicative feeling) as well as a conceptual component (the predicative pattern). Its datum is a proposition whose logical subject is the concrescence itself. This presupposes the peculiar operation Whitehead calls "self-functioning" or "immediacy" (PR 38). The "intrinsic reality" of an event, he says, consists in "the event as in its own prehension" (SMW 146). I take this to mean, in part, that in a later phase of a concrescence there are feelings that have an earlier phase of the concrescence as their datum. Such feelings might be regarded as a limiting case of physical feelings, the actual entity felt being the concrescence itself. And the function of this self-feeling might be compared with efficient causation. The latter occurs in the transition from one actual occasion to another. But *within* the internal process a sort of physical self-causation goes on. This self-feeling is part of the process by which, we might say, the occasion builds up the structure of its own feelings. Its feeling of one phase of the structure provides an indicative feeling, and this is integrated with a predicative pattern into the specific aim which guides the construction of a later phase.

Finally by this process of progressive integration the occasion becomes a concrete actuality. It becomes what it aims at. Then it must be taken account of and conformed to by its successors in the course of nature. It becomes a determinate fact and functions as an efficient cause in the formation of future concrescences.

The conditions an occasion must satisfy are given by the past actual world. The possibility it may realize is given by God. But the fact that it becomes at all, and that it becomes what it aims at, is not a necessary consequence of the past actual world, nor of God's primordial vision, nor of both taken together. This fact is the consequence of a "self-creative" (PR 38) act in which the concrescence actualizes its aim.

At the beginning of this section we asked whether the derivation of subjective aim from God compromised the real individuality of actual occasions and thus subverted Whitehead's pluralism. We have now seen that though an occasion depends on God in a crucial way it still has the freedom of self-causation. Over and above what God does, something remains to be done which even God cannot do. God cannot enact or even completely determine the occasion's valuation, specification, and actualization of its initial aim. This remains to be done by, and only by, the actual occasion itself. "Thus the initial stage of the aim is rooted in the nature of God, and its completion depends on the self-causation of the subject-superject" (PR 373). It is true that "an originality in the temporal world is conditioned, though not determined, by an initial subjective aim supplied by the ground of all order and of all originality" (PR 164). But to say that the occasion is not "determined" by God (or by anything else) is another way of saying that "Spontaneity, originality of decision, belongs to the essence of each actual occasion" (AI 332).

B. God and the Givenness of the Past

4. Givenness and the ontological principle

We saw in Part One how the transition from past to present is the crux of Whitehead's doctrine of social immanence. For this transition the givenness of the past for the present is essential. It is because of the stubborn factual character of the past that the new concrescence is obliged to conform to it and re-enact it.

Is it reasonable to ask for an ontological ground or reason for this givenness of the past? We recall the ontological principle: "That every condition to which the process of becoming conforms in any particular instance, has its reason *either* in the character of some actual entity in the actual world of that concrescence, *or* in the character of the subject which is in process of concrescence" (PR 36–7). And we ask whether this principle properly applies to the givenness of the past. Now it might well seem paradoxical to search for a "reason" for the givenness of the past, or for any givenness whatever. It is the nature of givenness, it seems, not to be penetrable by reason. What is given is *stubborn* fact. By definition, what is given does not permit reasons for its existence. Hence one might conclude that the ontological principle does not properly apply to the givenness of the past.

This objection fails to take account of a distinction which emerged in our discussion of causal efficacy, the distinction between explanation in the sense of logical demonstration of facts and explanation as categoreal analysis of facts. Whitehead thinks that stubborn facts cannot be explained in the former sense, but that they need to be explained in the latter sense. He does not begin by saying that the past *must* be given for the present, for such and such reasons, and then conclude that therefore it *is* given. Instead he begins by accepting what seems to him the obvious fact that the past *is* given now. The question then to be asked and answered is, *How* is it possible that the past is given now? This question, I suggest, is in accord with Whitehead's principles.

One of his basic principles, suggested by the relational character of experience, is "that there are no brute, self-contained matters of fact, capable of being understood apart from interpretation as an element in a system" (PR 21). There *is* stubborn fact in the sense that no particular matter of fact can be logically deduced from abstract principles. But the ideal of philosophy is a complete account of facts in their relations. Hence a philosopher cannot admit any particular matter of fact which is self-contained, entirely unconnected with other particular matters of fact. There are always connections and the philosopher's business is to seek them out. But the connections are between stubborn facts. To give a reason for the givenness of the past is not to prove that the past is given now. It is instead to show *how* it is that the past is given now.

Let us take the case of a simple physical feeling and consider what questions may reasonably be asked about its datum. Let the subject of the feeling be a concrescent occasion A, and let its initial datum be a past occasion X which is part of A's actual world. Now it is not reasonable, on Whitehead's principles, to ask why, of all possible worlds, it is this world that is actual. "No reason, internal to history, can be assigned why that flux of forms, rather than another flux, should have been illustrated" (PR 74). It is reasonable, however, to ask how X is related to the other actual entities which make up that actual world. And it is reasonable to ask for a reason for the character of the datum itself, if we mean by a "reason" some internal determination. What is given is "incapable of rationalization beyond the fact that within it every component which is determinable is internally determined" (PR 75). What is determinable is the character of the datum, and the character of this initial datum for A has been determined by the process of decision internal to X. In this way the ontological principle applies to the character of the datum.

Now I suggest it is also reasonable on Whitehead's principles to ask, How is it that what was decided in the past is given *now* for the present experience? This would apply the ontological principle not only to the character of the datum given for A but also to the fact that this datum is now given for A. And this means looking for some actual entity as the reason why X is now given for A. The importance of this question will appear as we look for its answer.

It might seem natural to suppose that the past occasion X is itself the ontological ground for the fact that it is now given for A. But this answer cannot be the right one. X is indeed the reason for the character of the initial datum. It is the reason for *what* is given. The immediate satisfaction of X is "a creative determination, by which the objectifications of the entity beyond itself are settled" (PR 130).

But X can hardly be the reason for the fact that the datum *is* now given for A. Because X has now perished and is no longer actual, whereas the only "reasons" according to the ontological principle are *actual* entities. This is not a merely verbal objection. According to the ontological principle, "any condition to be satisfied by one actual entity in its process expresses a fact either about the 'real internal constitutions' of some other actual entities, or about the 'subjective aim' conditioning that process" (PR 37). Past actual occasions do not now exist in their real internal constitutions. They are no longer subjectively immediate;

they are objectively immortal. Therefore they cannot serve as reasons for the fact that they are now given. This seems an inevitable consequence of the perishing of actual occasions, taken together with the exclusiveness of immediacy discussed in Chapter 3. It is only as the reason for the character of the datum that X functions as "part-creator of the transcendent world" (PR 130). What is yet to be explained in terms of the ontological principle is how a datum of this character is *now* given for A.

Certainly it is not possible that the present concrescence is the ground of the givenness of the past. The occasion for which the data are given cannot be the reason why the data are given. The essential nature of a datum is that it is given for the subject, not produced by the subject or dependent on the subject for its existence. At this point Whitehead's realism is clear: "Two conditions must be fulfilled in order that an entity may function as an object in a process of experiencing: (1) the entity must be *antecedent,* and (2) the entity must be experienced in virtue of its antecedence; it must be *given.* Thus an object must be a thing received, and must not be either a *mode* of reception or a thing *generated* in that occasion. . . . The process creates itself, but it does not create the objects which it receives as factors in its own nature" (AI 229–30).

It seems then that the reason for the givenness of the past is not to be found in the nature of past actual occasions, nor in the nature of the novel concrescence. Since future and contemporary actual occasions are obviously not relevant to the question, it seems that no actual occasion can be the ground of the givenness of a datum for a novel concrescence.

5. Is God the ground of givenness? The categories

The only remaining actual entity which might function as the ontological ground of the givenness of the past is God. I suggest that it is categoreally possible to assign this function to God. Later we must ask whether Whitehead does in fact assign this function to God.

God is actual, and thus fulfills the requirement that "actual entities are the only *reasons*" (PR 37). "God is an actual entity"

(PR 28). When viewed abstractly in his primordial nature God is "deficient in actuality" (PR 50), or "deficiently actual" (PR 521). (The primordial nature of God is not said to be *devoid* of actuality. See also PR 48, 530.) But in his consequent nature he is "fully actual" (PR 524). Properly speaking, God is a concrete unity of physical and conceptual prehensions from which his primordial nature and his consequent nature are abstractions.

Further, God is actual *now,* for any meaning of "now." He is "in unison of becoming with every other creative act" (PR 523), and is thus "everlasting." His existence as a concrete actuality is not timeless, in the sense of being out of relation to temporal process. He exists *formally* or immediately (which is to say actually) at all times (PR 524–5). Therefore at any time, that is to say with respect to any particular concrescence, it is categoreally possible for God to function as an ontological ground of some condition to which *this* concrescence conforms.

Further, relative to any concrescence, the actual occasions constituting the past actual world of that concrescence are objectively immortal in God (PR 134). Thus the consequent nature of God is, in a sense, cumulative.[1] It is enriched by the successive achievements of actual occasions in the course of nature. So any past occasion X will have been physically prehended by God and will be objectively immortal in God's immediate experience. As a consequence, the actuality of God relative to A will include the result of God's prehension of X.

Finally, God is not only a subject but also a superject like all other actual entities. As a subject God is self-creative, a concrescence of immediate feeling. As a superject God functions as an object for other subjects. "The 'superjective' nature of God is the character of the pragmatic value of his specific satisfaction qualifying the transcendent creativity in the various temporal instances" (PR 135. See 47–8, 377, 532; MT 128). The novel concrescence A will prehend God's satisfaction as now actual.

For these reasons it seems categoreally possible for God to be the ontological ground of the givenness of the past. One general

1. It is not cumulative in the sense that successive actual occasions retain, in the consequent nature of God, their own formal immediacy. Hence problems of temporal cumulation are avoided. See Chapter 17.

remark about this possible function of God needs to be made before we examine the relevant texts to see whether Whitehead does assign it to God.

Among the functions of God in Whitehead's system we might distinguish "metaphysical" from "religious" functions. A religious function of God presupposes a conscious religious interest on the part of some subject. God would be the object of religious contemplation or devotion. But most actual occasions do not have any conscious interests among their subjective forms of feeling. A metaphysical function would not require any conscious interest, such as a religious interest, in actual occasions. It would be a way of operating relative to all actual occasions without exception.

Now if God is the ontological ground of givenness, this would be a metaphysical not a religious function of God. Just as the subjective aim of *every* actual occasion needs to be accounted for, so the givenness of the past for *every* actual occasion would need to be accounted for. Just as the derivation of subjective aim from God would be a metaphysical function involving primarily his primordial nature, so God's function as ground of the givenness of the past would be a metaphysical function involving primarily his consequent nature. Now it is time to look at the relevant texts.

6. Is God the ground of givenness? Relevant texts

We have to ask whether Whitehead does in fact assign this function to God. The answer is not clear. In his more detailed and rigorous discussions of causal objectification there is scarcely a hint that he is even aware of the problem. Nor is there in those passages any explicit introduction of God as the ground of givenness.

The positive indications on which we have to rely occur mainly in passages where Whitehead is interpreting his scheme and relating it to experience, rather than in his more rigorous expositions of the categoreal scheme. For example, we have the general assertion that "the reasons for things are always to be found in the composite nature of definite actual entities—in the nature of God for reasons of the highest absoluteness, and in the nature of temporal actual entities for reasons which refer to a particular

environment" (PR 28). Here we are told that God does function as
an ontological ground. We might well infer that in one respect,
namely "for reasons of highest absoluteness," God is relevant to
any condition of a concrescence, including the givenness of its
past, as ontological ground of that condition. But this meaning is
not made explicit (see PR 75, 248-9).

The passage in which Whitehead comes nearest to saying that
God is the ground of givenness appears in *Modes of Thought* and
should be given in full:

> Finally [this follows a discussion of Time and Space], there
> is Deity, which is that factor in the universe whereby there
> is importance, value, and ideal beyond the actual. It is by
> reference of the spatial immediacies to the ideals of Deity
> that the sense of worth beyond ourselves arises. The unity
> of a transcendent universe, and the multiplicity of realized
> actualities, both enter into our experience by this sense of
> Deity. Apart from this sense of transcendent worth, the other-
> ness of reality would not enter into our consciousness. There
> must be value beyond ourselves. Otherwise every thing ex-
> perienced would be merely a barren detail in our own sol-
> ipsist mode of existence. We owe to the sense of Deity the
> obviousness of the many actualities of the world, and the
> obviousness of the unity of the world for the preservation of
> the values realized and for the transition to ideals beyond
> realized fact (MT 140).

The main problem about this passage is its reference to conscious
experience. If we could generalize to the experiences of all temporal actual entities, including nonconscious experiences, we might
conclude that the "otherness of reality" always enters into experience "by the sense of Deity." And since past occasions are the
only "actualities of the world" that are directly prehended as such,
we might conclude that past occasions are given for a subject by
reason of its prehension of God. But again this is not made explicit
(see MT 70).

A similar note is struck in the following passage: "The universe is at once the multiplicity of *rēs verae* and the solidarity of
rēs verae. The solidarity is itself the efficiency of the macroscopic

res vera, embodying the principle of unbounded permanence acquiring novelty through flux. The multiplicity is composed of microscopic *rēs verae,* each embodying the principle of bounded flux acquiring 'everlasting' permanence" (PR 254). The "macroscopic *res vera*" is God. The point of interest is that the solidarity of the universe, including presumably its continuity in time, is due to the efficiency of God. This might well be by way of his being the ground of the givenness of the past for a present concrescence. Once again, this interpretation goes beyond the explicit meaning of the passage.[2]

We have been asking whether Whitehead points to God as the reason for the givenness of the past. The most relevant passages have been adduced, but the evidence is certainly less clear, detailed, and ample than we might reasonably hope for, considering the importance of the question. No passage gives an affirmative answer in a clear and explicit way. But some passages do seem to point toward an affirmative answer.[3]

Further, without this explanation of the givenness of the past Whitehead's system is incomplete. This is so in the following way. A crucial feature of the theory of actual occasions is causal objectification. Now causal objectification is meaningless unless the past is given as stubborn fact. But this givenness of the past cannot be explained, in the sense required by the ontological principle, by reference to past occasions or to the novel concrescence itself. No actual entity which might serve as an explanation, except God, remains. Thus if this function is not assigned to God, then Whitehead's theory of actual occasions is incomplete. I take his failure to make this point clear as evidence of the unfinished character of the system set forth in his writings.

2. Whitehead's doctrine of an "impartial nexus" seems at first to have a similar bearing. A nexus remains for succeeding occasions what it was for the original percipient of the nexus. This impartial nexus requires God for its explanation. On closer examination of relevant texts it seems that God is the ground of the *unity* of the nexus as given for the succeeding occasions, not for the givenness as such of the nexus. But the bearing of these texts on our problem is not perfectly clear. See PR 351–3, 383–90.

3. In a conversation with Whitehead in 1942 I understood him to assent to the suggestion that God is the ontological ground of the givenness of the past.

7. How God might be the ground of givenness

Suppose this function should be assigned to God. Then we would need an explanation of just *how* God is the ontological ground of the givenness of the past. Such an explanation might begin as follows:

a. In the initial phase of A there is a prehension of X. In this prehension X is objectified by one of its own prehensions Xp. Thus Xp is the objective datum of A's prehension.

b. Relative to the concrescence of A, X has perished and is no longer a subjectively immediate actuality. Hence objectification of X by way of some such abstraction as Xp is possible. But this perishing of X also poses our problem about the givenness of X for A.

c. God in his consequent nature prehends X. Let us call this prehension GpX.

d. God, unlike X, does not perish but is in unison of becoming with A.

So far our path has been fairly clear. Now it becomes more obscure. A possible next step would be:

e. In the initial phase of A there is, in addition to A's prehension of Xp, a physical feeling of God in which God is objectified by his prehension of X. The objective datum of this feeling is thus GpX. This is a conformal feeling and its subjective form will conform to the subjective form of its datum GpX.

In this way the givenness of X for A, which is a condition of A's prehension of Xp, would be explained by reference to A's prehension of GpX. This seems a reasonably adequate explanation of the sort we need. But let us consider a further possibility.

f. In God's experience X persists with retention of its own subjective immediacy. Hence in prehending GpX, A is prehending X as now-actual. X-in-God is therefore the ground of its own givenness for A.

Against f there are several objections:

i. It would run counter to Whitehead's general theory of objectification, which seems to require loss of subjective immediacy in the objectified actual entity.

ii. In describing God's prehensions of actual occasions White-

head seems to imply that the general theory of objectification
applies to these prehensions. For example: "Each actuality in the
temporal world has its reception into God's nature. The corresponding element in God's nature is not temporal actuality, but
is the transmutation of that temporal actuality into a living, ever-
present fact." This seems to mean that what is "in God" is not X
in X's own subjective immediacy, but a "corresponding element."
X has made its particular and distinctive contribution to the data
and subjective form of God's own immediate satisfaction. X is
thus objectively immortal in God. Continuing with the passage
just cited: "An enduring personality in the temporal world is a
route of occasions in which the successors with some peculiar
completeness sum up their predecessors. The correlate fact in
God's nature is an even more complete unity of life in a chain of
elements for which succession does not mean loss of immediate
unison. This element in God's nature inherits from the temporal
counterpart according to the same principle as in the temporal
world the future inherits from the past" (PR 531–2). What is in
God is not the route of occasions which composes the society with
personal order. What is in God is a "correlate fact," a chain of
corresponding elements. What is in God is a "counterpart," which
inherits from the temporal world according to the same principle
as, in the temporal world, the future inherits from the past.

It is true that X is in God more completely than it is in A. As
we shall see in the following chapter, God's feeling of X is non-
eliminative. God prehends all of X and not merely some aspect of
it. Objectification of actual occasions for God does not mean
abstraction.[4] Still, Whitehead seems to say, objectification for
God entails loss of immediacy in the objectified entity. Thus
though X is completely in God, without eliminations from its
complete satisfaction, it is in God *objectivé*, not *formaliter*; it is
objectively immortal, not subjectively immediate. Though his
language is not always clear on this point (PR 517, 525), Whitehead seems to accept loss of immediacy as a *categoreal* require-

---

4. Judging from the categoreal scheme, objectification does not *categoreally* require abstraction. This requirement arises from the nature of
temporal actual entities.

ment of objectification, applying to God as well as to actual occasions.

iii. If we accept f there would be a serious problem about the unity of God's satisfaction. In God's experience actual occasions must be objects to which he responds with his own subjective forms of feeling, so as to achieve his own subjective aim in his satisfaction. To make room for God's own self-creative activity, which puts the stamp of his own unity on his experience, it seems that actual occasions must be prehended as *objectified* subjects.[5]

iv. If we accepted f we would "prove too much." In that case not only X but all of X's predecessors would be subjectively immediate in God. This would leave us with a problem about temporal cumulation in God's nature.

v. If f is true, then what is the sense of saying that X has perished? If X persists in God with retention of its own subjective immediacy, then is there any genuine sense in which X has perished? Would any real consequences of the doctrine of perishing, of which Whitehead makes so much (ESP 117), remain?

For these reasons, some of which will be amplified in the following chapter, it seems that we must reject f and fall back upon e as an explanation of how God might be the ground of the givenness of the past.

It might be thought that the resultant theory would amount to occasionalism. This would not be true. On an occasionalist theory the function of X is only to be an *occasion* for an exercise of divine causality. This theory, on the contrary, would assert that X is more than an instance of divine causality. X itself is a real causal agent. Its causal efficacy for A has been initiated by its real internal constitution as a self-creative act of becoming. God conforms to and sustains the influence initiated by X. Hence a full account of the ontological reason for the influence of X on A,

---

5. This objection is similar to the argument from the principle of creativity advanced in Chapter 3 against a literal interpretation of the "flow of feeling." It is different from the argument from the unity of the subject advanced there. That argument introduced the abstractive character of the physical prehensions of actual occasions. But God does not abstract, at least not in the same sense.

taking account both of *what* is given and *that* it is given, would have to refer both to X and to God. To refer to either alone would abstract from the concrete situation.

C. God and Contemporaneity

8. The causal independence of contemporaries

Charles Hartshorne has suggested that God influences actual occasions by effecting a mutual immanence of contemporary occasions. Thus, though apart from God contemporaries would be causally independent, this independence is overcome by God's influence upon them. He argues that Whitehead's doctrine of God implies a "cosmic present," which is "the *de facto* totality of actual entities as present in the divine immediacy." And from this it would follow, Hartshorne thinks, that contemporary actual occasions are not causally independent of each other. "Since they are all immanent in God, and he in turn immanent in them, must they not be immanent in each other?" In support of this deduction he argues as follows: "For, since God is not spatially separated from things, it seems no definite lapse of time can occur either between his prehension of them or theirs of him. There can be no transmission with the velocity of light from an event to the divine observer, or from the divine process itself to the creaturely events" (Schilpp 545).

The following comments are in order:

a. Is it supposed that actual entities "as present in the divine immediacy" retain their own immediacy? If so, then on the above argument contemporaries would be immanent in one another in a strong and direct way. Against this supposition there are serious objections, some of which have been presented. I suggest that actual occasions are *objectively* immortal in God, as data for his own immediate unity of satisfaction. If so, the only kind of immanence between contemporaries Hartshorne's argument could establish would be an indirect immanence, unlike the direct immanence of an actual occasion in its successors.

b. Even this milder version of the mutual immanence of contemporaries encounters a difficulty arising from the categories of subjective unity and subjective harmony. The categoreal reason for the mutual independence of contemporary actual occasions is that otherwise there could be no unified satisfaction and hence no completion of the concrescence. There must be a duration when the concrescence is closed to further physical data, so that the multiplicity of physical data in its initial phase may be inwardly absorbed into a unity of feeling.

c. This condition would have to apply, it seems, to the subject's prehensions of God as well as to its prehensions of other actual occasions. Otherwise the process of concrescence might go on and on, and never be satisfied and perish.

d. Hence we must suppose that God as prehended by A is God as conditioned by A's actual world but not by A's contemporaries. In its initial phase, A prehends God's specific satisfaction arising out of A's actual world. But in this initial phase A's contemporaries have not yet become and hence could not have been prehended by God.

e. Thus the lack of spatial separation between A and God is not sufficient reason for holding that A prehends God as conditioned by A's contemporary B. Therefore lack of spatial separation is insufficient to establish even an indirect immanence of contemporaries *via* God. Incidentally, the fact that light has a uniform, finite velocity is not the categoreal reason for the causal independence of contemporaries. This physical fact must be interpreted in terms of the categories but is not itself a categoreal condition in the system. Whitehead interprets space and time in terms of the experiences of actual occasions, not the other way around. Spatial separation is a reflection or consequence of a plurality of individual acts of experience.

f. One might say there is a *divine* present without saying there is a cosmic present. God is in unison of becoming with every actual occasion. God always has a present. The content of that present is relative to the creative advance of nature. But if there is mutual exclusiveness of immediacy between God and actual occasions, then at no time is there a single immediate experience which literally includes all other immediate experiences. In this sense there is no cosmic present. God's present is not the present of any or all of the actual occasions to which it is relative.

Now I shall state a different and, I think, more adequate interpretation of the temporal relations of God and actual occasions. For any concrescent occasion A, God is objectified as a specific satisfaction, which results from God's prehensions of all the occasions in A's past actual world. This unity of satisfaction which A prehends does not include God's prehension of any contemporary of A, as B, because B has not yet become. B like A is in process of concrescence and has not yet attained its satisfaction. Hence B cannot be objectified for God any more than it can be objectified for A. God does not prehend B until B has attained its satisfaction. Therefore A does not prehend God as conditioned by B.

God will prehend B when B has become. Thus for some later occasion M, God will be objectified as conditioned by A and by B as well as by the past actual worlds of A and B. But God *so* considered has himself not yet become. The occasions A and B have not yet been absorbed into the experience of his satisfaction. It follows that neither can be indirectly immanent in the other by way of an objectification in God. So the causal independence of contemporary occasions is not overcome by the influence of God.

Actual occasions are data for God's physical prehensions. They are given for God. But they are not *given* until they have *become*. They are not data for God's prehensions until they have achieved their satisfactions and thereby added new objective determinations to the course of nature. This is the inevitable consequence of Whitehead's epochal theory of time, which is itself a consequence of his theory of a multiplicity of real temporal individuals.

In this way Whitehead's principle of the mutual independence of contemporaries has to be extended so as to apply to God as well as to actual occasions. Since God is everlasting, there will be no actual occasion which will not be causally objectified for God, and for which God will not be causally objectified. In this respect God is unlike actual occasions. For in the case of any actual occasion there are other actual occasions, namely its contemporaries, which do not influence it and are not influenced by it.

It would remain true, however, that no actual entity, including God, influences another until it has achieved a definite and specific satisfaction. It must *become* before it is *given*. In this respect

God is like actual occasions. God as a superject effective for A is God as conditioned by A's *past*. God is in unison of becoming with A. But God *as* in unison of becoming with A is not causally effective for A. In this sense God and his contemporaries, as well as actual occasions and their contemporaries, are mutually independent.

9. Unison of becoming

The fact that God is in unison of becoming with every actual occasion does not require that any actual occasion should prehend God *as* being in unison of becoming with itself. We now ask the further question: Is God prehended by actual occasions *as* being in unison of becoming with them? If so, how? It seems that such a prehension could not be a direct causal objectification of God as contemporary. How else might God be prehended *as* in unison of becoming with A?

We might say in the first place that A prehends the *inclusive* quality of God's subjective aim. This quality will be an element in the subjective forms of God's prehensions which are data for A in A's initial phase. In this way there is conveyed to A the suggestion of God's transcendence of any finite set of possibilities and any finite state of affairs. God includes (by envisagement) all pure possibilities and (by physical prehension) all those actualities which, relative to A, have become. As an element in the subjective form of God's feeling, this quality of inclusiveness must be conformed to by the subjective form of A's prehension of God.

This does not amount to a direct awareness of God as in unison of becoming with A. A nearer approximation to such an awareness may occur in higher phases of experience. In a route of high grade occasions there may be a *judgment* that God is in unison of becoming with the finite subject. Let us revert to A's relation to B. B is not causally objectified for A. Yet the experience of A defines for it a "now" which extends beyond its own basic region and makes a there-now significant. The potentiality of contemporary occasions, the contemporary world as a locus of becoming, is given as a part of A's experience.

Reflection on the meaning and ground of "significance" may

now arise. What is the ontological ground of the "potential scheme of spatio-temporal extensiveness which is a datum for both *A* and *B*" (PR 188)? The inclusiveness of God's subjective aim, directly prehended as a quality of his experience, would suggest that God is in unison of becoming with the judging subject and that he is the ontological ground of the fact that "the real potentialities relative to all standpoints are coordinated as diverse determinations of one extensive continuum" (PR 103). In this way, from the inclusiveness of God's subjective aim and from the given fact of "becoming going on there-now," there might issue the judgment that divine becoming is going on now.

D. CONCLUSION

There is a significant parallel between the two salient features of the theory of actual occasions, namely the individuality and the influence of actual occasions. The real individuality of occasions is the basis for the doctrine of social transcendence. Causal objectification is the basis for the doctrine of social immanence. And in both cases the doctrine of God is required for an adequate explanation.

The individuality of an actual occasion depends on its subjective aim. And the existence of an initial aim requires explanation under the ontological principle. Whitehead's explanation is that the initial aim is derived from God. In this way his theory of finite individuality, and with it his doctrine of social transcendence, requires his doctrine of God.

Causal objectification depends for its meaning on the givenness *now* of the past which has perished. This givenness of the past, like the existence of an initial aim, requires explanation under the ontological principle. The only explanation open to Whitehead is that God is the ground of the givenness of the past. In this way his theory of influence, and with it his doctrine of social immanence, requires his doctrine of God.

At this point we can see how God makes possible an extensive continuum. The existence of God makes possible an *order* and a *continuity* of regions of actual occasions. Since his primordial nature is an envisagement of *all* possibilities, he makes available

for *any* situation the ideal possibility of a novel unity of experience. This novel unity of experience, as we saw in Chapter 4,
determines a unique extensive region, shared by no other actual
occasion. The unity and exclusiveness of the experience of an
occasion are reflected in the definiteness and exclusiveness of its
basic region. And since its unity of experience depends on its
subjective aim, and since in turn its subjective aim depends on
God, the definiteness and exclusiveness of its region depend on
God. In this way the order of the extended world requires Whitehead's doctrine of God.

Again, the continuity of the world in time requires the doctrine
of God. The past which has perished can be given for the present
and impose conformity on it, because God is the ontological
ground of its givenness. This givenness of the past for the present,
and the conformity of the present to the past, is the basis in experience for the continuity of time. The temporal contiguity of
standpoints of actual occasions is an abstract aspect of the influence of actual occasions on their successors. And since the influence of actual occasions requires God for its explanation, the
temporal continuity of the extended world requires the doctrine
of God.

In this way not only the categoreal conditions of acts of experience but also the order and continuity of the extended world,
which are derivative from these categoreal conditions, require
these functions of God. Thus in Whitehead's system God is an
explanation of the solidarity of the world. "The universe is at
once the multiplicity of *rēs verae* and the solidarity of *rēs verae*.
The solidarity is itself the efficiency of the macroscopic *res vera,*
embodying the principle of unbounded permanence acquiring
novelty through flux" (PR 254).

Finally, two general conclusions about Whitehead's conception
of God seem reasonably well established if the interpretation offered above is a fair one. (a) His theory of actual occasions requires his doctrine of God, if we accept his own principles of
explanation. It seems therefore that his conception of God is not
an *interpretation* of his metaphysical system, formulated after the
system had been constructed, for religious or other purposes
(though I would not deny that a religious interest may have in-

fluenced the construction of the system itself). I suggest that the conception of God is a part of the *structure* of the system. (b) The influence of God on the world leaves room for and is thus consistent with the freedom and creativity of actual occasions. The functions we may fairly attribute to God, on the basis of relevant texts and the categoreal scheme, do not nullify or supplant the real individuality and the influence of actual occasions.

CHAPTER 17

How the World Affects God

1. How God requires the world

IN THIS CHAPTER we come to a feature of Whitehead's theory
that sets it off more sharply from traditional theology. This feature might well have been anticipated since it follows from the
principle that God is the chief exemplification of the categories.
If every actual entity is affected by other entities, then God must
be affected by the world. But we shall see that God is not affected
by the world in the same way an actual occasion is affected by
other occasions, and emphatically not in the same way actual occasions are affected by God.

First we notice how the existence of God requires the existence
of many actual occasions. Then, in most of the chapter, we shall
explore the ways actual occasions influence God's experience—
and the ways they do not.

In God's experience, as in the experience of an actual occasion,
conceptual prehensions and physical prehensions are integrated
by a subjective aim into satisfaction. Physical prehensions are essential to his concrete actuality for without them God would have
no satisfaction. But his physical prehensions are of actual occasions. So if there were no actual occasions God would have no
physical prehensions and as a consequence would be deficient in
actuality (PR 50, 521). "The completion of God's nature into a fulness of physical feeling is derived from the objectification of the
world in God" (PR 523). In this way the existence of God as an
actual entity requires the existence of the world of actual occasions.

We may go a step further. God's satisfaction requires not merely
the existence of a world other than himself but, more specifically,
the existence of *many* real finite individuals other than himself. A
multiplicity of actual occasions is required for God's satisfaction.

This may be shown as follows: (a) The primordial nature of God is an envisagement of the unbounded multiplicity of eternal objects. God aims at the actualization of *all* pure possibilities. (b) Any actualization is finite, since the creative process involves decisions which exclude alternative possibilities. Therefore, for any particular actualization, some of the possibilities envisaged by God are incompatible for joint realization. (c) It follows that there cannot be any one real individual in which all eternal objects are physically realized. Hence more than one real individual other than himself is necessary for God's satisfaction. (d) Indeed there must be an infinite multiplicity of finite real individuals. For any finite set of finite actualities would exclude and fail to realize some pure possibilities. Therefore an infinite multiplicity of actual occasions is required for God's satisfaction. "This principle of intrinsic incompatibility has an important bearing upon our conception of the nature of God. . . . We must conceive the Divine Eros as the active entertainment of all ideals, with the urge to their finite realization, each in its due season. Thus a process must be inherent in God's nature, whereby his infinity is acquiring realization" (AI 357).

This conclusion is important because it illustrates Whitehead's aim at coherence in the development of his scheme. " 'Coherence,' as here employed, means that the fundamental ideas, in terms of which the scheme is developed, presuppose each other so that in isolation they are meaningless" (PR 5). In particular it means that the nature of God gives a "reason" of a sort why there are many finite real individuals. On this point he contrasts his philosophy with Spinoza's system of which he says, "The gap in the system is the arbitrary introduction of the 'modes' " (PR 10). In his own system the multiplicity of finite real individuals is required for the satisfaction of God's subjective aim.

We must avoid supposing this amounts to a deduction of the existence of many finite things. This is not an explanation of the world in that sense. He does not undertake to prove pluralism by demonstrating the existence of many finite things. On the contrary, the existence of many finite things is one of the facts of experience with which he begins to philosophize. He accepts it as an empirical fact. To recur to a distinction that has been useful at other points in this study, he offers a categoreal not a "meta-physical" explanation (SMW 249–50) of the existence of a world of many finite things.

A further qualification must be kept in mind. This is not a complete explanation of the particular actual occasions which *do* come into being. For as we saw in the preceding chapter God does not completely determine any actual occasion, though he conditions the becoming of every occasion in crucial ways. An actual occasion "is internally determined and is externally free' (PR 41). For this reason, if we were to construct an analogy between Whitehead's system and Spinoza's, we would have to construe actual occasions not as modes of God but as modes of creativity (SMW 248; PR 114, 125).

2. Are God and actual occasions mutually exclusive?

So far as we have seen that actual occasions make an essential contribution to the divine concrescence and satisfaction. Now we ask more specifically how this contribution is made. God requires actual occasions as data for his physical prehensions, without which his satisfaction would not be possible. How do actual occasions affect God by way of these prehensions? First we ask whether in his prehensions of actual occasions he shares their subjective immediacy. Considered as acts of experience, are God and an actual occasion mutually exclusive?

It seems perfectly clear that the data of God's physical prehensions are *objectified* actual occasions. "The completion of God's nature into a fulness of physical feeling is derived from the objectification of the world in God. He shares with every new creation its actual world; and the concrescent creature is objectified in God as a novel element in God's objectification of that actual world" (PR 523; see 134–5, 164 n). In this way God's prehensions of actual occasions exemplify the categoreal conditions of prehensions, and thus the conditions of immanence generally (PR 34, 38, 79–80). Now it was argued in Part One that the objectification of one occasion in another does not entail any sharing of immediacy, and that the experiences of the two occasions are mutually exclusive. The objectified occasion does not persist with its own

subjective immediacy into the new concrescence. Is this true of
the objectification of occasions in God also? Whitehead means to
apply the categories of explanation and obligation to God as well
as to actual occasions. Do the differences between God and actual
occasions require us to hold that there is sharing of immediacy
between God and actual occasions, though not among actual occasions? First we examine a number of texts that bear on this
question. Then we shall look at the implications of some fundamental principles.

When Whitehead discusses God's prehensions of actual occasions, and their prehensions of God, he uses much the same
language as when he discusses causal objectification within the
temporal world. The fundamental distinction between formal and
objective existence is applied to God (PR 47–8), and the immanence of God in other actual entities is identified with his objective immortality. "This function of creatures, that they constitute the shifting character of creativity, is here termed the
'objective immortality' of actual entities. Thus God has objective
immortality in respect to his primordial nature and his consequent nature" (PR 47; see 378). Hybrid physical feelings effect
"the objectification of God in a temporal subject" (PR 377). God is
"superjective" as well as "subjective" (PR 135). The immanence
of God in actual occasions is his objective existence in actual occasions. It is not God in his own subjective immediacy.

In turn, as we have seen above, actual occasions are objectified
in God. This clearly means, in most cases, that the objectified actual occasions have lost their subjective immediacy. Three problematical passages need to be noticed. The first occurs in the first
chapter of Part V of *Process and Reality,* a chapter composed almost entirely of presystematic discourse: "There is a unison of
becoming among things in the present. Why should there not be
novelty without loss of this direct unison of immediacy among
things? In the temporal world, it is the empirical fact that process
entails loss: the past is present under an abstraction. But there is
no reason, of any ultimate metaphysical generality, why this
should be the whole story" (PR 517). The second passage comes in
the following chapter, in a discussion of the consequent nature of
God: "In it there is no loss, no obstruction. The world is felt in a
unison of immediacy. The property of combining creative ad-

vance with the retention of mutual immediacy is what in the previous section is meant by the term 'everlasting' " (PR 524–5). The word "mutual" might suggest that actual occasions retain their immediacy when objectified in the consequent nature of God. The third passage is as follows: "Thus the consequent nature of God is composed of a multiplicity of elements with individual self-realization" (PR 531).

Several comments on these passages are in order. (a) The "unison of immediacy" referred to in the first two passages is God's own immediacy, as the second passage makes clear. (b) In the next section of this chapter some light will be thrown on the reference of the second passage to "abstraction." (c) In the third passage it might have been better to say the consequent nature of God "unifies" a multiplicity of elements. These elements, actual occasions, do have individual self-realization in their own immediate experiences. But God's own immediate experience is not a multiplicity but a unity, in which the multiplicity of occasions is objectified. (d) The suggestion that actual occasions retain their immediacy when objectified in God, which these passages might permit, is not consistent with some fundamental principles or with the plain meanings of other texts.

Some of these texts are as follows. Actual occasions *"obtain adequate representation* in the divine nature. Such representations compose the 'consequent nature' of God" (PR 18–19, my italics). This passage is particularly relevant to the third passage cited above, to which it may serve as a corrective. Again, God's physical experience is *"initially* derived from the temporal world" (PR 524, my italics). The nature of God "receives into its unity the scattered effectiveness of realized activities, *transformed* by the supremacy of its own ideals" (IMM 697–8, my italics). Another important passage should be given in full:

> Each actuality in the temporal world has its reception into God's nature. The corresponding element in God's nature is not temporal actuality, but is the transmutation of that temporal actuality into a living, ever-present fact. An enduring personality in the temporal world is a route of occasions in which the successors with some peculiar completeness sum up their predecessors. The correlate fact in God's

nature is an even more complete unity of life in a chain of elements for which succession does not mean loss of immediate unison. This element in God's nature inherits from the temporal counterpart according to the same principle as in the temporal world the future inherits from the past. Thus in the sense in which the present occasion is the person *now,* and yet with his own past, so the counterpart in God is that person in God (PR 531–2. See RM 155, 157; PR 164 n, 336–7).

It appears from these passages that when actual occasions are prehended into the consequent nature of God they do not retain their own immediacies. They obtain "adequate representation" in God's experience. They are "transmuted." The "living, ever-present fact," the "even more complete unity of life," is not the collective immediacies of the individual actual occasions. It is the everlasting subjectively immediate experience of God. The "correlate fact" in God's nature "inherits from the temporal counterpart according to the same principle as in the temporal world the future inherits from the past." This means, if causal objectification in the temporal world has been interpreted correctly, that actual occasions do not persist into God's experience with their own subjective immediacy. They are objectively immortal in God's own subjectively immediate experience.

In Chapter 3 certain arguments from Whitehead's categories were offered against interpreting causal objectification as literal transfer of feeling. We now ask whether these arguments apply to the objectification of actual occasions in God. If they do, they will add weight to the latter set of passages discussed above.

a. *Creativity.* If God is an actual entity then he must be, at least as much as an actual occasion, *causa sui* or self-creative. "To be *causa sui* means that the process of concrescence is its own reason for the decision in respect to the qualitative clothing of feelings" (PR 135). The way an actual entity exercises its creative freedom is by determining the quality of its responses to its environment. This is the way it "functions in respect to its own determination" (PR 38). It has the final decision about the subjective forms of its own feelings.

Now if the feelings experienced by actual occasions literally persisted, in their own subjective immediacy, into the divine concrescence, then this would seem to negate God's freedom. For then not only the data but also the "qualitative clothing" of some of his feelings would not be determined by himself. Whitehead's principles seem to require that God determines the subjective forms of his own feelings. The experiences of actual occasions, including the subjective forms of their feelings, are *data* for God's own feelings. *How* the subject feels its data must be decided finally by the subject itself.

b. *Time.* Actual occasions become and perish. This is the categoreal explanation of the epochal character of time. Therefore an occasion cannot literally and simply persist in the experience of a succeeding occasion. Now God does not perish but is everlasting, in unison of becoming with every occasion. Does God's everlastingness disqualify this argument from applying to God's prehensions of actual occasions? I suggest it does not.

Though God does not perish, Whitehead clearly means that actual occasions do. Now if actual occasions do not perish subjectively (PR 44) when objectified but retain their own immediacy in God, then it seems they would *never* perish subjectively. For there is no condition within God's experience that would thereafter require them to perish. But if actual occasions persisted everlastingly in God with retention of their own subjective immediacy, what meaning could be given to "perishing"? As a consequence, what meaning could be given to Whitehead's reiterated expression, taken from Locke, that time is a "perpetual perishing" (PR 43, 94)? His realistic view of time seems to require that actual occasions perish subjectively and become objectively immortal in God's experience as well as in the temporal world.

c. *The unity of the subject.* The first categoreal obligation clearly implies that every feeling in the concrescence of an actual entity has that actual entity as its subject (PR 39). If this applies to God as well as to actual occasions, then it follows that no feeling in the divine concrescence has any actual occasion as its subject. This would mean that no occasion literally persists in God with retention of its own subjective immediacy.

It is true that actual occasions always abstract from the data they objectify, whereas we shall see that God does not. That gives this argument additional strength when applied to actual occasions, as in Chapter 3. But the general consequences of the category of subjective unity seem sufficient to rule out literal transfer of feeling from an actual occasion to God. In the case of God, no less than in the case of actual occasions, privacy of experience is essential to unity of experience. And unity of experience is a necessary condition of an actual entity, temporal or divine.

I suggest that when actual occasions are prehended by God they lose their own immediacy of feeling. Their feelings are not literally transferred into God's experience. The divine immediacy and the immediacy of an actual occasion are mutually exclusive in the sense explained in Part One. Both the weight of the evidence from relevant texts and the implications of fundamental principles support this interpretation.

It is true that a contrary view may be suggested by some passages. Here as elsewhere in this study I do not argue that Whitehead is always self-consistent in his elucidation of the categoreal scheme, or that he never uses misleading expressions. I would suggest, however, that the misleading expressions usually occur when he is applying the scheme to experience and therefore must risk the ambiguities of ordinary language.

3. Does God abstract from actual occasions?
Negative prehensions

This question is closely connected with the preceding one. It asks further how actual occasions are data for God's physical prehensions. Here we find an important difference between the way God prehends actual occasions and the way actual occasions prehend one another.

Some of the passages cited above suggest that God's physical prehensions abstract from their data. Two other such passages may be cited:

> Every fact is what it is, a fact of pleasure, of joy, of pain, or
> of suffering. In its union with God that fact is not a total

> loss, but *on its finer* side is an element to be woven im-
> mortally into the rhythm of mortal things (RM 155, my
> italics).

> The consequent nature of God is his judgment on the world.
> He saves the world as it passes into the immediacy of his own
> life. It is the judgment of a tenderness which *loses nothing
> that can be saved* (PR 525, my italics).

This might mean that God's prehensions are selective, so that
something in the occasion he prehends is left out of his prehension. On this interpretation God would prehend every occasion but he would not prehend all of every occasion.

Other passages convey an opposite suggestion, namely that
God's prehensions do not eliminate anything from their data.
For example: "The perfection of God's subjective aim, derived
from the completeness of his primordial nature, issues into the
character of his consequent nature. In it there is no loss, no obstruction" (PR 524). Again, in the temporal world "objectification
involves elimination," for "In the temporal world, it is the empirical fact that process entails loss; the past is present under
an abstraction. But there is no reason, of any ultimate metaphysical generality, why this should be the whole story" (PR 517).
This suggests that in *God*'s prehensions of actual occasions there
is no abstraction.

Clearly some distinction is necessary in order to do justice to
these texts. Let us ask another question: Does God have any negative prehensions? This will put us on the way to the distinction
we need. The categoreal explanation of negative prehensions is:
"That there are two species of prehensions: (a) 'positive prehensions' which are termed 'feelings,' and (b) 'negative prehensions'
which are said to 'eliminate from feeling.' Negative prehensions
also have subjective forms. A negative prehension holds its datum
as inoperative in the progressive concrescence of prehensions constituting the unity of the subject" (PR 35, category of explanation
xii). Whitehead interprets this by taking an example of aesthetic
enjoyment, a kind of experience to which he often appeals for
interpretation of his philosophical categories.

Consider a good picture. It expresses a unity of mutual relevance. It resents the suggestion of addition. No extra patch
of scarlet can be placed in it without wrecking its unity.

The point is that the subjective unity of feeling and the
objective unity of mutual relevance express respectively a
relation of exclusion to the world beyond. There is a completion which rejects alternatives. Mere omission is characteristic of confusion. Rejection belongs to intelligible pattern
(ESP [1937] 130).

Negative prehension is more like rejection than omission because a negative prehension, like a positive prehension, has a
subjective form. And this subjective form affects the total complex of feeling, even though the datum of the prehension is
"eliminated" from feeling.

It is clear that there is always some negative prehension when
one actual occasion prehends another. In the temporal world
"objectification involves elimination" (PR 517). Some of the feelings belonging to the datum must be rejected for the sake of the
unity of the subject. By this elimination the initial datum becomes the objective datum.

This is necessary because the new subject cannot assimilate all
the content of its datum into its own unity of feeling. It aims at
a particular synthesis of feelings. From its finite standpoint, defined by its specific aim, it cannot handle all the experiences its
predecessors had. Hence some of these feelings must be excluded.
"This fact of the elimination by reason of synthesis is sometimes
termed the perspective of the actual world from the standpoint
of that concrescence" (PR 321; see 225, 251, 484).

When we turn from actual occasions to God, we find this reason for negative prehensions does not apply. God does not have a
limited perspective. Or, we might say, God shares all finite perspectives. The primordial nature of God "arises out of no actual
world" (PR 75). This makes it possible that God as consequent
"shares with every new creation its actual world." He is "in unison
of becoming with every other creative act" (PR 523).

Since his subjective aim is not constricted by a finite standpoint, the subjective forms of his feelings do not require elimina-

tions from his data. He has no absolute aversions (PR 48), though he prehends and values the aversions and adversions in the subjective forms of actual occasions. Unlike actual occasions, God never takes "the easy road of Anaesthesia by which discordant factors are dismissed into irrelevance" (AI 379).

To God all the feelings of actual occasions are relevant, acceptable, and important. He does not compete with any actual occasion for satisfaction. "God's role is not the combat of productive force with productive force, of destructive force with destructive force; it lies in the patient operation of the overpowering rationality of his conceptual harmonization" (PR 525–6). God's satisfaction does not require elimination of any feeling experienced by any actual occasion. On the contrary, every feeling in every actual occasion makes its positive contribution to his satisfaction. God's satisfaction does not require negative prehensions.

We now notice further that the categoreal scheme does not itself require that all actual entities have negative prehensions. It *defines* negative prehensions, in category of explanation xii (PR 35). But none of the categoreal obligations requires that every actual entity should have them. It is a derivative fact, not a categoreal condition, that actual occasions *do* have negative prehensions. Therefore to say that God has no negative prehensions would not conflict with the categoreal scheme. Here as elsewhere the categoreal scheme leaves room for differences between God and actual occasions.

Finally we ask whether Whitehead says that God has no negative prehensions. He makes it quite clear that there are no negative prehensions in God's conceptual experience. He says of the primordial nature: "It is therefore infinite, devoid of all negative prehensions" (PR 524; see 46, 48). When we come to God's physical experience the evidence from relevant texts is meager. There is no passage that tells us in so many words that the consequent nature of God does not include negative prehensions. This conclusion does seem to be implied by some of the passages cited above (PR 517, 524). In a similar passage he says that the revolts of destructive evil, purely self-regarding, "are dismissed into their triviality of merely individual facts; and yet the good they did achieve in individual joy, in individual sorrow, in the introduction of needed contrast, is yet saved by its relation to the completed whole. The image—and it is but an image—the image under which this operative growth of God's nature is best conceived, is that of a tender care that nothing be lost" (PR 525). And it is not clear how God could have a negative prehension of an actual occasion without having along with it a negative prehension of some eternal object.

The weight of the evidence, in my judgment, indicates that God's consequent nature does not include any negative prehensions, though he prehends positively the negative prehensions of actual occasions. Shortly I shall offer an interpretation, consistent with this conclusion, of certain problematical texts. But for this interpretation, and for an adequate answer to our initial question whether God abstracts from his data, we need a certain distinction for which we are now prepared.

We might distinguish between two senses of "abstraction": (a) abstraction as elimination by negative prehensions of part of the initial datum; and (b) abstraction simply as objectification, prehension of an actual entity as an object, understood as entailing loss of immediacy in the objectified entity as explained in Part One. We might then say that God's physical prehensions abstract from actual occasions in sense *b* but not in sense *a*. But Whitehead does not himself employ "abstraction" in sense *b* but only in sense *a*. Therefore it might be better to put our distinction another way. (A) Both for God and for actual occasions objectification means loss of immediacy in the objectified entity. (B) For actual occasions, but not for God, objectification *also* involves abstraction (sense *a*). God's physical prehensions objectify, but do not eliminate from, their data.

With this distinction we may now interpret certain problematical passages.

a. An actual occasion "contributes such elements as it can to a realization in God" (PR 134).

Its contribution is finite. It can contribute only what it has achieved. But *all* that it has achieved is prehended by God.

b. Actual occasions "obtain adequate representation in the divine nature" (PR 18–19).

They do not persist into God's experience with their own subjective immediacy. They have counterparts (PR 531) in God's own complex unity of experience. *All* of their feelings are adequately represented.

c. "In its union with God" a fact "on its finer side is an element to be woven immortally into the rhythm of mortal things" (RM 155).

From the perspective of some actual occasion a certain fact may be trivial or destructive. Hence the occasion must reject it. God is able to accept the fact for what it is. This potentiality for being accepted by God, and thereby making a contribution to existence, *is* "the finer side" of the fact. God accepts the *whole* of the fact.

d. God "loses nothing that can be saved" (PR 525).

Actual occasions perish. They cease to exist in the mode of subjective immediacy. Their subjective immediacy cannot be "saved" as such. They can be saved only by becoming objectified. By becoming objectified for God *all* the feelings of an actual occasion can be saved. Apart from God some of these feelings would be lost.

It seems fair to conclude that this interpretation is reasonably consistent with the categoreal scheme and with the relevant texts. And I suggest that it does more justice to the evidence than the opposite view would do. God does not abstract from actual occasions in the sense of eliminating some of their feelings from his initial data. None of the feelings experienced by actual occasions persists in God with retention of its subjective immediacy. But all of the feelings experienced by actual occasions become objectively immortal in God's experience.

4. Does God have conformal feelings?

To this point we have focused on the data of God's physical prehensions. Now we ask about the subjective forms of God's physical feelings. The question is: Do they conform to their data?

Notice how this contrasts with the question whether actual occasions persist into God with their own immediacy. There we asked whether God had a share in determining the subjective forms of his own feelings. Here we sail on an opposite tack. We ask whether actual occasions have a share in determining the subjective forms of God's feelings.

This problem arises in the following way. Whitehead tells us that actual occasions affect God's experience. But he does not tell us fully and clearly *how* their influence is effective. Now when we ask what the mechanism of influence on God might be, the most natural suggestion is the mechanism of conformity of subjective form in terms of which causal objectification in the temporal world is explained. As we saw in Chapter 7, the prehending subject (the effect) is obliged, categoreally speaking, to repeat in its own immediacy a subjective form of feeling encountered in its datum (the cause). In this way the subjective forms of the past occasion condition, but do not fully determine, the subjective forms of the new concrescence.

May this explanation of influence be applied also to the way actual occasions affect God? The following passage might suggest a negative answer: "This prehension into God of each creature is directed with the subjective aim, and clothed with the subjective form, wholly derivative from his all-inclusive primordial valuation" (PR 523). This sounds as though God's subjective forms are wholly determined by his primordial nature. If so, no room would remain for any effective conditioning of his subjective forms by the actual occasions he prehends. It would be impossible to say of God's physical prehensions that "the subjective form of a prehension is partly dictated by the qualitative element in the objective content of that prehension" (AI 326).

This produces a problem. If the subjective forms of God's physical feelings do not conform to their data, then how can we say that actual occasions are *given* for God? Part of the meaning of givenness is the imposition of conformity. What is given must be conformed to in some way or other. If actual occasions are not given for God, then it seems that the world of actual occasions does not really affect God's experience. Thus our question has considerable importance for interpretation of Whitehead's theory of God and the world.

It is possible that Whitehead has overstated his point. Certainly God's subjective aim is wholly derivative from his primordial nature. But is it not an exaggeration to say that the subjective forms of his physical prehensions are "wholly derivative" from his primordial nature? Would it be more exact to say they are "completely in harmony with" his primordial valuations? This may be compared with a sentence where, speaking of actual entities generally, the subjective form of a prehension is said to be "determined" by the subjective aim (PR 29). Since actual occasions certainly have conformal feelings, this must be understood as "partly determined." Perhaps neither passage means to rule out conformation.

Yet God's experience is plainly so different from the experiences of actual occasions that further exploration is needed. We should look more generally at what Whitehead's categories require about the subjective forms of God's physical prehensions. Let us interpret conformal feeling as in Chapter 7. And let us suppose provisionally that God's physical feelings are conformal. Then God's prehension of an actual occasion would differ from the prehension of one occasion by another in two intimately connected ways. Let us say that in God's feeling there is (a) perfect conformation and (b) perfect supplementation.

a. We have seen that God does not eliminate from his physical data any of their component feelings. God has no negative prehensions. This would mean that God conforms to all of the feelings of actual occasions in the creative advance of nature. All their feelings are re-enacted in his own immediacy and absorbed into his own satisfaction. His conformation is all-inclusive.

We would have to add now that his conformation is not only all-inclusive but perfect. He conforms to every feeling, and he conforms perfectly to each feeling. He not only feels all the feelings of actual occasions; he feels each feeling fully. There is perfect conformation.

When one actual occasion prehends another it eliminates some of the feelings composing the datum. Also it conforms imperfectly to those feelings in the datum that are positively felt. The new subject repeats or re-enacts the subjective forms of the object. "But the re-enaction is not perfect. The categoreal demands of the concrescence require adjustments of the pattern of emotional intensities. . . . [There is] partial equivalence of subjective form" (PR 363). An actual occasion has to compromise between actuality and ideality. It has an ideal of itself, its conceptual aim. But it also includes " 'given' components which exclude the attainment of the full ideal" (PR 128). This is why the initial aim needs specification, as explained in Chapter 16. The concrescence has to specify and limit its aim to what it may achieve in the given situation. This is one side, so to speak, of its compromise.

The other side of its compromise consists in elimination from and imperfect conformation to its datum. Even if A positively prehends X's feeling of some datum, A may not be able to entertain this feeling with the intensity it had in X. If A's repetition had an intensity equal to X's feeling, then X might be unassimilable into A's satisfaction. What is true of intensities in the datum is true also of qualitative patterns (PR 356) in the datum. Only by playing down certain intensities in the datum and simplifying its qualitative pattern can A achieve a satisfaction of its own.

This imperfect conformation of an occasion to the subjective forms of its datum is like the imperfect sympathy one human being may have with another. The full intensity of N's pain or pleasure may be too much for M to bear. The full richness of N's emotional response may be too complex for M to appreciate. The qualities and intensities of N's feeling thus pose a threat to M's integrity of experience, a threat against which M may defend himself by some mode of aversion or depreciation. In this way M may compete with N for satisfaction.

In God's experience this is not so. His aim is at the actualization of *all* possibilities, not at some definite and limited outcome.

> The primordial created fact is the unconditioned conceptual valuation of the entire multiplicity of eternal objects (PR 46).

> There is not just one 'ideal' order (PR 128. See RM 152–4; PR 48, 50, 75, 160–1, 521–2).

This unlimited valuation of possibilities means that God will have unlimited hospitality to those actualizations which do, as a matter of fact, occur in the process of nature. His hospitality will be unlimited, in the two ways mentioned above.

First, God will feel all feelings and eliminate none. Whatever possibilities are as a matter of fact realized, God wanted (so to speak) those possibilities actualized somehow, somewhere. Now they are realized, and God's prehension of all the feelings of each actual occasion is thus in harmony with his primordial appetition.

Second, God's re-enaction of these feelings will be without distortion and without exaggeration or diminution of intensity. Whatever the feeling may be, he can feel it for just what it is. No feeling need be distorted or depreciated to enter into his satisfaction. His full realization of what was felt and how it was felt will not threaten the unity of his experience. In his consequent nature "there is no loss, no obstruction" (PR 524). His reaction to each feeling can be fully appropriate. His subjective forms can be perfectly adequate to their data. God's conformation to his physical data, unlike the conformation of actual occasions, is perfect. In this way God is the "chief exemplification" (PR 521) of the conformity of subjective form.

b. This doctrine of unlimited divine hospitality and perfect conformation would stand alongside a companion doctrine, which we may call the doctrine of unlimited divine supplementation. The subjective forms of God's physical prehensions are perfectly supplemented in his satisfaction by the subjective forms of his prehensions of alternative possibilities. This is another respect in which God is the chief exemplification of the categories.

It is a general principle "That mental functioning introduces into realization subjective forms conformal to relevant alternatives excluded from the completeness of physical realization" (AI 333; see PR 280–7, 367). This principle holds for both actual occasions and God (PR 496). But the importance of mentality varies widely from subject to subject, and in many subjects the addition of contrasting alternatives is negligible. The extreme case at the lower limit is "pure conformation." "Such pure conformation involves the exclusion of all the contraries involved in the lure, with their various grades of proximity and remoteness" (PR 285). For practical purposes we assume pure conformation in the life history of a stone. This would be "undifferentiated endurance" with complete absence of mentality, an assumption reflected in the traditional doctrine of material substance. Whitehead adds that we have no direct evidence of undifferentiated endurance (PR 285). "Pure" (or we might say "mere" or "bare") conformation is at the (hypothetical) opposite extreme from what I have called "perfect" conformation.

In any actual occasion this enrichment of physical experience by mentality will be limited. Only part of the totality of contrasts that define the actual datum will be felt. Not all eternal objects will be effectively felt. Hence some contrasts will not be experienced. This is not the case with God's experience. Since he envisages all eternal objects, all possible contrasts will be felt, and with maximal intensity. God's experience is therefore at the opposite extreme from the hypothetical case of pure conformation. All the contraries in the "objective lure" (PR 281) are felt. None are excluded. God's supplementation of his physical data is unlimited or, we might better say, perfect.

This perfect supplementation of physical data by mentality enables God's hospitality and his conformation to be perfect. Every achievement of actuality can find its place in a meaningful pattern. Thus it can add something to the complex unity of God's satisfaction and hence to the richness of actuality. In God's experience, "The wisdom of subjective aim prehends every actuality for what it can be in such a perfected system. . . . the good they did achieve in individual joy, in individual sorrow, in the introduction of needed contrast, is yet saved by its relation to the completed whole" (PR 525).

In this way God, and God alone, can enter fully into every perspective and value fully every finite achievement. His conformation is perfect because his power of supplementation is unlimited. In both respects he is the chief exemplification of the categories. He does perfectly what actual occasions do imperfectly.

With this provisional explanation of how God might have conformal feelings let us turn to another side of our problem. One feature of Whitehead's account of causal objectification within the temporal world was the *obligation* on an actual occasion to repeat the subjective form of its datum. This was his interpretation of the efficacity of actual occasions. The datum imposes the obligation to conform. We found this feature added not as an additional part of the analytical mechanism of repetition but as an assertion of the dynamically efficient character of the process of transition.

Suppose we should say that actual occasions impose on God an obligation to conformity, that actual occasions make God repeat their subjective forms. How could this be interpreted? We would have to say that this obligation is not a limitation on God in just the same way it is a limitation on actual occasions.

The actual world limits an actual occasion in two senses. (i) The facts that confront its initial aim are results of "transcendent decision," not its own "immanent decision" (PR 248–9). The concrescence has no choice but to begin with these given facts. This is one way in which the data limit the occasion. (ii) Some of these facts are unwelcome to the concrescence. Hence it must eliminate from its initial datum and conform imperfectly to its objective datum. The data include obstructions to its satisfaction and thus limit its satisfaction in a stronger sense of limitation.

The obligation to conformity limits God's physical experience in the first sense but not in the second and stronger sense of limitation. The facts that confront God's subjective aim result from transcendent decision. An actual occasion does something God cannot do. It adds a creative determination to the world and thus imposes a limitation on God's experience. God has no choice but to begin his physical experience with these facts.

But we cannot say that God does not "want" these facts to be given. For the decisions of actual occasions are conditioned by initial aims derived from God himself. Certainly God is not completely "satisfied" by the decision of any one occasion, or indeed by the decisions of any finite set of actual occasions. But the satisfaction of his aim is not obstructed by any of the data he prehends. His hospitality is perfect and his satisfaction requires no eliminations or imperfections of conformation. In this sense the obligation to conformity is not a limitation on God's satisfaction.

Finally we may sum up in three stages an answer to the question with which we began, Does God have conformal feelings? (i) If there were no actual occasions God would have no physical feelings. We might say that actual occasions evoke God's physical feelings. (ii) God "repeats" or "re-enacts" or "reproduces" in his physical feelings the subjective forms he finds in the experiences of actual occasions. Indeed his power of unlimited conceptual supplementation enables him to re-enact them perfectly. (iii) An obligation to re-enaction is imposed on God by the decisions of actual occasions. But this is not a restrictive limitation on his satisfaction.

5. Do actual occasions alter God's satisfaction?

Let us recapitulate two main points already settled. First, actual occasions contribute data for God's physical feelings. Physical feelings are essential to God's satisfaction. Thus actual occasions are necessary to the constitution of God as an actual entity.

Second, actual occasions evoke appropriate subjective forms of feeling in God. The subjective forms of God's feelings conform to the achievements of actual occasions. In this way actual occasions affect the qualitative pattern of God's experience. They affect both the quality of his component physical feelings and the qualitative pattern of his satisfaction. In some degree every actual occasion affects the total quality of God's experience.

The *how* of God's feeling of satisfaction includes two elements, the qualitative pattern and the intensity of his feeling (see PR 356–7). We ask now whether actual occasions affect the intensity of God's satisfaction, as well as its qualitative pattern. Does the intensity of the divine satisfaction vary with variations in the intensities of actual occasions in the course of nature? Or is there some factor of compensation in the divine nature which operates to keep the intensity of God's satisfaction constant, whatever the course of nature may be?

Let us take the case of some large-scale change in nature. Suppose entropy operated to diminish the aggregate intensity of the actual occasions in some cosmic epoch (PR 139–41). Whitehead seems to think this is happening in our own epoch (RM 160;

FR 19–25, 28; ESP 118–19). And suppose the intensity of God's satisfaction varied directly with the aggregate intensity of finite satisfactions in the course of nature. Then it would follow that as entropy progressed the intensity of God's satisfaction would diminish.

Would it follow, further, that as the intensity of God's satisfaction diminished, the intensity of actual occasions would in turn diminish? If so there would be a reciprocal effect, accelerating the process of entropy. This is suggested by the fact that, in the derivation of initial aim from God, the subject's feeling conforms to God's subjective form of feeling.

We need not confine the problem to macroscopic changes in nature. For the aggregate intensity of actual occasions in some epoch depends on the intensities of the particular occasions in that epoch. If the intensity of God's satisfaction is affected by the aggregate intensity of occasions in some epoch, then it is affected by *each* individual satisfaction in some way or other. And this is the premise we need to consider. Does an actual occasion alter the intensity of God's satisfaction? An answer to this question might be affirmative or negative. Let us consider the consequences of each answer.

a. Suppose the intensity of an actual occasion *does* alter the intensity of the divine satisfaction. Then God's satisfaction would remain constant in intensity if, but only if, the aggregate intensity of finite satisfactions remained constant. Is there any principle in Whitehead's system which would guarantee this condition? I know of no such principle. If this condition were not guaranteed in some way, then the consequences of entropy pointed out above would be a real possibility. Does Whitehead's system countenance this possibility?

b. Suppose on the contrary that the intensity of an actual occasion does *not* alter the divine intensity. This is not an unreasonable supposition. For God's satisfaction is an integral feeling, to which both his physical feelings *and* his conceptual feelings contribute. His conceptual feelings supplement his physical feelings as we have seen. And the intensities of these supplementary feelings might compensate for variations in the aggregate intensity of finite satisfactions. In the "supplemental stage" that succeeds the stage of "pure reception" in a concrescence, "In the language of physical science, the 'scalar' form overwhelms the original 'vector' form: the origins become subordinate to the individual experience. The vector form is not lost, but is submerged as the foundation of the scalar superstructure" (PR 323). The influx of conceptual feelings gives the experience its own particular emotional character including, presumably, its final intensity.

Granted then (i) *some* physical feelings, and granted (ii) *unlimited* supplementation by propositions and other contrasts emotionally felt, then the intensity of God's satisfaction would be independent of the intensities of the occasions he prehends. It would not be a simple function of the intensities of his physical data.

Therefore it would not be diminished or increased by large-scale changes in the course of nature. The physical running down of the universe in a particular epoch, resulting in fainter and fainter intensities of finite satisfactions, would not diminish God's intensity. It might be the case that "The universe is laying the foundation of a new type [of order], where our present theories of order will appear as trivial" (ESP [1932] 118–19). Whether or not more complex types of order do emerge in the future, the *possibilities* of new types of order would add intensity to God's experience of his physical data.

Which of these two suppositions should we make, as an interpretation of Whitehead's theory? Should we suppose that an actual occasion alters the intensity of God's satisfaction, or that it does not? The second seems more in accord with Whitehead's principles. The only point in favor of the first is that actual occasions are clearly meant to affect God. But this is satisfied by the other effects we have noticed. Actual occasions contribute data for God's feelings and affect the qualitative pattern of his feeling.

In favor of the second supposition is the following passage and its implication: "Each occasion exhibits its measure of creative emphasis in proportion to its measure of subjective intensity. The absolute standard of such intensity is that of the primordial nature of God, which is neither great nor small because it arises out of no actual world" (PR 75; see 135, 160). I take this to mean that God's primordial aim is at absolute intensity. And if this aim is achieved in a satisfaction, then the satisfaction must have absolute intensity.

So I suggest that the qualitative pattern of God's satisfaction varies with the advance of nature, according to the specific qualities and intensities of finite satisfactions, but that the intensity of God's satisfaction is invariant. By the introduction of significant contrasts he avoids, in his own satisfaction, all those inhibitions (AI 329) which limit the intensities of actual occasions. It would follow that the progress of entropy—even though disastrous for human life and, more generally, ordered societies of actual occasions—would not alter the intensity of God's satisfaction.

Suppose on the other hand an evolutionary process in the opposite direction, a production of individuals and societies of greater complexity and intensity than those we now know. Then the aggregate intensity of the actual occasions in the universe might increase. Still this would not increase the intensity of God's satisfaction. For "all realization is finite" (AI 330) and the excluded alternatives are still infinite.

This conclusion bears on a question which has sometimes embarrassed evolutionary philosophers. If reality is an evolutionary process with a cumulative effect, and if past time is infinite, then it would seem that the universe must be now infinite in density or intensity of actuality. How then is further progress possible?

In Whitehead's system negative prehensions make it possible to interpret such principles as the conservation of energy in the temporal world. The intensity of a new concrescence is not a simple sum or product of the intensities of the past. For it will exclude some aspects of the past by negative prehensions. Thus the process of transition from one occasion to its successor *need* not result in cumulation of intensities.

But we have concluded that God has no negative prehensions. So the question still has point in reference to the consequent nature of God. If more and more actuality is achieved as time goes by, and if all is included in God and nothing is ever lost, then does God get "bigger and bigger"? Is the consequent nature of God cumulative? The answer to this question may be given in two parts.

a. The first part of the answer leads back to the theory of objectification. The objectification of actual occasions in God, effected by God's physical prehensions, does not mean "that one actual entity is added to another *simpliciter*" (PR 80). By now this should be abundantly clear. Actual occasions are not present in God with their own subjective immediacy. They are the objects of God's prehensions, and they exist *in* God only in the mode of objective immortality. They condition but they do not completely determine the subjective forms of God's physical feelings. The intensity of any one of God's physical feelings is not a simple function of the intensity of its datum. Therefore, in the first place, an increase in the aggregate intensity of a cosmic epoch need not result in an increase in the aggregate intensity of God's *physical* feelings.

b. The second part of the answer depends on the interpretation offered above. The intensity of God's satisfaction is not a simple product of the intensities of his physical feelings. Indeed, it is not altered by any changes in the temporal world. Therefore there can be no cumulation of intensity in the divine nature.

6. Actual occasions and the relevance of possibilities

So far we have concentrated on the consequent nature of God which "evolves in its relationship to the evolving world without derogation to the eternal completion of its primordial conceptual nature" (PR 19). But there is a sense in which even the primordial nature of God changes in its relationship to the changing world of actual occasions.

God's vision of pure possibilities is eternally complete. There are no new eternal objects. Pure possibilities do not *become*. But in the course of nature possibilities *become relevant* which were not relevant before (MT 130). More exactly, since all eternal objects are relevant in some way or other to every concrescence, possibilities become *effectively* relevant that were not so before. There are ideas whose hour has not yet come. They must wait for an actual world than can harbor them.

This is because a novel concrescence must conform to its actual world. Within *this* world it must achieve its satisfaction. Therefore the initial aim it derives from the primordial nature of God must bear some fruitful relation to its actual world. The possibility it prehends must be in an effective sense possible in this world. "The objectification of God in a temporal subject is effected by the hybrid feelings with God's conceptual feelings as data. Those of God's feelings which are positively prehended are those with some compatibility of contrast, or of identity, with physical feelings transmitted from the temporal world" (PR 377). This means that the effective relevance of the primordial nature of God for an actual occasion depends on the actual world of that occasion. Let us ask further how this is so.

Like any other actual entity God is a concrescence of conceptual and physical feelings. His primordial nature is conjoined with his consequent nature in a unity of experience. Functioning as an initial datum for an actual occasion A, God is a unified satisfaction, of which his conceptual and physical feelings are components.

Now compare A with an antecedent occasion X. In two complementary ways A's experience of God will differ from X's experience of God. In the first place X has laid down conditions to which the concrescence of A must conform. The actual world of A is thus different from the actual world of X, and as a result of this difference in actual worlds A prehends God from another perspective than that of X. In the second place, this difference of perspective is matched by a difference in the content of God's own experience. The divine satisfaction functioning as a datum for A includes a component prehension of X that was absent from the divine satisfaction functioning as a datum for X. Thus A's experience of God differs from X's experience of God in respect to its perspective and its datum.

As a consequence, ideal possibilities in God's conceptual experience which were not effectively relevant for X will be effectively relevant for A. For God's own experience is a systematic unity. The changing content of his physical experience effects a shift in the patterning of the relevance of eternal objects.

Now the reason for this difference in the relevance of eternal objects is the achievement of X. It is the self-creative activity of X that has made the difference, by presenting a condition for the new concrescence and by affecting the data and the qualitative pattern of God's satisfaction. Because of X, God's experience as given for A has a novel content, matching the novel standpoint from which A arises. As a further consequence A's hybrid feeling of God, by which its initial aim is derived, will prehend a possibility appropriate to its actual world. In this way X has affected the relationship of God's conceptual experience to the physical world.

Another way of putting this point is as follows. In Chapter 13 we saw how temporal orderings of eternal objects particularize the timeless ordering in God's primordial nature. Now the particular ordering of eternal objects in relevance to a particular concrescence is the "objective lure" for that concrescence. Here the concrescence finds the datum of its initial aim and the contrasts that enrich its physical feelings. And an objective lure is "that discrimination among eternal objects introduced into the universe by the real internal constitutions of the actual occasions forming the datum of the concrescence under review" (PR 281; see 131–6, 281–7). Notice that the discrimination is "introduced into the universe" by actual occasions. The primordial nature of God "includes in its appetitive vision all possibilities of order, possibilities at once incompatible and unlimited with a fecundity beyond imagination. Finite transience stages this welter of incompatibles in their ordered relevance to the flux of epochs. Thus the process of finite history is essential for the ordering of the basic vision, otherwise mere confusion" (ESP [1932] 118).

God's primordial envisagement ensures that all eternal objects are included in an objective lure. And God's consequent nature ensures that all temporal orderings are built into a systematically changing pattern. But *just what* A's objective lure shall be is determined by X and the other occasions in A's actual world. Thus X affects the relevance of God's conceptual experience for A.

Though actual occasions are thus effective in determining the relevance of God's primordial vision for future concrescences, they do not add to the pure possibilities God envisages. God's primordial nature is still eternally complete.

7. Summary

Actual occasions affect God in the following ways:

a. Actual occasions furnish data for God's physical prehensions, and thus are necessary to his existence as a complete actual entity.

b. The qualitative patterns and intensities of actual occasions affect, though they do not completely determine, the qualitative patterns and intensities of God's physical feelings. Indirectly they affect the qualitative pattern of God's satisfaction.

c. Actual occasions affect the relevance of possibilities in God's primordial nature for future concrescences.

The effects of actual occasions on God are qualified or limited in the following ways:

a. Actual occasions are not literally included in God with persistence of their own immediacy. They have perished and are objectively immortal.

b. Actual occasions do not alter the intensity of God's satisfaction.

c. Actual occasions do not add to God's primordial envisagement of eternal objects.

For a final comment I refer to one of Whitehead's deliberate paradoxes. "It is as true to say that God creates the World, as that the World creates God" (PR 528). From the results of this and the preceding chapter it might well seem doubtful whether the world affects God so radically as God affects the world, and whether God requires the world so crucially as the world requires God. Hence it might seem less true to say that the world creates God than that God creates the world.

But to be clear about the outcome of Whitehead's theory we need to spell it out analytically before giving it a final interpretation. That has been the aim of this chapter and the one before it. The next chapter will develop some further implications of these results.

CHAPTER 18

God and the World:
Transcendence and Immanence

WHITEHEAD's main positions on the nature of God and the world have been set forth, and some basic problems of interpretation have been explored. We can come now to some conclusions, on a higher level of interpretation, about what his theory amounts to and implies. In this chapter I shall apply the categories of transcendence and immanence to Whitehead's theory in a systematic way. In the next I shall discuss his criticism of traditional theology.

1. The principle of relativity

The philosophy of organism has no room for certain relations or properties that might be called "absolute transcendence" and "absolute immanence." By the statement, "M is absolutely transcendent," where M is an actuality not an abstraction, one or more of several meanings might be intended.

It might mean (a) that M is "beyond logic" in the sense that it cannot be the subject of any true proposition. It bears no logical relation to any entity, actual or nonactual, so that no concept is powerful enough to apply to it. It is beyond logical discourse.

It might mean (b) that M is "beyond the world" in the sense that it bears no "real" relation to any other actuality. No true propositions can be formulated to the effect that M causes, influences, conditions, *or* is caused, influenced, conditioned by, any other actuality.

It might mean (c) that M is "beyond experience" in the sense that there can be no direct apprehension of M by any experiencing subject.

Whitehead's rejection of absolute transcendence is contained in the principle of relativity. This fundamental principle appears in the categoreal scheme as follows: "That the potentiality for being an element in a real concrescence of many actualities into one actuality, is the one general metaphysical character attaching to all entities, actual and non-actual; and that every item in its universe is involved in each concrescence. In other words, it belongs to the nature of a 'being' that it is a potential for every 'becoming.' This is the 'principle of relativity'" (PR 33; see SMW 36–9, PR 42–3). This means that no actual entity is beyond logic, beyond the world, or beyond experience. Since eternal objects are ingredient in every actual entity, true propositions are possible. Since all actual entities contribute to the concrescences of others, none is isolated from others; each influences and is influenced by others. Since a concrescence is a process of experience, each subject experiences all the actual entities in its actual world.

In one sense this principle of relativity is an empirical principle and in another sense it is not. It is an empirical principle in the sense that, since some entities are experienced, it brings all entities into connection with experience. Whitehead's intention is to exclude any metaphysical conception that does not in some way refer to and characterize what we experience. "The elucidation of immediate experience is the sole justification for any thought; and the starting point for any thought is the analytic observation of components of this experience" (PR 6; see SMW 130).

But this is not an empirical principle in the sense that it is empirically demonstrable. It cannot be demonstrated from within experience that nothing transcends experience absolutely. Whitehead seems to realize this. He says that what does not communicate with immediate matter of fact "is unknowable, and the unknowable is unknown; and so this universality defined by 'communication' can suffice" (PR 5–6; see 288–9). Again, he says, "If anything out of relationship, then complete ignorance as to it. Here by 'ignorance,' I mean *ignorance;* accordingly no advice can be given as to how to expect it, or to treat it, in 'practice' or in any other way" (SMW 36–7). Insofar as he goes beyond these hypothetical statements and says there *is* no reality beyond experience, he must appeal to a ground other than experience. He is making the postulate of rationality. Reason cannot deal with anything out of all relation to experience. Absolute transcendence of experience cannot be rationally conceived. "Faith in reason is the trust that the ultimate natures of things lie together in a harmony which excludes mere arbitrariness" (smw 26. See 39; RM 24; PR 14, 67; AI 137).

The principle of relativity with its consequent denial of absolute transcendence is as true of God as of actual occasions. God is a "potential" for every finite becoming and every actual occasion is a potential for the divine becoming. God is not absolutely transcendent of the world or of any particular actual occasion. How serious is this denial of an absolutely transcendent deity, and what does it entail?

Certainly it does not imply there are no specific differences between God and actual occasions. Indeed we have had to ask whether or not these differences were so great that some categories fail to apply to God. This was the problem of Chapter 15. Denial of absolute transcendence leaves untouched some very strong senses of the "transcendence" of God, as we shall see. In the lecture on immortality he says, "Of course we are unable to conceive the experience of the Supreme Unity of Existence" (IMM 698).

Further, suppose this denial is understood—as it seems to be by Whitehead—as a consequence of the aim at "metaphysical rationalization" (RM 70). Then it remains a reasonable question whether even stronger senses of transcendence than we find in his system might be compatible with this aim, if it were carried out in some other way. Rejection of absolute transcendence leaves a good deal of room for theological debate.

Finally another sort of question is left open. Is the impulse to metaphysical rationalization itself subject to any judgment from beyond itself? As a matter of fact Whitehead's own rationalism is not unqualified, though it is very strong. I do not have in mind just now his genuine humility about his own system, though this is clear enough.[1] I am pointing to his humility about the enter-

---

1. It is nowhere clearer than in his letter to Professor Schilpp in 1941, when he was eighty years old, remarking on his inability to reply to the essays in *The Library of Living Philosophers*: "The absence of any direct

prise of speculative philosophy as such. This humility sprang from a healthy sense of human finitude, and kept him relatively free from that pride of intellect from which some rationalistic philosophers have suffered. He seems to have thought that reality transcended not only his own system but any possible system of metaphysics.[2]

This humility about the enterprise of speculative philosophy comes out in Whitehead's warnings against philosophical dogmatism. Any speculative scheme is but an imperfect account of the universe. No set of categories brings out all the aspects of actuality exactly and completely (RM 145). "Metaphysical categories are not dogmatic statements of the obvious; they are tentative formulations of the ultimate generalities" (PR 12). Philosophy can advance, but a final formulation of first principles is not to be hoped for. "The proper test is not that of finality, but of progress" (PR 21).

These warnings against dogmatic rationalism give no encouragement to intellectual timidity. They are consistent with that speculative boldness Whitehead advocated and exemplified. They are not designed to discourage speculation. They are designed to encourage criticism of the results of speculation. His sense of the limits of reason should not be overlooked in evaluating his denial of absolute transcendence.

The principle of relativity has another important consequence. It entails rejection of absolute immanence as well as absolute transcendence. "M is absolutely immanent in N," where M and N are actualities, might mean that M is included by N and in no sense excluded by N. For example one might say the world has

---

expression of my reaction to these chapters is but a slight loss. The progress of philosophy does not primarily involve reactions of agreement or dissent. It essentially consists in the enlargement of thought, whereby contradictions and agreements are transformed into partial aspects of wider points of view. Thus my own reaction to this book should consist in devoting many years to rewriting my previous works. Unfortunately this is impossible" (Schilpp 664).

2. In conversation in 1942 I was suggesting some possible inconsistencies in his writings. His reply was: "Yes, we must be systematic. Of course, when we are perfectly systematic we may be quite sure we have left out the fundamental principle of reality. Nevertheless we must be systematic."

no existence except as a part or aspect of God, or that God has no existence except as a part or aspect of the world.

But this possibility is ruled out. M cannot be absolutely immanent in N because no actual entity is merely something for some other actual entity or entities. An actual entity is also something for itself. It is an element in the concrescences of other actual entities, to be sure. But the converse is also true. Other actual entities are elements in its own concrescence. In this way the principle of relativity calls for a principle of real individuality according to which "every actual entity, including God, is something individual for its own sake; and thereby transcends the rest of actuality" (PR 135). It is with this consequence in mind that Whitehead says, "This principle of relativity is the axiom by which the ontological principle is rescued from issuing in an extreme monism" (PR 224; see SMW 38).

Thus the principle of relativity applied to actual entities requires both transcendence of others and immanence in others. An actual entity is both a subject and a superject. As a subject it transcends all other actual entities. As a superject it is self-transcendent; it transcends its own subjective experience by becoming immanent in other actual entities. In the remainder of this chapter I shall sum up the ways in which the world of actual occasions transcends God and is immanent in God, and the ways in which God transcends the world and is immanent in the world.

2. How the world transcends God: Actual occasions as subjects

Once more we ask, Does Whitehead's doctrine of God compromise the real individuality of actual occasions? Is the influence of God on actual occasions so potent and so intimate as to reduce actual occasions, in effect, to modes of the divine existence? We have seen how an actual occasion transcends other actual occasions. Are there also important ways in which an actual occasion transcends God? In preceding chapters we noticed two important and related ways in which an actual occasion transcends God.

a. An actual occasion transcends God by being self-creative. Its concrescence is conditioned by other actual occasions, which

determine the nature of the actual world to which it must conform. And in a special and crucial way it is conditioned by God.
For its conceptual aim, which initiates its unity, is derived from
God. In spite of this conditioning, the concrescence is not completely determined by its actual world even including God. It
is an instance of conditioned *freedom*. Its freedom vis-à-vis God
is expressed in three ways: (i) in the autonomy of the subjective
form with which it responds to the possibility that becomes its
subjective aim; (ii) in its specification of its subjective aim in relation to its given environment; and (iii) in its actualization of its
aim in concrete experience, terminating in its satisfaction. In
these ways the actual occasion does what even God cannot do for
it; it expresses the originative principle of creativity. For these
reasons, to say actual occasions are "derivative" from God is misleading.

b. In the second place an actual occasion transcends God by
excluding from its experience the subjective immediacy of God's
experience. The subjective immediacy of the concrescence is exclusive of the subjective immediacy of God. Even from God there
is no literal flow of feeling into the new concrescence. As a subject, the experience of the actual occasion is *private*. "An actual
entity considered in reference to the privacy of things is a 'subject' " (PR 443).

The categoreal necessity of this exclusiveness follows from the
aim at unity of experience. If the concrescence is to achieve its
own internal unity of satisfaction, other actual entities including
God must be objectified for it. They can be present in it only in
their objective immortality, not in their own subjective immediacy. So this second mode of transcendence is logically connected with the first mode. For if God's own prehensions were
present in the new concrescence with their own subjective immediacy there would be no room for the free self-determination
of the concrescence. Other actualities, including God, must be
objects for the new concrescence if it is to function creatively as
a *subject*. Privacy of experience is required for the freedom of
actual occasions.

In these ways, in its freedom and in its privacy, an actual occasion transcends God. For these reasons actual occasions cannot

be interpreted as organic parts of God. The universe cannot be construed as a divine organism, if this means that actual occasions are parts of God in the way the internal experiences of an actual entity are components of its own unity of satisfaction. Even though God conditions actual occasions in the very important ways explained in Chapter 16, a genuine meaning remains for the real individuality of finite actual entities.

3. How the world is immanent in God: Actual occasions as superjects

Actuality involves self-transcendence. Any actual entity transcends itself. In addition to being something for itself (a subject), it becomes something for other actual entities (a superject). Its self-transcendence consists in its immanence in other actualities. Here we are concerned with the immanence of actual occasions in God. We may say an actual occasion is present in God objectively, completely, and effectively.

a. Actual occasions are present in God *objectively,* not in their own subjective immediacy. Objectification means the perishing of immediacy. They are objectified data for God's physical prehensions and as such they enter into the complex datum of God's subjectively immediate satisfaction.

b. Though actual occasions are present in God's experience as objects, not as experiencing subjects, they are *completely* present in God's experience. God's subjective aim does not require eliminations from his physical data. Thus *all* of the feelings composing the integral satisfaction of the occasion are present objectively in God's experience. All that the actual occasion achieved is felt by God. The immanence of actual occasions in God is complete, though objective.

c. Actual occasions are *effectively* present in God's experience. The subjective forms of God's physical prehensions conform perfectly to their data. Thus the character of the actual occasion affects the quality of God's physical prehensions and consequently the qualitative pattern—though not the intensity—of his satisfaction. God's consequent nature thus varies with the creative advance of nature in accord with the finite achievements of actual occasions. Indirectly, by their effect on the consequent nature of God, actual occasions affect the relevance of the possibilities envisaged in God's primordial nature.

Finally it must be remembered that without the immanence of actual occasions in God's experience God would be abstract and deficient in actuality. His physical prehensions, by which actual occasions become immanent in God, are necessary to his being as a concrete actual entity.

4. How God transcends the world: God as subject

Like any other actual entity God is an experiencing subject, "something individual for its own sake." He is a unity of experience, from which his primordial nature and his consequent nature are abstractions. He is one being, not two. We ask how God as an experiencing subject transcends the world. We find that it is by virtue of the *freedom*, the *privacy*, and the *perfection* of his experience.

a. Like all actual entities God is self-creative. He is an embodiment or "creature" of creativity. He is *causa sui* (PR 135), an act of self-realization. It is true of God, as of actual occasions, that " 'decided' conditions are never such as to banish freedom" (PR 435). Actual occasions supply data for God's feelings, to which the subjective forms of his feelings conform. But they do not determine his subjective aim, and therefore do not determine how his subjective forms conform to their data. Actual occasions condition but do not determine God's experience. In this way the *freedom* of God's experience exemplifies the categories that apply to actual entities.

Further, in this respect as in others God is the chief exemplification of the categories. This is because his subjective aim, which determines the subjective forms of his feelings, is primordial, wholly derivative (PR 523) from his primordial nature. And his primordial nature is unconditioned (PR 46) by any actual world. "His unity of conceptual operations is a free creative act, untrammelled by reference to any particular course of things" (PR 522; see 47, 378). Therefore God is free to supplement his physical feelings from an infinite range of conceptual valuations, as we have seen. In these ways God's freedom contrasts with the limited though genuine freedom of actual occasions. God's freedom is freedom at a maximum.

b. Another way God's experience transcends actual occasions is by its *privacy.* Of God no less than of actual occasions it is true that "Prehensions have public careers, but they are born privately" (PR 444). No actual occasion shares God's own subjective immediacy. However crucial, inescapable, and decisive the influence of God in the world may be, his subjective immediacy of experience is something God does not and cannot share with any other actual entity. He enters into the composition of other actual entities, as they enter into the composition of his experience, only by objectification. In this respect God exemplifies the categories.

We ask, further, whether in this respect God is the *chief* exemplification of the categories. Is God's experience even more inaccessible to an actual occasion than are the privacies of other actual occasions? Certainly this would seem to be so. But it is so not because God has a different *mode* of existence from that of actual occasions, but because the *content* of his experience is unique. If we had no categories at all with which to indicate God's mode of existence within himself, we could form no conception of his being. *Qua* privacy God's experience is no more, and no less, accessible to actual occasions than are the experiences of other occasions. Privacy and publicity, subjective immediacy and objective immortality, are modes of existence. In this respect the categories do not seem to admit of more or less. But we now turn to the way God's experience differs from the experiences of actual occasions in content.

c. God as an experiencing subject differs from all other experiencing subjects in the *perfection* of his experience. His experience is perfect in *scope,* in *quality* of response, and in *intensity.*

i. God transcends actual occasions by the perfection of the *scope* of his experience, which is infinitely inclusive of fact and possibility. His conceptual experience excludes none of the unbounded multiplicity of eternal objects. He prehends and values all possibilities. His physical experience excludes nothing in the domain of finite actuality. He prehends all actual occasions, and he prehends all the components of the satisfaction of every actual occasion. No eliminations from the initial data, whether conceptual or physical, are necessary for the unity of his satisfaction. Hence God has no negative prehensions. Both in his primordial nature and in his consequent nature he is nonexclusive. His appetition for possibilities and his hospitality to facts are both unlimited.

In this way God transcends actual occasions. For they must eliminate some facts and possibilities from their experience to achieve a unified satisfaction. For example, an actual occasion does not experience the individual actualities of its contemporaries and successors. Also it selects only certain aspects of past actuality for positive prehension. Again, some pure potentials will be prehended only negatively.

God transcends these finite limitations. His experience is infinite in scope. It is true that, relative to some standpoint, God has not *then* experienced those actualities which will come into being in the future. But he eternally experiences all pure potentials, including those specially relevant to the future becomings. And since he is everlasting he will, in the future relative to that standpoint, experience the actualities of those becomings. He experiences every actuality in its own time. Thus his experience includes every other entity as a datum for feeling; possibilities are felt as possibilities, actualities are felt as actualities. Nothing is excluded. His satisfaction is "a Harmony of Harmonies" (AI 381), a unification of experience achieved out of an infinite diversity of facts and possibilities as data for feeling.

ii. The perfection of God's experience applies to the subjective forms of his feelings as well as to their data. His response to the data is perfect in quality, and his satisfaction is perfect in intensity. No greater adequacy or intensity of feeling is conceivable.

The perfection of the *quality* of God's response consists in the fact that he experiences every datum with perfect adequacy. An actual occasion responds imperfectly to its data. It cannot feel another actuality with complete sympathy, so to speak. For the sake of its own unity it must exclude some aspects of the datum. What remains is an abstraction from the full actuality of the past occasion. Some of the qualities of its feelings are not responded to and re-enacted. The conformation is imperfect.

God on the contrary can accept and value the achievement of each actual occasion for just what it is, without distortion or depreciation. His response is appropriate to the full richness of quality achieved in the occasion. His re-enaction of the feelings of actual occasions is in this way perfect.

This perfection of quality is made possible by the infinite scope of God's conceptual experience. Perfect conformation is possible because unlimited supplementation is available. God aims at the realization of *all* possibilities, each in its own time whenever that might be. Hence God can never be disappointed, so to speak, by whatever happens now, for any temporal "now." Whatever happens can be supplemented by contrasts derived from his conceptual experience, so as to lead to satisfaction. Here as elsewhere it is clear that the perfection of God's experience arises from the unity of his primordial with his consequent nature.

iii. God's experience is perfect in its *intensity,* as well as in its scope and quality. His subjective aim is at maximum realization. He values all eternal objects as possibilities for realization. This aim is unconditioned by any particular situation and transcends all limited objectives. No negative prehension, which would diminish the intensity of the aim, is included in the primordial nature of God. God's subjective aim is unconditioned and unlimited. "The absolute standard of such [subjective] intensity is that of the primordial nature of God, which is neither great nor small because it arises out of no actual world" (PR 75).

This aim is achieved in God's satisfaction. In this unified feeling an unimaginable complexity and diversity of data is felt with perfect qualitative adequacy and ordered into a harmony of contrasts. Since it is perfect in scope and in adequacy of quality it is also perfect in intensity. No inhibitions (AI 329–30) diminish its intensity. Just as the intensity of God's subjective aim is not conditioned by any particular happenings in the world, so the intensity of his satisfaction is not diminished or increased by particular happenings in the world. It is not affected by the varying intensities of actual occasions in the course of nature.

An actual occasion must aim at a limited objective. It can become only what its actual world permits it to become. The intensity of its satisfaction is restricted by the limited scope of its

physical feelings and by its limited capacity for conceptual supplementation of physical feeling. Since the scope of God's physical feelings is not thus limited, and since he is capable of unlimited
conceptual supplementation, his intensity as well as the scope
and quality of his experience is perfect. In this respect also he
transcends actual occasions.

To avoid misunderstanding we should notice certain senses in
which God's experience is *not* "perfect" as well as these senses in
which it *is* perfect. (a) God's experience is not perfect in the sense
of being *absolutely complete*. God is complete in the sense that
he is always satisfied, relative to any standpoint in the course of
nature. Though new prehensions are added to his being, in the
course of nature, they cannot increase or decrease the intensity
of his satisfaction. He is a complete unity of experience relative
to any "now" in the course of nature. But he is never complete in
an absolute sense, so that no new experiences could be added to
his being. He always has appetition for unrealized possibilities.

It follows (b) that God is not *absolutely independent* of the
happenings of the world. The qualitative pattern of his experience is affected by the qualities of actual occasions. And the structure of his satisfaction is affected by the intensities of actual occasions, determining the degree and kind of supplementation
necessary for his satisfaction. In these ways God's experience is
affected by the course of nature and therefore is not absolutely
independent of the world.

Though God is neither absolutely complete nor absolutely independent, this does not detract from his perfection if "perfection" is construed in Whitehead's way. In his system absolute
completeness and absolute independence are categoreally impossible. Hence to lack these attributes is not to lack any significant perfection.

God is relatively independent of the world, however. His existence, and the perfection of his experience in scope, quality, and
intensity, do not depend on any particular pattern of events. No
matter what actual occasions come into existence, God is in these
respects unchangeable. His relative independence of the world
follows from God's primordial character and is part of the meaning of his transcendence of the world.

5. How God is immanent in the world: God
   as superject

Like actual occasions God exists not only as subject but also as superject. He has objective immortality as well as subjective immediacy. He transcends himself, and his self-transcendence is his immanence in actual occasions. I shall summarize briefly three features of God's function in the concrescences of actual occasions.

a. The immanence of God in actual occasions is his *objective* existence. He is present in their experience as an object, not with his own subjective immediacy. Actual occasions prehend God as *being* an actual entity with his own subjective immediacy. But for them his experience is objectified. It is prehended from their own standpoints into their own subjectively immediate experiences. Furthermore, since for actual occasions objectification means abstraction, actual occasions prehend God abstractively. They can bring God into their experience only if they eliminate, by negative prehensions, some aspects of his concrete unity. This is true of one actual occasion's experience of another. It is all the more true of an actual occasion's experience of God, because of the infinite scope and complexity of God's experience.

b. God is immanent in the world as the *source of initial conceptual aim*. This is one specific way in which God is objectified for every actual occasion. He presents a possibility and evokes an appetition. "God's immanence in the world in respect to his primordial nature is an urge towards the future based upon an appetite in the present" (PR 47). But it would be a mistake to suppose this is a function of only the primordial nature of God. For the feeling by which the novel possibility is mediated to the concrescence is a hybrid *physical* feeling of God (PR 343). This reminds us that the two natures of God are abstract aspects of a concrete unity of experience.

The macroscopic effect of this function of God is that novelty and order are possible. God is immanent in the world as the necessary structural condition of novelty and order. "Apart from the intervention of God, there could be nothing new in the world, and no order in the world" (PR 377). He is the structural condition of novelty because he is the reservoir of unrealized potentiality.

If God did not exist, then only those forms of definiteness which had been realized in the past actual world would be available for a present concrescence. God makes novel possibilities available.

God is also the structural condition of order in the world. As prehended by some actual occasion, God is a determinate being. He is determined in part by his prehensions of the past actual world of that occasion. God, so determined, is the initial datum of the hybrid physical feeling from which the initial conceptual aim is derived. Because of the determinate nature of this initial datum, the objective datum of the feeling, namely one of God's own conceptual prehensions, will yield a possibility which is effectively relevant to *that* actual world. It will be a real possibility and not merely a pure possibility. The realm of eternal objects, though unordered in itself, has thus been ordered relative to the new concrescence by God's physical prehensions of the past actual world. Hence the novel actual occasion will bear some determinate relation to that world. Speaking of the spatiotemporal quantum or standpoint of a concrescence Whitehead says, "The quantum is that standpoint in the extensive continuum which is consonant with the subjective aim in its original derivation from God. Here 'God' is that actuality in the world, in virtue of which there is physical 'law' " (PR 434).[3] Here again the concrete unity of God's conceptual and physical experience is evident.

It may be added that while God is the necessary structural condition of novelty and order in the world, he is not the sufficient condition. The creativity of the new concrescence and the particular achievements of the past are also necessary conditions of a world characterized by novelty and order.

c. If the interpretation in Chapter 16 of what Whitehead's principles require is correct, then God is also immanent in the world as the *ground of the givenness of the past.* In a way not altogether clear God is essential for the continuity and solidarity of the world. Some implications of this mode of divine immanence will be noted in the following section.

3. See PR 315 on prehension of God as ground for nonstatistical judgments of probability.

6. How God transcends the world: God as superject

The immanence of God in the world of actual occasions is his objective immortality in actual occasions. Now Whitehead's theory of objectification is his account of influence or power. Thus an account of the objective immortality of God in actual occasions is in effect an account of the influence or power of God in the process of nature.

All actual entities have power. But when we compare the influence of actual occasions with the influence of God we find some striking contrasts. From these contrasts we derive another set of modes of divine transcendence. In an earlier section we dealt with what we may call God's transcendence in *being,* namely the ways in which God existing in himself, as subject, transcends actual occasions. Here we may speak of God's transcendence in *power,* namely the ways in which God existing for other actualities, as superject, transcends actual occasions. I shall mention three modes of God's transcendence in power and show how, on Whitehead's principles, divine power transcends the powers of actual occasions in degree and in kind.

a. God transcends actual occasions by the *universal extension* of his influence. His power transcends the powers of actual occasions by its omnipresence. He is effectively present throughout nature. He is "with all creation" and is objectified for every concrescence. The scope of his power is unrestricted.

The power of an actual occasion is on the contrary limited in scope. An occasion has no influence on its past actual world or on its contemporary world, but only on those occasions which succeed it. Its influence is also limited in space as well as in time. Generally speaking it will be stronger in its own neighborhood and weaker in more remote regions. Its power is restricted by the limitations of its standpoint.

God's power transcends these limitations. There are no spatiotemporal limitations on the extent of his influence. God has no temporal origin and he does not perish; he is everlasting. And no actuality anywhere, however faint and trivial, escapes his influence. Nor is any occasion more remote from his influence than any other. God exists everywhere and always, and his existence is always and everywhere effective. Throughout all cosmic epochs and for every act of becoming, God is the source of subjective aim and the ground of the givenness of the past.

b. God transcends actual occasions also by the *initiatory* quality of his power. Here the uniqueness and the activity of his role in the becoming of an actual occasion must be stressed. An actual occasion influences another by laying down conditions to which the succeeding occasion must conform. It exerts efficient causation. It demands repetition. It poses a problem. God on the contrary elicits novelty. He presents a novel possibility and by the intensity of his appetition evokes a responding intensity of novel feeling in the concrescence. He poses and evokes a solution to the problem set by the past.

I am aware of the need for caution in the description of this mode of divine transcendence. The self-creativity of the concrescence must be allowed for. Also the indispensability of a given actual world, achieved by the past, must be recognized. But when one considers the contrast between the kind of power exerted on the concrescence by the actual occasions of the given world, and the kind of power exerted on the concrescence by God, then it is not inappropriate for Whitehead to say that in a sense God can be termed "the creator of each temporal actual entity" (PR 343). He rightly adds qualifications to allow for the self-creativity of the concrescence, and to avoid confusion with traditional conceptions of divine creation. But it would be fair to say that in Whitehead's system this function of God has a place analogous to doctrines of divine creation in other systems (cf. Augustine, *City of God* XII, 25). The way this mode of divine activity transcends the activity of an actual occasion deserves careful consideration. God does what no temporal actuality can do, either for another actuality or for itself. He evokes novel actuality into being.

Does the traditional analysis of causation throw light on this mode of divine power? Some analogies are possible. God's evocation of novel actuality is like efficient causation in that God's concrete unity is a given fact, to which the new concrescence must conform. It is like formal causation in that a form of definiteness is presented for realization. And it is like final causation in that the novel possibility becomes an object of appetition for the concrescence itself. But it would be misleading to identify this act of divine power with any of the traditional modes of causation. It combines elements of each but is different from all. In this act the divine actuality elicits and evokes the self-creativity of the concrescence itself.

c. If the divine evocation of novel actuality is Whitehead's equivalent for the traditional doctrine of creation, God's function as ground of givenness might be called Whitehead's equivalent of the doctrine of divine preservation. In his everlasting nature God *preserves* the achievements of the past, which has perished, and thus gives continuity and solidarity to the world. God is the ground of the effective influence of temporal actualities as well as the ground of their novel individuality.

In this function also the power of God transcends the power of actual occasions. As we have seen, an actual occasion decides by its own achievement of satisfaction what shall be given for future becomings. But since it perishes it cannot be, in the future, the ground of its givenness *then*. There is thus a limit to its power to enforce its own givenness.

The power of God is not limited in this way. God is everlasting. And since his prehensions of the temporal actualities have entered into the composition of his everlasting satisfaction, he can be the ontological ground of their continuing influence on future becomings. In this sense he preserves the world in being, and in doing so transcends the temporal actual entities in power. Again God does what no temporal actuality can do.

7. Summary

The results of this chapter may be stated as follows:

a. Actual occasions (as subjects) transcend God by virtue of their freedom and their privacy.

b. Actual occasions (as superjects) are immanent in God objectively, completely, and effectively.

c. God (as superject) is immanent in the world objectively and effectively.

d. God (as subject) transcends the world by virtue of his freedom and his privacy.

e. God transcends the world also by virtue of his perfection.

His perfection in being (as subject) lies in the scope, the quality, and the intensity of his experience.

His perfection in power (as superject) lies in the unlimited extension of his power, his initiation of novel becomings, and his preservation of temporal achievements.

Finally it may be remarked that Whitehead's theory of God and the world has proved to be reasonably consistent and coherent. The functions of actual occasions supplement, and do not supplant or supersede, the functions of God. The converse is true also. God does not negate or inhibit or compete with actual occasions. On the contrary God evokes them into being and sustains their achievements.

CHAPTER 19

Whitehead and Traditional Theology

1. Introduction

IN THIS CHAPTER I shall assemble and discuss Whitehead's scattered criticisms of traditional theology, and raise some questions about the outcome of his own theory of God and the world.

Now and then one finds appreciative comments on traditional theology. For example he regards "the medieval insistence on the rationality of God" as one historical source of our modern faith in science (SMW 17–18; see 86, AI 145–6). In *Adventures of Ideas* he proposes a constructive program for modern Protestant theology (ch. 10, "The New Reformation"). And his own indebtedness to the past, most of all to Plato, is amply evident and explicitly acknowledged. "Plato's God is a God of this world. . . . Since then our concept of this world has enlarged to that of the universe. I have envisioned a union of Plato's God with a God of the universe" (DIAL 218 [dated 1943]). Notice also a remark that follows a brief recital of the life of Christ: "Can there be any doubt that the power of Christianity lies in its revelation in act, of that which Plato divined in theory?" (AI 214).

Even Plato comes in for occasional criticism, however, and most of his comments on traditional Jewish and Christian theology are unfavorable. In many cases they are hostile. The most severe comments are in the *Dialogues,* for example the following *obiter dictum:* "I consider Christian theology to be one of the great disasters of the human race" (DIAL 174). According to Price, Whitehead read "a great many books on theology" in a period of several years at Cambridge "early in their wedded life." "When he had finished with the subject," Price says, "for he *had* finished with it, he called in a Cambridge bookseller and asked what he would give for the lot" (DIAL 151). Judging from his later writings, it is not at all clear that he had "finished with the subject" as Price says, unless this means only that he stopped reading in it.

His critical remarks on traditional theology are scattered, unsystematic, and relatively undeveloped, since they are incidental to the development of his own theory. Their principal targets are: (a) unreflective supernaturalism; (b) the assumption that God is wholly unaffected by the world; and (c) the assumption that God is the sole determiner of the world. In explaining these criticisms I shall not raise questions about the accuracy of his historical interpretations. Our interest is in analysis of his own theory. These criticisms reveal some of his own philosophical and theological assumptions and give us a background for some questions about his positive doctrines.

2. Whitehead's criticisms: Unreflective supernaturalism

We begin with Whitehead's objection to explaining nature by reference to a divine "fiat" (PR 146, 519; AI 154). Part of his objection is to the use of personal categories to describe the divine being. This part of his objection will be discussed in section 9 below. Here we consider another part of his objection, his criticism of unreflective supernaturalism.

By a "fiat" he means an unconditioned act of will. His objection is thus directed against "the ascription of . . . arbitrary power to the nature of God" (IMM 697). Explanation of nature, or of a particular fact of nature, by reference to an arbitrary supernatural act is unreflective and unilluminating. It does not really explain what is to be explained.

He is not objecting to theistic explanations as such. He is objecting to unreflective explanations, which fail to connect specific features of the nature of God with the specific facts or features of the world to be explained. They fail to say *how* the existence and activity of God explain the facts. His objection to explanation by divine fiat is therefore part of his criticism of unreflective or "easy" appeals to the supernatural to explain nature. "My point is that any summary conclusion jumping from our conviction of the existence of such an order of nature to the easy assumption that there is an ultimate reality which, *in some unexplained way,* is to be appealed to for the removal of perplexity, constitutes the great refusal of rationality to assert its rights" (SMW 129–30, my italics).

A similar point appears in his criticism of Leibniz [1] and Berkeley for making "an appeal to a *Deus ex machina* who was capable of rising superior to the difficulties of metaphysics" (SMW 217; "Deus" for "Deux"). The fault of these philosophers is their failure to apply to God the fundamental categories of their systems. Appeal to God then becomes *ad hoc* explanation. Philosophers should not be content with this sort of explanation, since "metaphysics requires that the relationships of God to the World should lie beyond the accidents of will, and that they be founded upon the necessities of the nature of God and of the nature of the World" (AI 215).

His criticism of the "Semitic" concept of God (which he contrasts with the "Eastern Asiatic" and the "Pantheistic" concepts) is more severe. It "leaves God completely outside metaphysical rationalization. . . . He is undeniably useful, because anything baffling can be ascribed to his direct decree" (RM 70). Later on the early Christian theologians decided for the direct immanence of God in the world. But they failed to exploit their discovery by constructing a coherent metaphysical theory, because of an unfortunate presupposition. "The nature of God was exempted from all the metaphysical categories which applied to the individual things in this temporal world" (AI 216). Their conception of God was "a sublimation from its barbaric origin." To be content with the incoherence that results from this view of God is to lack faith in reason. "Faith in reason is the trust that the ultimate natures of things lie together in a harmony which excludes mere arbitrariness. It is the faith that at the base of things we shall not find mere arbitrary mystery" (SMW 26).

3. Is the existence of God irrational?

This is an appropriate place for comment on Whitehead's well-known remark that the existence of God is "the ultimate irrationality" (SMW 249). In the context he is presenting an argument

1. See also on Leibniz PR 289, AI 170–1. For a similar criticism of Descartes see FR 24, PR 289. On Plato see AI 215.

for the existence of God. The world of finite things is an "apparent irrational limitation" of the intrinsically boundless domain of possibility. Idealistic philosophies take this limitation "as a proof of illusion" and "look for reality behind the scene." Whitehead rejects idealism and accepts "the reality of actual occasions." He also accepts the need for some rational explanation of the existence of a temporal world. "If we reject this [idealistic] alternative [which places reality] behind the scene, we must provide a ground for limitation which stands among the attributes of the substantial activity" (SMW 249).

It is crucially important to understand just what kind of "explanation" of the temporal world can and must be given, on Whitehead's view. He accepts the necessity of a "principle of limitation." "Some particular *how* is necessary, and some particularisation in the *what* of matter of fact is necessary" (SMW 249). If we accept the reality of the temporal world, then we must be willing to explain *how* it is that there is such a world, and the general way in which particular matters of fact come into existence.

At the same time he is rejecting the rationalistic demand that the existence of a temporal world, and perhaps even the existence of *this* temporal world, be shown to be logically necessary. For if the world of nature were a product of logical necessity, then it would lose that character of givenness and "apparent irrationality" that we started out to explain. Instead of explaining the reality of the temporal world we would have explained it away. *That* the temporal world exists is a fact. The problem of speculative philosophy is not to deduce this fact "by abstract reason" but to construct a set of categories which will describe the conditions under which it *occurs*. "*How* is it that a world of finite things exists?" Whitehead accepts the demand of reason for a categoreal explanation of the temporal world. He rejects the demand for a "metaphysical" explanation of the temporal world. "In this argument the point to notice is, that what is metaphysically indeterminate has nevertheless to be categorically determinate. . . . The general principle of empiricism depends upon the doctrine that there is a principle of concretion which is not discoverable by abstract reason" (SMW 250).

It then follows that if God is the principle of limitation, "His existence is the ultimate irrationality" (SMW 249). For if the function of reason is to begin with facts and to understand their categoreal conditions, then reason is possible only because determinate facts exist. The real possibility of reasoning depends on the existence of nature. This is to say that reasoning depends on the existence of a principle of limitation which orders the boundless domain of pure possibility. "No reason can be given for the nature of God, because that nature is the ground of rationality" (SMW 250).

In saying that the existence of God is the ultimate irrationality, Whitehead is not saying it is irrational to believe that God exists. On the contrary, the existence of a principle of limitation is implied by the reality of the temporal world. He is not saying that no reason for belief in the existence of God can be given. He is only saying that no reason can be given for "the nature of God."

Nor is he saying that God himself is irrational in the sense that contradictory predicates must be applied to the divine being. On the contrary, Whitehead undertakes to present a consistent and coherent conception of the nature of God and his relation to the world.

Nor is he saying that God is irrational in the sense that God acts arbitrarily. Whitehead is not himself lapsing into the unreflective supernaturalism he criticizes. On the contrary, the function of God with which his argument is concerned is the altogether impartial function of a principle of limitation.

Whitehead is saying only that we have no pure and self-evident rational principles from which the existence of God, as the principle of limitation, could be deduced. Our belief in the existence of God is irrational only in the weak sense that it is logically based on the reality of the given temporal world, accepted as a fact.

4. Whitehead's criticisms: God as absolutely complete

A second criticism is leveled against the doctrine that God is absolutely complete and self-sufficient. This doctrine belongs to a more reflective phase of traditional theology. For the early Christian theologians, "He was internally complete" (AI 217; see RM

70). In the words of Descartes, God was "absolutely self-sustaining" (RM 106). God's existence required "no relations to anything beyond himself" (AI 217).

This last phrase carries the main point of the doctrine Whitehead is attacking. For there is a sense in which, in his own system, the satisfaction of every actual entity is "complete." Also God is complete in a way actual occasions are not. For God's primordial vision includes every eternal object and his physical experience includes every actual occasion, and this boundless reach of conceptual and physical experience is continually unified in an everlasting satisfaction. Even so this is not an *absolute* completion, for the being of God requires eternal objects, and God's satisfaction requires the production of novel actualities in the course of nature. God is intrinsically related to a boundless multiplicity of things beyond himself. Actual entities achieve internal completion but are not absolutely complete.

Whitehead seems to think this doctrine of the absolute completeness of God was encouraged, if not originated, by the theology of Plato and Aristotle.[2] It has since become part of the Western theological tradition, though it is inconsistent with other features of that tradition.

The direct consequence of this doctrine in early Christian theology was that "the World was not necessary to God" (AI 217). The indirect consequences of the doctrine may be put as follows, though Whitehead does not systematize them in this way. If the world is not necessary to God, then one of the following propositions is true:

a. The world is real and God is related to the world by unconditioned acts of will.

b. The world is unreal.

c. The world is real and is absolutely separated from God.

We have noticed Whitehead's criticism of the first of these views. We need not dwell on his criticism of the second. "The presupposition of the supreme reality as devoid of change" has the result that "the historic universe is degraded to a status of partial reality, issuing into the notion of mere appearance" (MT 109; see

2. See MT 111–12. On Plato, AI 215–7, IMM 684. On Aristotle's unmoved mover, PR 519.

PR 526). This view dismisses "the most evident characteristic of our experience." "We live in a world of turmoil" (MT 109).

If the third proposition were true there would be a gulf between God and the world. And "The worst of a gulf is, that it is very difficult to know what is happening on the further side of it. This has been the fate of the God of traditional theology. It is only by drawing the long bow of mysticism that evidences for his existence can be collected from our temporal World" (AI 217). Thus Descartes's argument for the existence of God fails, "because he abstracts God from the historic universe. Thus the conclusion depends upon meaningless phrases respecting the unknown" (MT 155; see RM 107). So serious objections lie against each of the indirect consequences of the doctrine that God is absolutely complete.

Instead of the major direct consequence of this doctrine, namely that the world is not necessary to God, Whitehead advances the principle of relativity. There is no entity, not even God, "which requires nothing but itself in order to exist" (RM 108; see IMM 687). Some of the concerns that lead him to advance this principle and apply it in theology are: (a) his concern to give full value to our experience of a world of many changing things, and of the connectedness of these things; and (b) his concern for rationality and his faith in reason.

5. Whitehead's criticisms: Unqualified omnipotence

The third of Whitehead's criticisms is aimed at the assumption that God is absolutely omnipotent. By "unqualified omnipotence" (AI 217) he means the property of being the only ultimate agent or determiner of things and events. He is objecting to the doctrine of God as "the one supreme reality, omnipotently disposing a wholly derivative world" (AI 213; see RM 68). By medieval and modern philosophers, "He has been conceived as the foundation of the metaphysical situation with its ultimate activity" (SMW 250). Thus the real target of this criticism is the view that God is omnificent, that all effective agency in the universe is to be ascribed to God.

For Whitehead the main consequences of this assumption—

though he does not organize them in this way—are: (a) that God's power is coercive power; (b) that God is responsible for evil in the world; and (c) that human effort becomes insignificant.

a. On this assumption God becomes "the supreme agency of compulsion" (AI 213). The glorification of God then becomes the glorification of power, a note Whitehead finds in Psalm 24 and regards as barbaric and morally dangerous (RM 55). In contrast, he says, the power of the life of Christ "lies in its absence of force" (RM 57).

Closely connected with this objection is the charge that the God of traditional theology is a divine tyrant (SMW 266; RM 55, 74–5), or despot (AI 218; DIAL 176, 198, 277), or dictator (MT 68). These epithets cover two distinguishable and logically independent lines of criticism. One is against arbitrary use of power. The tyrant acts from whims or passionate compulsions, not from a rational purpose arising from a rational nature. This line leads back to the criticism of unreflective supernaturalism and the notion of a divine fiat. The second line of criticism these epithets express is the one we are presently examining, namely the objection to conceiving the power of God as coercive power, excluding the freedom of temporal things. Thus even if God's activity were conceived as rational, not arbitrary, the present line of criticism would not be affected.

b. A second consequence is that God becomes responsible for evil:

> If this conception be adhered to, there can be no alternative except to discern in Him the origin of all evil as well as of all good (SMW 250–1).

> If the theory of complete determinism, by reason of the necessity of conformation with the nature of God, holds true, then the evil in the world is in conformity with the nature of God (RM 95; see 99).

In the *Dialogues* Whitehead expresses his disgust and horror at this consequence of the traditional doctrine, especially when God is conceived also as a personal will (DIAL 176, 189, 198).

c. A third consequence is that human effort becomes insignif-

icant. If the objectionable assumption is true, then man is "help-
less to cooperate" with God (SMW 105). In this respect, Whitehead
says, Augustinian theology and scientific mechanism have much in
common. Neither can give a genuine meaning to human freedom.
On neither view is human initiative and activity meaningful.
This assumption is incompatible with "our experience of responsibility, of approbation or of disapprobation, of self-approval or
of self-reproach, of freedom, of emphasis. This element in experience is too large to be put aside merely as misconstruction" (PR 74).

Because of these consequences Whitehead rejects the assumption that God is "unqualifiedly omnipotent." He turns to a suggestion he finds in Plato's later dialogues, namely "that the divine
element in the world is to be conceived as a persuasive agency
and not as a coercive agency" (AI 213). He thinks Plato wavered
between this view and the assumption of unqualified omnipotence
(AI 189–90, 213). His own development of Plato's suggestion needs
to be explored later. It means that God is not "omnipotent" (AI
189). God's action is conditioned by actual states of affairs of
which God is not the sole cause. "There is a general tendency in
the universe to produce worth-while things, and moments come
when we can work with it and it can work through us. But that
tendency in the universe to produce worth-while things is by no
means omnipotent. Other forces work against it" (DIAL 370; see RM
61–2). It would follow from this alternative view that God's action
is not coercive, that God is not responsible for evil, and that
human freedom and responsibility are significant. But "omnif-
icence" may be a better name than "omnipotence" for the attribute Whitehead is unwilling to assign to God.

6. Whitehead's alternative: The attributes of God

In earlier chapters we construed Whitehead's treatments of substance and of universals as revisions of traditional formulations of
those categories. It is possible to construe his critique of traditional
theology as a revision also. Let us look at his own doctrine of God
and lay it alongside traditional doctrines. In particular let us ask
how some of the attributes traditionally assigned to God would
be interpreted in the language of his own systematic categories.

We shall consider the unity, the immutability, the power, and the goodness of God.

a. *The unity of God.* First we notice those features of God's unity that follow from the categoreal conditions for all actual entities. In these ways his unity is like the unity of an actual occasion. Then we shall notice certain ways in which his unity is unlike that of an actual occasion.

i. The unity of an actual entity is not simple in the traditional theological sense. An actual entity is a concrescence of many physical and conceptual prehensions into an integral feeling of satisfaction. The multiplicity of the component prehensions is not annulled by this integration. The satisfaction is a harmony, not a simple unity of feeling. The data and subjective forms of the component feelings are synthesized into a *complex* unity. This is as true of God as of actual occasions.

ii. In the second place an actual entity is a *living* unity of feeling. It does not have the kind of self-identity that belongs to an abstract form. According to the categoreal scheme actuality means significance for self. Experience means an operation with reflexive significance, and this is what distinguishes concrete entities from abstract ones. This also is as true of God as of actual occasions. God is a complex and living unity.

iii. For this reason, though an actual entity is complex it is not "composite." It is true that Whitehead speaks of a concrescence as a process of "composition" (PR 223, MT 128). But here the term has a different sense. An actual entity is not composite in the sense of being an aggregate of discrete elements. It does not have parts in the ordinary sense of the term. It is composite only in the sense of being a concrescence of many prehensions.

For this question the tenth category of explanation is important: "That the first analysis of an actual entity, into its most concrete elements, discloses it to be a concrescence of prehensions, which have originated in its process of becoming. All further analysis is an analysis of prehensions" (PR 35). Other actual entities do not persist into the concrescence with their own immediacy. They are objectified as *data* for its prehensions. Likewise eternal objects are *ingredient* in but not parts of its experience. These other entities are not parts of the concrescent actual entity. It is a concrescence of *prehensions*.

This is as true of God as of an actual occasion. To say that God's prehensions are parts of God would be misleading. But it would be simply *wrong* to say that the actual occasions and eternal objects God prehends are parts of God. God is "composed" not of eternal objects and actual occasions but of prehensions of eternal objects and prehensions of actual occasions.

God's freedom and privacy require a distinction between his immediate subjective existence and all other entities. He experiences a multiplicity of other entities and thus, so to speak, knows and wills things other than himself. Also he is affected by other actual entities. But there is nothing *in* God except his own experience. Eternal objects and actual occasions are not parts of God.

iv. Though an actual entity is in a certain sense a process of composition and a unity of composition, it would have to be added that it is its own composer. An actual entity is "internally determined and externally free." It contributes to its own determination. In other words it is an instance of creativity. This also is as true of God as of an actual occasion.

In the above ways the unity of God is like the unity of an actual occasion and exemplifies the categoreal conditions of actual entities. God is a living and self-creative unity, complex but not composed of discrete and alien parts.

In other ways God is unlike actual occasions. He is unlike them in the scope of his experience and hence in the degree of its complexity. He prehends timelessly all eternal objects, and he prehends fully all the actual occasions that arise in the course of nature. We may say therefore that his experience is of infinite complexity. The question then naturally arises whether the unity of his experience is not a different mode of unity from that of an actual occasion.

To achieve its unity an actual occasion must prehend some of its data negatively. It must exclude some aspects of its world and some pure possibilities. We have seen how with God this is not the case. Because of the scope of his timeless subjective aim, his experience unifies an infinite multiplicity of data without any negative prehensions. God's unity is a unity without exclusions, and in this sense it may be said to be a *perfect* unity. In this way it differs from the unity of an actual occasion.

Finally we should notice that the unity of God differs in mode from that of an "enduring object," and in particular from that of a human person as interpreted in Whitehead's system (PR 50–2, 163–7). The unity of a human person is indeed a composite unity. Its parts are the actual occasions that are members of a complex society. The society is in fact "divided" by the discrete actual occasions that compose it. This is not true of God. He is not a society but a single actual entity with a unity of satisfaction. Hence his unity differs from the unity of a human person not in degree but in kind.

This categoreal contrast in Whitehead's system between the unity of God and the unity of a human person is particularly important for his relation to traditional theology. Traditional theology has been vitally concerned about the possibility of assigning to God such attributes as mind, thought, will, purpose, love, personality, etc. The clearest and most direct application of these terms, in ordinary discourse, is to human persons. May they be predicated of the divine being unambiguously? symbolically? analogically? To decide these questions it seems that we ought to be able to say, in *other* categories, how God is like and how he differs from human persons. Whitehead's categories make this logically possible. Later we shall explore his treatment of the question whether God is a "person." Here we notice only that in his own systematic terms the unity of God is categoreally different from the unity of a human person, remembering that while in this sense God is beyond personality he is not beyond the reach of all categories whatever. Of course objections to the adequacy of Whitehead's account of personality, as well as to his account of God, are still in order.

b. *God and extension.* Having in mind the traditional denial of composition in God, this may be an appropriate place to ask about the relation of God to space and time. It is not altogether clear what a systematic development of Whitehead's principles would require on this point. But I shall make several suggestions that bear on the problem. I suggest first that physical time and space are not in God. Then I suggest certain senses in which God is *not* in physical time and space and certain senses in which God *is* in physical time and space.

i. How physical time and space are not in God.

First consider God's relation to physical time. I suggest that though physical time is in the world, physical time is not in God. This is for the same reason that physical time is not in the concrescence of an actual occasion. For physical time transition or "passage" is required, and this is a relation between one actual entity that perishes and another that comes into being. In God there is a process of concrescence but no process of transition. God is always in concrescence and always satisfied, but there is no transition from one genetic phase of his experience to another such that one phase perishes before the other becomes. In God's experience there are durations but not transitions. Hence there is no physical time within God's experience.

Second, I suggest that physical space is in the world but not in God. This is so for a reason that also applies to the previous point about time. It is because God does not have any region or extensive standpoint which might include finite and externally connected regions. In passing it is worth noting that the concepts of extension and regions do not appear in the categoreal scheme but are treated as "derivative notions." Thus the categoreal scheme leaves room for an actual entity without a region. Suppose we should say God does have a region analogous to that of an actual occasion, as explained in Chapter 4. How might this be interpreted?

Since God's unity as an actual entity forbids our treating his region as a simple aggregate of finite regions, our only recourse is to identify God's region with the extensive continuum. Whitehead does not seem to make this identification. The extensive continuum is the relational unity of the regions of actual occasions considered as potentially divisible. Since God is the supreme ground of order he is an essential condition of there being an extensive continuum. But the continuum itself is constituted by actual occasions, not by God.

The denial that physical space and time are in God has an important implication, namely that God has no spatiotemporal parts. Just as actual occasions are not parts of God, so also the regions of occasions are not parts of God. And this is entirely consistent with Whitehead's theory of extension. For the region of an occasion is an abstraction from its existence as an act of experience.

ii. How God is *not* in physical time and space.

Though physical time is not in an actual occasion, an actual occasion is in physical time. At a certain time it has not yet come into being. At a later time it has perished. Thus it has temporal boundaries marking transitions between the physical past and the present, and between the present and the physical future. But God is not in physical time in this way. For God has no temporal beginning or end. He is primordial and everlasting. Unlike actual occasions he does not come into being or perish. There was no time when God was not and there will be no time when God is not.

Similarly, though physical space is not in an actual occasion, still an actual occasion is in physical space. Its experience has spatial as well as temporal boundaries. Though all of its experience goes on "here," the "thereness" of a contemporary world spatially external to itself is significant. This is true even though the occasion does not directly discern the structure and character of what in fact is "there." Now for God's experience this is not the case. Since he has no finite region defining his "here," his experience has no spatial boundaries in the way actual occasions do. In this sense God is not in physical space.

iii. How God *is* in physical space and time.

Though physical time and space are not in God, and though there are senses in which God is not in physical time and space, there are three senses in which God *is* in physical space and time. They are as follows: (a) Physical prehensions are necessary for his actuality. His being as an actual entity is not independent of events in space and time. (b) He prehends actual occasions in their spatiotemporal contexts. He prehends the "real essence" and not merely the "abstract essence" (PR 93–4) of an actual occasion. He prehends not only its "definiteness" but also its "position," where "position" means "relative status in a nexus of actual entities" (PR 38). In this way God's experience is conditioned by space and time. (c) God is prehended by actual occasions in the contexts of their respective actual worlds. As prehended by a certain actual occasion, God is *that* unity of feelings which results from the integration of his primordial nature with his prehensions of the past actual world of *that* actual occasion. In this way the objectifications of God for temporal subjects are conditioned by space and time.

Then may we say of God, as we said of an actual occasion, that he "enjoys extendedness"? Certainly we would have to construe this differently than in an actual occasion. The "thickness" and "spread" that qualify an occasion's experience have some definite meaning because of the experiential boundaries of the occasion. But God's experience has no such boundaries except toward the future. No actuality is in God's "past" in the sense that it existed when God did not. And no actuality is spatially remote from God.

I have argued that the categoreal conditions of concrescence entail exclusiveness of immediacy between God and an actual occasion. But the objectification of an occasion for God is complete, not abstractive. For this reason it is not meaningful to attribute to God a finite region as a standpoint for his experience. He is not limited by a finite perspective. He prehends every here-now, but he has no here-now of his own. Hence we might say that God enjoys the extendedness of the occasions he prehends but not his own immediate experience as extended. In an even stronger sense than is true of an actual occasion, God is complex but not composite.

c. *The immutability of God.* Since God is a living unity of experience he does not have the pure self-identity of a timeless form. Nor does he have the undifferentiated endurance attributed in classical physics to a material particle. His immutability cannot be construed in either of these ways.

Unlike other actual entities his subjective aim is not affected by conditions external to himself. No event in the course of nature, no matter how massive in importance, could affect his aim at intensity. Since it is a primordial appetition, it cannot be augmented, diminished, or diverted by temporal happenings. Consequently no event could change the unlimited hospitality and the perfect conformity of his response to finite becomings.

His subjective aim is immutably constant because it is independent of the changing course of nature.

Unlike other actual entities God does not perish. He is everlasting. Nothing could happen that would entail the final completion and perishing of God. God is always in concrescence and always satisfied. Thus it would be fair to say that the structure of God's experience, as a concrescence of conceptual and physical feelings into satisfaction, is immutable.

Finally, it is true that, unlike other actual entities, the content of his satisfaction is continually changing in its qualitative pattern, as he initiates and responds to novel actual occasions. But this change in God's experience is not a change for the better or for the worse. Changes originating in the world do not make God more perfect or less perfect. He is immutable in the perfection, as well as in the structure, of his experience. His subjective aim at maximum intensity is always achieved in his satisfaction.

Thus though on Whitehead's theory God is not absolutely complete, absolutely self-sufficient, and absolutely simple, yet there are intelligible and important senses in which he is one and immutable. He is immutable in the character of his aim, the structure of his experience, and the perfection of his experience.

d. *The power of God.* Whitehead rejects the doctrine of the *absolute* omnipotence of God. The freedom of God, like that of every other actual entity, is conditioned. But the conditions on God's activity are construed not as restraints but as occasions for activity. What is it that God cannot do?

i. God cannot make compatible an intrinsic *incompatibility*. Relative to any given situation, some pure possibilities envisaged by God are incompatible for joint realization (AI 357). But God can and does hold all eternal objects in view, with appetition for each to be actualized in its due time and place. He is thus the timeless lure for the creative process of nature, which is "the way by which the universe escapes from the exclusions of inconsistency" (MT 75).

ii. God cannot supplant *the freedom of actual occasions.* But as the ground of order he can and does ensure to every occasion an aim relevant to its actual world. He makes anarchic freedom impossible. Further, he "persuades" the self-creative activity of the concrescence toward the maximum satisfaction its actual world permits.

iii. God cannot prevent the *perishing* of actual occasions. But he can and does give every occasion an objective immortality in his own everlasting experience. And as the ground of the givenness of the past he makes possible its objective immortality in future actual occasions.

iv. God cannot annul the *past*. He cannot make the past not to have been what it was. But from any actual world he can and does evoke a novel and constructive outcome. By his presentation of a novel and relevant aim, he transforms the past world from being an obstruction into a condition of novel creative achievement. In this way God can never be defeated by the course of nature.

Properly understood therefore we might say that in Whitehead's theory the power of God is conditioned but not limited. From the point of view of God's subjective aim, the conditions we have noticed are not restraints preventing God from doing what he wills to do. They are rather conditions in the sense of opportunities or occasions for the operation of his power. The nonsystematic character of the realm of eternal objects, the self-creativity of finite subjects, the reality of transition, the stubbornness of given facts, all these are categoreal conditions for the existence of a world of finite actualities other than God. Without such a world, on Whitehead's view of the universe, no field for the operation of God's power would remain, and "the power of God" would have no meaning.

Some theologians have said that God can do anything that is not "absolutely" impossible. Understood in his own systematic terms Whitehead could assent to this proposition. The conditions on God's action are categoreal conditions, not some "order of nature" eternally established and immutable. This is illustrated by his interpretation of "Laws of Nature" in chapters 7 and 8 of *Adventures of Ideas*. He adopts the view that laws of nature are "immanent" not "imposed," which means that "the order of nature expresses the characters of the real things which jointly compose the existences to be found in nature" (AI 142). One important consequence is that "since the laws of nature depend on the individual characters of the things constituting nature, as the things change, then correspondingly the laws will change. . . . Thus the conception of the Universe as evolving subject to fixed eternal laws regulating all behaviour should be abandoned" (AI 143; see PR 139). This view of the order of nature is consistent with the primacy of creativity, the unbounded and unstructured character of the multiplicity of eternal objects, and the all-embracing scope of God's primordial envisagement, as we saw in Chapter 14.

It follows that questions about whether certain events have occurred, or might occur, are empirical questions. Such questions cannot be finally settled by appeals to any eternally established laws of nature, though judgments of probability must take full account of the laws of nature in a given epoch. In particular, theological questions about particular "acts of God" have to be decided in the light of history and experience.

In one way Whitehead's principles give more scope to God's power than it might have in other systems. On his view there are no absolute incompatibilities in God's primordial vision. Incompatibilities are always and only relative to some particular situation in the course of nature. The scope of his vision makes it possible for the process of nature to "escape the exclusions of inconsistency" (MT 75). This does not mean that every real possibility will as a matter of fact be actualized. It does mean that in one sense nothing is absolutely impossible to God.

e. *The goodness of God.* I suggest that in respect to this as well as other attributes the gap between traditional theology and Whitehead's theory is not as wide as his criticisms might lead us to suppose. He charges traditional theology with obscuring the goodness of God by its assertion of unqualified omnipotence. But certainly on his own theory God is not good in any very simple sense. We should begin by distinguishing between the goodness of God as subject and the goodness of God as superject.

God as a subject of experience means God as he is in himself. So considered, his goodness consists in the perfection of his experience. Three aspects of the perfection of God's experience may be discriminated.

i. God's experience synthesizes into a unity of satisfaction all pure potentials and all actual occasions, without exclusion. Thus he transcends in perfection the unities of experience of actual occasions, which require exclusions.

ii. God's experience is perfect also in the adequacy of his response to his data. The infinite richness of his experience of satisfaction is the result not only of an infinite multiplicity of data positively felt but also of his perfect re-enaction of the experiences of actual occasions. His subjective forms of feeling are perfectly responsive to his data. Thus he transcends the experiences of actual occasions, which re-enact their physical data imperfectly.

iii. God's experience is perfect also in its intensity. His subjective aim is at maximum intensity of experience. This aim is continually achieved in his satisfaction, the intensity of his satisfaction being independent of any particular course of events in the temporal world. Thus he transcends the limited and contingent intensities of the satisfactions of actual occasions.

God as a superject is God as he is for other subjects. So considered, his goodness must be seen in his effects on other subjects. These effects we have examined in some detail. To summarize, he evokes new subjects into being and preserves their achievements. God is the supreme condition of all finite experiences of value, and thus the source of finite goodness.

His goodness as superject follows from his goodness as subject. He is good for the world because he is good in himself. Because he is all-inclusive in his valuation of possibilities, he can present to any situation a relevant ideal. Because of the intensity of his experience he can evoke a creative response in any situation. Because of the infinite richness of his experience he can give objective immortality to the complete achievement of every finite subject.

7. The problem of evil

At this point we must see how the problem of evil takes shape in the context of Whitehead's theory. Since actual occasions have freedom, God is not the sole ultimate cause of all things, including experiences of pain, deprivation and degradation, and morally wrong decisions and deeds. But does not God share in the production of such experiences and decisions and deeds? This question arises in the following way.

God envisages all pure possibilities with appetition for their realization. It seems therefore that his appetition includes those forms of definiteness which in the course of history characterize evil experiences and decisions and deeds. Then God must share in their production of these experiences, decisions, and deeds, since his appetition evokes conformal appetition in finite concrescences.

Similarly God prehends and values all the feelings of actual occasions, including their feelings of pain, deprivation, and degradation, and including those intentions and decisions which constitute moral evil. It seems that in doing so he accepts and consents to these feelings. He does not reject them but aims at harmonizing them in the unity of his experience. It seems therefore that God has a share in the preservation as well as the production of evil experiences and decisions.

Two remarks are in order. The first is that on Whitehead's theory God is certainly not morally good, judged by those standards of behavior that are necessary for the peace and prosperity of a human community. The question is whether these standards properly apply to his nature, and whether it is reasonable to judge God by them. There is a considerable consensus in traditional theology to the effect that it is not.

Whitehead's explanation is as follows. To achieve unity of satisfaction an actual occasion must exclude some components of its initial datum. Translated into human psychology and sociology this means that inhibitions and exclusions are inevitable in human life, for the person and for the community. The problem of moral conduct arises from the necessity of deciding what to inhibit and what to exclude: "The nature of evil is that the characters of things are mutually obstructive" (PR 517; see RM 94-9, AI 333-9). To a finite being all things are not possible. Some desires must be restrained or denied so others may be fulfilled; some actions must be avoided or punished so that other actions may be possible.

God is different from other actual entities in that no exclusions are needed for his satisfaction. Therefore God has no moral problems as human beings do. It seems to follow that the moral standards evolved to guide decisions in the world of finite things are not appropriate for human valuation of God.

The second remark is that though the goodness of God is not moral goodness still it is a kind of goodness. God's aim is at maximum intensity of satisfaction and hence at the production of maximum depth and richness of actuality in every situation. Because of the all-inclusiveness and the intensity of his aim God ensures that *some* positive value, some novel act of experience, will come out of every situation. God cannot and does not ensure that out of every situation there will come what is best, abstractly considered. God cannot prevent the occurrence of evil experiences and decisions. For just those experiences and decisions may be the only constructive outcomes really possible in those situations. Anything is better than nothing. "This function of God is analogous to the remorseless working of things in Greek and in Buddhist thought. The initial aim is the best for that *impasse*. But if the best be bad, then the ruthlessness of God can be personified as Atè, the goddess of mischief. The chaff is burnt" (PR 373).

This does not imply the unreality of evil. Experiences of pain, deprivation, and degradation, and morally evil decisions and deeds do occur. These are real facts. For their subjects they are qualities of immediate experience. They become stubborn facts, requiring conformation and thus acting as real causes. They affect not only their temporal successors but God's own physical experience. It is difficult to see how facts could be more "real" than this.

God's aim is to evoke some constructive response to these facts and so to overcome them (RM 155). But this is possible only if they are accepted precisely as stubborn facts, and valued as evil, by finite subjects and by God. Only thus can some good come out of evil. The overcoming of evil does not mean the annulment of evil. Rather it strictly implies the reality of that which is overcome. It also implies the existence of goodness as well as evil in the initial situation. And if out of every situation some constructive outcome is possible, this implies some infinite source of possibility.

In this way God's aim and function in the temporal world, though not morally good, is yet good in a sense intelligible to finite minds. His aim is indeed not a sufficient rule for human conduct. Moral aims must be projected in specific actual situations and directed toward limited objectives if they are to be effective. Exclusions are necessary for finite satisfactions. Also our knowledge of the world in which we act and our vision of its possibilities are, to say the least, very incomplete. Hence moral decisions require reference to relative standards. Apart from such relative standards moral decisions have no meaning. But our very consciousness of their relativity requires us to hold them in some relation to an aim which transcends them.

8. Is Whitehead a pantheist?

By this time it should be abundantly clear that Whitehead does not mean to be a monist. In his cosmology there is no room for a self-sufficient entity. According to the principle of relativity, every entity essentially refers to entities other than itself. More specifically, there is no *actual* entity which does not require other actual entities for its own existence. Therefore it is categoreally impossible to reduce actuality to one entity, whether this be called the universe, the absolute, or God.

Whitehead enforces this point when he speaks of his substitution of creativity for Spinoza's one substance (PR 10–11, 125). For creativity is not an entity. It is not to be found among the categories of existence. Much less is it an actual entity. Rather it is a name for a general fact, namely that the universe is made up of novel concrescences.

He enforces it further by his comparison of his system with Bradley's. In a discussion of propositions and judgments he says:

> According to Bradley, the ultimate subject of every judgement is the one ultimate substance, the absolute (PR 304).

> In the philosophy of organism . . . Bradley's doctrine of actuality is simply inverted. The final actuality is the particular process with its particular attainment of satisfaction. The actuality of the universe is merely derivative from its solidarity in each actual entity (PR 305; see 224).

We might say that this is the "realistic basis" onto which he transforms "some main doctrines of Absolute Idealism" (PR viii). Instead of saying that the actuality of finite things is derivative from the actuality of the universe, he takes the precisely opposite view and holds that the actuality of the universe is "merely derivative from its solidarity in each actual entity."

From this rejection of monism it would follow that neither God nor any other entity is identical with a totality of real things. If pantheism is the assertion that God is identical with the totality of real things, that God is "essentially immanent and in no way transcendent" (AI 154), then Whitehead is certainly not a pantheist (RM 68–9, AI 303).

Usually, however, pantheism is not construed in this simple way. The Stoics and Spinoza distinguished God from the aggregate of finite things. He is the *soul* of the world. He is *natura naturans*, not *natura naturata*. Therefore we must consider whether Whitehead's theory of God and the world approximates certain views less simple than pantheism as defined above. In particular, is Whitehead a panentheist?

Panentheism asserts that the world exists only in God and that God is more than the world. God includes the world. This view has been subtly developed and ably defended by Charles Hartshorne,[3] who attributes it to Whitehead also. This is not the place to assess its merits and demerits, but we must ask whether it can be fairly attributed to Whitehead.

Hartshorne contrasts panentheism with other views in the following way: "Thus there are logically the three views: (1) God is merely the cosmos, in all aspects inseparable from the sum or system of dependent things or effects; (2) he is both this system and something independent of it; (3) he is not the system, but is in all aspects independent" (DR 90). He identifies the first view with traditional pantheism, the second view with panentheism, and the third view with traditional theism. Two features of panentheism must be noticed. One is that "God literally contains the universe" (DR 90). This seems to mean that "God literally has our enjoyments" (DR 91). God has all the experiences

3. See *The Divine Relativity,* New Haven, Yale University Press, 1948 (cited here as DR).

that finite things have. He is "the subject of all change," though not the only subject of change, since there are finite subjects of change also.[4] Thus God includes all the experiences of finite subjects, which is to say that God includes the world.

The other feature of panentheism is that though God includes the world he is also independent of the world. But, Hartshorne explains, it is not in his concrete actuality but only in his abstract or "individual" or "personal" essence that God is independent of the world.

> The total actual state of deity-now, as surrelative to the present universe, has nothing outside itself, and in that sense is the All. But the individual essence of deity (what makes God God, or the divine divine) is utterly independent of this All, since any other possible all (and there are infinite possibilities of different totalities) would have been compatible with this essence. The divine personal essence in this fashion infinitely transcends the de facto totality, and every moment a partly new totality contains and embodies the essence (DR 88–9).

Thus God as a concrete actuality includes both the world and his own individual essence. But the individual essence of God is "utterly" or "infinitely" independent and transcendent of any particular state of affairs.

Is Whitehead a panentheist? I suggest he is not, since his theory of God and the world differs in essential respects from the view Hartshorne proposes. God does not literally include or contain the world. And he transcends the world not merely in his "essence" but in his concrete actuality. Two considerations support this interpretation of Whitehead's theory.

a. God prehends actual occasions, but he does not share their immediacy. Actual occasions enter into God's experience, but they do so as *objects* of his physical prehensions. God's prehension of an actual occasion is the objectification of that actual occasion for God. And an objectified entity has perished and lost its subjective immediacy. It is functioning as an object and not as a subject. It is an objectified subject.

4. *Man's Vision of God* (Chicago, Willett, Clark & Co., 1941), ch. 8.

This interpretation of objectification has been explained, supported, and applied to the experiences of actual occasions and to God's experience. It means that, though there is a sense in which God includes the world, there is also an important sense in which God excludes the world. Just as the subjectively immediate experiences of two actual occasions are mutually exclusive, so the immediate experience of God and the immediate experience of an actual occasion are mutually exclusive. Between God and an actual occasion there is no sharing of immediacy. In this respect God does not include the world but excludes it. God is not the subject of all change. There are real processes of change of which God is *not* the subject.

b. God prehends an actual occasion only when it has achieved its satisfaction. For any incomplete "now," God has not yet prehended the actual occasion that defines that "now." God and that occasion are in "unison of becoming," and the occasion cannot be prehended by God until it has achieved its satisfaction and become fully determinate. In this way the principle of the nonprehension of contemporaries as concrete individuals applies to God's experience as well as to the experiences of actual occasions. Every actual occasion is objectified for God, but only when it has achieved its satisfaction.

This interpretation of God and contemporaneity applies the epochal theory of time to the relation between actual occasions and God. It yields an additional sense in which God does not include the world. It followed from a that God never includes any actual occasion "literally," though he includes every actual occasion objectively. It follows from b that for any incomplete "now" God does not include the world even objectively, though he will include that world objectively when it has become complete. God's experience and action participate in the rhythm of creativity. In this further sense God excludes and thus transcends the world.

It follows from these considerations that God transcends the world not merely in respect to his abstract "essence," however that might be interpreted in Whitehead's categories, but also in respect to his concrete actuality as an actual entity. As a result Whitehead's theory of God and the world is somewhat nearer traditional theism than panentheism is.

I suggest therefore a fourth logical possibility, in addition to the three views defined by Hartshorne. This fourth view may be stated as follows: (a) God is not the cosmos, nor does he include (in Hartshorne's sense) the cosmos; and (b) his activity is always conditioned though never determined by the cosmos. This view agrees with traditional theism, against traditional pantheism and panentheism, in asserting that God is neither identical with nor inclusive of the world. It agrees with panentheism and traditional theism, against traditional pantheism, in asserting that God transcends the world. And it agrees with traditional pantheism and panentheism, against traditional theism, in asserting that God is conditioned by the world. I suggest further that this fourth view in the theory of God and the world that Whitehead's categories imply.

Now we can take up a question left unanswered toward the end of Part One (Chapter 9, section 2). At that point we were asking whether relations between actual occasions are "organic." One possible interpretation was that actual occasions are related to one another as are cells in an organism. One translation of this view into Whitehead's categories is that actual occasions are cell-like parts of nexūs. We examined this version and found only a very limited sense in which relations among members of a nexus are "organic." Another version, mentioned but not examined at that time, was that God is an organism of which actual occasions are cell-like parts. This would yield another sense in which Whitehead might be a pantheist, and we ought to ask whether this is a tenable interpretation of his theory of God and the world.

If actual occasions are to God as cells are to a body then the universe might be called a divine organism. Do Whitehead's principles imply that the universe is a divine organism in this way? Are actual occasions parts of God in the way cells are parts of a living organism?

First let us see how this might be expressed in Whitehead's own systematic terms. The most plausible interpretation would be that God is a society of actual occasions with personal order.[5] Does Whitehead's theory permit this description of God? It seems very clear that it does not.

5. For Hartshorne's discussions of this view see DR 29–31, 157–8; Schilpp 555; with W. L. Reese, *Philosophers Speak of God* (Chicago, 1953), p. 274.

A society is a certain sort of nexus, namely a nexus with social order (PR 50, 136). And category of explanation xiv is: "That a nexus is a set of actual entities in the unity of the relatedness constituted by their prehensions of each other, or—what is the same thing conversely expressed—constituted by their objectifications in each other" (PR 35). Now actual entities and nexūs belong to different categories of existence, which is to say mutually exclusive classes of entities. And since God is an actual entity, he is not a nexus and hence not a society of any kind.

This distinction between God and societies means that God has a unity of experience which an animal body, for example, does not have. An animal body does not as such have a satisfaction. Only actual entities have satisfactions. The satisfactions achieved in the course of the existence of the body are the satisfactions of the actual occasions that compose it. "All the life in the body is the life of the individual cells" (PR 165). God on the contrary has his own satisfaction, which is one, continuous and everlasting. It does not seem possible to give a plausible interpretation of the statement that the universe is a divine organism in Whitehead's own systematic terms.

Let us ask next whether "The universe is a divine organism" has a good use, as an interpretation of the outcome of Whitehead's theory, granting that it cannot be translated plausibly into his own systematic terms.[6] Certain obvious qualifications spring to mind at once. Ordinarily speaking, an organism has an environment. This "divine organism" would not. Ordinarily speaking, an organism has a beginning and an end. This divine organism would not.

These qualifications might not rule out our statement. But more serious objections have to be considered. Ordinarily speaking, an organism has "organic" unity, a mutual immanence among its cells, within each of its durations, as well as a persistent pattern of unity in time. This divine organism would not have this sort of unity. Again, ordinarily speaking, an organism

6. His characterization of his theory of actual occasions as "a cell-theory of actuality" (PR 334; see 347) is a way of stressing the real individuality of an occasion, not a way of suggesting it is a component of a unity of a higher order.

occupies a region of space-time which is the sum of the regions
of its cells. Its region includes the regions of its cells. This divine
organism would not have this kind of spatiotemporal relation to
its members. God does not include actual occasions in the way an
organism includes its cells. Finally, ordinarily speaking, the cells
of an organism have a fundamentally different structure from the
organism of which they are parts. This divine organism would
have the same fundamental structure as the actual occasions that
function as its "cells."

It seems there are some good reasons for *not* saying that, as the
outcome of Whitehead's theory of God and the world, the universe is a divine organism. Certainly actual occasions become immanent in God, and God becomes immanent in actual occasions.
But this relation of immanence is the outcome of prehensions.
And a prehension is not a symmetrical relation; it is a one-direc-
tional function. A subject prehends an object. Conversely an entity is objectified for a subject. The immanence of the world in
God and of God in the world is a shorthand expression for a multiplicity of asymmetrical operations of which both God and actual
occasions are agents.

The experiences of actual occasions are not literally parts of
God's experience. Actual occasions are *in* God only as objectified.
In God they have objective immortality not subjective immediacy. God and God alone is the subject of his experiences, just
as an actual occasion and it alone is the subject of its experiences.
Thus the relation between God and the world is not the relation
between a whole and a part. It is a relation between (a) an actual
entity in unison with every becoming with a continuous though
changing satisfaction, and (b) actual entities which become and
perish at particular where-whens in the course of nature. And,
"every actual entity, including God, is something individual for
its own sake; and thereby transcends the rest of actuality" (PR
135).

9. Is God a person?

Personality is not one of Whitehead's systematic categories. It
is a presystematic term calling for interpretation by means of the

categories of existence, explanation, and obligation which make up the categoreal scheme. Human persons are systematically interpreted as highly complex societies of actual occasions of a special sort. But clearly God is not a person in this systematic sense. God is an actual entity.

Further, Whitehead is very reluctant to speak of God as a person, even in a presystematic way. He wants to avoid misleading ambiguities (RM 78, DIAL 301). And he connects traditional conceptions of God as a person with unreflective supernaturalism. The idea of God as a person seems too simple to be true (RM 68, 72, 76). The only explanatory value he can see in this idea consists in an appeal to an unconditioned will. He finds such explanations unsatisfactory as we have seen.

Though he rejects simple attribution of personality to God, he also rejects the opposite extreme, namely thinking of God as "sheer infinity" (MG 675) or as "the impersonal order of the universe" (RM 150; see SMW 18). He proposes his theory as a view that avoids both these extremes.

In some of the more interpretative passages in his writings he uses personal images in referring to God. For example he speaks of the wisdom (PR 525, 527), the patience (PR 525), the love (SMW 268, PR 532), and the tender care (PR 525) of God. God is "the ideal companion" (RM 154). At the same time, he makes it quite clear that this is unsystematic and interpretative discourse. These are images only (PR 525). He is using these terms in a symbolic way.

Some theologians have spoken of God as a person in order to do justice to the mystery of the divine nature. The image of a person with freedom of will has been used to suggest a being whose ways are "past finding out." This intention need not conflict with Whitehead's principles or with the outcome of his theory.

The systematic development of a categoreal scheme need not dispel mystery from that to which it applies, unless a sense of mystery is nothing more than a state of intellectual confusion. Indeed perhaps it is just when we think most clearly and coherently about reality that we see how "mysterious" it is. Certainly remarks like the following are not out of keeping with the theory we have examined.

> The depths of his existence lie beyond the vulgarities of praise or of power (RM 154).

> Of course we are unable to conceive the experience of the Supreme Unity of Existence (IMM 698).

Whitehead also offers an interpretation of the freedom of God and thus locates, so to speak, the mystery of his being. Indeed the perfection of God's power implies the perfection of his freedom. His primordial aim is not conditioned by events in the course of nature. His power of conceptual supplementation is unlimited. He never fails to achieve satisfaction. And his power of initiating novel becomings is unbounded though always conditioned. He is the supreme instance of creativity.

But Whitehead's deep concern for rationality and his faith that "at the base of things we shall not find mere *arbitrary* mystery" (SMW 26, my italics) keep him from attributing to God an arbitrary freedom, a freedom expressed in absolutely unconditioned action. And we might well ask whether freedom of this latter sort is apt to be suggested by the image of a "person." It seems that if by divine freedom a power of absolutely unconditioned action is meant, then to speak of God as also a "person" is to use the term in a symbolic way or to invite confusion, or both.

Two final remarks on this topic remain to be made. The first is that on Whitehead's theory God is an actuality that exists through time without loss of immediacy. His unity is not of a persistent pattern of definiteness with a continuity *between* individual immediacies. It is a continuing unity *within* an individual immediacy. In this one respect Whitehead's conception of God fits our common-sense notion of personal existence better than actual occasions and nexūs do. The second remark is that, as Whitehead tells us plainly, the categoreal notion of an actual entity, which applies both to God and to actual occasions, is itself an imaginative generalization from instances of human experience.

10. Conclusion

In this chapter we have laid Whitehead's theory of God and the world alongside some traditional doctrines. The outcome of his theory may be closer to traditional theology than some interpreters have taken it to be. But it would not do to argue that, in spite of himself, he is in agreement with traditional theology. It is plain enough that he diverges from it at important points.

One problem is just how to formulate and characterize these disagreements. This calls for theological analysis, an enterprise to which this chapter might be a contribution. This enterprise is important because it may lead us to invent distinctions that put old questions in new and clearer ways. As a result, whatever our own answers to these questions may be, we may acquire a sharper perception of what those answers amount to, what they presuppose and entail, and the alternatives they exclude.

Beyond the questions about meaning we have asked in this and the preceding chapters of this study lies the question of truth. I have not argued that Whitehead's system is true or that it is untrue. This is not because the question is irrelevant or unimportant. On the contrary it is both a fair and an important question, though not a simple one.

What sort of truth-claim does Whitehead's system make? Certainly not the sort of truth-claim made by a scientific or common-sense statements. Whitehead has done his best to make it clear that speculative philosophy is not a substitute for science or for common sense. It is the truth-claim of a speculative scheme. Let us see what this means. Suppose we should grant that the system is, in his words, *logical* and *coherent*. Suppose we should agree that his systematic terms are reasonably well defined and explained, and that the categoreal scheme is elaborated in a reasonably coherent way. How then might we go about deciding whether what he proposes is true or untrue?

First, I suggest, we will ask whether there are any propositions we believe to be true which can be stated adequately in his systematic terms. If we find any such proposition and continue to believe it, then we will judge the scheme is *applicable*. If on the contrary we find no true proposition, in ordinary discourse or in science or in theology or in any other mode of discourse, which can be stated adequately in the terms of the categoreal scheme, then we will judge that the scheme is not applicable.

Second, we will ask whether there are any propositions we believe to be true which can*not* be stated adequately in Whitehead's systematic terms. For example take one of the following sentences: "I am the same person I was yesterday." "No purposes are effective." "Stones have no feelings." "There is no divine being." "God is unchangeable." If we decide after reflection that the proposition stated by some such sentence is true, and if we judge that this proposition cannot be expressed adequately by using Whitehead's terms, then we will judge that his system is not *adequate* to the facts. That is to say it is untrue. If on the contrary we find no such proposition, then we will judge that the system is adequate to the facts we have considered. That is to say, tentatively, that it is true.

Good judgments depend on understanding the categoreal scheme, and we do not understand it fully until we find out how it can be used. Going on beyond our study of the groundwork of Whitehead's system, we need to see how well it could be used to explain the various sorts of objects we encounter, for example stones and human beings, and the various modes of experience we have, for example physical motion and moral decision. Good judgments depend also on readiness to reconsider the beliefs we happen to have, before judging the system, as we must, by what we believe to be true. In it Whitehead offers a new view of things, not just a new way of saying what we already see. This view of things deserves to be taken seriously. Taking it seriously means, in part, looking again for ourselves at the world we experience.

Index